THE RIGHT TO SCIENCE

That everyone has a human right to enjoy the benefits of the progress of science and its applications comes as a surprise to many. Nevertheless, this right is pertinent to numerous issues at the intersection of science and society: open access; "dual use" science; access to ownership and dissemination of data, knowledge, methods and the affordances and applications thereof; as well as the role of international cooperation, human dignity and other human rights in relation to science and its products. As we advance towards superintelligence, quantum computing, drone swarms and life-extension technology, serious policy decisions will be made at the national and international levels. The human right to science provides an ideal tool to do so, backed up as it is by international law, political heft and normative weight. This book is the first sustained attempt at turning this wonder of foresight into an actionable and justiciable right. This title is also available as Open Access on Cambridge Core.

Helle Porsdam is Professor of Law and Humanities and UNESCO Chair in Cultural Rights at the University of Copenhagen, Denmark. She holds a PhD from Yale University in American Studies, has held fellowships at Harvard Law School; Wolfson College Cambridge; and was a Global Ethics Fellow with the Carnegie Council for Ethics in International Affairs. Her publications include *Legally Speaking: Contemporary American Culture and the Law* (1999), *From Civil to Human Rights: Dialogues in Law and Humanities on the United States and Europe* (2009), and *The Transforming Power of Cultural Rights: A Promising Law and Humanities Approach* (2019).

Sebastian Porsdam Mann is a DPhil researcher at the Faculty of Law at Oxford. He was educated in philosophy, psychology, and neuroscience at the University of Cambridge, where he did his first PhD in neuroethics. Sebastian has held postdoctoral positions in bioethics at Harvard Medical School and, as Carlsberg Foundation Postdoctoral Fellow, at the Universities of Copenhagen and Oxford.

The Right to Science

THEN AND NOW

Edited by
HELLE PORSDAM
University of Copenhagen
SEBASTIAN PORSDAM MANN
University of Oxford

CAMBRIDGE
UNIVERSITY PRESS

University Printing House, Cambridge CB2 8BS, United Kingdom

One Liberty Plaza, 20th Floor, New York, NY 10006, USA

477 Williamstown Road, Port Melbourne, VIC 3207, Australia

314–321, 3rd Floor, Plot 3, Splendor Forum, Jasola District Centre,
New Delhi – 110025, India

103 Penang Road, #05–06/07, Visioncrest Commercial, Singapore 238467

Cambridge University Press is part of the University of Cambridge.

It furthers the University's mission by disseminating knowledge in the pursuit of education, learning, and research at the highest international levels of excellence.

www.cambridge.org
Information on this title: www.cambridge.org/9781108478250
DOI: 10.1017/9781108776301

© Helle Porsdam and Sebastian Porsdam Mann 2022

This work is in copyright. It is subject to statutory exceptions
and to the provisions of relevant licensing agreements;
with the exception of the Creative Commons version the link for which is provided below, no reproduction of any part of this work may take place without the written permission of Cambridge University Press.

An online version of this work is published at doi.org/10.1017/9781108776301 under a Creative Commons Open Access license CC-BY-NC-ND 4.0 which permits re-use, distribution and reproduction in any medium for non-commercial purposes providing appropriate credit to the original work is given. You may not distribute derivative works without permission. To view a copy of this license, visit https://creativecommons.org/licenses/by-nc-nd/4.0

All versions of this work may contain content reproduced under license from third parties. Permission to reproduce this third-party content must be obtained from these third-parties directly. When citing this work, please include a reference to the DOI 10.1017/9781108776301

First published 2022

A catalogue record for this publication is available from the British Library.

ISBN 978-1-108-47825-0 Hardback

Cambridge University Press has no responsibility for the persistence or accuracy of URLs for external or third-party internet websites referred to in this publication and does not guarantee that any content on such websites is, or will remain, accurate or appropriate.

Contents

List of Contributors		*page* vii
Acknowledgments		ix
Foreword *Lea Bishop*		xi
	Introduction Helle Porsdam and Sebastian Porsdam Mann	1
	PART I THE RIGHT TO SCIENCE, THEN	
1	The Dawning of a Right Science and the Universal Declaration of Human Rights (1941–1948) Mikel Mancisidor	17
2	The Origins of the Right to Science The American Declaration on the Rights and Duties of Man Cesare P. R. Romano	33
3	IP Rights and Human Rights What History Tells Us and Why It Matters Aurora Plomer	54
4	"Fostering a Love of Truth" Conceptions of Science in UNESCO's Early Years Ivan Lind Christensen	76
5	The Right to Science and the Evolution of Scientific Integrity Roberto Andorno	91

PART II THE RIGHT TO SCIENCE, NOW

6 On the Right to Science As a Cultural Human Right 107
   Farida Shaheed and Andrew Mazibrada

7 Mainstreaming Science and Human Rights in UNESCO 124
   Yvonne Donders and Konstantinos Tararas

8 Considering the Right to Enjoy the Benefits of Scientific Progress and Its Applications As a Cultural Right
   A Change in Perspective 140
   Mylène Bidault

9 Implications of the Right to Science for People with Disabilities 150
   Valerie J. Bradley

10 Science in the Times of SARS-CoV-2 166
   Stjepan Orešković and Sebastian Porsdam Mann

PART III DISSEMINATING, IMPLEMENTING, AND PUTTING INTO PRACTICE THE RIGHT TO SCIENCE

11 "Fight the Fear with the Facts!" 195
   Ranga Yogeshwar

12 The Right to Science
   From Principle to Practice and the Role of National Science Academies
   Jessica M. Wyndham, Margaret W. Vitullo, Rebecca Everly, Teresa 211
   M. Stoepler and Nathaniel Weisenberg

13 The Right to Science in Practice
   A Proposed Test in Four Stages 231
   Sebastian Porsdam Mann, Yvonne Donders and Helle Porsdam

14 The Right to Science
   A Practical Tool for Advancing Global Health Equity and Promoting the Human Rights of People with Tuberculosis 246
   Mike Frick and Gisa Dang

15 A Proposal for Indicators of the Human Right to Science 268
   Andrea Boggio and Brian Gran

16 Epilogue
   Tensions in the Right to Science Then and Now 286
   Christine Mitchell

Index 298

Contributors

Mikel Mancisidor is a Member of the United Nations Committee on Economic, Social and Cultural Rights. He holds a Doctorate in International Relations from the Geneva School of Diplomacy and International Relations (DIR GSD), Washington College of Law.

Cesare P.R. Romano is a Professor of Law, Loyola Law School, Los Angeles, USA.

Aurora Plomer is a Professor of Law, University of Bristol, School of Law, Wills Memorial Building Queen's Road Bristol BS8 1RJ, UK.

Ivan Lind Christensen is an Associate Professor, Department of Politics and Society, Aalborg University, Denmark.

Roberto Andorno is an Associate Professor of Biomedical Law and Bioethics at the School of Law of the University of Zurich, Switzerland.

Farida Shaheed is an Executive Director, Shirkat Gah – Women's Resource Centre, Pakistan.

Andrew Mazibrada PhD Fellow, Centre for Interdisciplinary Studies of Law, University of Copenhagen.

Yvonne Donders is a Professor, International Human Rights and Cultural Diversity and Head of the Department of International and European Public Law at the Faculty of Law of the University of Amsterdam.

Konstantinos Tararas is a Program Specialist, Inclusion and Rights Section, UNESCO.

Mylène Bidault is a Member of the Friborg Group, Switzerland and has a doctorate in law, University of Paris X Nanterre, University of Geneva.

Valerie J. Bradley is the founder and President Emerita of Human Services Research Institute.

Stjepan Oreskovic is a Professor, University of Zagreb School of Medicine, Croatia.

Sebastian Porsdam Mann is a Postdoctoral Research Fellow at Harvard Medical School's Center for Bioethics and the University of Copenhagen.

Ranga Yogeshwar is a Professor for Ethics and Science Communication, Center for Ethics and Responsibility (ZEV), Hochschule Bonn-Rhein-Sieg, University of Applied Sciences, Germany.

Jessica Wyndham is the Director of the Scientific Responsibility, Human Rights and Law Program. She also serves as coordinator of the American Association for the Advancement of Science (AAAS).

Margaret W. Vitullo is the Deputy Director, American Sociological Association, USA.

Rebecca Everly is the Executive Director, International Human Rights Network of Academies and Scholarly Societies.

Teresa M. Stoepler is executive director of the InterAcademy Partnership for Research (IAP-R), USA.

Nathaniel Weisenberg is the Program Associate, American Association for the Advancement of Science (AAAS), USA.

Helle Porsdam is Professor of Law and Humanities at the Centre for Interdisciplinary Studies of Law (CIS), Faculty of Law, University of Copenhagen, Denmark.

Mike Frick is Tuberculosis Project Co-director, Treatment Action Group, USA.

Gisa Dang is Health and Human Rights Concultant, Treatment Action Group, USA.

Andrea Boggio is a professor in the Legal Studies department at Bryant University, USA.

Brian Gran is a Professor, Case Western Reserve University, Department of Sociology, Law School, and School of Applied Social Sciences, USA.

Christine Mitchel is the Executive Director, Center for Bioethics, Harvard Medical School, Boston, MA.

Acknowledgments

The editors wish to extend special thanks and acknowledgment to Andrew Mazibrada, without whose unfailingly rapid, high-quality editorial support, and language revision this volume would have been much impoverished.

The editors wish to thank Josu Guevara for generously allowing us to use his work, 'ArteRia', for our volume. Originally part of an exhibition titled 'Giza Eskubideei Begira' (Insights into Human Rights) and organized by the Basque Government in 2017 on the occasion of the 70 anniversary of the Universal Declaration of Human Rights, Guevara's work specifically addresses Article 27 of the Universal Declaration.

Foreword

Lea Bishop

Freedom of scientific enquiry. Integrity of research. Universal access to science education. Sharing knowledge and discoveries as a public good. Open access to academic research. International cooperation through scientific collaboration. Scientifically sound public policy. Broad participation in scientific enquiry. Attention to the needs of vulnerable communities. Widespread access to new technologies. Patent policy as a means to this end. Free and informed participation in experiments and new technologies. These are among the central themes of the internationally recognized human right to participate in the process of scientific discovery and to share in the benefits of technological progress – what has only very recently come to be shorthanded as "the right to science." As the book now in front of you will make clear in greater detail, the right to science is a philosophical ideal, a legal promise, a political discourse, and – perhaps – a social movement.

Its seed was firmly planted in Article 27 of the Universal Declaration of Human Rights, now over 80 years ago. Some three decades later, the young shoot was transplanted into Article 15 of the International Covenant on Economic, Social and Cultural Rights. The philosophical ideal thus became a legal promise. Yet, for many decades, this promise had little practical impact. The right to science received too little light and nourishment to grow into its potential. Even human rights experts remained unsure how to interpret and apply these most obscure of all the international human rights treaty provisions. About two decades ago, however, the seedling finally found fertile soil at the American Association for the Advancement of Science, the University of Connecticut Human Rights Institute, and the Information Society Project at Yale Law School. At these institutions, Jessica Wyndham and Professor Audrey Chapman provided the critical care at a tender stage. They inspired and welcomed me to join in the work. When I published *The Right to Science and Culture* in 2010 – then using a different last name – I *hoped* to provide a conceptual trellis to enable the Article 15 rights to one day achieve a firm foothold within the United Nations human rights system.

That dream has now been realized by the collective efforts of a global network of human right scholars and advocates. Each has grasped his or her own conceptual offshoot and carefully cultivated it. "The right to science and culture" is now the subject of an ample and growing body of scholarship, multiple United Nation Special Rapporteur reports, and at least one ICESCR interpretative commentary. I am reminded of the gardener's adage about planting and caring for vining plants: "First they sleep. Then they creep. Then they leap!" *The Right to Science: Then and Now* represents this third stage of accelerating growth. So much is now being written about Article 15, it has become impossible to do justice to both the scientific and cultural aspects in a single volume! The vine is mature. It now depends upon human rights advocates to seize its fruit. A social movement is needed to lay claim to the right, leveraging these new conceptual and legal tools to continuously promote the right to science and defend it from threats.

If you will permit me a second extended metaphor, let us leave the vineyard for wilder land. For contributing authors, participating in an edited volume is a bit like embarking upon a camping trip with very old friends. Most of the writers have known each other for a long time, formed friendships over many an academic gathering, and drawn inspiration from each other's writings and constructive feedback. Coming together in such a massive collective effort is exciting – and often exhausting – and always exhilarating. Of course, every camping trip succeeds or fails based on the efforts of its organizers. Until you have had the editorial experience yourself, it is impossible to guess at the enormous investment of time and energy required to bring such a volume together. Ironically, it is vastly easier to write one's own book than to edit a collection of essays! The editors of *The Right to Science: Then and Now* have been particularly ambitious in including such a diversity of contributors. This scale multiplies the complexity of the conceptual task and organizational labor ... but also the richness of the final outcome. For the reader seeking a comprehensive introduction, such a thorough survey of the field is a treat indeed. As you enjoy the volume that follows, I hope you will appreciate the labor of love that it represents, and find your own way to pay it forward.

Introduction

Helle Porsdam and Sebastian Porsdam Mann

1. Everyone has the right freely to participate in the cultural life of the community, to enjoy the arts and to share in scientific advancement and its benefits.

2. Everyone has the right to the protection of the moral and material interests resulting from any scientific, literary or artistic production of which he is the author.

Article 27, Universal Declaration of Human Rights (UDHR)

[Everyone has] the right (a) to take part in cultural life;

(b) to enjoy the benefits of scientific progress and its applications;

(c) to benefit from the protection of the moral and material interests resulting from any scientific, literary or artistic production of which he is the author.

Article 15 (1) International Covenant on Economic, Social and Cultural Rights (ICESCR)

The International Covenant on Economic, Social, and Cultural Rights (ICESCR) from 1966 turned the rights enshrined in the 1948 Universal Declaration of Human Rights (UDHR) into binding obligations under international law for ratifying states.[1] One of these rights is the right to enjoy the benefits of scientific progress and its applications, referred to here as the right to science. Both instruments mention the right to science alongside the rights to take part in cultural life and authors' rights. Together with the right to education, these three rights constitute the core of the so-called cultural rights and, ideally, interact to enable the flow of human creativity and understanding.[2] The drafters of the UDHR counted Articles 23 through 27 UDHR, outlining the four core cultural human rights, among the most fundamental and

---

[1] As a declaration, rather than a treaty or covenant, the UDHR originally bore no force of law but rather expressed an ideal standard held in common with and by nations around the world. Today, it is generally considered as reflecting customary law, which is binding upon all states.

[2] See Helle Porsdam, *The Transforming Power of Cultural Rights: A Promising Law and Humanities Approach* (Cambridge University Press, 2019).

argued that these rights "aim at the realization of the right to the full development of one's person."[3]

Due to its classification as a cultural right, the vastness of its subject matter, and its physical location near the end of both the UDHR and ICESCR, the Right to Science (RtS) has long been overlooked. Indeed, when we conducted a systematic review of the extant literature with colleagues, we found a total of only seventy-eight publications.[4] As the American Association for the Advancement of Science has stated, "governments have largely ignored their Article 15 obligations and neither the human rights nor the scientific communities have brought their skills and influential voices to bear on the promotion and application of this right in practice."[5]

This neglect is surprising given both the relevance of science to the fulfilment of other human rights and the current political climate of hostility to facts, scientists, and experts. In a world where Harvard University libraries, the wealthiest in the world, have to declare insufficient funds to afford journal subscriptions; where President Putin expresses the opinion that "whoever becomes the leader in [artifical intelligence and quantum computing] will rule the world";[6] where the Chinese state jails the first scientist to edit human embryos using CRISPR/Cas9; where democratically elected politicians preface their comments with the reminder that they are "not a scientist,"[7] yet speedily proceed to call into question the most basic of scientific tenets – in such a world, the fact that enjoyment of the benefits of scientific progress and its applications has been recognized as a human right is of great practical, legal, and normative relevance.

Fact-based knowledge and evidence no longer exert the rational pull they once did. At the same time, progress in science becomes ever more arcane, specialized, and difficult to comprehend. Moreover, people are increasingly afraid of the "dual use" of emerging technologies involving for example artificial intelligence or human genetic modification. Digital exclusion and a lack of scientific literacy furthermore add to the distrust in science. Public access to scientific information primarily involves the digital media. Today, this essentially means making digital versions of new research publicly available by means of, for example, open-access journals, repositories, and mandatory open-access policies. Especially the latter policies ensure that publicly funded research is shared

---

[3] Johannes Morsink, *The Universal Declaration of Human Rights: Origins, Drafting, and Intent* (University of Pennsylvania Press, 1999), p. 212.

[4] S. Porsdam Mann, V. J. Bradley, M. F. Chou, G. Church, M. Mann, C. Mitchell, Y. Donders, and H. Porsdam, "On the Human Right to Enjoy the Benefits of Science and Its Applications" (2018) *Proceedings of the National Academy of Science* 115(43), pp. 10820–10823; updated in S. Porsdam Mann, Y. Donders, and H. Porsdam, "Sleeping Beauty: the Human Right to Science." (2020) 42(2) *Human Rights Quarterly* 332–356.

[5] AAAS Scientific Responsibility, Human Rights, and Law Program website, quoted in Porsdam Mann, Bradley, Chou, Church, Mann, Mitchell, Donders, and Porsdam, p. 10820.

[6] R. Gigova, "Who Vladimir Putin Thinks Will Rule the World," CNN Online, https://edition.cnn.com/2017/09/01/world/putin-artificial-intelligence-will-rule-world/index.html.

[7] This tendency is true of several and diverse global leaders and is wonderfully laid out in D. Levitan, *Not a Scientist: How Politicians Mistake, Misrepresent, and Utterly Mangle Science* (Norton & Company, 2017).

across the world. Nevertheless, digital divides in computer or cell phone use and in access to the internet exist "for reasons of income, education, gender and geographic location."[8]

Even in areas of the world where people do have access to scientific knowledge on as well as off the internet, there is a lack of scientific literacy. Many simply do not know enough science to be able to distinguish proper from fake or pseudoscience. "Not only can people find it difficult to grasp new knowledge (largely due to the digital divide), but they also lack the necessary critical tools to question this knowledge (in terms of source and content) and assess its reliability."[9] The resulting disbelief in science and science-based reasoning constitutes a problem for democratic societies, which crucially rely on rational and evidence-based decision-making.

The right to science adds a normative and judicial dimension to issues at the intersection of science and society. The right to science thus provides a perfect tool not only for presenting evidence-based knowledge, but also for highlighting the complexity and uncertainty of the questions raised, thereby reflecting the fact that science and its applications are part of the cause as well as the cure. Yet despite its potential for defending science and the freedom to think, question, and share scientific ideas, the right to science has not received the attention it deserves. It has remained an inefficient legal norm, which neither informs major policy and governance issues, nor gives guidance to practicing scientists and the public.

The historical neglect of the right to science has in part been due to the difficulty in interpreting its implications, both normative and practical.[10] In April 2020, during the COVID-19 pandemic, the Committee on Economic, Social and Cultural Rights (CECSR), the independent UN body monitoring the implementation of the ICESCR, published General Comment No. 25 on Science, a document to help governments and courts understand the duties imposed on States Parties by those parts of Article 15 ICESCR that especially concern science.[11] Like other General Comments, this document is vested with considerable authority and will heavily influence how international law in areas relevant to science and scientists will be developed and interpreted.

Several of the contributors to this volume participated as experts on the General Day of Discussion on the new General Comment on Science, which took place on October 9, 2018 at the UN Human Rights Office of the High Commissioner in

---

[8] Report of the UN Special Rapporteur in the field of cultural rights, A/HRC/20/26, para. 37.
[9] Cécile Petitgand, Catherine Régis, and Jean-Louis Denis, "Is Science a Human Right? Implementing the Principle of Participatory, Equitable, and Universally Accessible Science" (Ottawa, Canada: the Canadian Commission for UNESCO's Idealab, 2019), p. 6.
[10] See e.g. Porsdam Mann, Bradley, Chou, Church, Mann, Mitchell, Donders, and Porsdam, pp. 10820–10823.
[11] CESCR, General comment No. 25 (2020) on science and economic, social and cultural rights, UN Doc. E/C.12/GC/25, April 30, 2020.

Geneva.[12] Mikel Mancisidor de la Fuente, member of the CESCR and coauthor of the General Comment on Science, is among the contributors to the present volume. This book is therefore the first to contain the perspective of the primary author of the new General Comment. Moreover, it is the first to contain the reactions and reflections upon the General Comment by the leading academic experts and human and science rights advocates out there, as nearly all fifteen chapters have been adapted to fit the content and release of the General Comment.

The Right to Science: Then and Now reflects the most current and leading perspectives on the right to science. Its ambition is to elucidate both the theory and the practical significance of the right. The fifteen contributions touch on several challenging conceptual questions. Among these are the issues of dual use science and how we might ensure that potentially harmful impacts of scientific and technological developments are minimized or avoided. Embodying "principles that are intended to inform the conduct of science,"

> at its core, Article 15 requires that science be used as an instrument for human benefit, and that the process of doing scientific research and the development of applications from that science be consistent with fundamental human rights principles such as nondiscrimination and equal treatment, participation and transparency in decision-making, and free and informed consent to participation in research.[13]

Article 15 also touches upon complicated and important issues of access to and participation in science, science policy, and priority setting within science. Together with the larger cultural rights and ICESCR framework, the Article 15 rights present a helpful instrument of analysis for issues that are already pertinent but will only increase in importance over time. These include access to, ownership, and dissemination of, data, knowledge, methods, and the affordances and applications thereof; as well as the role of international cooperation, human dignity, and other human rights in relation to science and its products. Backed up by both international law and public morality, Article 15 provides a unique and powerful perspective on these intricate issues.

Unless it is legally defined, guidance for full implementation of the right to science may never be established.[14] When it comes to the significance of this and other cultural rights, moreover, we need to look not only at the level of each individual person or group; we also need to explore the importance of the right to science at the societal level. From a personal perspective, the main issue is the possibility that the right to science gives for each individual and/or group to develop

---

[12] See www.ohchr.org/EN/HRBodies/CESCR/Pages/Discussion2018.aspx.
[13] AAAS, "Right to Science: FAQs" – available at www.aaas.org/programs/scientific-responsibility-human-rights-law/resources/faqs.
[14] See e.g. Jessica M. Wyndham and Margaret Weigers Vitullo , "Define the Human Right to Science," Editorial, *Science*, Nov. 30, 2018, Vol. 362, Issue 6418, pp. 975 DOI: 10.1126/science.aaw1467: http://science.sciencemag.org/content/362/6418/975.

and acquire knowledge – and thereby to get a better life. But the general welfare of democratic society, too, depends on an educated and open-minded citizenry. For the framers of the UDHR, an enlightened and well-informed citizenry constituted the best defense against hatred and bigotry – and for democracy. It also formed the basis for human rights education, and what later became known as education for democratic citizenship.

When Farida Shaheed became the first mandate holder as UN Special Rapporteur in the field of cultural rights in 2009, she was met by skepticism on the part of many states. This skepticism most of all had to do with the uncertainty surrounding the exact nature of cultural rights – were these rights a distinct area of human rights, were they universal like other human rights and not relativistic? Part of the problem, she relates in her reflections on the significance and challenges of the mandate, "stemmed from the paucity of previous work on cultural rights, reflected in the frequent comment prior to my mandate, that cultural rights were a generally underdeveloped area in comparison to other human rights."[15] This situation has since been remedied somewhat. On cultural rights in general, the last few years have seen the publication of various monographs and edited volumes.[16]

More specifically to the right to science, Aurora Plomer published *Patents, Human Rights and Access to Science* in 2015.[17] This, along with Richard Pierre Claude's *Science in the Service of Human Rights* (2002), represents the most thorough book-length treatments to date.[18] Anna Maria Andersen Nawrot's *The Utopian Human Right to Science and Culture* (2014) addresses the topic from a postmodernist perspective, while Philipp Aerni explores the intersection between economic rights and the right to science in his *Entrepreneurial Rights as Human Rights* (2015).[19]

---

[15] Farida Shaheed, "The United Nations Cultural Rights Mandate: Reflections on the Significance and Challenges," in Lucky Belder and Helle Porsdam (eds.), *Negotiating Cultural Rights: Issues at Stake, Challenges and Recommendations* (Cheltenham: Edward Elgar, 2017), p. 22.

[16] See e.g. Helaine Silverman and D. Fairchild Ruggles, *Cultural Heritage and Human Rights* (Berlin: Springer, 2007); Yvonne Donders and Vladimir Volodin (eds.), *Human Rights in Education, Science and Culture* (Burlington, VT and Ashgate, UK: UNESCO and Ashgate, 2007); Francesco Francioni and Martin Scheinin, *Cultural Human Rights* (Leiden, NLD: Martinus Nijhoff, 2008); James A. R. Nafziger, Robert Kirkwood Paterson, and Alison Dundes Renteln (eds.), *Cultural Law: International, Comparative, and Indigenous* (Cambridge: Cambridge University Press, 2010); Olivier de Schutter (ed.), *Economic, Social and Cultural Rights as Human Rights* (Cheltenham: Edward Elgar, 2013); Federico Lenzerini, *The Culturalization of Human Rights Law* (Oxford: Oxford University Press, 2014) Ana F. Vrdoljak, *The Cultural Dimension of Human Rights* (Oxford: Oxford University Press, 2014); Lucky Belder and Helle Porsdam (eds.), *Negotiating Cultural Rights: Issues at Stake, Challenges and Recommendations* (Cheltenham: Edward Elgar, 2017); and Helle Porsdam, *The Transforming Power of Cultural Rights: A Promising Law and Humanities Approach* (Cambridge: Cambridge University Press, 2019).

[17] Aurora Plomer, *Patents, Human Rights and Access to Science* (Cheltenham: Edward Elgar, 2015).

[18] Richard Pierre Claude, *Science in the Service of Human Rights* (Philadelphia, PA: University of Pennsylvania Press, 2002).

[19] Anna Maria Andersen Nawrot, *The Utopian Human Right to Science and Culture: Toward the Philosophy of Excendence in the Postmodern Society* (London: Routledge, 2014); Philipp Aerni,

STRUCTURE AND CHAPTERS

The Right to Science: Then and Now is an interdisciplinary endeavor. When it comes to the setting of the right to science as well as other cultural and human rights – the way in which they are formulated in international treaties and domestic and international law, and applied in practice in national constitutional and legal systems – law is obviously a key discipline. Yet it is not the only one; a purely legal approach fails to take into account the ethical, historical, political, economic, anthropological, as well as the scientific, technical, and health-related dimensions. These are just as important and it is only by integrating data, tools, perspectives, and theories across faculties and disciplines that we can begin to get a sense of the full right to science picture.

The volume is divided into three parts. Following the editors' Introduction to the volume, Part I concerns the history of the right to science: how this right was developed, and the lessons we may learn from this. This first part consists of five chapters. In the first chapter, "The Dawning of a Right: Science and the Universal Declaration of Human Rights (1941–1948)," **Mikel Mancisidor** explores how and under what circumstances the right to science entered the UDHR, and what the *travaux préparatoires*[20] of the Declaration may tell us about why those who drafted the Declaration chose these precise words – what they intended to say, and what they avoided saying.[21] The Universal Declaration of Human Rights started out as a succession of working drafts over one and a half years. The first draft was prepared by the Canadian jurist John Peters Humphrey, who had been appointed the first Director of the United Nations Division of Human Rights. This first draft, which is a very complete list of the rights that had been recorded in other declarations and reference texts, was then rearranged and converted into a more consistent declaration by the French jurist René Cassin. That draft subsequently had to pass the drafting Committee and the sessions of the Human Rights Commission before being approved by the ECOSOC and finally, on December 10, 1948, by the General Assembly in session at the Palais Chaillot in Paris, resulting in the Universal Declaration of Human Rights that we know today.

Entrepreneurial Rights as Human Rights: Why Economic Rights Must Include the Human Right to Science and the Freedom to Grow Through Innovation (Cambridge: Banson, 2015).

[20] Johannes Morsink, *The Universal Declaration of Human Rights: Origins, Drafting and Intent* (Philadelphia PA: University of Pennsylvania Press, 1999); Mary Ann Glendon, *A World Made New: Eleanor Roosevelt and the Universal Declaration of Human Rights* (New York: Random House, 2001); and William A. Schabas : *The Universal Declaration of Human Rights. The travaux préparatoires* (New York: Cambridge University Press, 2013).

[21] As established by article 32 of the 1969 Vienna Convention on the Law of Treaties, "the preparatory work of the treaty and the circumstances of its conclusion" are not principle resources for interpreting the texts as regards their application, but are "supplementary means of interpretation" which can be used to find out more about this right.

Humphrey's first draft already included a right to science in the same article as culture and arts. According to René Cassin,[22] the article was included per request from several cultural organizations, including UNESCO,[23] which was represented at this time before the Commission on Human Rights by Jacques L. Havet. Why did the drafters not include any mention of the purposes of science? What was UNESCO's role in those debates? What were the impacts of the Nuremberg Trial? And how were the two thematic elements, the right to take part in science and the right to enjoy the benefits of scientific progress and its applications, introduced in the final version?

In Chapter 2, "The Origins of the Right to Science: The American Declaration on the Rights and Duties of Man," **Cesare P. R. Romano** begins by noting the distinction between the "right to benefit from advancements in science and technology" (i.e. the Right to Science) and the so-called "rights of science" (e.g. rights to academic freedom, to conduct research, to reap the fruits of one's own inventions etc.). Romano proceeds to discuss the roots of these two sets of rights. The roots of the rights of science run deep, all the way to Bacon and Galileo, and intertwine with other more well-known rights, such as the right to education and freedom of expression. The roots of the Right to Science are relatively more recent and can be traced to the work of the Inter-American (I-A) Juridical Committee, the expert body that drafted the American Declaration of Human Rights. This chapter tells the story of the debates between the members of the I-A Committee on the right to science, the various wordings they considered, and the influences and considerations that shaped their choices. Finally, it explains how and why the wording of Article XIII of the American declaration morphed into Article 27 of the Universal Declaration and, later, Article 15.1.b, 15.2–4 of the ICESCR.

Aurora Plomer's chapter (Chapter 3), "IP Rights and Human Rights: What History Tells Us and Why it Matters," investigates how human rights have been a critical counterweight to the social and economic costs of the global extension of intellectual property (IP) rights. The Universal Declaration of Human Rights provides the foundational values which are at the heart of this critique. Plomer retraces the origins and normative foundations of the rights of authors and inventors in the Universal Declaration of Human Rights. She argues against recent scholarship which questions the relevance of human rights to current debates about IP rights, shows how this scholarship conflates IP rights with human rights, and demonstrates why human rights were never intended to be equated with IP rights. Resetting the history of human rights and IP rights reveals why human rights

---

[22] Morsink, p. 218.
[23] On the UNESCO's intellectual contribution to the drafting of the Universal Declaration, see UNESCO/PHS/3(rev) Paris, July 25, 1948, with contributions by J, Maritain, M. Gandhi, E. H. Carr, B. Croce, R. P. Teilhard de Chardin, A. Huxley and two specific papers on scientific matters: "Rights and Duties Concerning Creative Expression, in particular in Science", by J. M. Burgers, and "Science and the Rights of Man", by W. A. Noyes.

continue to have a meaningful role to play in protecting public goods and addressing the grave injustices caused by the global extension of IP rights today.

The title of **Ivan Lind Christensen's** chapter (Chapter 4) is "Fostering a Love of Truth: Conceptions of Science in UNESCO's Early Years." Apart from publishing *Recommendation on the Status of Scientific Researchers* and the subsequent *Recommendation on Science and Scientific Research* (1974 and 2017, respectively), UNESCO has been a significant agent in international science cooperation since 1945. The 'S'cience in UNESCO was, however, a last-minute addition, which was closely tied to the beginning of the nuclear age, and the creation of the previously unthinkable, annihilative power of the nuclear bomb. The science department of UNESCO was thus created at a time when science did not only promise endless, modern progress to the broader public as well as to many politicians, but also threatened world destruction. In the following decades, the onset of the Cold War posed its own challenges to the idealized norms of science as proposed by Robert K. Merton in 1942 (universalism, communality, disinterestedness, and organized skepticism), as well as to the ideas of international science cooperation in general. In this chapter, Christensen traces the different ideas of science as they were articulated within UNESCO, thereby illustrating what the organization itself understood by the concept of science and its relations to concepts of modernity, progress, and development.

Roberto Andorno's chapter (Chapter 5), "The Right to Science and the Evolution of Scientific Integrity," presents the history of the development, in the United States as well as in Europe, of ethical concerns in science. Science is one of the highest expressions of human thought and makes a crucial contribution to the well-being and progress of society. This is why the right to freely conduct science is expressly protected by international human rights law (Article 15, paragraph 3, ICESCR). As the object of this right is "science," activities conducted by scientists are protected by this right insofar as they satisfy the requirements set up by ethical guidelines and professional standards. Practices that involve fabrication or falsification of data and plagiarism contradict the very essence of science, as they encompass acts of deception of the scientific community and society. Over the past few decades, awareness has grown about the importance of adhering to ethical standards in the conduct of science. Scientific misconduct became the subject of significant public attention beginning in the 1980s, which led to public statements and guidelines by academic and funding agencies, as well as to procedures for dealing with allegations of misconduct in science.

In Part II, the right to science now, that is to say at the present time, is explored in five chapters. Chapter 6, "On the Right to Science As a Cultural Human Right," is an essay written by former UN Special Rapporteur in the field of cultural rights, **Farida Shaheed**, and **Andrew Mazibrada**, based on an interview with Shaheed conducted by the editors. Among the topics covered are the challenges Shaheed faced in developing the broad normative contents for the right of science for the

Human Rights Council; why this right should be embedded within cultural rights at all – a question that has itself engendered significant debate – and how the thread connecting the apparently disparate fields of culture and science is in fact human creativity, which lies at the heart of cultural rights. The chapter underlines the importance of adopting a "public good" approach to knowledge innovation and diffusion, illustrating the critical relevance of the right to science today by reference to a few selected issues. It concludes with the need to have robust discussions involving all parties, including in particular the private sector, whose voices have historically been nearly or entirely missing from human rights discussions.

In Chapter 7, "Mainstreaming Science and Human Rights in UNESCO," **Yvonne Donders** and **Konstantinos Tararas** explore the unique mandate UNESCO has in the UN system to "contribute to peace and security by promoting collaboration among the nations through education, science and culture in order to further universal respect for justice, for the rule of law and for the human rights and fundamental freedoms." (Article 1 of UNESCO's Constitution). The advancement of human rights is an explicit goal of UNESCO, that is; and science is one of the fields through which UNESCO ought pursue this goal. Indeed, UNESCO has adopted legal instruments and has developed programs and activities in the field of science and human rights, most notably in the fields of bioethics and ethics of science. Donders and Tararas discuss several ways, including instruments and policies, in which UNESCO has worked on human rights in relation to science, and on science in relation to human rights. They attempt to bring to the fore the core approaches underpinning these efforts; to highlight the evolution in the Organization's thinking; and to show the extent to which these are aligned to and promote the advancement of the right to enjoy the benefits of scientific progress as included in human rights instruments, in particular the dimensions of scientific freedom, protection against harm, benefit sharing and international cooperation.

"Considering the Right to Enjoy the Benefits of Scientific Progress and Its Applications As a Cultural Right: A Change in Perspective," is the title of Chapter 8. **Mylène Bidault** presents a set of criteria allowing us to consider science as being part of culture, and to rethink the right to benefit from scientific progress and its applications as an emanation and specification of the right to participate in cultural life. Such an approach deeply influences our understanding of the "right to science," now commonly mentioned in academic and human rights circles. It may be time, though, Bidault suggests, also to refer to a right to "participate in scientific life," meaning the right of everyone to access and contribute to the development of science, as well as to practice their scientific and critical spirit in everyday life. This does not mean that everyone ought suddenly to become a scientific researcher nor that we all should be regarded as such, but rather that everyone may be a researcher in their own spheres of interest, using and refining knowledge for the sake of their own personal development and aspirations.

Chapter 9 concerns "Implications of the Right to Science for People with Disabilities." In her contribution, **Valerie J. Bradley** explores the unique and powerful importance of the right to science for people with intellectual, physical and mental health disabilities. The human rights of people with disabilities articulated in the Convention on the Rights of People with Disabilities (CRPD) (2006) directly connect to the principles and aspirations of the right to science. As noted in the 2014 meeting of the American Association for the Advancement of Science on *Disability Rights and Accessing the Benefits of Scientific Progress and Its Applications*, access to science and technology can have both a positive and negative impact on the rights of people with disabilities. Bradley begins with a review of the human rights of people with disabilities both in the CRPD and as articulated and reinforced in public policy and judicial rulings. Those rights, which have specific affinities to the right to science, include the ability to live independently, to be employed, to enjoy health and well-being, to receive adequate education, to have access to habilitation and rehabilitation, and to be free from degrading treatment. The intersection of the right to science and its applications and the realization – or abridgement – of these rights are explored. Further, the unique vulnerability of people with disabilities as subjects of scientific research and experimentation, including a history of exploitation and the application of now discredited interventions, are described, just as the barriers, physical as well as educational, to people with disabilities as students and practitioners of science are examined. Finally, for people with disabilities, access to technology holds the promise of more independent functioning, a reexamination of the construct of disability, and increased community participation.

Stjepan Orešković's and **Sebastian Porsdam Mann's** chapter (Chapter 10), "Science in the times of SARS-CoV-2," explores the applicability of the right to science to the 2020 coronavirus pandemic. The disproportionate impact of the virus on minorities and the socioeconomically disadvantaged highlights the importance of the fundamental human rights principles of equality, nondiscrimination, and international cooperation. The rise of government surveillance powers occasioned in some countries due to the need for contact tracing and public health measures give rise to dual use concerns. The woefully inadequate preventive measures taken before the pandemic illustrate the need for States Parties to progressively realize their obligations under the right to science before disaster strikes. Yet the current, global response to the pandemic also represents an unprecedented degree of international collaboration, and the evidence-based responses of some individual nations have saved countless lives.

Orešković and Porsdam Mann draw a distinction between "fast" and "slow" science. Whereas the latter involves rigorous and laborious adherence to the scientific method, the former represents the reality that much scientific work faces time pressures which at times force shortcuts. The distinction can be seen to operate in contemporary research into the coronavirus pandemic: whereas the development of vaccines and treatments usually requires years of meticulous laboratory work and several more years of clinical testing, the many millions suffering from the disease need a treatment *now*. However, by taking too many safeguards off the treatment discovery and testing pipelines, or by refusing to act in accordance with scientific advice, governments risk sacrificing the public's trust not only in the government's scientific bona fides but in the scientific process itself. This is a heavy price to pay, argue Orešković and Porsdam Mann, and point to evidence indicating that the success of Germany and Japan in combating COVID-19 can be traced to public trust in science and government, as well as scientifically informed and respectful national leadership.

The five chapters of Part III look at various ways in which the right to science is disseminated, implemented, and put into practice. **Ranga Yogeshwar**, in Chapter 11, "Fight the Fear with the Facts!," investigates current shifts in the grammar of communication of social networks and media, some of which contribute to the avalanche of fake news and alternative facts which we are currently experiencing. This shift begins to dissolve the base of enlightenment and questions science as such. How do we deal with complexity and how do we communicate science in a world with easy-to-use interfaces? Social networks act like fire accelerators, for their characteristic feature is the reversal of the flow of direction of media: they lend every citizen a voice and a great deal of steam now flows out of this valve. Former mass media now become the media of the masses, and this networked flow of news runs unembellished, unedited, and superficially free of charge. Even within science and among scientists, we encounter similar patterns with novel publishing models. Some questionable open access publications seem likewise to profit by, and therefore contribute to, the dissemination of fake science.

This is why science has to act on its own in a sound and professional way, Yogeshwar argues. Little is known in this field and we could develop a science of communicating facts based on knowledge rather than instinct. How do we present statistical data to the wider population in a more understandable way? How do we communicate risk without inducing fear? What is the best graphic approach to give people a sense of relevance? How do we display complexity? According to Article 15(2) ICESCR, the dissemination of science is a constitutive element of the right to science. Our aim should be to strengthen the language of enlightenment, and to fuel the open and critical dialogue that is the foundation of every civilized society.

Chapter 12, "The Right to Science – From Principle to Practice and the role of National Science Academies," by **Jessica M. Wyndham, Margaret Weigers Vitullo, Rebecca Everly, Teresa M. Stoepler,** and **Nathaniel Weisenberg**, examines points of convergence and disconnect between scientists across the globe and States party to the ICESCR regarding the key benefits of science and the key obligations of states. Without widespread recognition among scientists and the public and without implementation at the level of governments, the right to science has little meaning in practice. Wyndham et al. introduce the idea that national academies of science within States Parties may have a central role to play in the implementation of this right, serving as an intermediary to distill and frame key priorities regarding the right to science within their national context, and providing locally relevant and feasible recommendations for how their government might fulfill its obligations under Article 15.

The chapter draws from three stages of empirical inquiry into what the right to science means from the perspectives of scientists, engineers, and health professionals; action required to realize the right in practice; as well as barriers to its implementation. The first stage involved seventeen disciplinary-specific focus groups of US-based scientists which informed the development of a new conceptual framework for understanding "access" in the context of the right to science. This contributed to an expansive vision for the benefits of science as being both tangible and intangible. The second stage involved a global questionnaire of scientists, engineers, and health professionals to identify regional variations particularly in the actions necessary to ensure realization of the right to science, as well as targeted interviews of public health professionals about the value of the right in practice. The third stage is informed by qualitative research carried out specifically for this chapter. This empirical work involved interviewing representatives of science academies in countries that are a party to the ICESCR to determine how the right to science could be used as a tool of policy and advocacy to address core concerns at the intersection of science and society, for example, access to quality STEM education, health care, and/or climate change.

Together with **Sebastian Porsdam Mann, Yvonne Donders** and **Helle Porsdam** look at the interpretation of the right to science and its normative implications in Chapter 13, "The Right to Science in Practice: A Proposed Test in Four Stages." The Right to Science adds an important legal and ethical dimension to fundamental issues in science. The authors propose a four-step framework, derived from Articles 2, 4, and 15 of the International Covenant on Economic, Social and Cultural Rights, which may be used as a practical means of testing policy choices and implications against the obligations derived from the right to science. The first step consists in identifying whether a given policy, product, or aspect of science constitutes a "benefit of scientific progress" or "its applications." Where this is the case, Article 15(1)(b) establishes a prima facie right to the aspect of science in question. However, the RtS is not absolute, and the second step of the framework involves testing the prima facie right against competing rights claims and the Article 2 and 4 limitation criteria. These establish that limitations to the right must be (1) determined by law; (2) compatible with the nature of the ICESCR rights; (3) invoked solely for the purpose of promoting the general welfare in a democratic society; (4) and consistent with fundamental human rights principles of inclusion, participation, nondiscrimination, and dignity.

The third step specifies the obligations of States towards ensuring the respect, protection and fulfilment of the right in light of the duties imposed by Article 2 to "undertake to take steps, individually and through international assistance and cooperation, especially economic and technical, to the maximum of [States'] available resources, with a view to achieving progressively the full realization of the rights recognized in the present Covenant by all appropriate means, including particularly the adoption of legislative measures." Finally, the fourth step aims, using other associated human rights principles and further Articles of relevant treaties, to delineate the steps needed to achieve these aims in practice by identifying the policy option which is both (1) most likely to maximize benefits and (2) consistent with the limits and obligations imposed by the right to science and fundamental human rights principles.

In Chapter 14, **Mike Frick** and **Gisa Dang** investigate "The Right to Science: A Practical Tool for Advancing Global Health Equity and Promoting the Human Rights of People with Tuberculosis." Tuberculosis (TB) has killed more people than any other infectious disease in human history and remains the leading cause of death from a single infectious agent globally. The deadly persistence of TB reflects decades of underinvestment in research and development and insufficient efforts by governments (i.e. duty bearers) to make the benefits of scientific progress and its applications available to all people with and at risk of TB. The prevailing orientation of biomedical innovation – defined by a maximalist approach to intellectual property protection – does not prioritize the health of poor and marginalized communities which bear the greatest burden of TB. Nor do many governments' health laws and policies keep up with scientific progress, resulting in outdated TB programs with negative outcomes for the health and human rights of individuals with TB.

Frick and Dang examine how the Treatment Action Group (TAG) has applied the right to science as the primary frame for analysis, activism, and community mobilization aimed at promoting TB research and ensuring equitable access to its benefits. They first illustrate how TB stands as a paradigmatic example of the consequences of state inattention to the development, diffusion, and conservation of science. Then, they describe how TAG has applied right to science principles and concepts in pursuit of three overarching questions in the context of TB: (1) What does access mean under the right? (2) What does participation under the right look like in practice? (3) How can advocates hold governments accountable for upholding their obligations under the right?

Finally, in Chapter 15, "A Proposal for Indicators of the Human Right to Science," **Andrea Boggio** and **Brian Gran** discuss how indicators may be used to monitor realization of the human right to science articulated in Article 15 ICESCR. Measuring the extent of the gap between universally acknowledged standards and implementation efforts of national governments contributes to the realization of the human right to science for different countries at different times. Indicators are widely used to monitor how well states live up to the standards necessary for the advancement of human rights. Following a review of relevant literature on human rights indicators, Boggio and Gran propose a definition of the normative content of the human right to science and identify indicators which can be used to measure the realization of the right. They discuss several challenges and limitations of their approach yet ultimately argue for the utility of indicators. Such indicators can be used to (1) facilitate monitoring of compliance with Article 15 of the Covenant on Economic, Social and Cultural Rights by UN bodies as well as human rights advocates; (2) refine the essential attributes of the human right to science, which are still not well defined; and (3) assist national governments in implementing policies that contribute to the realization of the human right to science.

The Right to Science: Then and Now ends with an "Epilogue" by **Christine Mitchell**.

PART I

The Right to Science, Then

1

The Dawning of a Right

Science and the Universal Declaration of Human Rights (1941–1948)

Mikel Mancisidor

1.1 INTRODUCTION

The United Nations (UN) Committee on Economic, Social and Cultural Rights has recently adopted General Comment No. 25 on Science and Economic, Social and Cultural Rights (E/C.12/GC/25), a process in which the author of the present chapter has been intimately involved for five years.

This General Comment, which has normative implications for 170 countries, is an interpretation of the obligations contained in the UN International Covenant on Economic, Social and Cultural Rights (ICESCR) of 1966, which came into effect in 1976. It is also an important step on a long journey that began at the dawn of the Universal Declaration of Human Rights and has not yet finished.

This chapter reviews the origins of that story. To do so, it charts the background from President Franklin D. Roosevelt's famous Four Freedoms speech, delivered in January 1941, to the adoption of the Universal Declaration of Human Rights at the Palais Chaillot in Paris on December 10, 1948, with many steps in between and beyond.

A careful reading of the background and the historical context of the Universal Declaration, supplemented by a study of the *travaux préparatoires*, will reveal to us that many of the debates, dilemmas, and challenges that we face today were already known in an inchoate form and discussed by our predecessors. Absorbing the lessons of those debates and reflecting on their ideas is not only to pay due homage, but also to undertake an exercise of extraordinary relevance and practicality.

1.2 THE HISTORICAL CONTEXT AND BACKGROUND

The Right to Science,[1] as we will refer to it in this chapter, was recognized in the 1948 Universal Declaration of Human Rights ("the Declaration") as follows:

---

[1] This denomination is the source of some conflict and is not shared by all scholars in the field. Still, due to its general nature, it will help us to start. We will make the terminology more precise during the course of this chapter.

27 (1) Everyone has the right freely to participate in the cultural life of the community, to enjoy the arts and to share in scientific advancement and its benefits.

Having read article 27, we may refer to the *travaux préparatoires*[2] of the Declaration to discern why its drafters chose those precise words and what they thereby intended to say and leave unsaid.[3] At first sight, this may seem like a question with a short, straightforward answer. On reflection, however, it is clear that further inquiry is necessary to fully grasp the drafters' intentions.

To fulfil this goal, we must go back in history to January 1941. Eleven months prior to the United States' entry into World War II, President Roosevelt made reference, in his famous "Four Freedoms" speech, to the "enjoyment of the fruits of scientific progress" in a context which allows us to consider it a direct precedent of the Right to Science. The speech is widely recognized as one of the main intellectual precursors of the post-war international system and as one of the foundations of the Universal Declaration. Roosevelt's reference here to science is not secondary or circumstantial. Science is given center stage as President Roosevelt places it amongst the six "basic things" of a "healthy and strong" democracy enabling the enjoyment of the Four Freedoms. These Freedoms, in turn, provide the foundations of human rights:

> For there is nothing mysterious about the foundations of a healthy and strong democracy. The basic things expected by our people of their political and economic systems are simple. They are: Equality of opportunity for youth and for others. Jobs for those who can work. Security for those who need it. The ending of special privilege for the few. The preservation of civil liberties for all. The enjoyment of the fruits of scientific progress in a wider and constantly rising standard of living.
>
> These are the simple, the basic things that must never be lost sight of in the turmoil and unbelievable complexity of our modern world. The inner and abiding strength of our economic and political systems is dependent upon the degree to which they fulfil these expectations. ...In the future days, which we seek to make secure, we look forward to a world founded upon four essential human freedoms.[4]

---

[2] For this historical analysis, I have referred to two essential classics (Morsink and Glendon) and a more recent book which will surely soon become a new and essential classic, also written by one of the leading experts on the Right to Science (Schabas): Johannes Morsink, *The Universal Declaration of Human Rights: Origins, Drafting and Intent*, University of Pennsylvania Press, 1999; Mary Ann Glendon, *A World Made New: Eleanor Roosevelt and the Universal Declaration of Human Rights*, Random House, 2001; and William A. Schabas, *The Universal Declaration of Human Rights. The travaux préparatoires*, Cambridge University Press, 2013.

[3] According to article 32 of the 1969 Vienna Convention on the Law of Treaties, "the preparatory work of the treaty and the circumstances of its conclusion" are not principle resources for interpreting the texts as regards their application, but are "supplementary means of interpretation" which can be used to "in order to confirm the meaning resulting from the application of article 31, or to determine the meaning when the interpretation according to article 31: (a) leaves the meaning ambiguous or obscure; or (b) leads to a result which is manifestly absurd or unreasonable." See for example *LaGrand (Germany v. United States)* [2001] ICJ Rep 466, paras. 104–109 and Julian Davis Mortenson, "Is the Vienna Convention Hostile to Drafting History?" (2013) *Am. J. Int'l L.* 107.

[4] The Franklin D. Roosevelt Presidential Library and Museum: www.fdrlibrary.org/archives.

The key aspect science played in Roosevelt's vision was confirmed in his famous letter to Vannevar Bush,[5] the wartime head of US military research and development, in November 1944, in which Roosevelt imagined a better world after the war thanks to science and asked Bush for a specific plan to carry out this mission:

> There is no reason why the lessons to be found (in times of war) cannot be profitably employed in times of peace. ... What can be done ... to make known to the world as soon as possible the contributions which have been made during our war effort to scientific knowledge ... New frontiers of the mind are before us, and if they are pioneered with the same vision, boldness, and drive with which we have waged this war we can create a fuller and more fruitful employment and a fuller and more fruitful life.[6]

The President, however, died soon after and in the post-war period that followed two circumstances were to have serious influence on the debates regarding science. The first was the long-standing memory of the two atomic bombs dropped on Hiroshima and Nagasaki in August 1945, which placed science, its limits, its control, and the social responsibility of scientists at the forefront of many debates.[7] The second was the new Cold War rivalry between the United States and the Soviet Union which, as we shall see, would have a profound impact on the issue of science and its role in the international arena.

Nevertheless, the role of science in the humanities was gaining traction, a concept that can clearly be seen in the evolution of the institution that we now know as the United Nations Educational, Scientific and Cultural Organization (UNESCO). The origins of UNESCO, as we know it, lie in a little-known debate which is however key to understanding the interplay between science and politics. UNESCO came into being on the initiative of the Conference of Allied Ministers of Education (CAME), following a proposal made by the United States to set up a United Nations Organisation for Educational and Cultural Reconstruction, and afterwards a United Nations Organisation for Education and Culture, UNECO. It was only later in a Conference in November 1945 that UNECO, entirely without any reference to science in its acronym, was revamped to create UNESCO. This conference, held in London and chaired by the British Minister for Education, Ms. Ellen Wilkinson, saw a group of scientists led by the biochemist Joseph Needham and the biologist Julian Huxley, both British, fight for the inclusion of science in the name and mandate of the new organization. Their commitment to the new organization would lead Needham to be installed as the Director of the Natural Sciences Section and Huxley to be inaugurated as the first Director General

---

[5] On the Roosevelt-Bush relationship and its impact on the development of basic science see Jacques Mirenowicz, *Sciences et démocratie: le couple impossible?*, Ed. Charles Leopold Mayer, 2000.

[6] The Scientific War Work of Linus C. Pauling website. Oregon State University. http://scarc.library.oregonstate.edu/coll/pauling/war/corr/sci13.006.4-roosevelt-bush-19441117.html.

[7] For a history of scientists and the atomic bomb, see Diana Preston, *Before the Fall-Out. From Marie Curie to Hiroshima*, Walker & Company, 2005.

(in fact one of only two Director Generals in UNESCO's history to be a scientist, along with Federico Mayor Zaragoza, from Spain).

Encouraged by these two scientists, at the plenary session of the London Conference, Minister Wilkinson defended the position with the following very significant words:

> Although the Organisation's original name does not mention science, the British delegation will present a proposal for the name to be Organisation for Education, Science and Culture. In these days, when we are all wondering, perhaps apprehensively, what the scientists will do to us next, it is important that they should be linked closely with the humanities and should feel that they have a responsibility to mankind. I do not believe that any scientists will have survived the world catastrophe, who will say that they are utterly uninterested in the social implications of their discoveries.[8]

The reason for briefly digressing into the creation history of UNESCO is to demonstrate the state of distrust ("what the scientists will do to us next") which pervaded the debate on the development of science when fully disconnected from values and aims. The role of science and technology in Nazi war crimes, and in the atomic bombs mentioned above, was still very present in their thoughts.[9] Bearing in mind that the Nuremberg Doctor's Trial,[10] with its 140 days of gruesome and horrendous evidence, was held during 1947, and that seven defendants found guilty were given the death penalty and hanged in June 1948, that is, right in the middle of the negotiation process for the Declaration, we can appreciate René Cassin's observation that this trial "influenced the debate on how or whether to connect human rights and science in the Universal Declaration."[11]

Nevertheless, despite current affairs and developments, UNESCO's Constitution puts science at the service of other objectives (peace and security) and does not treat it as a purpose in itself:[12]

> The purpose of the Organization is to contribute to peace and security by promoting collaboration among the nations through education, science and culture in order to

---

[8] C. Atlee, E. Wilkinson, J. T. Bodet, R. Cassin (1985) The Life of the Mind. UNESCO Courier Oct: 8–9.

[9] It is interesting how for many authors the experience of a political and moral catastrophe was in fact the central prior condition not only for the creation of this article 27 but for the entire Declaration. Hence one cannot comprehend either the fact, structure, or the dynamic of the expansion of human rights after 1945 without interpreting it as a result of the experience of a political and moral catastrophe. Christoph Menke and Arnd Pollmann, *Philosophie der Menschenrechte*, Junius Verlag GMBH, 2017.

[10] *United States of America v. Karl Brandt et al.* Nov. 21, 1946–Aug. 20, 1947, Accession Number: 1995.A.0970, RG Number: RG-30.001M (https://collections.ushmm.org/search/catalog/irn504191).

[11] Professor Richard Pierre Claude. Science in the Service of Human Rights. An Introductory Class for Science, Technology and Public Health. Princeton University Syllabus, 2002.

[12] See the same idea in Fernando Valderrama, *Historia de la UNESCO*. UNESCO Reference Works. UNESCO Publications, Paris, 1995: "for UNESCO, education, science and culture are not purposes in themselves but rather means and tools for a spiritual enterprise and a moral conduct or effort. The final objective, declared in its Constitution, is peace based on respect for human rights", p. 29.

further universal respect for justice, for the rule of law and for the human rights and fundamental freedoms which are affirmed for the peoples of the world, without distinction of race, sex, language or religion, by the Charter of the United Nations.

In this context, the Universal Declaration of Human Rights started out as a succession of working drafts over one and a half years. The first draft was prepared by the Canadian jurist John Peters Humphrey, who had been appointed the first Director of the United Nations Division of Human Rights. This draft is a very complete list of the rights which had been recorded in other declarations and reference texts. It was then rearranged and converted into a more consistent draft by the French jurist René Cassin. That draft had to then pass the drafting Committee and the sessions of the Human Rights Commission, before being approved by the United Nations Economic and Social Council (ECOSOC) and finally, on December 10, 1948, by the General Assembly in a session at the Palais Chaillot in Paris, leading to the Universal Declaration of Human Rights as we know it today.

Humphrey's first draft already included a Right to Science under the same article as a Right to Culture and to the Arts. According to René Cassin[13] the article was included on request from cultural organizations, including UNESCO,[14] which was represented at this time before the Commission on Human Rights by Jacques L. Havet. Already in this first version, we find that the choice of wording of the text is an important matter to consider.

In Humphrey's draft, the right is formulated as the right "to share in the benefits of science." This formulation appears to have been inspired by the Inter-American Juridical Committee for the American Declaration of the Rights and Duties of Man,[15] as the Chilean delegation was keen to point out.[16] This Declaration had been approved in Bogotá a few months before the Universal Declaration and it stated in its article XIII that "[e]very person has the right to take part in the cultural life of the community, to enjoy the arts, and to participate in the benefits that result from intellectual progress, especially scientific discoveries."

---

[13] Morsink, p. 218.
[14] On the UNESCO's intellectual contribution to the drafting of the Universal Declaration, see UNESCO/PHS/3(rev) Paris, July 25, 1948, with contributions by J. Maritain, M. Gandhi, E. H. Carr, B. Croce, R. P. Teilhard de Chardin, A. Huxley and two specific papers on scientific matters: "Rights and Duties Concerning Creative Expression, in particular in Science," by J. M. Burgers, and "Science and the Rights of Man," by W. A. Noyes.
[15] Richard Pierre Claude looks for the origin of that contribution in the Inter-American Conference on the Problems on War and Peace, Mexico, 1945 (Richard Pierre Claude, "Scientists' Rights and the Human Right to the Benefits of Science" in Audrey Chapman and Sage Russel, *Core Obligations: Building a Framework for Economic, Social and Cultural Rights*, Intersentia, 2002. p. 250)
[16] Mikel Mancisidor, "El Derecho Humano a la Ciencia", Anuario de Derechos Humanos. Universidad de Chile, 2017.

1.3 DEBATE ON THE PURPOSE OF SCIENCE IN THE DECLARATION

The end goal of science is and has long been a topic of perennial debate. As such, it should come as no surprise that this debate took on some importance during the negotiation of the Declaration in the political context of the Cold War. The debate started during the first rounds of drafting and discussion when the Soviet delegation, led by Alexei Pavlov, nephew of the well-known Russian scientist Ivan Pavlov, proposed a new text to the effect that this right should protect and promote certain objectives. The proposal stated that: "the development of science must serve the interest of progress and democracy and the cause of international peace and cooperation."

The proposal was reasonable enough on its face given that, as the Soviet delegation argued, the preceding article in the Declaration on the Right to Education had been given a new second paragraph on the objectives of education. In its final formulation, article 26 states:

> 26. 1. Everyone has the right to education. ... 2. Education shall be directed to the full development of the human personality and to the strengthening of respect for human rights and fundamental freedoms. It shall promote understanding, tolerance and friendship among all nations, racial or religious groups, and shall further the activities of the United Nations for the maintenance of peace.

If it had been considered appropriate under the Right to Education to refer to the objectives or aims of education (human development, human rights, understanding, tolerance, peace, and so on), the Soviet proposal of including the objectives of science to be protected and promoted by the Right to Science appeared logical on the same grounds. However, in the end, the three ideas contained in the proposal (progress, democracy, and peace and international cooperation) were voted on separately and all three were rejected. Some States considered that science, and therefore the Right to Science, should not be subject to any purpose, however noble, given that its aim could only be to seek the truth.[17]

The Ecuadorian delegate explained his vote during the debates on the Declaration by saying that "science should serve the interests of life rather than death, of peace rather than war." The Soviet proposal seemed reasonable enough,

---

[17] See the Belgian position ("the USSR amendment was an attempt to assign science a political mission. While he (the Belgian delegate) wanted science to serve the cause of peace and co-operation among nations, he thought it was not for the declaration of human rights to define its role. In any case, if it had to be done it would have been better to say that the aim of science was the search for truth") or in even stronger terms by the Cuban stance (the delegation "was convinced that science should remain entirely free and that the State should not interfere at any stage in scientific or literary creation. On the contrary, it was democracy which should be placed at the service of science, the latter itself the servant of truth. Those who had faith in man could not fear truth. That was the spirit underlying the declaration of human rights.") Cassin was concerned about the possibility of the idea being "invoked to justify the harnessing of science to political ends". And Chile feared that "it might in practice lead to the control of scientific research for political ends". Citations taken from Morsink.

certainly, except when considered under the perverse Cold War logic dominant at the time.[18] The fact was that other delegations distrusted the concept of democracy being defended by the USSR and its satellites. Eleanor Roosevelt, for example, feared a right "applied to abstract ideas for which no uniform interpretation existed. It seemed dangerous to adopt a text which could be interpreted as a pretext for the enslavement of science. The US delegation would under no circumstances agree that science should be placed at the service of politics. Yet that might be the practical effect of the USSR amendment."[19] Similarly, the British delegation added that "unfortunately, the conception of democracy and of progress did not seem to be the same everywhere. The word 'democracy' could be interpreted in many ways ... science should not be at the service of an ideology."[20]

The Soviet delegation warned about the danger of a "science subservient to militarism and where intellectual forces were concentrated on producing a terrible weapon"[21] twelve years before Eisenhower denounced:

> the acquisition of unwarranted influence, whether sought or unsought, by the military industrial complex. The potential for the disastrous rise of misplaced power exists and will persist ... Akin to, and largely responsible for the sweeping changes in our industrial-military posture, has been the technological revolution during recent decades.
>
> In this revolution, research has become central; it also becomes more formalized, complex, and costly ... a government contract becomes virtually a substitute for intellectual curiosity ... Yet, in holding scientific research and discovery in respect, as we should, we must also be alert to the equal and opposite danger that public policy could itself become the captive of a scientific technological elite.[22]

A neutral observer might have considered the Soviet concern as being along the right lines, or even seen it as visionary, although, with the benefit of historical hindsight, the reluctance of the other countries might also appear justified, given that they were faced with Stalin's militarized Soviet Union at the beginning of the Cold War.

As we now know, the final formulation, for good or ill, rightly or wrongly, avoided references to the purposes of the Right to Science, or of science itself, beyond enjoying the "benefits which derive from it."

---

[18] "The United Nations General Assembly adopted the Universal Declaration of Human Rights ... in the midst of an especially bitter phase of the Cold War." Dr John F. Sears, available at www.fdrlibrary.org/documents/356632/390886/sears.pdf/c300e130-b6e6-4580-8bf1-07b72195b370.

[19] Morsink considers this position "spurious" although this author is not so sure. The author does however go on to recall that once the proposal had been rejected Eleanor Roosevelt generously declared that "during the war science in the United States had been placed at the service of Government and it might be recalled that all the allies, including the USSR, had profited therefrom." (pp. 62–63)

[20] Morsink, p. 63.

[21] Morsink, p. 62.

[22] Public Papers of the Presidents of the United States Dwight Eisenhower, Published by the National Archives of the United States, 1961. Doc. N°. 421, pp. 1035–1040.

1.4 PRIMARY OBJECTS OF THE RIGHT ACCORDING TO THE DECLARATION

At one stage of the Declaration negotiation process the formulation of the right was modified from the initial version based "on the benefits that result from scientific discoveries" to the wider idea of the right to "share in scientific advancement." This significant change was approved on a proposal from China, based, according to the delegate Peng Chun Chang, on the authority of Francis Bacon.[23][24][25]

This change and the loss of the word "benefits" did not last long and it was soon restored.[26] The Soviet delegation had already voiced its support for the idea of "benefits": "the benefits of science were not the property of a chosen few, but the heritage of mankind ... that the task of science was to work for the advancement of peaceful aims and to make human life better."[27] However, the word was recovered on submission from Cuba with the argument that "not everyone was sufficiently gifted to play a part in scientific advancement" and that what was needed was for the text to state that everyone has the right "to share in the benefits that result from scientific advancement."[28] Chile supported the Cuban proposal emphasizing that, as the Inter-American Juridical Committee had proposed, the key concept was the idea of "benefits."

To this both the Chinese and Saudi Arabian delegation added that even if one does not have the capacities to contribute to scientific knowledge, we all nevertheless possess the capacity for certain enjoyments of science beyond just its direct, material benefits.[29]

In the end, however, Cassin agreed with the Cuban vision and declared that "even if all persons could not play an equal part in scientific progress, they should indisputably be able to participate in the benefits derived from it."[30]

---

[23] William A. Schabas "Study of the Right to Enjoy the Benefits of the Scientific and Technological Progress and its Applications" in Yvonne Donders and Vladimir Volodin (eds.) *Human Rights in Education, Science and Culture*, UNESCO Ashgate, 2007. p. 276; and Morsink, p. 219.

[24] It is curious that we cite here Dr. P. C. Chang as if his great contribution was based on the authority of a Western classic, when "Dr. Chang was one of the few members of the Commission who consistently reminded his colleagues that a Universal Declaration had to incorporate philosophical systems other than those of the West, and he himself frequently cited Confucian principles to inform the discussion. Humphrey credits him with using his mastery of Confucian philosophy to find compromise language at particularly difficult points." M. Glen Johnson and Janusz Symonides, (eds.), *The Universal Declaration of Human Rights: A History of its Creation and Implementation 1948–1998*. Preface by Federico Mayor Zaragoza. UNESCO, 1998. p. 22.

[25] The importance of Chang's contribution was seen differently to how it is seen here by Richard Pierre Claude: "the elitist tone of the original article, appearing only to protect scientists, was thus overcome by Mr Chang's proposal that everyone has the right not only to share in the advancement of science (scientists and students of science) but also to share in their benefits (the general public)" (Claude, "Scientists ..." pp. 253–254).

[26] On which see generally Morsink and Schabas.

[27] Morsink, p. 219.

[28] Morsink, p. 219.

[29] Morsink, p. 219.

[30] Morsink, p. 219.

This back-and-forth exchange of ripostes nonetheless ended with the concept of the benefits of science being restored by consensus and added to, rather than substituted into, the Chinese text, which is more important than it may seem.

This historical debate helps explain the prevalence of the misapprehension that the scope of this right is limited to participating in "the benefits of science" which means, among other things, the ability to "be able to receive affordable medicine."[31] One of this chapter's intentions is to provide a more comprehensive and ambitious interpretation of this key phrase than the mere idea of "[being] able to receive." The word "share" in the phrase "everyone has the right freely ... to share in scientific advancement and its benefits," may appear at first sight to be of a high level of generality, and as connoting less engagement or activity than the alternative phrases to "participate" or "take part." However, given the background above the phrase must in my judgment be taken to indicate an idea of action or agency, of active participation in an enterprise or endeavor, and must therefore be considered in this regard to have the same meaning as "participate" or "take part."

Against this statement one could argue that since article 27 opens with the expression "everyone has the right freely to participate in the cultural life of the community," that had the authors intended to use this same idea of active participation also in science, then they would have used the same word; however, this was not the case as "share in" was chosen instead, possibly precisely to reduce this association with action. However, the French and Spanish versions of the Declaration, which are equally valid, clearly opt for the idea I propose by including the words "participer" and "participar," which are without doubt identical synonyms of their French and Spanish counterparts, "prendre part" or "tomar parte," which are used to open the article.

If we examine international law criteria for interpreting identical texts in two or more languages,[32] we see that "the text is equally authoritative in each language," that "[t]he terms of the treaty are presumed to have the same meaning in each authentic text" and that "when a comparison of the authentic texts discloses a difference of meaning ... the meaning which best reconciles the texts, having regard to the object and purpose of the treaty, shall be adopted." I propose without doubt that we should opt for an interpretation of "to share in" that is synonymous with "to participate in" or "to take part in" through which we achieve the equivalence of meanings between language versions necessary to "reconcile the texts."

Further support for this position may be derived from General Comment No. 21 on the Right to Participate in Cultural Life, and the work of the Committee for Economic, Social and Cultural Rights (CESCR), which have previously analyzed

---

[31] Here I use an expression borrowed from Morsink, p. 219.
[32] Article 33 of the Vienna Convention on the Law of Treaties states that when a treaty has been authenticated in two or more languages, the text is equally authoritative in each language, unless the treaty provides or the parties agree that, in case of divergence, a particular text shall prevail. The terms of the treaty are presumed to have the same meaning in each authentic text.

the meaning and scope of the term "to participate" or "to take part" in and indicated that "they have the same meaning" and include both "access" and "contribution."[33] The same idea applies to interpreting the Right to Science.[34]

Although this reflection delves deeply into semantics, this analysis is essential to framing our vision of a right which goes beyond "benefit from" and advocates broader concepts of "participation in;" a right which includes participation in scientific creation[35] (citizen science),[36] and participation in scientific policy,[37] among other things. The recent approval of the General Comment No. 25 by CESCR[38] provides enough guiding elements to revisit this question with new tools.

1.5 A BRIEF CONSIDERATION OF THE NAME OF THE RIGHT

Up to this point we have referred to this right as the Right to Science, which might appear to some as lacking in technical precision. Many authors outright reject this framing. It does however merit further consideration.

We could refer to this right in the terms of the Universal Declaration as the "right to share in scientific advancement and its benefits" (RSSAB) or in terms of the ICESCR as the "right to enjoy the benefits of scientific progress and its applications" (REBSP), but it is clear these are both unwieldy and of limited usefulness as formulae if we wish to develop this right, disseminate it, and hope for its uptake

---

[33] "15. There are, among others, three interrelated main components of the right to participate or take part in cultural life: (a) participation in, (b) access to, and (c) contribution to cultural life."

[34] E/C.12/GC/21Committee on Economic, Social and Cultural Rights. Forty-third session. 2–20 November 2009. General comment No. 21: Right of everyone to take part in cultural life (art. 15, para. 1 (a), of the International Covenant on Economic, Social and Cultural Rights).

[35] "Ground is being made in the idea that knowledge is a matter of all, work to which ... all citizens contribute. Little by little the capacity has been recognised of all human beings to participate in research, invent and do science, or at least judge some of its conclusions. At the beginning of the nineties organisations like the American Association for the Advancement of Science (AAAS) and UNESCO proclaimed the slogan 'science for all', which can be summarised as follows: not only science in the service of all, but science for all." (Daniel Innerarity, *La democracia del conocimiento. Por una sociedad inteligente*, Paidós, Barcelona, 2011. p. 130).

[36] "The idea of "civic science" (Alan Irving, *Citizen Science: A Study of People, Expertise and Sustainable Government*, London, Routledge. 1995) or of a "scientific citizen" (Frank Fisher, *Citizens, Experts and Environment. The Politics of Local Knowledge*, Durham NC, Duke University Press Books, 2000) refer to the current challenges regarding how to introduce nonscientific agents into the decision-making processes, how to take local knowledge and experience into consideration, how to report risk in a transparent manner or other similar democratisation requirements." (Innerarity, p. 114).

[37] On participation in decision-making and its problems and solutions, with important ideas and interesting examples, see Daniel Lee Kleinman, "Democratization of Science and Technology" in Daniel Lee Kleinman (ed.), *Science, Technology & Democracy*, State University of New York Press, 2000.

[38] E/C.12/GC/25, Committee on Economic, Social and Cultural Rights. Sixty-seventh Session, 30 April 2020. General comment No. 25 (2020) on science and economic, social and cultural rights (article 15 (1) (b), (2), (3) and (4) of the International Covenant on Economic, Social and Cultural Rights).

and use by the broader society. General Comment No. 25 chooses to use another, more complete, wording which might still suffer some practical problems in the everyday, and certainly oral, usage: "the right to participate in and to enjoy the benefits of Scientific Progress and its Applications (RPEBSPA)."

Some may find in its abbreviated formulation, the Right to Science, opportunities for humor. For example, science is not accessed as of right but through effort and intellectual energy, which is clearly true (since Euclid we have known that "there is no Royal Road to geometry"). Yet, putting cynicism aside, the fact remains that when we speak about the Right to Health,[39] technically what we are speaking about is the right to the "enjoyment of the highest attainable standard of physical and mental health," and not about a right to be healthy by decree. The same applies to the Right to Science. A simple name does not simplify or caricature a right's normative contents, but is instead intended to offer practical cognitive advantages facilitating familiarity with the concept and easing the cognitive burdens of its use. We are interested in a shorter, more manageable, and more easily popularized formulation than the RSSAB or the REBSP or RPEBSPA. Lea Shaver has suggested a very interesting name, the Right to Science and Culture, which includes the artistic, cultural, and scientific contents of article 27 of the Declaration. For Shaver, "[a]lthough 'science' and 'culture' are invoked separately in both UNESCO's name and the Article 27 text, there is no clear dividing line between these two fields …. This integrated approach is captured by my emphasis on the unifying concept of the 'Right to science and culture.'"[40]

There are substantial grounds for this unified approach to science and culture, not the least of which can be discerned from the points this chapter has already made above and in chapters by several other distinguished commentators on the right to science contained within this volume. That said, for practical reasons, and to most effectively develop the contents of science and culture, it is arguably most appropriate to continue, at least for now, working in pursuit of an autonomous Right to Science within the field of cultural rights. Shaver's proposal still appears to me to be an attractive option full of suggestive possibilities.

Another short-form name for the right, the "right to access to knowledge," has been suggested, backed by the authority of B. Boutros-Ghali,[41] although it could be said that this formulation only refers to some of the possible normative contents of the Right to Science.[42] The Information Society Project at Yale

---

[39] I am grateful for the example given at public lectures by Lea Shaver and Jessica Wyndham.
[40] Lea Shaver, "The Right to Science and Culture," Wisconsin Law Review 2010, no. 1, 121–184, at p. 156.
[41] B. Boutros-Ghali, "The Right to Culture and the Universal Declaration of Human Rights" at the UNESCO's Meeting of Experts on Cultural Rights as Human Rights, Paris, 1968. Subsequently published under the title *Cultural Rights as Human Rights*, UNESCO, Paris, 1970. Cited by Shaver, p. 153. The expression "right to knowledge" did at least have a precedent in the Declaration of Principles of International Cultural Cooperation de 1966 (Shaver, p. 156).
[42] The conceptual idea put forward by Boutros-Ghali back in 1968 might now be considered somewhat limited: "(Art. 27) assumes firstly that the individual has attained a 'standard of living adequate' … For, if the individual has not reached this standard because he is undernourished or even starving,

Law School has opted for solid arguments based on the ICESCR for the same formulation of a "right of access to knowledge" or more briefly still, "the right to knowledge."[43] Here, the more flexible and practical "Right to Science" is advanced as the most appropriate, encouraged by the fact that it has already been accepted by a considerable number of authors,[44] scientific and academic associations, social organizations, the first Special Rapporteur in the Field of Cultural Rights, Farida Shaheed,[45] UNESCO,[46] and some countries.[47]

Some may say that what is gained in flexibility is lost in rigor when considered against the REBSP, but it could be said that the short formulation is at once more ambitious because it contains all the contents of a right to actively access science beyond merely passively participating in its benefits. It is this framework that is defended in this chapter. What we shorten in title we increase in contents.

The commitment to an autonomous and differentiated Right to Science must not prevent it from being read together and in harmony with other human rights and in particular with the cultural rights of which it forms part,[48] and with which it is

because he has no decent lodging or lacks the possibility of receiving the most elementary medical attention, it is evident that he will have neither the desire nor the possibility of taking part in the cultural life of his community and there can be no question of his enjoying the arts and literature, still less of participating in scientific advancement." Shaver, p. 73.

[43] "Article 15 contains three provisions addressing (a) cultural participation, (b) access to the benefits of science and technology, and (c) protection of authorship. A careful reading, however, makes clear that these must be understood as three aspects of a single right, as the text continues: 'the steps to be taken by the States Parties to the present Covenant to achieve the full realization of this right shall include those necessary for the conservation, the development and the diffusion of science and culture.' The Covenant's use of the singular noun 'this right' indicates that the 15(1)(a–c) provisions are intended as three interrelated aspects of a single human right: the right of everyone to participate in the advancement and share in the benefits of human knowledge – both scientific and cultural. This scope is best captured by the phrase 'the right of access to knowledge,' or more briefly still, 'the right to knowledge.'" www.yaleisp.org/sites/default/files/publications/article15.pdf.

[44] S. Porsdam Mann, V. J. Bradley, M. F. Chou, G. Church, M. Mann, C. Mitchell, Y. Donders and H. Porsdam, "On the human right to enjoy the benefits of science and its applications" Proceedings of the National Academies of Science, October 23, 2018, 115 (43) 10820–10823; S. Porsdam Mann, Y. Donders and H. Porsdam, "Sleeping beauty: the Human Right to Science," Human Rights Quarterly, Volume 42, Number 2, May 2020, 332–356.

[45] A/HRC/20/26, Human Rights Council, Twentieth session, 14 May 2012, Report of the Special Rapporteur in the field of cultural rights, Farida Shaheed: The right to enjoy the benefits of scientific progress and its applications, "this right, referred herein as the right to science," para. 3.

[46] https://en.unesco.org/commemorations/worldscienceday2018.

[47] XXVI Cumbre Iberoamericana de Jefes de Estado y de Gobierno. Declaración Final. Guatemala, 16 November, 2018. Para. 45, www.segib.org/wp-content/uploads/00.1.-DECLARACION-DE-LA-XXVI-CUMBRE-GUATEMALA_VF_E.pdf.

[48] "Five human Rights are understood – according to Elsa Stamapopulou – as cultural rights under International Law: 1. The Right to Education; 2. The Right to Participate in Cultural Life; 3. The Right to Enjoy the Benefits of Scientific Progress and its Applications; 4. The Right to Benefit from the protection of the moral and material interest resulting from any scientific, cultural or artistic production of which the person is the author, and, 5. the freedom for scientific research and creative activity." Elsa Stamatopoulou, *Cultural Rights in International Law. Article 27 of the Universal Declaration of Human Rights and Beyond*, Matrinus Nijhoff, 2007.

"inherently interlinked"[49] as the Special Rapporteur on Cultural Rights rightly says, or as the Information Society Project argues in favor of the right of access to knowledge.

It seems that over time, the use of the expression "Right to Science" will become a familiar shorthand, making this type of nominalist explanation no longer necessary, and it will be used for ease of exposition in the same way we speak about the Right to Health, the Right to Work, or the Right to Housing, which are at least as problematic as the Right to Science when it comes to the gulf existing between a simplistic reading of their formulation and their real contents.

1.6 THE RIGHT TO SCIENCE AS A CULTURAL RIGHT

The importance of science for the enjoyment of other human rights and for sustainable human development is thankfully beyond doubt. Thousands of pages have been written on science's importance for the challenges facing our societies and our planet, and plenty more on science's importance for our wellbeing and for the opportunities and possibilities currently in our hands.

Thanks to scientific and technological advancement we have managed, in global terms, to double life expectancy, vanquish much suffering and disease, and we are also able to produce sufficient food to feed the world (the fact that we do not have sufficient institutional, economic, political, or ethical resources to make the most of this capacity is altogether another matter). Bertrand Russell once said that "science can confer two kinds of benefits: it can diminish bad things, and it can increase good things."[50] Nowadays, we have access to information and knowledge which was previously unimaginable, at a speed and price which surprises us every day. All of this provides us with the opportunity to be free, to choose, to learn, to investigate, ... to develop ourselves as persons and as communities, because "the knowledge society has more possibilities for personal freedom than all previous social forms."[51]

It is true that this development has brought with it new problems that were previously unknown: new diseases; novel risks and threats like the loss of biodiversity, climate change, contamination; how to apportion and manage control over the continually expanding mass of useful information; loss of privacy; the dilemmas of bioethics; and many others. It is not suggested that science alone can solve these challenges; it is certain, however, that without science they cannot be successfully and responsibly tackled. Science is not therefore ultimately responsible for these challenges, but it is an essential element in meeting them. The response to these

---

[49] Farida Shaheed A/HRC/20/26 (n. 45): "the Special Rapporteur views these rights inherently interlinked, since both relate to the pursuit of knowledge and understanding and to human creativity in a constantly changing world" (para. 3) and "the rights to science and culture are interlinked" (para. 16).

[50] Bertrand Russell, *The Impact of Science on Society*, London, 1952. p. 104.

[51] Innerarity, p. 73.

challenges must be social, political, economic, ethical,[52] and also scientific, because the response must be based on scientific knowledge on our side.[53]

Science is directly related to various rights up to the point where they have common contents. Take, for example, its interconnections with the Right to Education: education is necessary for the performance of science, and science is essential to any proper education from primary school level and beyond. Consider the Right to Health: the right to enjoy the highest possible level of physical and mental health relies in large part for its fulfilment on the right to benefit from the advancement of scientific progress, and especially its applications. With respect to the Right to Food or the Right to Water and Sanitation, it is clear that science and technology must be allies for progress in the universalization of the enjoyment of those basic needs. As for Rights of Association, Information, and Expression, these are all essential requirements for the smooth and efficient workings of the scientific community. The UNESCO representative at the Commission on Human Rights, Jacques L. Havet, pronounced very clearly on this matter at the Seventh Session: "The right of everyone to enjoy his share of the benefits of science was to a great extent the determining factor for the exercise by mankind as a whole of many other rights."[54]

The relationship between gender equality (or the principle of nondiscrimination on the grounds of gender) and science is also important. Scientific and technological advancement favor equality. Advancements ranging from progress in sexual and reproductive health, to the facilities provided by technology in areas traditionally (and in many places still currently) identified with women, through to scientific evidence of the persistence of the wage gap and continued implicit biases against women in some professions, have been of great practical usefulness in the fight for access by women to other previously taboo, or even vetoed, social and labor areas. Equality is also one of the contents of the Right to science which makes it crucial given there is still considerable imbalance in access to education by women in general and above all to professional technical scientific work in particular. This is so even in countries which are considered advanced in this issue. Inequality also leads to a loss of talent and capacity for science itself, which, given the reflections above on the interconnections between science and several human rights, must necessarily compound to the greater loss of humanity.

[52] "The increasing gap opening between technology and human needs can only be reduced by turning to ethics" states the eminent physicist Freeman Dyson in his delightful collection of learned articles *The Scientist as a Rebel*, New York Review Books, 2006.

[53] "Des choix sont à faire, les plus démocratiques possible, et les plus éclairés aussi. Mais une chose est sûre: nous ne préserverons pas la biodiversité avec la biologie de Pline l'Ancien, ni ne stabiliserons le climat avec la physique d'Aristote." The humorous ending to the fine book by Étienne Klein, *Allons-nous liquider la science? Galilée et les Indiens*, Flammarion, 2008. p. 120.

[54] Cited by William A. Schabas : "Study of the Right to Enjoy the Benefits of Scientific and Technological Progress and Its Applications" in Yvonne Donders and Vladimir Volodin, *Human Rights in Education, Science and Culture. Legal Development and Challenges*, UNESCO Publishing/Ashgate, Paris, 2007. p. 281.

Finally, the relationship between democracy and science is also important. Experience has shown that science flourishes more easily in settings with freedom and participation. In turn, science becomes a force for democracy by providing citizens with the knowledge needed to act responsibly in the political debate, and by providing better technological tools for participation.[55] The relationship between science and human development, the Sustainable Development Goals, and a great many other issues could be easily developed. Not much of value, though, would be added to the debate that has not been covered above. What should be highlighted is that intentional emphasis has been placed on the idea of an interrelationship or interdependence between science and other rights and interests. We must not frame a vision of science solely as an instrument for other more valuable objectives, but rather as an interaction between human assets.

This is because the need for a Right to Science is often justified by reference to science's importance for the enjoyment of other rights and this is exactly the idea I want to challenge: evidently not because it is false, but because it is insufficient for the basis of science as a human right. If science's role is purely instrumental, for the attainment of other rights, the right to science would in the best of cases be a derivative, instrumental or secondary right. I advance the argument that this right should go much further, and indeed has its own objectives and inherent value which justify it standing alone as a separate human right. In this sense, scientific knowledge makes us more human, it allows us to know ourselves and our environment better, to make better individual and collective decisions, and to enjoy life and its beauty more fully.

There is furthermore a logical, internal reason derived from the UDHR which should be stressed here: the Right to Science is contained within provisions dedicated to cultural rights, in the same category as the right to "participate in the cultural life" and the right to "enjoy the arts." There is no argument that suggests participation in cultural life or the arts should be justified as human rights by reference to their service to other ulterior or higher purposes, and they are accepted as objectives in themselves. Nor is anyone asked to explain the use of poetry, dance, or music to defend their right to create and enjoy them. The same should be said of science: its relationship to creativity, aesthetic and intellectual enjoyment, and

---

[55] The scientist and ex-Director General of UNESCO, Federico Mayor Zaragoza, often insists on the importance of "the possibility of remote participation thanks to the information and communication technology" ("Invest in the future." El País, 21 August 2012). "Technology to disseminate values, to realise the basic principle of human rights: equal dignity for all, without exceptions. Technology to disseminate the risk, to avoid fear, dogmatism, fanaticism, extremism ... Technology to create a global awareness which allows is to better appreciate what we have and the precarious situation of others. Technology to see the invisible and thereby contribute towards making what it impossible today possible in the future. Technology to mobilise, to arouse the dormant, the numb, those who are tired of waiting, the silenced and the silent, so that they can dream again, so that they spare no efforts in showing that the radical changes which are so desired are, in fact, feasible." "Women, technology and democracy for social change." http://federicomayor.blogspot.com.es/2012/10/mujer-tecnologia-y-democracia-para-el.html.

human curiosity and understanding, should suffice in order to justify it as a human right.[56] We might say that the right "to share in scientific advancement" is an objective in itself, additional to "shar[ing] in ... its benefits," where the latter of these expressions is concerned mainly with the useful effects of science on the enjoyment of other rights. More colloquially, we might say that people have a right to science for the same reason as they have a right to literature (read and write), because they are objectives in themselves, universally realizable assets, a human necessity; but that perhaps they have the right to benefit from science, in principle, because they have the right to health or to food. Had the intention been otherwise, the Right to Science would be more of an instrument of economic and social rights, and its logical position would be amongst these. It has, however, right from the beginning, been set amongst the cultural rights because, as stated by a well-known scientist and commentator, "science is culture in capital letters."[57]

Science is a basic human necessity and, as already stated, not only due to its effects on other rights but as a necessity in itself. Science makes us human, just like literature or music, or history or linguistic diversity, and this is why it is a necessity associated with the concept of dignity.

1.7 FINAL CONSIDERATIONS

This chapter examined the debates and dilemmas that led to the creation of a right that included elements both of participation in and the enjoyment of the benefits of science. It is a right that has profound political implications. It was always a means to achieve other goods and goals, but it was above all a cultural right; that is to say, a good in itself. As a book chapter it was finalized in the middle of the COVID-19 confinement. The current relevance of the right to science is therefore greater than ever.[58] It is a human right that adds key dimensions, some of them previously undervalued, to the debate around science and human rights, from access to knowledge to citizen participation, from transparency to quality, and from promoting the role of women and minorities in science to balancing intellectual property and facilitating universal access to its applications. It includes the need for the promotion of research, development & innovation, public funding and, in conclusion, it puts science at the service of citizens and the world, through international scientific cooperation. There are few challenges more pressing than to revisit the spirit of article 27 of the 1948 Universal Declaration of Human Rights, and to ensure its revival and enhance its influence in the contemporary era.

[56] Due to its different subject matter, the right to science will have different practical implications and will be handled differently to the rights to participate in culture and the arts, but here we are only talking about the basis as a human right.
[57] Interview with Juan Ignacio Perez Iglesias. DEIA, 03.11.13 www.deia.com/2013/11/03/bizkaia/bilbao/juan-ignacio-perez-la-ciencia-es-cultura-con-mayusculas.
[58] See Stjepan Oreskovic and Sebastian Porsdam Mann's Chapter 10, "Science in the times of SARS-CoV-2," for more on this topic.

2

The Origins of the Right to Science

The American Declaration on the Rights and Duties of Man

Cesare P. R. Romano

2.1 INTRODUCTION

If one were to pinpoint a day and place where the "right to science" was born, it would be December 31, 1945, in Rio de Janeiro, Brazil. On the last day of the year that saw the end of World War II, four members of the Inter-American Juridical Committee gathered to adopt the first draft of the future American Declaration on the Rights and Duties of Man (American Declaration).[1] In it, they described a new human right, never articulated before: the right to benefit from progress in science and technology, also known more succinctly as "the right to science". Although reworded and re-elaborated, the right survived two drafts and the negotiating process to end up in Article XIII of the American Declaration. In turn, that provided the essential wording for Article 27.1 of the Universal Declaration of Human Rights (Universal Declaration),[2] which then led to Article 15 of the International Covenant on Economic, Social and Cultural Rights (ICESCR),[3] and several other human rights treaties and declarations.[4]

This chapter tells the story of the drafting and adoption of the American Declaration, and in particular of its provisions on the right to science and the "rights of science (i.e. the human rights that are most crucial for the work of scientists and inventors, such as freedom of thought, academic freedom, intellectual property, and others).

---

[1] American Declaration of the Rights and Duties of Man, adopted on May 2, 1948 by the Ninth International Conference of American States, OAS Res XXX, reprinted in Basic Documents Pertaining to Human Rights in the Inter-American System, OEA/Ser L V/II.82 Doc 6 Rev 1, at 17 (1992).
[2] Universal Declaration of Human Rights, adopted December 10, 1948, UNGA Res 217A (III) (UDHR).
[3] International Covenant on Economic, Social and Cultural Rights, adopted December 16, 1966, entered into force January 3, 1976, 993 UNTS 3.
[4] Additional Protocol to the American Convention on Human Rights in the Area of Economic, Social, and Cultural Rights (Protocol of San Salvador), November 17, 1988, OASTS No. 69, Art. 14.1.b; (Revised) Arab Charter on Human Rights, May 22, 2004, reprinted in 12 Int'l Hum. Rts. Rep. 893 (2005), Art. 42.1; Association of Southeast Asian Nations (ASEAN) Human Rights Declaration, November 18, 2012, Art. 32.

The American Declaration is the first broad and detailed enumeration of human rights to be adopted by an intergovernmental organization. Although the Universal Declaration is hailed as the founding document of international human rights, it is often forgotten that it was preceded and inspired by the American Declaration.[5] While the Universal and the American declarations were largely drafted in parallel, the drafting of the American Declaration was always a couple of steps ahead. Indeed, the Inter-American Judicial Committee adopted the first draft of the American Declaration at the end of December 1945, only six months after the San Francisco conference, which established the United Nations, had concluded (June 1945). The first draft was published in March 1946, before the UN Preparatory Committee tasked with drafting the Universal Declaration had even held its first meeting. The American Declaration was completed before the second round of drafting of the Universal Declaration, and was adopted on May 2, 1948, almost eight months before the Universal Declaration (December 10, 1948). There is no doubt that the American Declaration heavily influenced the drafting process and final wording of the universal one.[6]

The fact that the American Declaration is the source of the language used in the corresponding provisions of the Universal Declaration, and, partly, of the ICESCR, is already sufficient to warrant a chapter in this book. However, there is also an operative and autonomous justification for this exposé. Indeed, in the Western hemisphere there are some major states, such as the United States and Cuba, which have not ratified the American Convention or the ICESCR. Because of that, the Universal Declaration and the American Declaration are the only codified international human rights standards applicable to them. While the Universal Declaration does not have a specific mechanism to ensure compliance other than the generic Universal Periodic Review,[7] the American Declaration can be invoked before a specific quasi-judicial body, the Inter-American Commission on Human Rights.[8] Although, to the best of my

---

[5] On the contribution of the American Declaration to the construction of the international system of protection of human rights, see, in general: Kathryn Sikkink, "Latin American Countries as Norm Protagonists of the Idea of International Human Rights", *Global Governance*, Vol. 20 (2014), p. 396; Tom Farer, "The Rise of the Inter-American Human Rights Regime: No Longer a Unicorn, Not Yet an Ox," in David Harris and Stephen Livingstone, eds., *The Inter-American System of Human Rights*, Oxford University Press, 1998, p. 35; Ana Elizabeth Villalta Vizcarra, "La Contribución de América al Derecho Internacional," in Organización de los Estados Americanos, XXXIII *Curso de Derecho Internacional (2006): El Derecho Internacional en las Américas: 100 años del Comité Jurídico Interamericano*, 2006, pp. 167–187; Claudio Grossman, "American Declaration of the Rights and Duties of Man (1948)," in *Max Planck Encyclopedia of Public International Law* (hereafter MPEPIL); Johannes Morsink, *The Universal Declaration of Human Rights: Origins, Drafting, and Intent*, University of Pennsylvania Press, 1999, pp. 130–134; Paolo Carozza, "From Conquest to Constitutions: Retrieving a Latin American Tradition of the Idea of Human Rights," *Human Rights Quarterly*, Vol. 25, 2003, p. 281; Mary Ann Glendon, "The Forgotten Crucible: The Latin American Influence on the Universal Human Rights Idea," *Harvard Human Rights Journal*, Vol. 16, 2003, p. 27.

[6] Morsink, supra note 5, p. 130.

[7] Christian Tomuschat, "Universal Periodic Review Procedure: Human Rights Council," *MPEPIL*.

[8] The Inter-American Commission on Human Rights and the Inter-American Court of Human Rights have maintained that the American Declaration has acquired legally binding force. When the OAS

knowledge, to date there has been no petition brought before the Inter-American Commission claiming a violation of the right to science or the rights of science the possibility exists.

2.2 THE DRAFTING HISTORY OF THE AMERICAN DECLARATION

From August 21, 1944 to October 7, 1944, as the Allied forces were inching closer to Berlin and Tokyo, the "Four Policemen" (the U.S., UK, USSR and China) met at the Dumbarton Oaks estate, in Washington D.C., to discuss the creation of future international organizations to ensure international peace and security, leading eventually to the creation of the United Nations. Despite being members of the Allied coalition, Latin American countries were not invited. That snub, and also because discussions at Dumbarton Oaks did not include various issues of their concern, including human rights,[9] caused Latin American countries to move ahead on a parallel track to discuss the creation of similar institutions for the Western hemisphere, eventually leading to the creation of the Organization of American States (OAS).

Thus, from February 21 to March 8, 1945, twenty members of the Pan-American Union gathered near the park of Chapultepec, in Mexico City, to discuss the "Project of Organic Pact of the Inter-American System," with the goal to reorganize

Charter was amended in 1967, several references to human rights were included. Yet, at that time, the only exhaustive list of human rights in the OAS system was the American Declaration. Because of that, the Commission and the Court have concluded that the OAS members must have had the intention to incorporate it into the OAS Charter. Moreover, the OAS members accepted the 1967 OAS Charter amendments, and the General Assembly of the OAS has repeatedly declared that the American Declaration is a source of international obligations for its members. *Interpretation of the American Declaration of the Rights and Duties of Man Within the Framework of Article 64 of the American Convention on Human Rights*, Advisory Opinion, OC-10/89, Inter-Am. Ct. H.R., (Ser. A) No. 10 (July 14, 1989), paras. 39–43; Christina Cerna, "Reflections on the Normative Status of the American Declaration of the Rights and Duties of Man," *University of Pennsylvania Journal of International Law*, Vol. 30, 2009, p. 1212.

Although the U.S. government insists the American Declaration does not bind it legally, it has participated in proceedings before the Commission when individuals have brought petition accusing it of having violated the Declaration, and, in several cases, it has taken steps to get back into compliance when the Commission found it in violation of the Declaration. Elizabeth Abi-Mershed, "The United States and the Inter-American Court of Human Rights," in Cesare Romano (ed.), *The Sword and the Scales: The United States and International Courts and Tribunals*, Cambridge University Press, 2009, pp. 185–209. Although U.S. courts hold that they are not bound to give effect to the reports on petitions of the Inter-American Commission, they stop short of saying they are not binding at all. They rather say that they are aimed at the executive and legislature, and not the judiciary. For one example of this consistent approach, see *Thompson v. State of Tennessee*, 134 S.W. 3d 168.

[9] "Latin American countries felt betrayed because they had not been involved in the Dumbarton Oaks discussion about a postwar organization, and also because the Dumbarton Oaks draft did not incorporate various ideals they supported, including human rights." Sikkink, supra note 5, p. 393, citing Paul Gordon Lauren, *The Evolution of International Human Rights: Visions Seen*, University of Pennsylvania Press, 1998, pp. 174–179.

inter-American cooperation and to coordinate with the soon-to-be United Nations.[10] At the Chapultepec conference, the participating states decided that the Organic Pact would be accompanied by two declarations: one on the "rights and duties of states" and a second on the "rights and duties of man".[11] The first was to be a declaration of rights and duties of states vis-à-vis each other, codifying principles of nonintervention, prohibition of aggression, peaceful settlement of disputes, and the like. The second, however, was to lay down duties states had vis-à-vis their citizens and other persons within their jurisdiction, that is to say human rights, as well as duties that those individuals owed to the states.[12] The drafting of the former was entrusted to the Governing Board of the Pan American Union (a body made of representatives of member states), while the Inter-American Juridical Committee (Comité Jurídico Interamericano – Comissão Jurídica Interamericana) was given the task to draft the latter.[13]

2.2.1 *The Work of the Inter-American Juridical Committee*

The Inter-American Juridical Committee was – and still is – a group of independent jurists, headquartered in Rio de Janeiro, Brazil.[14] Its function is to develop and coordinate the work of the codification of international law, and in particular "American international law," meaning the rules of international law specific to

[10] They were Bolivia, Brazil, Chile, Colombia, Costa Rica, Cuba, Dominican Republic, Ecuador, El Salvador, Guatemala, Haiti, Honduras, Mexico, Nicaragua, Panama, Paraguay, Peru, Uruguay, USA, and Venezuela. Argentina, despite being a member of the Union, was not invited because it had not joined the Allied side until late during the war. However, it signed the final resolution of the Chapultepec Conference. Canada and the various European territories and colonies in the Caribbean were not part of the inter-American system and did not participate to the Chapultepec conference, nor the Bogotá conference, which created the OAS and adopted the American Declaration of the Rights and Duties of Man. Josef Kunz, "The Inter-American Conference on the Problems of War and Peace at Mexico City and the Problem of the Reorganization of the Inter-American System," *American Journal of International Law*, Vol. 39, No. 3 (1945), pp. 527–533.

[11] U.S. Department of State, *Ninth International Conference of American States, Bogotá, Colombia, March 30–May 2, Report of the Delegation of the United States of America with Related Documents*, Department of State Publication 3263, Division of Publications, Office of Public Affairs, Washington D.C., November 1948 [hereinafter Ninth International Conference], p. 3. At an earlier meeting of the Inter-American Bar Association in Mexico City in 1944, resolutions had also emphasized the "necessity" of a declaration of rights of man, and the importance of international machinery and procedures to put the principles in the declaration into action. Sikkink, supra note 5, pp. 393–394.

[12] In particular, Resolution XL of March 7, 1945 on the International Protection of the Essential Rights of Man proclaimed that "the American Republics" would adhere to "the principles established by international law for safeguarding essential rights of man," and declared, in its preamble, the need to define such rights and duties, calling for the creation of a regional system for their protection. U.S. Department of State, *Report of the Delegation of the United States of America to the Inter-American Conference on Problems of War and Peace*, U.S. Government Printing Office, Washington 1946, pp. 108–109.

[13] *U.S. Report, Ninth International Conference*, supra note 11, p. 3.

[14] On the Inter-American Juridical Committee, see, in general, Fernanda Millicay, "Inter-American Juridical Committee," *MPEPIL*.

The Origins of the Right to Science 37

the Americas. However, it is obvious that drafting a declaration on the rights and duties of man was an exercise that required going beyond mere codification of international law. It was squarely a matter of progressive development. Although during the interwar and war years, a number of projects of international declarations of human rights and freedoms had been prepared by various organization and societies, many of which were in Latin America,[15] at that time state practice was, at best, vague and scant or, in the case of the right to science, completely nonexistent.[16]

The Committee started working in earnest right after the closing of the Chapultepec conference. Within nine months, they had produced a first draft titled "Anteproyecto de declaracion del los derechos y deberes internacionales del hombre" (Preliminary Draft of a Declaration on the Rights and Duties of Men).[17] A second draft, titled "Proyecto Definitivo" (Final Draft) took two more years, since state members of the Inter-American system had been given the opportunity to comment. It was adopted on December 8, 1947.[18]

At the time the America Declaration was drafted, the Committee was composed of seven members (as opposed to eleven nowadays) nominated by the governments of Argentina, Brazil, Chile, Cuba, Mexico, the United States, and Venezuela.[19] The Chapultepec Conference added two more members (Colombia and Peru).[20] However, in total only six members signed the two drafts the Committee produced (and presumably participated in their preparation).[21] Charles Fenwick (United

---

[15] See Hector Gros Espiell, *Derechos Humanos y Vida Internacional*, Instituto de Investigaciones Jurídicas, Comisión Nacional de Derechos Humanos, México, 1995, p. 16, note 9.

[16] Richard Pierre Claude, *Science in the Service of Human Rights*, University of Philadelphia Press, 2002, p. 35.

[17] Comité Jurídico Interamericano, "Anteproyecto de declaración de los derechos y deberes internacionales del hombre, Rio de Janeiro, 31 dicembre 1945," in Comité Jurídico Interamericano, *Recomendaciones e informes, Documentos Oficiales (1945–1947)*, Departamento de Imprensa Nacional, Rio de Janeiro, 1950, pp. 49–59. For the commentary, see "Informe anexo al anteproyecto de declaración de los derechos y deberes internacionales del hombre", *ibid.*, p. 61–115. The English version of the Draft Declaration, including a commentary, can be found in Pan American Union, *Draft Declaration of the International Rights and Duties of Man and Accompanying Report, Formulated by the Inter-American Juridical Committee in accordance with Resolutions IX and XL of the Inter-American Conference on Problems of War and Peace held at Mexico City, February 21–March 8, 1945*, Pan American Union, Washington DC, March 1946 [hereinafter First Draft].

[18] Comité Jurídico Interamericano, *Declaración de los derechos y deberes internacionales del hombre*, Rio de Janeiro, December 8, 1947, in Comité Jurídico Interamericano, *Recomendaciones e informes, Documentos Oficiales (1945–1947)*, pp. 185–193. The English version of the second draft can be found in *Ninth International Conference*, supra note 11, pp. 115–120, or in Thomas Buergenthal and Robert E. Norris, eds. *Human Rights: The Inter-American System*, Oceana Publications (loose-leaf format), Part I, Chapter IV, p. 9 (Section C). The Commentary of the second draft can be found at p. 195 ff and in Ministerio de Relaciones Exteriores de Colombia, *IX Conferencia Internacional Americana, Bogotá, 1949, Actas y Documentos*, Bogotá, 1953, Vol. V, pp. 454–458 [hereinafter IX Conferencia].

[19] José Joaquín Caicedo Castilla, *The Work of the Inter-American Juridical Committee*, Pan American Union, OAS, 1964, p. 4.

[20] Ibid.

[21] It is not clear why not all members of the Committee participated in the preparation of the drafts. José Joaquín Caicedo Castilla, who was member of the Inter-American Juridical Committee for thirty-three

States) and Francisco Campos (Brazil) signed both drafts, while Felix Nieto del Río (Chile) and Antonio Gómez Robledo (Mexico) signed the first draft, and José Joaquín Caicedo Castilla (Colombia) and Eduardo Arroyo Lameda (Venezuela) the second. They were all scholars and diplomats, each bringing their own unique perspective to the task.[22] Curiously, many of them were not formally trained in law or had never practiced law.[23]

A Brazilian, as a tribute to the country hosting it, traditionally chaired the Committee.[24] At the time of the drafting of the Declaration, the Brazilian member was Francisco Luís da Silva Campos, a jurist, attorney, legal scholar, and politician. A scion of families that dominated the economic, political, and social life of Brazil of the late XIX century, Campos was the author of Brazil's Constitution of 1937, and of the criminal and criminal procedural codes of Brazil, which, in substance, are still in force in Brazil to this day.[25] That, and the fact that history remembers him for his authoritarian and anti-liberal views of the state and democracy, made him an unlikely author of a declaration of human rights.[26]

Although he was a political scientist by training (Ph.D. in political science from Johns Hopkins University, in 1912) and never earned a law degree, Charles Ghequiere Fenwick was considered one of the distinguished international lawyers and scholars of his time.[27] He was professor of political science at Bryn Mawr College from 1918 to 1947 and President of the American Society of International Law (1953–1954).[28] After having worked on the draft of the American Declaration at the Inter-American Juridical Committee, he became director of the Department of

---

years, from July 3, 1946 to his death, on December 15, 1979, suggests it might be because not all members where in Rio at that time. "At first the Committee met all through the year and the members lived in Rio. However, although apparently paradoxical, experience showed that this was not the best system, because the necessary quorum for the adoption of a decision was often lacking." *Ibid.*, p. 13.

[22] As it has been noted, Latin American scholars and politicians are neither fully Western nor non-Western. The West/non-West dichotomy in international relations scholarship hides unique Latin American contributions. Louise Fawcett, "Between West and Non-West: Latin American Contributions to International Thought," *International History Review*, Vol. 34, no. 4 (2012), pp. 679–704. Instead, Liliana Obregón Tarazona speaks of a "creole" legal consciousness that blends elements unique to the Latin American experience with international legal traditions of the time. Liliana Obregón, "Between Civilization and Barbarism: Creole Interventions in International Law," *Third World Quarterly*, Vol. 27, no. 5 (2006), pp. 815–832.

[23] Yet, as Charles Fenwick noted while commenting the Committee's statute, "the members of the Committee should be jurists [and] should have "no other duties than those pertaining to the Committee." This provision was directed against the appointment by several Governments of their diplomatic representatives in Rio as members of the Committee". Charles G. Fenwick, "The Inter-American Juridical Committee," *American Journal of International Law*, Vol. 37, no. 1 (1943), pp. 5–29, at 7 and 8.

[24] Caicedo, supra note 19, p. 12.

[25] https://cpdoc.fgv.br/producao/dossies/AEraVargas1/biografias/francisco_campos

[26] *Ibid.*

[27] www.nytimes.com/1973/04/26/archives/charles-g-fenwick-dies-at-92-was-international-law-expert.html.

[28] *Ibid.*

The Origins of the Right to Science 39

International Law of the Pan American Union, and later of the Organization of American States.[29]

Felix Nieto del Río studied law but never practiced or taught it. He had a career as a journalist and writer first, and then as a diplomat.[30] He entered public service as employee of the National Library and later of the Ministry of Foreign Affairs.[31] He became a diplomat, representing Chile in several capitals in Europe and the Americas. He was Chile's ambassador to Brazil (1936–1939) and to the U.S. (1947–1952),[32] and, crucially, he represented Chile at the first meeting of the UN Human Rights Commission, the body that drafted the Universal Declaration of Human Rights, ensuring continuity between the two.

Like Nieto del Río, Antonio Gómez Robledo was also a diplomat by trade.[33] Yet, he was a philosopher and legal scholar of the first order, too.[34] Born from a wealthy family in Guadalajara, Mexico, he read law at the University of Guadalajara.[35] Before joining the Mexican diplomatic service, in 1936, he earned a doctorate in philosophy from the Universidad Nacional Autónoma de Mexico, and studied in Paris, The Hague, New York (Fordham University) and Rio.[36] After retiring from the diplomatic service, he went back to academia and scholarly writing, publishing on Plato and Socrates, on the origins of international law and its early writers, and various works on catholic issues.[37]

In 1946, after the first draft had been adopted and before the second and final one was prepared, José Joaquín Caicedo Castilla and Eduardo Arroyo Lameda replaced Nieto del Río and Gómez Robledo in the Committee.

Arroyo Lameda was a poet and writer, with a respectable publishing and prizes record, member and director of the Venezuelan Academy of Language (*Academia Venezoelana de la Lengua*).[38] He studied literature first, and then obtained a doctorate in Political Science from the Central University of Venezuela.[39] The study of law, which he undertook subsequently, seemed to be an afterthought. Later he became professor of diplomatic history and international relations.[40]

[29] *Ibid.*
[30] Sergio Martínez Baeza, "En el cincuentenario de su muerte. Félix Nieto del Rio, 1888–1953," *Boletín de la Academia Chilena de la Historia*, no. 133, 2004; https://es.wikipedia.org/wiki/F%C3%A9lix_Nieto_del_R%C3%ADo.
[31] *Ibid.*
[32] *Ibid.*
[33] Marta Morineau, Antonio Gómez Robledo, Vida y Obra, *Anuario mexicano de historia del derecho*, no. 17, 2005, pp. 219–239; https://es.wikipedia.org/wiki/Antonio_G%C3%B3mez_Robledo.
[34] *Ibid.*
[35] *Ibid.*
[36] *Ibid.*
[37] *Ibid.*
[38] Jose Román Duque Sanchez, "Homenaje al Dr. Eduardo Arroyo Lameda con motivo del centenario de su nacimiento," *Boletín de la Academia de Ciencias Políticas y Sociales*, Vol. 67, no. 123, 1991, pp. 241–246.
[39] *Ibid.*
[40] *Ibid.*

Of the six men who participated in the drafting of the American Declaration, José Joaquín Caicedo Castilla probably had the strongest international law credentials.[41] He graduated in law and political science from the National University of Colombia.[42] He was Judge ad hoc of the International Court of Justice in the *Haya de la Torre* case[43] and served both as elected member of both the parliament and the Senate of Colombia, as minister of the government (Work and Social Affairs first, and then Foreign Affairs), as Ambassador (to Italy, Costa Rica, Honduras, and Nicaragua).[44] He published copiously in international law, both public and private, and founded the Instituto Hispano-Luso-Americano de Derecho Internacional. He was also member of the Inter-American Juridical Committee from July 3, 1946 to his death, on December 15, 1979.[45]

Of these six men, we do not know who was actually responsible for the provision on the right to science. We know that the essence of the right to science was written during the redaction of the first draft and remained largely unchanged in the final draft. We know who signed the first and second drafts. We know that Fenwick and Campos were the two members of the Committee who authored both the first and second, and that Campos was the Chairman of the Committee. However, we do not know much more than that. The hunt for the intellectual father(s) of the right to science is probably one of the most interesting puzzles for historians of international law.

We do know a little more about the documents that inspired the members of the Committee. Writing the first international declaration of human rights was a daunting intellectual and political task. Articulating key concepts and finding the best words was both a legal and a linguistic challenge, and the Committee had little in the way of wording from which to borrow. The Chapultepec Conference had given the Committee limited guidance. The only language that could remotely connect to the right to science is found in Resolution XI: "The goal of the state is the happiness of man within society. The interests of society must be harmonized with the rights of the individual. The American man does not conceive to live without justice. Nor does he conceive to live without freedom."[46] Granted, the Committee did not work in a vacuum. It could draw from a rich tradition of human rights and rule of law nurtured in the West since the Enlightenment, and on specific Latin American tradition. They had at their disposal several drafts and projects on human

---

[41] Haroldo T. Valladão, "Un jurista das Americas: José Joaquín Caicedo Castilla," in *Séptimo Curso de Derecho Internacional Organizado por el Comité Jurídico Interamericano*, OAS, 2006, pp. 12–16.
[42] Ibid.
[43] Ibid.
[44] Ibid.
[45] Ibid.
[46] "El fin del Estado es la felicidad del hombre dentro de la sociedad. Deben armonizarse los intereses de la sociedad con los derechos del individuo. El hombre americano no concibe vivir sin justicia. Tampoco concibe vivir sin libertad." Declaración de México (Resolución XI) del 6 de marzo de 1945, inciso 12.

rights that had been prepared since the 1920s by various organizations. Specifically, the Committee acknowledged having taken into consideration at least four main sources while drafting the Declaration:[47]

(1) The Declaration of International Rights of Men (Déclaration des droits internationaux de l'homme) of the International Law Institute (Institut de Droit International) (October 12, 1929);
(2) American Law Institute Statement of Essential Human Rights (1942–1945);
(3) Preliminary Report of the Commission to Study the Organization of Peace (1940);
(4) Declaration of Philadelphia of the International Labor Committee (1944).

Yet, none of these contained anything about a right to benefit from progress in science and technology. The ILI Declaration of International Rights of Men was a short document of only six articles, providing only for a generic duty not to discriminate and few basic freedoms, but made no mention of the right to science or "rights of science," such as freedom of speech and expression.[48] The American Law Institute Statement of Essential Human Rights included the right to education (Article 11), albeit without mentioning academic freedom, and several other economic, social, and cultural rights, but made no mention of the right to science either.[49] It addressed freedom of expression, opinion, and dissemination, dedicating an article each to Freedom of Opinion and to Freedom of Expression.[50] However, these articles focused on the press and media and no mention was made to the freedom to investigate. Neither the 1944 Declaration of Philadelphia of the International Labor Committee mentioned the right to science or the rights of science. All it did was "reaffirm the fundamental principles on which the Organization is based and, in particular, that: (b) freedom of expression and of association are essential to sustained progress."[51] Finally, the 1940 Preliminary Report of the Commission to Study the Organization of Peace contained a general statement on the positive and negative effects of science on international life and the need for international institutions to solve the problem. However, it did not contain a list of rights, and certainly nothing that could be borrowed by the drafters of the American Declaration.[52]

---

[47] First Draft, supra note 17, pp. 18–20.
[48] Institut de Droit International, *Annuaire de l'institut de droit international*, New York session, 1929, Vol. 35-II, 1929, pp. 110–138.
[49] American Law Institute, Committee of Advisers on Essential Human Rights, *Statement of Essential Human Rights* (1945), Americans United for World Organization, New York, 1945, Art. 11.
[50] Ibid., Arts. 2 and 3.
[51] International Labor Committee, *Declaration Concerning the Aims and Purposes of the International Labour Organisation*, adopted at the 26th session of the ILO, Philadelphia, 10 May 1944, Art. I.
[52] Commission to Study the Organization of Peace, "Preliminary Report, November 1940," in Commission to Study the Organization of Peace, *Building Peace: Reports of the Commission to Study the Organization of Peace* (1939–1972), Vol. I, Scarecrow, NY, 1973, pp. 2–3; Smith Simpson,

Thus, it seems the members of the Committee drew mostly from their own experience and readings to draft the articles addressing the right to science and the rights of science. The question of whether and how a statement of worldwide rights and fundamental freedoms should refer to science and technology was new to global discourse. The fact that the members of the Committee were independent experts and not State representatives is noteworthy, as their personal character and idiosyncrasies probably had a heightened impact on the drafts. As we will see, the Bogotá conference adopted a final text that was considerably more succinct and more tightly worded.

As to the right to science in specific, the first draft (*Anteproyecto*) articulated it as follows:

> Article XV: Right to Share in Benefits of Science.
>
> Every person has the right to share in the benefits accruing from the discoveries and inventions of science, under conditions which permit a fair return to the industry and skill of those responsible for the discovery or invention.
>
> The state has the duty to encourage the development of the arts and sciences, but it must see to it that the laws for the protection of trade-marks, patents and copyrights are not used for the establishment of monopolies which might prevent all persons from sharing in the benefits of science. It is the duty of the state to protect the citizens against the use of scientific discoveries in a manner to create fear and unrest among the people.[53]

The first draft set several of the key issues regarding the right to science that will determine its future shape and the discourse about it. First, it affirmed the "right to science," that is to say, the "right to share in the benefits accruing from the discoveries and inventions of science."[54] However, the draft did not discuss the "rights of science" other than declaring that: "The state has the duty to encourage the development of the arts and sciences."[55] Arguably, that included the duty of the state not to arbitrarily interfere with the development of science and technology too, but it would be several years before the rights of science would be spelled out in Article 15.3 of the Covenant on Economic, Social and Cultural Rights.

The first draft also introduced the principle that there should be limits to science, and the more controversial idea that science should develop in a certain direction. The issue of whether science should have a direction and limits, still very hotly debated to this day, would have its first full discussion during the drafting of the Universal Declaration, but it surfaced here first. Actually, the draft seems to see

---

"The Commission to Study the Organization of Peace," *American Political Science Review*, Vol. 35, no. 2 (Apr. 1941), pp. 317–324, p. 321. See also James T. Shotwell, *A Discussion of the Preliminary Report*, Reprint of Radio Broadcast delivered November 9, 1940 over the Columbia Broadcasting System.

[53] First Draft, supra note 17, Art. XV, p. 48.
[54] *Ibid.*, Art. XV, first paragraph.
[55] *Ibid.*, second paragraph.

science as a threat ("It is the duty of the state to protect the citizens against the use of scientific discoveries in a manner to create fear and unrest among the people"), but this needs to be put in its historical context.

In the Commentary to the first draft, the Committee noted:

> The last sentence of the article, referring to discoveries which create fear and unrest among the people, is obviously directed against the recent discovery of the means of making atomic energy available for destructive purposes. Here the protection to be given by the state to its nationals will be contingent upon the cooperation of other states in taking similar action. In the presence of this newest discovery of science it may be said that the first and foremost international right of man is now no longer the right to his own personal existence or to his own personal liberty or other associated rights, but rather his right to the existence of the civilization of which he is part and without which life would be intolerable even if he himself personally survived destruction. The "freedom from fear" which the Atlantic Charter contemplated as one of the results of the peace to be established after the war takes on a larger meaning in the light of the newly-discovered means of carrying the devastation of war to its logical extreme.[56]

The first draft was also the first international legal document to attempt to strike a balance between the right to benefit from science and the need to ensure those who develop science and technology have a fair return. "Every person has the right to share in the benefits accruing from the discoveries and inventions of science, under conditions which permit a fair return to the industry and skill of those responsible for the discovery or invention."[57] It was the first salvo in the long battle between the right to benefit from progress in science and technology and intellectual property rights. In the Committee's own words:

> The principle upon which Article XV of the draft Declaration proceeds is that the democratic state is a cooperative commonwealth, in which the opportunities for discovery and invention are the result of many generations of progressive effort, and that each generation is the heir of the civilization which preceded it and as such is entitled to share collectively in the benefit which its men of greater genius are able to draw from the conditions placed at their disposal. At the same time the Article recognizes the necessity of rewarding the industry and skill of the discoverer or inventor and thus encouraging the patient study and research which may lead to new advances in the field of science.[58]

Yet, mindful of having potentially opened a Pandora's box, the Committee hastened to add that the need to ensure a fair return to those who advance science and technology must not come at the expense of the duty to ensure all persons could share in the benefits of science.[59] Again, from the Commentary:

---

[56] First Draft, supra note 17, pp. 48–49.
[57] Ibid., Art. XV, first paragraph, p. 9.
[58] Ibid., p. 48.
[59] Ibid., Art. XV, second paragraph, p. 9.

Here, as in the case of the right to work, a balance must be sought between encouragement of individual initiative by the grant of patents and copyrights and the protection of the public against the abuse of the special privileges thus granted. The duty of the state to protect the individual against monopolies in the exploitation of natural resources of the state is recognized in the legislation of all American states; and it is equally the duty of the state to control the use of trade-marks and patents so as to prevent similar monopolies in the production or distribution of the articles thus protected against competition.[60]

As to the right to freedom of expression and opinion, a right particularly important for scientists and inventors, the Preliminary Draft contained a very long and detailed Article (III). For sake of brevity, it will not be discussed here. The text can be found in Table 2.2. All that needs to be said here is that nothing suggests that the Committee considered the right to freedom of expression and opinion to be particularly relevant for scientific inquiry and research. The Commentary of the Preliminary Draft discusses the media at length, including the press, radio, and cinema, and limits to the freedom of expression and opinion and censorship, but it does not touch upon scientists and their special needs.[61]

The Committee transmitted the first draft, accompanied by a "long and very carefully written report, in which the subject of the rights of man was analyzed in general, the precedents in jurisprudence and the acts of international bodies set forth, and one by one, the proposed clauses were commented upon and justified,"[62] to the States members of the Inter-American system for comment.[63] Once they received the comments back, they produced the second and final draft. Article XV changed little between the first and second draft. Table 2.1 highlights the changes. They were minimal, either because it was as good as it could be or, more likely, because states preferred focusing on more crucial rights and did not attach to this one particular importance. Thus, the core of the right to science, as well as most of the freedom of information and opinion, was set by December 1945.

It is remarkable that the first draft gave the right to science its own dignity, separate and distinct from the "right to culture," and that this survived to the second draft. However, at the same time, the Inter-American Juridical Committee nodded towards the subsequent, momentous development, when they stated that: "The state has the duty to encourage the development of the arts and sciences."[64]

---

[60] *Ibid.*, p. 48.
[61] *Ibid.*, pp. 25–29.
[62] Caicedo Castilla, supra note 19, p. 31.
[63] IX Conferencia, supra note 18, p. 456.
[64] First Draft, supra note 17, Art. XV, second paragraph.

TABLE 2.1 *Comparison of the provisions on the right to science in the drafts of the Inter-American Juridical Committee and the final text of the American Declaration* (differences between previous and subsequent versions are in italics)

Preliminary Draft by the Inter-American Juridical Committee (31 Dec. 1945)	Final Draft by the Inter-American Juridical Committee (8 Dec. 1947)	American Declaration of the Rights and Duties of Men (30 April 1948)
Article XV: Right to Share in Benefits of Science. Every person has the right to share in the benefits accruing from the discoveries and inventions of science, under conditions which permit a fair return to the industry and skill of those responsible for the discovery or invention. The state has the duty to encourage the development of the arts and sciences, but it must see to it that the laws for the protection of trademarks, patents and copyrights are not used for the establishment of monopolies *which might prevent all persons from sharing in the benefits of science*. It is the duty of the state to protect the citizens against the use of scientific discoveries in a manner to create fear and unrest *among the people*.	Article XV: Right to Share in Benefits of Science. Every person has the right to share in the benefits accruing from the discoveries and inventions of science, under conditions which permit a fair return to the industry and skill of those responsible for the discovery or invention. The state has the duty to encourage the development of the arts and sciences, but it must see to it that the laws for the protection of literary and artistic copyrights, *patents, and industrial and commercial trademarks* are not used for the establishment of monopolies. It is the duty of the state to protect the citizens against the use of scientific discoveries in a manner to create fear and unrest.	*Article XIII: Right to the Benefits of Culture.* Every person has the right to *take part in the cultural life of the community, to enjoy the arts, and* to *participate* in the benefits *that result from intellectual progress, especially scientific discoveries.* *He likewise has the right to the protection of his moral and material interests as regards his inventions or any literary, scientific or artistic works of which he is the author.*

2.2.2 *The Ninth Conference of American States (Bogotá, Colombia, Spring 1948)*

The second draft of the Inter-American Juridical Committee was considered at the next conference of the American States, the ninth. Twenty-one states, all the American Republics, as they were called, participated.[65] Most were represented at

---

[65] Honduras, Guatemala, Chile, Uruguay, Cuba, USA, Dominican Republic, Bolivia, Peru, Nicaragua, Mexico, Panama, El Salvador, Paraguay, Costa Rica, Ecuador, Brazil, Haiti, Venezuela, Argentina, and Colombia. Canada did not participate, nor any of the European territories and colonies in the Caribbean.

TABLE 2.2 *Comparison of the provisions on the Freedom of Investigation, Opinion, Expression and Dissemination in the drafts of the Inter-American Juridical Committee and the final text of the American Declaration*

Preliminary Draft by the Inter-American Juridical Committee (31 Dec. 1945)	Final Draft by the Inter-American Juridical Committee (8 Dec. 1947)	American Declaration of the Rights and Duties of Men (30 April 1948)
Article III: Right to Freedom of Speech and of Expression Every person has the right to freedom of speech and of expression. This right includes freedom to form and to hold opinions and to give expression to them, in private and in public, and to publish them in written or printed form. The right to freedom of speech and of expression extends to the use of whatever means of communication are available: freedom to use the postal service, the public utilities of telegraph, telephone and radio communication; freedom to use the graphic arts, the theater, the cinema and other agencies for the dissemination of ideas. The right to freedom of speech and of expression includes freedom of access to the sources of information, both domestic and foreign. The right to freedom of speech and of expression includes the special highly privileged right to freedom of the press.	Article III: Right to Freedom of Speech and of Expression Every person has the right to freedom of speech and of expression. The right to express ad to maintain opinions extends to the use of the postal services and the public utilities of radio communication and telephone; freedom to use the graphic arts, the theater, the cinema and other agencies for the communication and dissemination of ideas. The right to freedom of speech and of expression includes freedom of access to the sources of information, both domestic and foreign. The right to freedom of speech and of expression includes the special highly important right to freedom of the press. In the case of immoral or libelous publications, or such as incite to violence, only measures of a civil or penal character may be applied, in accordance with due process of law. Censorship of the cinema may be in advance of publication.	Article IV: Right to Freedom of Investigation, Opinion, Expression and Dissemination Every person has the right to freedom of investigation, of opinion, and of the expression and dissemination of ideas, by any medium whatsoever.

TABLE 2.2 *(continued)*

Preliminary Draft by the Inter-American Juridical Committee (31 Dec. 1945)	Final Draft by the Inter-American Juridical Committee (8 Dec. 1947)	American Declaration of the Rights and Duties of Men (30 April 1948)
The only limitations which the state may impose upon this freedom are those prescribed by general laws looking to the protection of the public peace against slanderous or libellous defamation of others, and against indecent language or publications, and language or publications directly provocative of violence among the people. Censorship of the press is prohibited, whether by direct or indirect means, and all limitations imposed in the interest of public order shall only be applied subsequently to the publication of the material alleged to be of the offensive character described in the law. Censorship of the cinema may be in advance of publication, taking into account the particular form of publication and the necessity of protecting the public against matters offensive to accepted standards of conduct. The state may not retain a monopoly of radio broadcasting so as to deny to the individual the opportunity for the free expression of opinion through that instrumentality of communication.		

a high level. Eleven delegations were headed by their Minister of Foreign Affairs or the equivalent.[66] The task of the drafting the declaration was entrusted to the VI Committee (Juridical-Political Issues), and from it to a working group (Sub-Committee A) consisting of representatives of Argentina, Bolivia, Brazil, Colombia, Cuba, Mexico, Peru, the U.S., Uruguay, and Venezuela.[67] The working group met first on April 17, 1948. It started from the "fairly acceptable draft"[68] produced by the Inter-American Juridical Committee, but produced a new text, quite different from the one prepared by the Committee, taking into account the amendments and proposals presented by numerous delegations, and discussions had within the working group.[69] Besides the draft of the Inter-American Juridical Committee (the Final Draft), and the amendments and proposals presented by numerous delegations, the working group considered also the draft of the Universal Declaration of Human Rights circulated at the Human Rights Commission's second session, in December 1947.[70] The text hammered out by the working group then went back to the VI Committee, where it was approved.[71] It is said that the discussions on social, economic, and cultural rights, including the right to science, were particularly intense.[72] Finally, on May 2, 1948, the Plenary unanimously approved the text sent by the VI Committee without discussion and as a nonbinding resolution of the Conference.

The U.S. delegation participated at all stages of the drafting of the Declaration (Working Group, VI Committee and Plenary). It obtained a modification of the article on the right to health, to ensure it would not contain any preference between public and private control of health and sanitation facilities, and it

[66] The United States was represented by the U.S. Secretary of State, George C. Marshall, who was present for most of the conference and left only on April 24, when all key decisions had been taken. Ninth International Conference, supra note 11, p. 4.

[67] Report of the Working Group on Human Rights: Report of the Rapporteur of the Working Group on Human Rights, Ninth International Conference (Bogotá, 1948), in Buergenthal and Norris, supra note 18, Part I, Chapter IV, p. 15 (Section D.1.1) [hereinafter Report of the Working Group on Human Rights]. Uruguay ended up not sending a representative to sit in the working group because they had not enough diplomats to attend all meetings. Ibid., p. 16 (Section D.1.3). These are the representatives who sat in the working group: Luis Fernan Cisneros (Peru) and Guy Pérez Cisneros (Cuba), respectively as President and Rapporteur. Gerardo Melguizo served the Group as Secretary. Then, Enrique V. Coreminas (Argentina); Alberto Salinas López (Bolivia), Camillo de Oliveira (Brazil), Luis López de Mesa (Colombia), Edward A. Jamison (United States), German Fernandez del Castillo (Mexico) and Melchor Monteverde (Venezuela), as members. Ibid., pp. 15–16 (Section D.1.3).

[68] "Memorandum by the Secretary of State to Diplomatic Representatives in the American Republic, Washington, March 9, 1948," in Foreign Relations of the United States, 1948, The Western Hemisphere, Volume IX.

[69] The text of all amendments and proposals presented at the Ninth Conference (CB 101, 112, 125, 139, 163, 194, 328, 337, 400, 401 and 420) can be found in IX Conferencia, supra note 18, pp. 440 ff.

[70] UN Economic and Social Council, E/600, 17 December 1947, Annex A, Part I; Report of the Working Group on Human Rights, supra note 67, p. 15 (Section D.1.3).

[71] The text and the report of the Rapporteur are included in IX Conferencia, supra note 18, pp. 494–504, 510.

[72] Report of the Working Group on Human Rights, supra note 67, Chapter IV, p. 22.

successfully opposed a proposal for including a statement on the right of resistance to oppression.[73] However, it unsuccessfully opposed the inclusion of a statement on the right to protection of authors and inventors in the article on the "right to culture."[74] The U.S. representative (Jack B. Tate) argued that it was not an essential human right.[75] However, strongly supported by Cuba, the article was left unchanged.[76]

In the end, the Conference produced a "lengthy document whose principal defect is considerable verbiage," as the U.S. Ambassador to Colombia sneeringly noted.[77] It consists of a preamble and two chapters. The preamble sets forth general principles, chapter one contains rights (both civil and political and, crucially, economic, social, and cultural rights) and chapter two contains duties. To limit our discussion only to the provisions regarding the right to science, these are the relevant provisions in the final text of the American Declaration on the Rights and Duties of Man:

> WHEREAS: The American peoples have acknowledged the dignity of the individual, and their national constitutions recognize that juridical and political institutions, which regulate life in human society, have as their principal aim the protection of the essential rights of man and the creation of circumstances that will permit him to achieve spiritual and material progress and attain happiness;
> . . .
> Preamble: . . . Since culture is the highest social and historical expression of that spiritual development, it is the duty of man to preserve, practice and foster culture by every means within his power; And, since moral conduct constitutes the noblest flowering of culture, it is the duty of every man always to hold it in high respect.
> . . .
> Right to freedom of investigation, opinion, expression and dissemination.
> Article IV. Every person has the right to freedom of investigation, of opinion, and of the expression and dissemination of ideas, by any medium whatsoever.
> . . .
> Right to the benefits of culture.
> Article XIII. Every person has the right to take part in the cultural life of the community, to enjoy the arts, and to participate in the benefits that result from intellectual progress, especially scientific discoveries.

---

[73] Ninth International Conference, supra note 11, p. 81.
[74] U.S. Department of State, Office of the Historian, "The Ambassador in Colombia (Beaulac) to the Secretary of State, 25 April 1948," in Foreign Relations of the United States, 1948, The Western Hemisphere, Volume IX [hereafter Beaulac 25 April]; IX Conferencia, supra note 18, p. 582.
[75] Beaulac 25 April, supra note 74; Ninth International Conference, supra note 11, p. 81; IX Conferencia, supra note 18, p. 582.
[76] Beaulac 25 April, supra note 74; IX Conferencia, supra note 18, p. 582.
[77] "The Ambassador in Colombia (Beaulac) to the Secretary of State, 26 April 1948," in Foreign Relations of the United States, 1948, The Western Hemisphere, Volume IX.

He likewise has the right to the protection of his moral and material interests as regards his inventions or any literary, scientific or artistic works of which he is the author.[78]

Tables 2.1 and 2.2 compare the final text of the American Declaration with the drafts produced by the Inter-American Committee. The resulting Article XIII, on the right to science, and Article IV, on freedom of investigation, of opinion, and of the expression and dissemination of ideas, are considerably terser than the corresponding articles in the drafts of the Inter-American Commission of Jurists. That should be no surprise since the text adopted in Bogotá was the result of a diplomatic effort rather than an intellectual project, as the drafts of the Inter-American Commission of Jurists had been.

The differences between the draft declaration and the final one are many and significant. In the Inter-American Commission's drafts, Article XV was entitled "Right to Share in Benefits of Science." In the final text adopted in Bogotá, the right to science ends up in Article XIII, entitled "Right to the Benefits of Culture." Thus, the right to science became part of the broader right to "take part in the cultural life of the community, to enjoy the arts, and to participate in the benefits that result from intellectual progress."[79] It was a significant demotion of the right to science, which from then on would be lumped together with other cultural phenomena, like figurative arts, literature, sport, or cuisine. Article XIII treats science almost as an afterthought ("especially scientific discoveries").[80] On the other hand, Article III of the Inter-American Commission's drafts, entitled "Right to Freedom of Speech and of Expression," was retitled to "Right to Freedom of Investigation, Opinion, Expression and Dissemination" (Article IV). The particular addition of the "freedom of investigation" is notable as it opened the door for the extension of the freedom of expression to scientists, *qua* scientist and not as mere citizens.

Second, the "right *to share* in the benefits accruing from the discoveries and inventions of science" of the drafts, became the "right *to ... participate* in the benefits that result from intellectual progress, especially scientific discoveries" of the American Declaration. The Universal Declaration reverted to the language of the drafts, speaking of "right *to ... share* in scientific advancement and its benefits."[81] The distinction is crucial. The *travaux préparatoires* of the Universal Declaration show a debate took place on whether the right should be understood as being only about enjoying passively the benefits or is also about taking part in the scientific enterprise in a broader sense.[82] As Mikel Mancisidor has remarked, the word "share" in the phrase "the right to share in scientific advancement and its benefits" indicates

---

[78] American Declaration, supra note 1, preamble, Arts. IV and XIII.
[79] Ibid., Art. XIII, first paragraph.
[80] Ibid.
[81] Universal Declaration, supra note 2, Art. 27.1.
[82] Morsink, supra note 5, pp. 217–222.

an idea of action or agency.[83] According to him, the Draft and the Universal Declaration, but not the American Declaration, advocate "a view of 'participation' which includes science popularization, participation in scientific creation and in scientific policy, citizen science, gender equality, the freedoms of those doing science and some other aspects which are in addition to the right to 'benefit from scientific applications'."[84]

As the drafts, the Declaration recognized the need to ensure fair return to those who advance science, but it did it in more succinct and subtly different terms: "[Every person] has the right to the protection of his moral and material interests as regards his inventions or any literary, scientific or artistic works of which he is the author." Compare this with lengthy provision in the first:

> Every person has the right to share in the benefits accruing from the discoveries and inventions of science, under conditions which permit a fair return to the industry and skill of those responsible for the discovery or invention. The state has the duty to encourage the development of the arts and sciences, but it must see to it that the laws for the protection of trade-marks, patents and copy-rights are not used for the establishment of monopolies which might prevent all persons from sharing in the benefits of science.[85]

Note that the American Declaration does not speak of "fair return" but rather of "protection of moral and material interests."

As has been said, this particular aspect of the right to science was one of the few, if not the only, to be discussed in Bogotá. The U.S. delegation strongly opposed the inclusion of a right to "protection of moral and material interests" on the ground that it not consider it an essential human right, but lost to the Latin American bloc. Considering the contemporary debates between the Global North and the Global South, where the former advocates for strong intellectual property rights, while the latter argues that intellectual property protection robs them of the right to benefit from scientific progress, the debate in Bogotá over the inclusion of a right to "protection of moral and material interests" is surprising. What pushed Latin American countries to insist on the need to protect them?

According to Lea Shaver,

> [t]he enduring controversy over the protection element reflects an underlying international disagreement about the underpinnings of copyright law. Within the common law tradition, the exclusive rights of authors to control publication of their works are considered solely in economic and utilitarian terms as providing incentives for creativity. Within the civil law tradition, the natural law concept of *droit d'auteur* recognizes additional, inalienable rights of authors grounded in the ethical

---

[83] Mikel Mancisidor, "Is there Such a Thing as A Human Right to Science in International Law?," *ESIL Reflections*, Vol. 4, No. 1, April 2015, p. 2.
[84] Ibid.
[85] First Draft, supra note 17, Article XV.

conception of the creative product as an extension of the creator's personality. From the civil law perspective, then, authors' rights were grounded in the same basis as other human rights and should sensibly be included in the Declaration. From the common law perspective, a moral rights provision risked introducing a complex area of disagreement that more appropriately belonged to the realm of economic and trade law.[86]

The debate continued in the context of the drafting of the Universal Declaration, as well as in that of the Covenant on Economic, Social and Political Rights. The United Kingdom, a country of the common law tradition, joined the argument on the side of the United States, while France, from the civil law tradition, sided with the Latin American states, sharing their view of the issue. Nevertheless, "protection of moral and material interests" remained a feature of the right to science and the rights of science in all subsequent articulations of the rights. That is because of the numeric superiority of civil law countries over common law countries, and because the USA, UK, and other developed countries eventually adopted strong intellectual property and copyrights protection in the 1980s.

Finally, although the Latin American bloc was successful in ensuring the final text of the American Declaration contained the duty to protect "moral and material interests" of scientists, inventors and authors, lamentably the duty of states to ensure that "laws for the protection of trade-marks, patents and copy-rights are not used for the establishment of monopolies which might prevent all persons from sharing in the benefits of science" was lost, never to resurface again. One can only wonder how, had that wording of the Draft made it to the American and the Universal Declarations, international and national intellectual protection regimes might have developed.

The "duty of the state to protect the citizens against the use of scientific discoveries in a manner to create fear and unrest among the people" was lost, too, but it came back again during the drafting of the Universal Declaration in the form of a lively debate between the East and the West on the purpose and limits of science.

2.3 THE AFTERMATH OF THE AMERICAN DECLARATION

The wording of the right to science proposed by the Inter-American Committee was fundamentally changed by the American States' meeting in Bogotá, to the point of being almost unrecognizable. However, the wording proposed by the Committee came back into play during the drafting the Universal Declaration. John Humphrey, the Director of the United Nations Division of Human Rights, who prepared the first draft of the Universal Declaration, relied on the drafts prepared by the Committee. Chile suggested relying on the Committee's drafts, too. However, in the end, the Third Committee of the General Assembly opted to essentially copy and paste

---

[86] Lea Shaver, "The Right to Science and Culture," *Wisconsin Law Review*, Vol. 2010, 2010, p. 147.

Article XIII of the American Declaration into Article 27 of the Universal Declaration.

Although the current standard wording of the right to science departs from the one chosen by the members of the Inter-American Committee, there is no doubt that the right to science came to be first in Rio de Janeiro, on December 31, 1945. There is no sign of it before then and it went a long way after then. Since Rio is famous for its extravagant celebrations of New Year's Eve, one can imagine the four members of the Committee to be in a rush to adopt the Preliminary Draft of a Declaration on the Rights and Duties of Men, with the new right to science in it, before joining the festivities. One might wonder whether they suspected how far the idea would have gone.

3

IP Rights and Human Rights

What History Tells Us and Why It Matters

Aurora Plomer

3.1 INTRODUCTION

The right to access the benefits of science in Article 27 of the Universal Declaration of Human Rights (UDHR) had received little attention until the spectacular expansion of patents in the life sciences at the turn of the twentieth century. The international legal backdrop which secured this expansion was the adoption of the TRIPS Agreement in 1994 which imposed a legal obligation on all World Trade Organization (WTO) members to grant patents on inventions in all fields of science providing they met certain minimum requirements. The controversies which erupted over the appropriation of human genes by for-profit organizations led to a resurgence of interest in Article 27 UDHR and its sequel, Article 15 of the International Covenant on Economic, Social and Cultural Rights (ICESCR). Scientists and civil society struggled to understand how genes and cells could be classified as "inventions." Many feared that patent holders would become the gatekeepers of science and that patents would delay and obstruct scientific research, ultimately compromising the right of everyone "to share in scientific advancement and its benefits" proclaimed in Article 27(1) UDHR and its counterpart in Article 15(1)(b) ICESCR.

Yet Article 27 UDHR does not set out an unqualified right of access to share in the benefits of science. The second paragraph of Article 27 requires protection of "the moral and material interests of authors and inventors resulting from any scientific, literary or artistic production of which he is the author." The language of Article 27(2) is reminiscent of the language of the Berne Convention of 1928, the first international treaty on copyright, prompting confusion as to whether Article 27 UDHR was intended to proclaim that intellectual property rights are fundamental human rights. Against this background, some scholars have recently begun to question the relevance of Article 27 UDHR and Article 15 ICESCR to address the social and economic challenges raised by IP rights, partly on the grounds that human rights proclaimed therein reflect individualist, Western, and Eurocentric values. This chapter argues that this scholarship attaches undue weight to Western, classical liberal conceptions of human rights and overlooks the influence of the Latin American social justice vision of human rights in the Bogota Declaration of 1948, which greatly influenced the drafting of the UDHR's inclusion of social and economic rights.

This chapter draws on the Travaux Preparatoires for the Bogota Declaration, only recently published in full, to show the influence of the Bogota Declaration on the drafting of the provision on moral and material interests of authors and inventors in Article 27(2) UDHR. The analysis is combined with a study of the origins and aims of protecting the "moral" rights of authors in the Berne Convention to draw out the similarities, differences and overlap. The first part of the chapter sets out the controversy which has erupted about the interface between IP rights and human rights and the human rights sceptics' arguments. The second part retraces the origins and purpose of the "moral" rights of authors in the Berne Convention 1928, revealing how its contested and ambiguous meaning facilitated its partial transplant in Article 27(2) UDHR. The final part contrasts the provisions on protection of intellectual property rights in Berne, with the aims of the Bogota Declaration adopted by socialist South American countries whose delegates pressed for the inclusion of the moral and material interests of authors in Article 27(2). This novel, comparative study of the genesis and normative foundations of Article 27 UDHR charts an interpretive route towards recovering the Latin American ideals of universal human rights as foundations of social and economic justice which animated its drafting.

3.2 THE ORIGINS AND GROWTH OF INTERNATIONAL IP RIGHTS

The starting point from which to gain an understanding of the nature of the rights protected in Article 27 UDHR and the interface between IP rights and human rights is the adoption of the Trade Related Agreement on Intellectual Property Rights (TRIPS) in 1994[1] and its enforcement by the World Trade Organization. Intellectual property rights are known as "negative" rights because they confer on holders the right to exclude everyone from using the protected matter without the holder's consent for a fixed number of years. Until the adoption of TRIPS, the legal requirements for protection of IP rights, including patents, copyright, and trademarks were to be found primarily in national laws and were enforced by national courts. The first initiatives to create international legal standards took place in the second part of the nineteenth century with the rapid growth of industrialization in developed countries

---

[1] General Agreement on Trade in Services (GATS), Annex 1B of the WTO Agreement (Marrakesh, April 15, 1994, 1869 UNTS 183); Agreement on Trade Related Aspects of Intellectual Property Rights (TRIPS), Annex 1C of the WTO Agreement (Marrakesh, April 15, 1994, 1869 UNTS 299. For a detailed discussion of the origins of TRIPS and the protection of intellectual property in international law see Henning Grosse Ruse-Khan, *The Protection of Intellectual Property in International Law*, Oxford University Press, 2016.

and the related international trade fairs. These factors exposed exhibitors to the risk that their innovative machines and artifacts could be copied by competitors with no means of redress.[2]

Two important international multilateral treaties were adopted: the Paris Convention on the Protection of Industrial Property (1884)[3] and the Berne Convention on the Protection of Artistic and Literary Works (1886).[4] The Paris Convention applies to "industrial property" in the broadest sense, including patents, trademarks, and utility models (Article 1). It was intended to enable inventors to enforce their IP rights abroad.[5] This power was mainly secured by Article 2 which establishes the principle of national treatment, enabling nationals of any country to enjoy in all the contracting countries the same protection and same legal remedy against infringement of their rights. However, the Paris Convention did not harmonize legal requirements for the grant of patents. These, along with exclusions and exceptions, continued to be the preserve of States. Similarly, the principle of national treatment was replicated in the Berne Convention for the Protection of Literary and Artistic Works, adopted two years later in 1886. Article 2 provided that authors enjoy in all the contracting States the same rights of exclusivity as nationals over translations, adaptations, performances in public, broadcasts, communications to the public, and reproductions. Formal requirements and terms of protection remained the preserve of contracting States.

The Berne Convention was amended in Rome in 1928 with the addition of Article 6bis protecting the "moral rights" of authors. The turning point for international IP law came in 1994 with the adoption of the TRIPS Agreement which imposed on all contracting members of the WTO obligations regarding the nature, scope, and term of protection for intellectual property rights. Unlike previous treaties, the obligations in TRIPS "had teeth" with the creation of an international enforcement machinery through WTO panels.[6] For the purposes of the discussion in this chapter, there are two critical points to note. As regards copyright, TRIPS incorporated the provisions in Berne, except for the moral rights of authors, underscoring the economic and commercial value of the legal rights of exclusivity conferred by international intellectual property law on authors (and their estate) for the duration of their lives and fifty years thereafter. As regards patents, TRIPS imposed on all contracting States an obligation to grant patent protection for a minimum of twenty years (Article 33) in

---

[2] London: Great Exhibition. Crystal Palace 1851 Paris: Exposition Universelle, 1855, 1867, 1868.
[3] Paris Convention on the Protection of Industrial Property (PC) (Paris, March 20, 1883, last revised at Stockholm on July 14, 1967 and amended in 1979, 828 UNTS 306. On the origins of the Paris Convention see Alfredo C. Jr. Robles, "History of the Paris Convention," 15 *World Bull.* 1 (1999), p. 15.
[4] Berne Convention on the Protection of Literary and Artistic Works (BC) (Berne, September 9, 1886, last revised at Paris on July 24, 1971 and amended in 1979, 1161 UNTS 30).
[5] Through the establishment of the principle of national treatment (Article 2), rights of priority (Article 4) and the requirement that members should provide IP protection for exhibits at international fairs (Article 11).
[6] Laurence R. Helfer, "Regime Shifting: The TRIPs Agreement and New Dynamics of International Intellectual Property Lawmaking" (2004) 29 *Yale J Int'l L* 1.

"all fields of technology for inventions which are new, involve an inventive step and are capable of industrial application" (Article 27[1]). Patent holders enjoy the right "to exclude others from making, using, selling or importing patented product" (Article 28). As this brief history shows, the essence of international intellectual property rights thus lies in the grant to authors and inventors of legal rights to have and retain exclusive use and control of their works/inventions for a specified term (twenty years for patents, lifetime plus fifty years after death for copyright). One of the most profound impacts of TRIPS was to radically alter existing national patent laws. At the time, a large number of countries did not have intellectual property laws and the laws of many others, including developing countries like India, known as the "pharmacy of the world," excluded patents on pharmaceuticals.[7] The knock-on effects of TRIPS on developing countries were catastrophic.[8] At the height of the AIDS crisis, the government of South Africa was sued by a consortium of thirty-nine pharmaceutical companies alleging that South Africa's importation of antiretroviral generics was a violation of the country's TRIPS obligations.[9] The legal suit was dropped following a global outcry, mobilization of civil society movements across borders, and UN institutions reclaiming the primacy of human rights over trade rights.[10]

The adoption of TRIPS also coincided with the race to sequence the human genome. Article 27(1) TRIPS not only permits but makes it obligatory for States to grant patents "in all fields of technology." Were WTO States under an obligation to grant patents on human genes? Who owned science?[11] The controversy over ownership of science prompted a revival of interest in the right science enunciated in Article 27 UDHR and Article 15 ICESCR, pioneered by Audrey Chapman at the AAAS.[12] Several reports on Article 15 ICESCR have since been produced by the UN

---

[7] Amy Kapczynski, "Harmonization and its Discontents: A Case Study of TRIPS Implementation in India's Pharmaceutical Sector" (2009) 97 *Calif. L. Rev.* 1571.
[8] See for instance Susan K. Sell. *Private Power, Public Law: The Globalization of Intellectual Property Rights*. Vol. 88. Cambridge University Press, 2003 and Duncan Matthews, *Globalising Intellectual Property Rights: The TRIPS Agreement*. Routledge, 2003, Peter K Yu, "TRIPS and Its Discontents" (2006) 10 *Marq Intell Prop L Rev* 369.
[9] See also Ellen Hoen, "TRIPS, Pharmaceutical Patents, and Access to Essential Medicines: A Long Way from Seattle to Doha" (2002) 3 *Chi. J. Int'l L.* 27.
[10] The role of civil movements is mobilizing global support for access to medicines at the height of the AIDS crisis is recorded in "Life in the Blood," a documentary which won the Sundance Grand Jury Prize in 2013: www.imdb.com/title/tt1787067/.
[11] The US team of scientists led by J. Craig Venter wanted to patent the genome. By contrast, the international team of scientists led by John Sulston in Cambridge argued that science was a public good. In a relentless campaign against gene patents, Sulston warned that the appropriation of the human genome would result in the closure of traditionally collaborative and open fields of science to the benefit of private, profit making companies. See John Sulston and Georgina Ferry, The Common Thread: A Story of Science, Politics, Ethics, and the Human Genome. Random House, 2002 and Joseph Stiglitz and John Sulston, "The Case against Gene Patents." Wall Street Journal (2010).
[12] Audrey R. Chapman, "A human rights perspective on intellectual property, scientific progress, and access to the benefits of science." *WIPO/OHCHR, Intellectual Property and Human Rights, A Panel Discussion to Commemorate the 50th Anniversary of the Universal Declaration of Human Rights*, Geneva, Switzerland (1999): 127–168.

(most recently by the then-UN Special Rapporteur in the field of cultural rights, Farida Shaheed).[13]

The unequivocal, strong recurrent theme of the UN reports is that the human rights of authors and inventors protected in Article 27 UDHR and Article 15 ICESCR are not identical to, and should not be confused with, intellectual property rights.[14] In short, IP rights are bound by time and place. By contrast, human rights enunciate moral ideals based on the primacy and dignity of each human being. They are universal and hold irrespective of place and time. They articulate the spheres of civil, political, social, economic, and cultural protection which are required for the full realization and development of each human being's personality. It is this ethos of human self-realization which animates the right to science in Article 27 UDHR and Article 15 ICESCR.[15] Notwithstanding, legal scholars have recently argued that the nature of the rights protected in these articles is not only problematic but indicative of the limited relevance of human rights as counterweights to the global injustices created by the international expansion of IP rights. The next section sets out the arguments of the(se) sceptics before retracing the drafting history of Article 27 UDHR to show that they are based on a limited understanding of the aims of the drafters.

3.3 CONFLATION OF IP RIGHTS WITH HUMAN RIGHTS IN THE UDHR AND ICESCR?

The main arguments questioning the relevance of human rights to IP rights are deployed in a recent article by Okediji.[16] They are threefold. First, it is claimed that the addition of human rights ideals to IP regimes can actually strengthen IP rights in socially harmful ways. The second argument is that human rights-driven global challenges to IP, mainly in the health field, are not neutral but reflect the values of the Western and Eurocentric liberal regimes of developed countries. Lastly, it is argued that the limited effect of human rights on IP is due to a narrow vision of human rights which excludes social and economic rights.[17] To be clear, Okediji does not claim that human rights cannot have a beneficial role to play. Instead, her argument is that they do not offer "a meaningful pathway" as a counterweight to IP rights in the absence of serious engagement with the full panoply of economic, social, and cultural group rights.[18] This notwithstanding, according to Okediji, the

---

[13] These reports are discussed in other contributions to this volume.
[14] As detailed in Part III.
[15] See Aurora Plomer, *Patents, Human Rights and Access to Science*. Edward Elgar Publishing, 2015.
[16] Ruth L. Okediji, "Does Intellectual Property Need Human Rights?" (2018) 51 *NYUJ Int'l L. & Pol.* 1, p. 4.
[17] Ibid. p. 5.
[18] Ibid. p. 6.

human rights framework "has largely operated as a justification for the core architecture of the international IP system"[19] because of the "unequivocal recognition of authorial interests found in Article 15 of the ICESCR and Article 27 of the UDHR."[20] The rights of authors and inventors, she argues, have operated as "the formal hook" on which strong support for international IP rights have been hung by UN General Comments and reports, as well as by academic commentary,[21] buttressed by utilitarian and liberal ideals of freedom and property as an expression of the human personality.[22] As a result, Okediji argues, whilst General Comment 17 cautions not to conflate IP rights with human rights and claims that IP rights should be subordinated to human rights, the report's recommendations are based on the foundational premise that rights of authors need to be balanced against other interests and may only be limited by States subject to strict legal requirements, reinforcing IP rights.[23] In this way, the "hard" guidance on the legal interpretation of the rights of authors and inventors in General Comment 17 reflects an instrumentalist vision of IP and liberal values of freedom and dignity in Western, Eurocentric, developed countries. Moreover, as rightly noted by Okediji, several writers conflate IP rights with human rights. The World Intellectual Property Organization (WIPO) and the UN Commission for Human Rights have also somewhat confusedly asserted that "intellectual property rights are enshrined as human rights in the UDHR."[24] Okediji acknowledges that a more nuanced position is adopted by the UN former Special Rapporteur in the field of cultural rights in 2015, Farida Shaheed, who explicitly stated that protection of the moral and material interests of authors and inventors "cannot be used to defend patent laws that inadequately respect … scientific progress and its applications."[25] However, in her view, the "hard" guidance in General Comment 17 is likely to prevail over the "soft" guidance in the UN Special Rapporteur's reports.

Yet, on closer examination, the distance between the various UN reports is perhaps not as great as claimed. As mentioned by Okediji in a footnote, General Comment 17 and Shaheed's report concur that "[i]n contrast to the perpetual moral interests of authors … the material interests of authors need not necessarily be protected forever, or even for an author's entire life."[26] Under both reports, human rights have primacy and, in the event of conflict, must prevail over time-limited legal rights of ownership and exclusivity. Furthermore, neither General Comment 17 nor Farida Shaheed's reports provide justification for the view that Article 27 UDHR (or

---

[19] Ibid. p. 20.
[20] Ibid. p. 18.
[21] Ibid. p. 18.
[22] Ibid. footnote 59 p. 20.
[23] For instance, Okediji cites Daniel Gervais highlighting the "stringent" standard for assessing state limitations on the rights in the ICESCR (at p. 21).
[24] p. 19, footnote 56 and p. 23.
[25] 2015 Shaheed Report, UN. Doc A/70/279 (Aug. 4, 2015).
[26] General Comment No. 17, para. 16.

Article 15 ICESR) imply that intellectual property rights are the foundation on which authorial rights are premised or the presumption that human rights can only limit IP rights at the margins. It is true that Article 27(2) could be read as reflecting liberal, utilitarian, or Hegelian conceptions of property and personhood. It is also true, although not specifically discussed by Okediji, that the rights of authors and inventors over their intellectual creations could be read as reflecting Lockean, natural rights theories of property.[27] However, as will be argued below, to privilege the liberal, utilitarian or natural rights reading of authors rights one has to disconnect the text of Article 27(2) from the intention of the drafters as revealed in its drafting history and one has to read Article 27 in isolation from the full spectrum of interconnected civil, political, social and economic rights encompassed by the UDHR.

By contrast, as shown in the next section, the story of the genesis of Article 27(2) reveals that the insertion of the rights of authors and inventors in Article 27 UDHR was never intended to signal that authors and inventors have a fundamental human right to ownership and exclusivity over their works/inventions or a human right to patents and copyright.

3.4 ARTICLE 27 UDHR: THE INFLUENCE OF BERNE AND BOGOTA

There is no question that reference to the "moral" interests of authors and inventors in 27(2) UDHR is a *renvoi* to the "moral" rights of authors in the revisions of the Berne Convention adopted in Rome in 1928 which provided that:

> Article 6 bis: (I) Independently of the author's economic rights, and even after the transfer of the said rights, the author shall have the right to claim authorship of the work and to object to any distortion, mutilation or other modification of, or other derogatory action in relation to, the said work, which would be prejudicial to his honor or reputation.

As mentioned above, the Berne Convention is an international treaty on copyright law, raising the question of whether the drafters of the UDHR were aware of the risk of conflating IP rights with human rights and if so, why the text was nevertheless adopted. The analysis of the drafting history of Article 27 shows that the drafters were aware that the concept of the moral rights of authors and inventors was to be found in international copyright law. Moreover it was precisely for that reason that many delegations, mostly from Western liberal countries, opposed the inclusion of authors rights. However, there was limited understanding of international IP law and some confusion over the legal concept of "moral rights," a term whose constructive ambiguity facilitated the final acceptance of 27(2) UDHR. by the General Assembly.

---

[27] General Comment No. 17, para. 16

3.4.1 *The Origins and Aims of Article 27(1)*

The origin of Article 27 is in the preliminary Draft Convention prepared by the Canadian lawyer John Humphrey, as Director of the UN Secretariat's Division for Human Rights.[28] From the very beginning, and in contrast with the list of the classical, liberal list of "negative" rights of the Enlightenment, Humphrey's text was intended to go well beyond the civil and political rights enunciated in the texts of the French Declaration of Human Rights or the US Bill of Rights and Constitution. We know from Humphrey's biography, and from scholarship on the UDHR,[29] that Humphrey had drawn inspiration for the inclusion of social, economic, and cultural rights in the preliminary draft list from the text of the human rights bill submitted by the Inter-American Juridical Committee. The forty-eight rights enumerated in Humphrey's draft[30] included the immediate predecessor of "the right to science" (Article 44, now Article 27 UDHR) which Humphrey had listed as follows:

> Everyone has the right to participate in the cultural life of the community, to enjoy the arts and to share in the benefits of science.[31]

Humphrey's wording closely matches the first part of Article XV of the bill submitted by Chile on behalf of the Inter-American Juridical Committee which stated that "everyone has the right to share in the benefits accruing from the discoveries and inventions of science."[32]

---

[28] For further details on the composition of the drafting committee and the evolution of the text see: http://research.un.org/en/undhr/draftingcommittee.

[29] The leading commentary on the drafting history of the UDHR is by Johannes Morsink, *The Universal Declaration of Human Rights: Origins, Drafting, and Intent*. University of Pennsylvania Press, 1999.

[30] UN, ECOSOC, Commission on Human Rights Drafting Committee: International Bill of Rights, E/CN.4/AC.1/3. Amongst the list of socioeconomic rights in Humphrey's list was a right to health (Article 35), the right to free education irrespective of race, gender, language, or religion (Article 36), the right to work (Article 37), the right to equitable share of the national income in proportion to the contribution each makes to society (Article 39), the right to social security (Article 41), the right to food and housing (Article 42) and the right to leisure (Article 43). https://undocs.org/E/CN.4/AC.1/3/ADD.1

[31] Ibid. Article 44

[32] Morsink's claim that Humphrey had almost no other constitutional sources is not strictly correct. Other sources mentioned by Humphrey include the United States' suggestion that the categories of rights to be included should extend to the right to "enjoy minimum standards of social, economic and cultural well-being." Humphrey also mentioned Articles 163 and 164 of the Bolivian Constitution (1938) which asserted the State's obligations to protect artistic, cultural, and archeological heritage and to promote culture. Another source was the Brazilian Constitution of 1946 which imposed an obligation on the State to promote culture through the creation of research institutes particularly in connection with establishments of higher education (Article 174) and further stated that "science, letters and the arts are free" (Article 173). Similarly, Uruguay's Constitution of 1942, declared that education, including artistic and "industrial" skills were social needs which should be freely accessible to all and called for the creation of libraries as well as scholarships in the arts and sciences (Article 62). Finally, the Constitution of Yugoslavia provided that "[t]he state assists science and art with a view to developing the people's culture and creativity" (Article 37).

The original text of Article 27 produced by Humphrey was thus an amalgam of the Inter-American Juridical Committee's text submitted by Chile and some provisions in national constitutions calling for protection of the arts and sciences which should be freely accessible to all. Moreover, Humphrey's "right to arts/science" was conceptually embedded in and interconnected with other social and economic rights, most notably rights to education and rights to leisure. The interdependence and indivisibility of civil, political, social, and economic rights was preserved in the final list of rights enumerated in the UDHR, along with the obligation of States to facilitate access to the benefits of the arts and sciences as a means of securing the social and economic rights which are indispensable for the free and full development of the human personality (in Articles 22, 26, and 29). In addition, the interdependence of the individual and society and the correlation of individual rights and duties is further reflected in Article 29(1) of the final UDHR text, which explicitly links individual rights to communal duties: "Everyone has duties to the community in which alone the free and full development of his personality is possible." As indicated by one of the delegates, the term "alone" stresses "the essential fact that the individual could attain the full development of his personality only within the framework of society."[33]

In short, the origins of Article 27 and its conceptual and normative links to the rest of the Declaration clearly indicate that the original purpose of what was to become the first paragraph of Article 27 was to enjoin States to facilitate free access to the arts and sciences as a means to promote the full development of each individual human being.

In this light, the question which arises is why Humphrey's original text was amended and qualified by the addition of a second paragraph whose wording and purpose appears prima facie at odds with the first paragraph of Article 27?

3.4.2 *The Origins and Aims of Article 27(2)*

The starting point for the second paragraph of Article 27 may be traced back to the full text submitted by Chile on behalf of the Inter-American Juridical Committee. The sections omitted by Humphrey can be seen retrospectively to show awareness of a possible tension between public rights to participate and share in the benefits of science and intellectual property rights. The full text of Article XV of the Inter-American Juridical Committee's bill was as follows (with italics added to highlight the text omitted by Humphrey):

> Everyone has the right to participate in the cultural life of the community, to enjoy the arts and to share in the benefits of science *under conditions which permit a fair*

---

[33] The second paragraph of Article 29 further reinforces the mutuality of individual and society in specifying the conditions under which individual rights may be legitimately limited.

return to the industry and skill of those responsible for the discovery of the invention . . .

The state has the duty to encourage the development of the arts and sciences, but it must see to it that the laws for the protection of trademarks, patents and copyrights are not used for the establishment of monopolies which might prevent all persons from sharing in the benefits of science. It is the duty of the state to protect the citizen against the use of of scientific discoveries in a manner to create fear and unrest among the people.[34]

The omitted sentences arguably indicate that, whilst the Inter-American Juridical Committee accepted the legal obligation imposed on States to protect patents, trademarks, and copyright, the Committee thought that the overriding duty of the State was to protect the human right of everyone to participate and share in the benefits of science. The potential risks to public access to science posed by the monopolies created by IP rights are explicitly acknowledged. Moreover, the profits derived from ownership of IP are subject to a test of fairness, in line with the overarching values of the Draft Declaration of the International Rights and Duties of Man (1947) proposed by the Inter-American Juridical Committee which assumes the interdependence of the individual and society.[35] For instance, in addition to rights to work (XIV), social security (XVI), and education (XVII), Article VIII on the right to own property limits the right to attaining "the minimum standard of private ownership of property based upon the essential material needs of a decent life, looking to the maintenance of the dignity of the human person and the sanctity of home life."[36] Article VII further envisaged that "[t]he state may determine by general laws the limitations which may be placed upon the ownership of property, looking to the maintenance of social justice and to the promotion of the common interest of the community."[37]

When compared to the text of the Berne Convention and the second paragraph of Article 27, it is clear that the text of the Draft Inter-American Bill on which Humphrey had based the original formulation of Article 27(1) on the right to science had a very different intent from Berne. It was largely at the insistence of the French delegation that "moral" rights of authors had been added to the revision of the Berne Convention in Rome in 1928. The "moral" rights of authors were further extended in the Brussels revision of Berne, in a meeting from June 5 to June 26, 1948 which overlapped with the third Session of the Human Rights Commission from May 24 until June 18, 1948. The next section sets out the ambiguities surrounding the concept of "moral" rights and its contested addition to the Berne Convention in 1928 as a backdrop to the origins of the second paragraph in Article 27.

---

[34] Article XV, E/CN.4/AC1/3/Add.1, at p. 356.
[35] E/CN.4/2, https://digitallibrary.un.org/record/560759.
[36] Ibid. E/CN.4/2.
[37] Ibid.

3.4.2.1 The "Moral" Rights of Authors in Berne

As mentioned earlier, international intellectual property law had begun to emerge in the last quarter of the nineteenth century and accelerated in the last part of the twentieth century with the adoption of the TRIPS Agreement in 1995 and the enforcement machinery of the WTO panels. When the Berne Convention was originally adopted in 1886 there was no reference to the "moral" rights of authors in the text. Legal scholarship on the origins of the addition of "moral" rights of authors shows that the revisions of the Berne Convention in 1928 rested on confused and contested legal concepts whose inclusion were the result of complex factors and historical accidents.

The rights originally protected in Berne were economic rights, enabling the author/inventor to commercially exploit publication and reproduction of the work for the duration of the copyright term which was originally left to national laws. In 1928, Article 6bis added a new provision entitled "moral rights" which were said to reflect the personality of its creator, just as the economic rights reflect the author's need "to keep body and soul together".[38] The text of Article 6bis has remained virtually unchanged since 1928, although the revisions of 1948 made it mandatory for States to protect the "moral" rights for the duration of the life of the author and in 1967 this was further extended to a minimum of fifty years after the life of the author.[39] Article 6bis stipulated that:

> (1) Independently of the author's economic rights, and even after the transfer of the said rights, the author shall have the right to claim authorship of the work and to object to any distortion, mutilation or other modification of, or other derogatory action in relation to, the said work, which would be prejudicial to his honor or reputation.

The rights therein protected are commonly referred to as rights of attribution and integrity. They require, inter alia, that the author's name be mentioned in a publication and they entitle authors to object to mutilation or distortion of their works.

Whilst the justifications for "moral rights" are typically drawn from French and German philosophical theories, in practice, in nineteenth-century France, authors assigned their rights to publishers who were the real beneficiaries of the profits generated by publications.[40] In a seminal article on the origins of moral rights in Berne, the legal scholar Rigamonti shows that the doctrine of "moral rights" in the nineteenth century attempted to address two central issues.[41] Could creditors force

---

[38] www.wipo.int/edocs/pubdocs/en/copyright/615/wipo_pub_615.pdf at 41.
[39] Ibid.
[40] Ronan Deazley, *Rethinking Copyright: History, Theory, Language*. Edward Elgar Publishing, 2006 and Ronan Deazley, Martin Kretschmer, and Lionel Bently, *Privilege and Property: Essays on the History of Copyright*. Open Book Publishers, 2010.
[41] Cyrill P. Rigamonti, "Deconstructing Moral Rights" (2006) 47 *Harv. Int'l LJ* 353. See also Alexander Peukert, *A Critique of the Ontology of Intellectual Property Law*, CUP, 2021 questioning the transplant of the legal paradigm for tangible property to intangible, 'immaterial' objects in 'intellectual' property law.

publication of a work in debt collection and bankruptcy cases? Secondly, could publishers publish the work without the author's name or modify it without the author's consent? There were no specific legislation or codes dealing with these questions in most European countries and, whilst rules had been developed by courts, systematizing and codifying the rules was challenging because national laws were based on Roman law which recognized only *tangible* forms of property or personality rights which were inalienable.[42]

The solution adopted by Germany in 1906 was to merge these rules in the copyright statutes of 1901 and 1907, effectively creating a new legal category of property – *intangible*, intellectual property – which merged rights of attribution and integrity with economic rights. Although the merging of personality rights with economic rights was described, as "the chronic disease of copyright scholarship in Germany," as argued by Rigamonti, the disease ultimately prevailed.[43] Meanwhile, common law countries had addressed the same issues through a patchwork of rules mostly derived from tort or contract without recourse to the ambiguous concept of "moral" rights in intellectual property. According to Rigamonti, theorization of "moral" IP rights in Europe gained momentum at the turn of the century, and this facilitated their inclusion in the Berne revision of 1928 together with the historical accident of Italy hosting the conference.[44]

The legal history of the concept of moral rights in copyright law thus shows that, in substance, the concept was ambiguous and contested. Moral rights are supposedly universal, inalienable personality rights. As such, they are conceptually distinct from the time limited, proprietary, economic rights of authors and inventors to exclusive commercial exploitation of their work protected in international law. Unfortunately, these legal and conceptual complexities were lost on French and South American delegations leading the debates on the inclusion of Article 27(2) in the UDHR.

---

[42] For an overview of the nineteenth-century debates see Fritz Machlup and Edith Penrose, "The Patent Controversy in the Nineteenth Century" (1950) 10(1) *The Journal of Economic History* 1–29

[43] Cyrill P. Rigamonti "The Conceptual Transformation of Moral Rights" *American Journal of Comparative Law*, Winter, 2007, Vol. 55, No. 1 pp. 67-122 at p. 108 referring to Josef Kohler, Zur Literatur des Autorrechts, 21 Kritische Vierteljahresschrift f?r Gesetzgebung und Rechtswissenschaft 189, 197 (1879).

[44] Rigamonti shows that moral rights were not originally in the agenda for the 1928 Berne conference in Rome, but Italy had recently modelled its own copyright laws on the German copyright statutes. Moral rights were added to the agenda by Italy as it seized the opportunity to enhance its international reputation. Unsurprisingly, Italy's proposal was resisted by common-law countries because "moral" IP rights were not part of their legal tradition and because the legal issues that "moral" rights sought to address were already addressed through common law rules. Changes to Berne had to secure unanimous approval. Australia, reflecting a different common law tradition, opposed the addition of "moral" rights, but ultimately relented because of the constructive ambiguity of Article 6bis which defined the content of moral rights as protection of honour and reputation which common law countries already protected.

3.4.2.2 The Latin American Approach to IP Rights

Apart from Brazil, Latin American countries were not parties to the Berne Convention whose members at the time where mainly former European colonial powers.[45] Instead, Latin American countries had developed their own regional copyright treaty, the Inter-American Convention on the Rights of the Author in Literary, Scientific and Artistic Works, concluded in Washington on June 22, 1946. There was no mention of the ambiguous "moral rights" or its theoretical scaffold in that text. The legal lacunae concerning rights of attribution and integrity which had prompted the inclusion of moral rights of authors in Berne were addressed pragmatically as follows:

> **Article XI**
> The author of any copyrighted work, in disposing of his copyright therein by sale, assignment or otherwise, retains the right to retain the paternity of the work and to oppose any modification or use of it which is prejudicial to his reputation as an author, unless he has consented . . .[46]

There was another important difference between the Inter-American Convention and Berne. By contrast to the mandatory term of protection of life of the authors introduced in Berne in 1948, the Inter-American Convention left the duration of copyright to the discretion of member states. Whilst there were significant variations, in general, protection lasted for twenty years (Mexico, Chile, and Peru) and therefore significantly less than Berne.[47] This, together with provisions enabling States to create exceptions and limitations on copyright, reflected the socialist vision of the Latin American republics to promote access to books and, more generally, to the arts and science. As argued by Cerda Silva

> in highly simple terms, the European copyright system ... provided automatic protection to authors for their lives plus at least fifty years, but not that much flexibility for meeting public interest needs. The Inter-American system, which was limited to countries of the Americas, provided international protection for a discretionary term to authors who had complied with formalities set forth by countries of origin.[48]

As noted earlier, the Latin American vision that protection of authorial rights should be subject to a fairness test in order to promote social justice was reflected in

---

[45] See Alberto J Cerda Silva, "Copyright Tradition in Latin America: From Independence to Internationalization" (2014) 61 *J Copyright Soc'y USA* 57 7.
[46] www.oas.org/juridico/english/treaties/b-28.html.
[47] Twenty years in Chile, Mexico, and Peru; twenty-five years in El Salvador; thirty years in Argentina, Bolivia, Dominican Republic, and Venezuela; forty years in Uruguay; fifty years p.m.a. in Costa Rica and Ecuador; sixty years in Brazil; eighty years in Colombia, Cuba, and Panama; cited by Cerda Silva at p. 597, footnote 117.
[48] Alberto J Cerda Silva, "Copyright Tradition in Latin America: From Independence to Internationalization" (2014) 61 *J Copyright Soc'y USA* 577 at p. 598

the full text of the bill prepared by the Inter-Juridical Committee in 1945. The overriding importance of protection of social and economic rights as fundamental human rights was further affirmed in the American Declaration on the Rights and Duties of Man (Bogota Declaration) adopted in Bogota on May 2, 1948, six months before the UDHR in 1948. Unfortunately, by then the ambiguous language of Berne on the "moral" rights/interests of authors had also made its way into the text of Article XIII which provided that:

> **Article XIII.**
> Every person has the right to take part in the cultural life of the community, to enjoy the arts, and to participate in the benefits that result from intellectual progress, especially scientific discoveries.
>
> He likewise has the right to the protection of his moral and material interests as regards his inventions or any literary, scientific or artistic works of which he is the author.

The final text of paragraph 2 of Article 27 UDHR is almost identical to the text of Article XIII of the Bogota Declaration. If read in isolation from the rest of the Declaration the second paragraph of Article XIII's reference to the "moral and material interests" of authors could be seen as a *renvoi* to the IP rights protected in Berne and, more generally, as an assertion that intellectual property rights are fundamental human rights.[49] It was precisely for this reason that many countries opposed the addition of paragraph 2 to Article 27 UDHR which, they feared, risked conflating IP rights with human rights.[50] Cassin, representing the French delegation, and the Latin American countries who supported the addition of the second paragraph, insisted that this was not the case. In order to understand their reasons, one has to go back to the full text of the Bogota Declaration and read Article XIII holistically in the light of the values enunciated in the Preamble and the full list of social and economic rights which were included.

3.4.2.3 The Meaning of "Moral and Material Interests" in the Bogota Declaration

The Bogota Declaration was based on a humanist vision of human rights grounded in social justice. If the "material" interests of authors are to be understood as the economic rights of authors to exploit their intellectual property, then as a species of property rights, these rights are subject to the limitations in Article XXIII on the right to property which stipulates that "[e]very person has a right to own such private property as meets the essential needs of decent living and helps to maintain the dignity of the individual and of the home." As such, Article 27(2) UDHR (and its

---

[49] See Mary W. S. Wong, "Toward an Alternative Normative Framework for Copyright: From Private Property to Human Rights" (2008–2009) 26 *Cardozo Arts & Ent. L.J.* 775 and J. Janewa OseiTutu, "Corporate Human Rights to Intellectual Property Protection" (2015) 55 *Santa Clara L. Rev.* 1.

[50] Aurora Plomer, "The Human Rights Paradox: Intellectual Property Rights and Rights of Access to Science" (2013) 35 *Hum. Rts. Q.* 143.

counterpart Article 15 1(c) in the ICESCR) would at most permit authors and inventors to receive a fair remuneration for their intellectual property.[51]

But there are also indications that the term "material" at the time was used in a different sense to refer to the physical needs and well-being of each human being. For instance, the 1944 Philadelphia Declaration of the International Labour Organization, one of the sources for the Bogota Declaration,[52] provides in Article II that:

> a) all human beings, irrespective of race, creed or sex, have the right to pursue both their *material well-being* and their spiritual development in conditions of freedom and dignity, of economic security and equal opportunity; [emphasis added].

The language of *material* wellbeing is echoed in the Preamble of the Bogota Declaration which states that the aim of the Declaration is to acknowledge the dignity of the individual and to facilitate the creation of conditions which: "permit him to achieve *spiritual and material progress* and attain happiness" [emphasis added]. Here, the word "material" is used to distinguish the physical from the spiritual/mental well-being and needs of each person. The word "material" is also used to distinguish physical from mental wellbeing in the *Travaux Preparatoires* of the Philadelphia Declaration, in the text of the right to education which states that "illiteracy prevents individuals from full participation in the political and economic life of the state and to avail themselves of the opportunities for *material and cultural development*" (author's translation from the original Spanish, emphasis added).[53]

The delegates' views on protection of the "moral and material interests" of authors in Article XIII of the Bogota Declaration are consistent with this interpretation of "material" as denoting the physical needs and well-being of the human person as distinct from the individual's mental/spiritual needs. As mentioned earlier, Article XIII provides that:

> Every person has the right to take part in the cultural life of the community, to enjoy the arts, and to participate in the benefits that result from intellectual progress, especially scientific discoveries.
>
> He likewise has the right to the protection of his moral and material interests as regards his inventions or any literary, scientific or artistic works of which he is the author.

---

[51] As argued in General Comment 17 – see also Peter K. Yu, "Reconceptualizing Intellectual Property Interests in a Human Rights Framework" (2007) 40 *U.C. Davis L. Rev.* 1039.

[52] As shown by Paúl, Álvaro (2017). *Los trabajos preparatorios de la Declaración Americana de los Derechos y Deberes del Hombre y el origen remoto de la Corte Interamericana*. Mexico: Instituto de Investigaciones Jurídicas UNAM. p.1, p. 110.

[53] Álvaro Paúl, *Los trabajos preparatorios de la Declaración Americana de los Derechos y Deberes del Hombre y el origen remoto de la Corte Interamericana*. Mexico: Instituto de Investigaciones Jurídicas UNAM, 2017, Article XVII, p. 135. Spanish text: "No se necesita de ningun argumento para demostrar que el analfabeto no puede participar plenamente de la vida politica, economica y social del Estado, y que no puede aprovecharse de las muchas posibilidades de desarrollo material y cultural que se le presentan . . ."

The *Travaux Préparatoires* on the Bogota Declaration and Article XIII, recently published in Spanish, show that the main rationale for the second paragraph of Article XIII of the Bogota Declaration was provided by Fernandez del Castillo, the delegate from Mexico. In answer to the delegate from the USA (Tate), who spoke against the inclusion of rights of authors on the grounds that the rights of authors were not fundamental human rights, Fernandez del Castillo said that intellectual creations were the product of the human genius.[54] They were the main distinctive attributes of human beings which are essential to his person even though they may not have been recognized as such in national constitutions for political reasons.[55] Perez Cisneros, the delegate from Cuba, said that he understood and agreed with the spirit of the Mexican point, but he thought that since the second paragraph of Article XIII referred to intellectual property rights, it did not belong to an Article on the right to science and culture.[56] He was also concerned that a special category of individuals were singled out. Fernandez del Castillo's reply was that the words "paternity" and "property" in relation to intellectual creations were being used by analogy to denote the natural creative attributes of human beings. For this reason, the rights protected therein were universal and not confined to a special category, but extended to all creative human beings who made a fundamental contribution to society through the arts and sciences.[57] As such, protection of the creations of the mind was essential to the advancement of culture. Fernandez del Castillos's arguments prevailed and Article XIII was ultimately approved with the addition of the second paragraph in the Bogota Declaration. The representative of the Mexican delegation at the UN in the discussions on the UDHR turned out to be one of the strongest supporters of Cassin's proposal to add a second paragraph on protection of the rights of authors.

3.5 THE FINAL STAGES OF THE DRAFT OF ARTICLE 27(2) IN THE UDHR

The proposal to add a paragraph on the "moral" interests/rights of authors and inventors was driven by Rene Cassin, on behalf of the French delegation. On May 21, 1948, at the Second Session of the Drafting Committee at Lake City,[58] Cassin proposed an amendment to what by then had become Article 30 stating that:

> Authors of creative works and inventors shall retain, apart from financial rights, a moral right over their work or discovery, which shall remain extant after the financial rights have expired.[59]

[54] Ibid., p. 275.
[55] Ibid.
[56] Ibid., p. 276.
[57] Ibid.
[58] The second session of the Drafting Committee of the Commission on Human Rights opened on Monday, May 3, 1948, at the Interim Headquarters of the United Nations, Lake Success, New York. The Drafting Committee held twenty-five plenary, meetings and terminated its work on Friday, May 21, 1948.
[59] Report of the Drafting Committee to the Commission on Human Rights, E/CN.4/95, p. 13.

Cassin explained that the provision reflected a similar provision recently adopted in the Bogota Declaration. The French amendment was discussed and rejected by the Commission on Human Rights on June 11, 1948. The concerns raised by the critics mirror the arguments previously voiced by other delegates at Bogota. Mehta (India) and Wilson (UK) thought that it was inappropriate to single out a special category of persons in a universal declaration on human rights.[60] The representative from Uruguay disagreed. Uruguay had also supported the Mexican amendment in Bogota. He thought that without the amendment "intellectual workers" would be left without protection. The French amendment also received strong support from Larrain (Chile) who was gratified that it was based on the Bogota Declaration. The Chair (Roosevelt), speaking for the USA, opposed the French amendment on the grounds that it dealt with copyright which was the subject matter of international IP law.[61] Cassin's amendment was rejected by six votes to five, with five abstentions.

Thus, at the close of the 3rd Session of the Commission on Human Rights (held May 24 to June 18, 1948), the draft bill submitted by the Commission for consideration to the UN General Assembly included only the predecessor to the first paragraph of Article 27, then Article 25, stating that:

> **Article 25** Everyone has the right to participate in the cultural life of the community, to enjoy the arts and to share in scientific advancement. (E/800, p. 13).

Speaking in support of the draft Declaration to the plenary meeting held by the Economic and Social Council at its 7th Session on August 25, 1948, Cassin urged the Council to submit the draft Declaration for approval to the General Assembly notwithstanding the fact that it did not give sufficient prominence to certain rights, notably rights of asylum for stateless persons, limited right to equal pay; and that "[t]he Declaration gave no place to scientific and artistic pioneers, although those who contributed to the advance of civilization were entitled to have their interests protected."[62]

On September 24, 1948, the General Assembly referred the draft International Declaration of Human Rights to the Third Committee. The Third Committee considered Article 25 at its 150th to 152th Meetings from November 20 to November 22, 1948.[63] By then Cassin had gained the support of Mexico and Cuba which had submitted amendments to Article 25 calling for the insertion of an additional clause protecting the moral and material interests of authors and inventors.[64] The three delegations agreed to join their amendments ahead of the

---

[60] Commission on Human Rights, Summary of the 70th Meeting held at Lake City on June 11, 1948, https://undocs.org/E./CN.4/SR.70, p. 6.
[61] Ibid. p. 7.
[62] E_SR.215 215th Meeting, held on Wednesday, August 25, 1948: 25/08/1948 at pp. 649–650.
[63] A/C.3/SR.150 records the deliberations and votes of the Third Committee on Article 25.
[64] A/C.3/266 (Mexico); A/C.3/261 (Cuba), A/C.3/244/Rev.1)- (France).

IP Rights and Human Rights 71

Third Committee's meeting. The joint amendment proposed to add the following text to Article 25:

> Everyone has, likewise, the right to the protection of his moral and material interests in any inventions or literary) scientific or artistic works of which he is the author.[65]

Cassin's persistence paid off as the three delegations were now able to convince a majority of the delegates of the Third Committee to accept the amendment.

Campos Ortiz (Mexico) explained that the Mexican amendment was based on the text on the protection of intellectual property proposed by Mexico in Bogota which had been unanimously adopted.[66] In Campus Ortiz's view, only a small number of artists, scientists, writers, and independent researchers were salaried workers. Without recognition of their work, no social progress was possible. National and international legislation safeguarding the rights of authors' and inventors' patents was not always effective. Likewise, Cassin claimed that although royalties and patents might provide some reward for authors and inventors the aim of the amendment was to go further and protect the spiritual and moral interests of authors who are often not interested in profits but want recognition by posterity and for their work to be free from distortion. His amendment, he said, took account not only of the "material" aspect of the question but was also designed to protect the spiritual and moral interests of artists and inventors.[67]

On their face, Cassin's arguments were based on a double conflation or confusion of:

(1) the economic rights of exploitation protected by international IP law with the material/physical well-being of authors in Bogota and
(2) the "moral" rights of authors (in Berne) directed at legal protection of the integrity of creative works with the "spiritual" well-being of intellectuals in Bogota.

A similar conflation between the legal conceptions of intellectual property protection in Berne and the moral objective of encouraging and protecting intellectual creativity is evident in the contributions of the South American delegates who supported Cassin. Perez Cisneros (Cuba), who had expressed reservations on the counterpart addition to Article XIII in the Bogota Declaration, said that Cuba had submitted an amendment in the same spirit as Mexico, which Perez Cisneros praised for being the first to raise the question of protection of intellectual property rights in Bogota.[68] Protection of intellectual property was new and important and should be included in the UDHR.[69] The "material" conditions of "men of learning"

[65] A/C.3/360.
[66] A/C.3/SR.150 at p. 617.
[67] Ibid. p. 620.
[68] A/C.3/SR.150 at p. 618.
[69] Perez Cisneros (Cuba) said that Cuba's amendment was similar in substance to the amendment proposed by the French delegation "phrased with admirable perfection and style." Cuba withdrew its amendment in favor of the French.

and artists were limited and required equitable protection. Artistic and scientific works should be made accessible to the people directly in their original form, but for this to happen it was necessary that "the moral rights of the creative artist are protected."[70] Zuloaga (Venezuela) supported the joint amendment of France, Cuba, and Mexico because the government "regarded as one of its most important duties the development of the cultural level of the masses in order to enjoy scientific, literary and artistic works" and the terms were identical to the American Declaration of the Rights of Man.[71] Jimenez de Arechaga (Uruguay) noted with satisfaction that the French, Mexican, and Cuban amendment were based on a principle adopted by the Uruguay government in Bogota. Artistic property was covered by special laws in most countries and did not therefore fall into Article 15 which protected rights to property in general.[72] The delegate from Belgium (Count Carton de Wiart) concurred. The right to property protected by Article 15 was not applicable because, he claimed, the right in question was "an intellectual right."[73] Beaufort (Netherlands) agreed. Intellectual works were not adequately safeguarded by a general right to property as illustrated by Marie Curie's works. They were more abstract and liable to infringement.[74]

By contrast, Carrera Andrade (Ecuador) was concerned that, as amended, the article was one of the most confused and contradictory that the committee had had to examine but recalled that South American Republics had recently taken measures to protect artistic and literary ownership which were defined in a very flexible manner which did not restrict cultural development. The aim of the article was to make arts and culture freely accessible to all by granting access to museums and libraries and to further education. Rights of authors and inventors were a form of property right which would curtail humanity's access to books and scientific works. He proposed that 25 should be deleted in its entirety.[75]

Roosevelt (USA) was opposed because the proposed amendment "reproduced almost word for word the article in the Bogota Declaration" which she thought dealt with patents and copyright. The USA thought that patents and copyright were out of place in the Declaration and, as an aspect of the right to property, were covered in Article 15 UDHR.[76] Similarly, Corbet (UK) argued that Cassin had run together two very different concepts. On the one hand, proprietary rights of ownership which attached to an invention and on the other, rights of attribution and recognition due to the author of an invention. She thought it was unwise to have a provision which had already been dealt with by international conventions on copyright, in an Article on the right of an individual to participate in cultural life. Copyright was not a basic

---

[70] A/C.3/SR.151 at p. 628.
[71] A/C.3/SR.151 at p. 627.
[72] A/C.3/SR.150 at p. 621.
[73] Ibid. at p. 622.
[74] A/C.3/SR.151 at p. 630.
[75] A/C.3/SR.150 at p. 618.
[76] Ibid. at p. 621.

human right.[77] Likewise Carter (Canada) thought that copyright and patents did not belong in a declaration but in a covenant and, for that reason, rejected the joint amendment. Lunde (Norway) also voted against the second paragraph for the same reason. Watt (Australia) opposed the amendment on the grounds that the rights of artists and scientists were the concern of national and international conventions and should not appear together with fundamental rights of a more general nature.[78] It was not appropriate to include rights of intellectual workers alongside freedom of thought, religious freedom, and the right to work.[79] Santa Cruz (Chile) concurred, adding that protection of the rights of intellectual workers "conflicted to a certain extent with that of freedom of access to all literary, artistic or scientific output" and affected a special category of persons only.[80] Ecuador too thought it inappropriate to include in a declaration a right to which only a small minority of mankind was entitled.[81] The same was true of Kayaly (Syria) who voted against the second paragraph and Azkoul (Lebanon) who voted in favour of the first paragraph but considered it inappropriate to include rights applying to a minority and abstained.[82]

The first and second paragraph as amended were put to separate votes. The first paragraph was adopted unanimously.[83] Eighteen countries voted in favour, the majority from Latin America. Thirteen countries voted against: Sweden, Syria, UK, USA, Yemen, Australia, Canada, Chile, Denmark, Ecuador, India, Norway, and Pakistan. Ten countries including the USSR and most soviet satellite countries abstained on the second paragraph: Saudi Arabia, Ukrainian Socialist Republic, Union of Soviet Socialist Republics, Yugoslavia, Afghanistan, Byelorussian Soviet Socialist Republic, Czechoslovakia, Lebanon, New Zealand, and the Philippines.

The whole of Article 25 as amended, was put to a separate vote and adopted by thirty-six votes to none with four abstentions.[84] Santa Cruz, who had voted against the second paragraph, voted in favour of the article as a whole as he thought it was not sufficiently important to warrant rejection of the whole article. The same was true of Roosevelt (USA) who also voted against the second paragraph but in favour of article as a whole. New Zealand also voted in favour of the whole article having

---

[77] Ibid. at p. 624.
[78] A/C.3/SR.151 at p. 630.
[79] Ibid.
[80] A/C.3/SR.151 at p. 632.
[81] A/C.3/SR.152 at p. 635.
[82] Pavlov, the Soviet delegate, supported the principle on which the original Article 25 was based, namely, that everyone had the right to participate in the cultural life of the community, to enjoy the arts and to share in scientific advancement. But the USSR's main concern was to press for the inclusion of amendments which would require that science should be used for peaceful purposes or in the interests of progress and democracy only. These were endorsed by Poland and Ukraine but overwhelmingly rejected by countries fearing that it would provide a platform for state control of science and interfere with freedom of research.
[83] A/C.3/SR.152 at p. 634.
[84] A/C.3/361.

abstained on the second paragraph which was viewed as belonged to Article 15. . The overall text adopted by the overwhelming majority thus read:

(1) Everyone has the right freely to participate in the cultural life of the community, to enjoy the arts and to share in scientific advancement and its benefits.
(2) Everyone has the right to the protection of the moral and material interests resulting from any scientific, literary or artistic production of which he is the author.

The final text included Peru's amendment to include the word "freely" in the first paragraph and the Chinese delegate's amendment to add the words "and its benefits" after "share in scientific advancements" in acknowledgment that whilst not everyone has the ability to take part in the creation of artistic, literary, and scientific works everyone had the right to enjoy the benefits of science and the arts.[85] It was this core ideal of free, universal access to the arts and science which animated the inclusion of the original Article 25 on which delegates were unanimously agreed. It was also this core ideal of the universal right of every human being to access the benefits of human creativity which facilitated the adoption of the final text notwithstanding the confusions, tensions and contradictions introduced by the second paragraph.

3.6 CONCLUSION

The analysis of the historical record reveals the original rationale for the inclusion of of "moral" rights om in the Berne Convention revisions of 1928 and the very different purpose of its mirror wording in Article XIII of the Bogota Declaration which inspired the inclusion of Article 27 in the UDHR. Thanks to the recent publication of the *Travaux Preparatoires* of the Bogota Declaration it is now possible to understand how he constructive ambiguity of the terms "moral" and "material" resonated with the Latin American ideals of social justice who understood these terms to refer to the "spiritual/mental" and "material/physical" *well-being* of each human being to which fundamental rights are directed. The humanistic ideals of spiritual and physical human self-development, were thought by advocates of Article 27(2) to be sufficiently clear if Article 27(2) was read as an integral part of the full, interconnected spectrum of social and economic rights in the UDHR. An integrative, contextual reading would displace the risk of conflating time-bound, exclusionary proprietary IP rights with universal human rights centered on development of the human personality.

In retrospect, it seems that regional political alliances prevailed over clear analytical thinking and won the day in Bogota and in the final stages of the drafting of the UDHR in Paris. Nonetheless, in the midst of the conceptual fog introduced by

[85] A/C.3/SR.151 at 627 and A/C.3/361.

Article 27(2) it is also true that those who insisted on its inclusion were not moved by an individualist, Western, liberal vision of human rights. On the contrary, their overarching vision of human rights, as reflected in Bogota, was founded on a vision of the interdependence of the individual and society and on the idea that fulfilment of human rights in democratic States has a cooperative basis which entails individual duties as well as individual rights. Their vision of human rights stood in contrast with the Western liberal classical conception of human rights of the Enlightenment, as negative rights, limited to civil and political liberties. The Bogota Declaration self-consciously sought to distance itself from that vision in its explicit embrace of social and economic rights and ideals of distribute justice. The same ideals found their way in the full spectrum of rights enunciated in the Universal Declaration of Human Rights and are captured in the first paragraph of Article 27. It is in the light of these ideals that Article 27(2) should ultimately be read and not as an affirmation that intellectual property is a fundamental human right.

4

"Fostering a Love of Truth"

Conceptions of Science in UNESCO's Early Years

*Ivan Lind Christensen**

4.1 INTRODUCTION

The right to enjoy the benefits of scientific progress and its applications was first included (inter alia) in Article 27 of the Universal Declaration of Human Rights in 1948, and later in Article 15(1)(b) of the International Covenant on Economic, Social and Cultural Rights (ICESCR) in 1966. The Right to Science thus has a long history in the UN family and in UNESCO in particular. Beneath the ideas about the right to participate in science and to access the body of knowledge produced via science, stands the concept of science itself. The UNESCO General Conference at its thirty-ninth session in 2017, adopted the Recommendation on Science and Scientific Researchers (which replaced the 1974 Recommendation on the Status of Scientific Researchers) and in doing so it stated, among other things, that:

(1) the word "science" signifies the enterprise whereby humankind, acting individually or in small or large groups, makes an organized attempt, by means of the objective study of observed phenomena and its validation through sharing of findings and data and through peer review, to discover and master the chain of causalities, relations, or interactions; brings together in a coordinated form subsystems of knowledge by means of systematic reflection and conceptualization; and thereby furnishes itself with the opportunity of using, to its own advantage, understanding of the processes and phenomena occurring in nature and society;

(2) the term "the sciences" signifies a complex of knowledge, fact, and hypothesis, in which the theoretical element is capable of being validated in the short or long term, and to that extent includes the sciences concerned with social facts and phenomena.[1]

---

* I would like to take the opportunity to sincerely thank Assistant Professor Sarah Awad (Alborg University), for her substantial comments on and willingness to discuss earlier drafts of this chapter

[1] Recommendation on Science and Scientific Researchers, November 13, 2017, UNESCO. Available at: http://portal.unesco.org/en/ev.php-URL_ID=49455&URL_DO=DO_TOPIC&URL_SECTION=201 .html. When I in the following use the term science, it is in a broader understanding of science as both "the enterprise" and the disciplines.

While these definitions may seem commonplace for many present-day readers, they are in fact the result of substantial debates and conceptual negotiations, which have been ongoing throughout the history of UNESCO. This chapter takes a closer look at what the concept of science meant in the early years and how it influenced the initiatives carried out by the Natural Science Section of UNESCO.

The S(cience) in UNESCO was added very late in the process of the organization's founding. In the original plans for its creation, UNESCO was to be an organization for education and culture only. That it became UNESCO and not UNECO was due to several factors, but especially the persistent pressure exhorted by Joseph Needham (1900–1995), who was to become the first head of the Natural Science Sector in UNESCO, and the first Director-General Julian Huxley. Their visions of science strongly influenced the conceptualization and direction of science in UNESCO.[2] On a structural level, another current undoubtedly played a crucial role in getting the "S" in UNESCO, and that was the unset of the Nuclear Age. If science still retained any enlightenment innocence in the eyes of the global public before the end of the second world war, it was hard pressed by the invention and use of the nuclear bombs dropped over Hiroshima and Nagasaki in 1945. The harnessing and destructive use of atomic energy left the broader public with an attitude characterized by both hope and fear.[3] These sentiments were well captured by the UK Minister of Education, Ellen Wilkinson, at the Conference for the establishment of UNESCO in 1945, as she said:

> In these days, when we are all wondering, perhaps apprehensively, what the scientists will do to us next, it is important that they should be linked closely with the humanities and should feel that they have a responsibility to mankind for the result of their labours. I do not believe any scientists will have survived the world catastrophe, who will still say that they are utterly uninterested in the social implications of their discoveries.[4]

As I will return to later, this conflicted public opinion towards science after 1945 was seen as a real and important problem by UNESCO's science section in the early years. In what follows, I focus first on the conceptualization of science in the formative years from 1945–1965 in UNESCO. I trace the different ideas of science as they were articulated within UNESCO to illustrate what the organization itself understood by the concept of science and its relationship to concepts of modernity, progress, and development. This will shed light on the significant role that UNESCO was to continuously play in international science cooperation from that point on. Taking up the legacy from the League of Nations, UNESCO became, and remains, a central

---

[2] Petitjean (2006). Petitjean, Zharov, Glaser, Richardson, de Padirac, and Archibald (2006), pp. 43–47.
[3] See Weart (2012). For the American context see: Boyer (1985/1994). For the British context: Grant Matthew (2009).
[4] UK Minister of Education, Ellen Wilkinson: Conference for the establishment of the United Nations Educational, Scientific and Cultural Organisation, Held at the Institute of Civil Engineers, London, from the 1st to the 16th November, 1945, ECO/CONF./29, p. 24. UNESCO Archive, Paris.

place for science and science policy discussions. An exploration of how views on science developed within UNESCO may therefore offer useful background to the historical routes that the development and establishment of the Right to Science took.

4.2 HISTORIES OF SCIENCE IN UNESCO (HISTORIOGRAPHY)

Throughout the last three decades, the history of the way in which UNESCO conceptualized science has received much needed attention. This is not least due to the persistent and admirable work of Patrick Petijean. Today Petijean stands as one of the central figures within the historiography of UNESCO and science, and was one of the central editors behind the celebratory anthology *Sixty Years of Science at UNESCO 1945–2005*.[5] This anthology still stands as one of the central works on science in UNESCO. Bringing in both historians and former UNESCO science employees, the book gives a detailed and vivid account of the historical development of the science section in UNESCO. Despite its celebratory starting point, the anthology is not merely a narrative of triumph. It acknowledges the hardship, the failures, and the frustrations as well as the success and fruitful cooperations that were fostered within the UNESCO science section.

The historical role of UNESCO in international science cooperation has generally been highlighted, not least by Elzinga (1996), Krieger (2006) and to some extent Finnemore (1993). While interpretations of the effect of the Cold War divide the historical accounts of UNESCO's role in the realm of international science cooperation, there is a general consensus that the natural science section did do important work by bringing together and funding different international science communities. The disagreements occur along the more traditional lines of antagonism between the realist and idealist approaches to international politics and the role of international organizations within the Cold war setting.[6] Some argue that UNESCO and its science initiatives willingly or unwillingly became part of the "western" (that is, US-dictated) battle for the hearts and minds of people during the Cold War (Krieger 2006). Others, like Finnemore, ascribe more autonomy and (moral) power to UNESCO (Finnemore 1993), especially in relation to international norm setting and knowledge accumulation. Since this chapter deals with the conceptualization of science in UNESCO and less with the specific initiatives and their impact, I will not venture further into this discussion here.[7] The literature on UNESCO's

---

[5] Petitjean et al. (2006).
[6] In the realist approach to international politics, the states are traditionally seen as the central actors in an international political system in which there are no transnational authority. The states act (only) based on rational self-interest and in pursuit of power (self-preservation). The liberalist approach, on the other hand, rejects the idea that power politics is the only possible outcome of international relations and hence gives a significantly bigger role for international organizations to play in the international system, See e.g. Baylis, Smith and Owens (2017).
[7] For a more detailed discussion, see Christensen (2016). For the broader discussion on science and the cold war, see e.g. Doel (1997).

"Fostering a Love of Truth"

conception of science is rather limited. There seems to be a general agreement that it was strongly influenced, during the period covered here, by what Sluga describes as an "Enlightenment-coddled trust in the universal power of knowledge and education."[8] And as Elzinga has argued, it functioned "within an overall framework of western bias."[9] We may however come even closer to understanding the concept by looking more closely at actual usages of the concept within UNESCO.

4.3 APPROACH

My approach will be that of conceptual history which rests on several important assumptions that should be stated upfront. The first assumption is that our understanding of the present is created in the continual interactions between our past experiences and our expectations of the future. Furthermore, it assumes that this fundamental relationship between past, present, and future manifests itself in the concepts through which we try to make sense of our world. If we are correct in assuming this, then the conceptual architecture of our source material lends itself as prism, giving insight into pasts, presents, and futures past. In other words, the concepts are made up of spaces of experience and horizons of expectation.[10] Thus, through the analysis of concepts we gain an understanding of how historical agents understood their past, what they found relevant in their present, and how they imagined their future. The concepts function as both indicators of past ideas and as factors affecting contemporary events, pointing towards a horizon of expectation.

In this study, the conceptualization of science has been tracked from 1945 to 1965 in documents produced by and around the Natural Science Section in UNESCO.[11] In order to analyze and interpret the various concepts of science in these documents special attention has been paid to concurrent concepts and counter-concepts, which is to say concepts that, through their oppositional character, codefine the concept of science (such as the concepts of magic and religion). Through this conceptual mapping, the semantic field of the concept of science in UNESCO 1945–1965 emerges, which in a condensed and simplified form could be presented as in Figure 4.1 below:

This initial mapping of the semantic network of the concept of science in UNESCO forms a starting point for the following sections. These will elaborate on the different meanings attached to the concept and the ways in which it has

---

[8] Sluga (2010), p. 397.
[9] Elzinga (1996), p. 166.
[10] Koselleck (2004).
[11] The search has been conducted in the UNESCO online archive Unesdoc (https://unesdoc.unesco.org/) using the search terms "Science*," "Scientific*," "Natural Science*." The extensive amount of documents yielded by this search was surveyed and exemplary documents selected for analysis. These documents have been supplemented with documents gathered from research visits to the UNESCO Archive in Paris. There were several collaborations between The Section of Natural Science and other UNESCO departments, and these have been included although they may not have originated from the Science section itself.

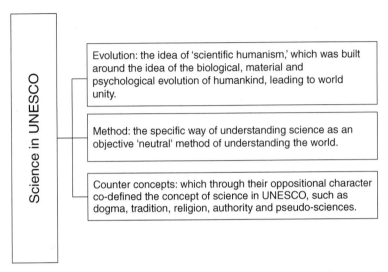

FIGURE 4.1 Semantic field of the concept of science in UNESCO 1945–1965

shaped how science was understood within the organization, and how it has been communicated to the wider public through UNESCO's Natural Science Section.

4.4 SCIENCE, EVOLUTION, AND WORLD UNITY

On the threshold of the nuclear age, public opinion towards science in general, and natural science in particular, was ambivalent. Fear of global destruction and hope of utopian futures were mingled together in unclear discourses of modernity and progress, in which science played a crucial but also ambiguous role. In the view of Julian Huxley (the first Director General of UNESCO) and Joseph Needham (the first head for the Natural Science Section) science, however, had a completely different status. For them, science was an ideologically neutral prerequisite of progress for the benefit of humankind.[12] This was manifested not least in Huxley's idea of "scientific humanism," which was constituted around a notion of (the) biological, material, and psychological evolution of humankind, leading to world unity:

> the unifying of traditions in a single common pool of experience, awareness, and purpose is the necessary prerequisite for further major progress in human evolution. Accordingly, ... unification in the things of the mind is not only ... necessary but can pave the way for other types of unification. Thus in the past the great religions unified the thoughts and attitudes of large regions of the earth's surface; and in recent times science, both directly through its ideas and indirectly through its

[12] Elzinga (1996), p. 166.

applications in shrinking the globe, has been a powerful factor in directing men's thoughts to the possibilities of, and the need for, full world unity.[13]

Huxley's scientific humanism was in all relevant aspects a scientific evolutionism. As Elzinga has also noted, his conception of science and human evolution was ripe with ideas about progress and cultural stratification. UNESCO should seek to lift up the culturally "backward" countries and races, Huxley argued,[14] and this should be done not least through the distribution of science and education. He saw in science the promise for social development and progress of different nations, rather than the fear of the consequences of scientific developments in relation to wars and destruction. On this last subject Huxley was ad idem with Needham. From the onset in 1945, the science section of UNESCO had a strong focus on the distribution of scientific knowledge from the Western to the Third World countries.

The third-world focus in UNESCO's science efforts in the post-war years was due in large part to the personal commitment of Needham. Needham had a background, like Huxley, in the UK-based "Social Relations of Science Movement" (SRSM). Needham opposed the scientific Eurocentrism that he saw in Western intellectual circles. His focus was on the distribution of advanced scientific knowledge and applied sciences to third world countries. This ambition manifested itself in the establishment of the Field Science Cooperation Offices in Asia, Africa, and Latin America. These offices were to become important sites for later efforts to promote science policy implementation in the Third-World member states. Science was the key (along with basic, and particularly science-focused, education) to entering modernity and lifting the living standard of humankind. What was needed was the free flow of ideas (and intellectuals) on a global scale. Within this scientific ethos, the fear and reluctance among the broader public towards science could only be seen as irrational, if not childish. Pierre Auger, the next head of the Natural Science Section after Needham, put it starkly:

> Again and again we have heard people criticize the advances of science, labelling their effects dangerous, destructive and baneful. ... They want to turn back the clock, to return to the Gods they lament, but there is no longer any question of doing so, and no answer is called for; we are caught up in an automatic process, a natural process which we men are powerless to arrest.[15]

Belief in a scientific evolutionism was thus very strong and the ideas of an inevitable (scientific) process seem central to the understanding of science within UNESCO in the early years.

However, both Needham's idea of a grand international science cooperation and Huxley's vision of UNESCO as Mannheim's "free floating intellectuals" were

[13] Huxley (1947), p. 17.
[14] Elzinga (1996), p. 172.
[15] Auger (1950), p. 108.

eventually stifled by the onset of the Cold War.[16] As the Cold War accelerated, a tight web of secrecy was spun around so-called "sensitive information," especially the nuclear programs, and the desire for an international "free flow of ideas" was partly subdued under the weight of national security interests. However, these factors – important as they were – did not stop ambitions to organize international science cooperation and to support scientific communities through such international cooperation. That said, the tense political situation may have still influenced how science was conceptualized and communicated by UNESCO. This could be seen in their efforts to highlight the "neutral," objective nature of science, which was particularly emphasized through a specific way of understanding the scientific method. This brings us to the second theme in the semantic field of the conceptualization of science in UNESCO, that of scientific method and objectivity.

4.5 "ONE CANNOT TRIFLE WITH NATURE": SCIENCE AND OBJECTIVITY – METHOD AND WORLDVIEW

Objectivity and science emerge as co-occurring concepts in this period, to the extent that we may be allowed to conclude that they were in fact seen as largely defining each other. Comtean positivism was still untouched by deconstruction, social constructivism, or linguistic turns, and objective truth was therefore also a relatively unproblematic and potent idea.[17] In the preamble to UNESCO's constitution, the member states thus verified that:

> For these reasons, the States Parties to this Constitution, *believing in full and equal opportunities for education for all, in the unrestricted pursuit of objective truth, and in the free exchange of ideas and knowledge,* are agreed and determined to develop and to increase the means of communication between their peoples and to employ these means for the purposes of mutual understanding and a truer and more perfect knowledge of each other's lives.[18]

In their conceptual architecture, tight lines linking the concepts of objectivity, science, and method were drawn. The scientific method was seen as the foundation of objective knowledge and as the driving force in the progress experienced by modern society and in the peace and solidarity of humankind. As in Auguste Comte's understanding of proper science, the core of the scientific method had

---

[16] Karl Manheim (1893–1947) had in the early-twentieth century proposed the idea that the intellectuals unlike other groups in modern society could (and should) form a relatively classless stratum, which would be able to function as a dynamic mediator between left and right wings of the European political spectrum. See e.g. Heeren (1971).

[17] The term Comtean positivism refers to the epistemological principles proposed by August Comte (1798–1857), which sets outs the methods of the classical physics experiment as the goal for all types of science including the human and social sciences.

[18] Emphasis added. UNESCO Constitution available at: http://portal.unesco.org/en/ev.php-URL_ID=15244&URL_DO=DO_TOPIC&URL_SECTION=201.html.

the experimental method as its ideal. Science, one of the UNESCO representatives stated: "requires verification by experiment – the experiment is the final arbiter. No quantity of words can be used successfully to camouflage a disproven idea or belief."[19] It was due to the scientific method that scientists had now "tamed the atom" and a strong belief prevailed among the scientific community in and around UNESCO that:

> The accelerating pace of man's progress in the natural sciences is to a great extent brought about by the power of the scientific method. A method that was developed over the centuries and followed by more and more men, beginning with Galileo in the 16th century ... Always, the scientist and technician strives for objectivity and honesty – prejudice and falsification have been found to be disastrous. One cannot trifle with nature.[20]

It is thus safe to say that the epistemological grounds beneath the concept of science were strongly influenced by a Comtean-inspired positivism and scientific rationalism. To Needham, Auger, and their staff, the Natural Science Section was taking up a proud heritage, not only from an epistemological point of view, but also from the point of view of international scientific cooperation. Here UNESCO (in its own narrative) came to represent the apex of a development begun by European intellectuals in the seventeenth century, manifested in the astronomers' conferences in the early-nineteenth century, institutionalized in the League of Nations and now, in the mid-twentieth century, continued in an international "brotherhood" spearheaded by UNESCO. The prerequisite of this brotherhood was freedom, as Bart Bok mentioned, and here science and the newly established Universal Declaration of Human Rights joined forces: "As long as science is free, scientists are almost automatically joined in a world brotherhood and it is fervently hoped that the scientists of the world will realise that in the Universal Declaration of Human Rights lies the promise of a guarantee for their cherished freedoms."[21] Apart from being an evolutionary process, a method, and an international brotherhood, science was also conceived of as a worldview in a broader sense.[22] The function of science was not limited to the actual inventions or methods produced and used. Its function extended into the realm of what is best captured by the German term *bildung*, meaning both creation and education. Science teaching was seen as the key to disseminate this scientific attitude to life:

> Science, and Physics especially, is better fitted than other subjects to develop the ability to distinguish fact from opinion, and to form judgements and base conclusions on the known data. Prejudice, superstition and dogmatic assertion are the

---

[19] Frank (1947), p. 3.
[20] Ibid.
[21] Bart Bok cited in The UNESCO Courier's article "The Scientist and Human Rights." (1950) III (11), p. 2.
[22] Christensen (2016).

enemies of progress and vigorous development. The scientific spirit implies belief in a rational universe, and scientific studies should form the basis of an attitude to life.[23]

Science was a way of understanding the world and forming opinions and judgments about different matters. Science was also the primary defense against the enemies of progress and development, and it had to be taught from an early stage in order to form the "right" worldview. The time had passed, or so it was argued in UNESCO circles, where young people could get along in life without a proper understanding of science.[24] In 1954, at the General Conference in Montevideo, resolutions were thus adopted in order to advance science teaching in general and "to stimulate the extension and improvement of science teaching."[25] The values believed to be inherent to the scientific worldview went far beyond the classroom. It constituted a prerequisite for life in the modern world and could assist in producing useful citizens and wise parents.[26] Some even argued that the teaching of science could alter fundamental preferences and: "awaken [the] capacity to observe, describe, and evaluate (discovering, investigating, comparing, classifying) thus fostering a love of truth and intellectual honesty, pleasure in work well done and a liking of order."[27] Science was presented as a way of seeing the world, and a way of distinguishing fact and reality from opinions and prejudgments. Superstitions and dogmatic assertions were therefore positioned as the enemy of science and progress. This brings us to the third theme in the semantic field of the concept of science in UNESCO, that of counter concepts – not what science is, but also what it is not.

4.6 SCIENCE AND "THE ENEMIES OF PROGRESS"

UNESCO's conception of science found its antithesis in concepts such as dogma, tradition, authority, and pseudoscience. Regarding the latter, the pseudosciences, it was clear that the scientific community in and around UNESCO felt a need to distinguish their conception of science, "true science," from other less methodologically sound practices. Huxley had already taken up the subject of "borderline fields" such as "parapsychology," "Hindu yogi body control," and "eugenics" in his 1947 publication.[28] Huxley argued that while science should remain open to the possibility of radical extensions of our knowledge from these borderline fields, UNESCO should disregard or even oppose that which is unscientific:

---

[23] Boulind (1957), p. 3.
[24] Gillett (1957).
[25] UNESCO Eighth Session, Montevideo 1954, General Conference Resolutions IV.1.2.321 and 1.2.322.
[26] Joseph (1953).
[27] "A Proposed Programme in Science Teaching," UNESCO, WS/104.70, November 5, 1954, Paris, p. 4.
[28] Huxley (1947), p. 37. Regarding Eugenics, Huxley firmly believed it should be brought entirely within the preserve of science, as he believed that scientific eugenics would be a necessity in the not too distant future (ibid., p. 38).

Such facts may be modified and extended, but not overthrown. Though not dogma, they may, perhaps, properly be described as scientific doctrine. Unesco must see that its activities and ideas are not opposed to this body of established scientific doctrine, just as it must encourage the use of the scientific method wherever it is applicable. Thus it cannot and must not tolerate the blocking of research or the hampering of its application by superstition or theological prejudice. It must disregard or, if necessary, oppose unscientific or anti-scientific movements, such as antivivisectionism, fundamentalism, belief in miracles, crude spiritualism, etc.[29]

What was at stake was the drawing of borders around a broad, "scientific" epistemic community, and this was by no means an easy task. Once again, the scientific method lent itself as a possible demarcation line and became the primary weapon in the fight against pseudo-sciences. In order to oppose these practices effectively, Huxley argued "widespread popular education is required in the facts of science, the significance of the scientific method, and the possibilities of scientific application for increasing human welfare."[30] Almost a decade later, Huxley's views were echoed at the UNESCO conference on the Dissemination of Science in Madrid in 1955. At this point in time, it was particularly the growing popularity of numerology, astrology, hypnotism, and clairvoyance that troubled the scientific community. They lamented the "'average man's' relative or total lack of culture" which made him an easy target for the pseudosciences.[31] It was well known, they argued, that: "the pseudo-science recruits no followers among those who recognize the value of scientific experiment; and it is confidence in scientific experiment that we must inculcate in people today."[32] The concern was twofold. Firstly, pseudoscience and similar practices pretended to be somehow "scientific" and attempted to convince followers of the veracity of this claim. Secondly, there were those practices that did not claim to be scientific, yet still proclaimed dogmatic authority over their followers, such as religions. The question of religion was a difficult and contentious one. When Huxley would argue that science "is by its nature opposed to dogmatic orthodoxies and to the claims of authority" then a conflict with religion seemed imminent and inevitable. Auger, the second director of the Section of Natural Science, offered a somewhat more diplomatic position when he, in his writings in 1950, addressed the issue:

> the religions which, in the course of time, have reached the highest pitch of refinement, have realized the absolute barrier of dogma. They have accordingly removed dogma to a different plane, where it runs no risk of coming into conflict with the discoveries of science. And with that plane, where it may not set foot, science is not concerned.[33]

---

[29] Ibid., p. 37.
[30] Ibid.
[31] Ibid.
[32] Bessemans and Hougardy (1955).
[33] Auger (1950), p. 108.

Religion was, according to Auger, simply to be relegated to "a different plane," where the dogmas would not come into conflict with science. Auger (wisely) did not elaborate on whether the religions had willingly removed dogma, or to what "plane" they had been moved. However, he reaffirmed that it was in science that we could all work together with the same language, "since Science is the same in every land" and through this scientific common ground of communication, "a common attitude of mind, inspired by the common goal of the advancement of science, is maintained throughout this society."[34]

4.7 CONCLUDING REMARKS: ACTIONS AND RIGHTS

Looking back at the intense efforts made within UNESCO to define and promote a particular definition of science in the early years, one can of course wonder why these efforts seemed to be of such crucial importance. Several things are, however, at stake when defining a key concept like science. As touched upon above, the definition of science helped to demarcate the borders of an epistemic community. These borders were established through highlighting what science was in terms of biological, material, and psychological evolution of humankind, objective knowledge seeking, and a scientific methodological approach. Just as important, these borders were established through highlighting what science was not, as such science was defined in opposition to dogma, tradition, religion, authority and pseudosciences.

Furthermore, the definition manifests a certain understanding of the past: where we came from and, in line with this, where we are going in the future. The definition thus creates specific horizons of action within which some paths of action seem rational and others are deemed illogical and contrary to human progress. The understanding of science in UNESCO, as outlined above, became the conceptual background for the impressive amount of actions carried through by UNESCO and its Natural Science Section. In line with the understanding of science as a prerequisite for development and progress, UNESCO, immediately after the war, set out to rebuild the science infrastructure in war-devastated regions. They sought to facilitate already existing science organizations, and international cooperation, both financially and organizationally, and published a great variety of science material. One such piece was the very popular "Suggestions for Science Teachers in the Devastated Countries" by J. P. Stephenson, which by the early 1960s had been expanded and translated into more than thirty languages. The book contained detailed instructions on how to conduct "good science teaching" despite a lack of proper materials, and instructions on how to build cheap apparatuses from everyday materials.

The strong focus on science teaching in UNESCO becomes more evident when we look at it in light of exactly what science meant to the organization, and how it

[34] Ibid.

was conceptualized and distinguished from other practices. In understanding science not only as a set of methods of inquiry, but as a worldview and an attitude to life, the science teaching classroom becomes the ideal place to form the mindset of the new generations from an early age. This was indeed an enculturation process, although it was not conceived as such by the scientist involved in the science teaching planning. The classroom could not only be used to install this scientific gaze in the pupils. It could also be used to correct what many scientists believed was the (misunderstood) image of the scientist in the broader public. As Boulind stated in the UNESCO House:

> the teaching should be such as to prevent pupils from thinking of scientists in general and nuclear physicists in particular as Frankensteins, hell-bent on producing monstrous machines they cannot control. Instead they should realize that science and magic are poles apart, that scientists are ordinary human beings who are the servants of mankind, and not its masters.[35]

In this manner, the teaching of science was also an arena well suited to combat what scientists saw as the unrealistic fears (and hopes) of the broader public in the nuclear age. In relation to this, we can also see that the Natural Science Section in UNESCO cooperated cross-departmentally many times, with both the Division of Dissemination of Science, the Department of Mass Communication and the Department of Education.[36]

Another UNESCO science-initiative, the establishment of the Field Science Cooperation Offices in Asia, Africa, and Latin America, likewise takes on a deeper significance when we understand it in light of the fundamental definitions of science in the early years of UNESCO. These offices represented not only a means to distribute scientific knowledge from a Western center to the developing countries, but also an institutionalization of the world brotherhood to which scientists were imagined to belong, and an establishment of a common world language of science that is oriented towards world development.

From the definition of science as a vocation, a worldview, and an ideologically neutral knowledge that benefits all humankind, springs also the claim for rights for scientists. This came in the wake of the massive influx of state control, censorship, and secrecy that especially nuclear scientists were subjected to during World War II, and which only increased during the Cold War.[37] Huxley took up the subject in 1949 and posted the question in both *Nature* and the *Bulletin of the Atomic Scientists*:

> How should men of science act in the face of the increasing concern of the State with science, and the subsequent increasing pressure of the State on science? Can they accept the existence of an official scientific policy? Can they accept the possibility that the majority of men of science shall be paid by the State and that

---

[35] Boulind (1958), p. 4.
[36] Christensen (2016).
[37] Krige (2006).

the major cost of scientific work shall be borne on government funds? Can they accept official direction as to what subjects shall be investigated?[38]

Huxley was lashing out at both the Soviet Union and the Western allies for their attempts to control their respective science communities. The answer to Huxley's question (or one of them), came from Bart Bok, Chairman of the National (US) Research Council's Committee on Science in UNESCO. Under the headline "Freedom of science and the Universal Declaration of Human Rights" Bok argued that scientists had been given a powerful weapon in their fight for basic rights in the Declaration, and he urged his fellow scientists to seize the opportunity given:

> The Universal Declaration of Human Rights is issued at a time when the freedom of science is under attack from many sides. Scientists have reason to be grateful to the drafters of the Declaration, for we have been given an inspiring restatement of basic principles to guide us in the fight for the freedom of science.[39]

Thus, looking at the conceptualization of science by UNESCO, and the different ideas of science as they were articulated within UNESCO, we see what the organization itself understood by the concept of science and its relations to the concepts of modernity, progress, and development. UNESCO defined its borders concretely with the firm commitment to the "S" in its name, which made it better able to defend those borders when it came to asserting scientific freedom in opposition to state control, censorship, and secrecy that scientists, particularly nuclear scientists, faced during the Cold War. It was that definition and UNESCO's strong defense of science, that was put into practice when the onset of the Cold War posed its own challenges to the Mertonian norms of science and to the ideas of international science cooperation in general.

LITERATURE

Auger, P. (1950) "Scientific Progress in the Present-Day World," in *Impact of Science on Society*, Vol. 1. No. 3–4, October–December, pp.108–111.
Baylis, John, Steve Smith and Patricia Owens (eds.) (2017) *The Globalization of World Politics. An Introduction to International Relations*. 7th ed. Oxford: Oxford University Press.
Bok, Bart (1949) "Freedom of Science and the Universal Declaration of Human Rights," in *Bulletin of the Atomic Scientists*, August, p. 211–217.
Boulind, H. F. (1957) *The Teaching of Physics in Tropical Secondary Schools – Being Volume VIII of the UNESCO Handbooks on the Teaching of Science in Tropical Countries* ed. F. Smithies. London: Oxford University Press.

---

[38] Huxley (1949), p. 209.
[39] Bok (1949). Bok also published his thoughts on the subject in the UNESCO publication "La Liberté de la science" in 1949.

Boulind, H. F. (1958) "'Atomic energy and education', Unesco House, 15–19 September, Paris" UNESCO Archive, Paris, UNESCO/AEP/8.

Bessemans, A. and Hougardy, A. (1955) "The Pseudo-sciences: How to Recognize and Guard Against Them" Conference on the Dissemination of Science, Madrid, 1955, NS/DIF/2, WS/075.68, UNESCO Archive, Paris.

Boyer, Paul (1985/1994) *By the Bomb's Early Light American Thought and Culture At the Dawn of the Atomic Age*. Chapel Hill: The University of North Carolina Press.

Christensen, I. L. (2016). "The Role of Science Education in the Nuclear Age: UNESCO's Promotion of 'Atoms for peace' in 1946–1968," in I. A. Kulnazarova and C. Ydesen (eds.), *UNESCO Without Borders: Educational Campaigns for International Understanding*. New York: Routledge. Routledge Research in Education, Nr. 172, Bind. 1, pp. 75–92.

Doel, Ronald E. (1997) "Scientists as Policymakers, Advisors, and Intelligence Agents: Linking Contemporary Diplomatic History with the History of Contemporary Science," in Thomas Söderqvist (ed.), *The Historiography of Contemporary Science and Technology*. Amsterdam: Harwood. pp. 215–244.

Elzinga, Aant. (1996) "UNESCO and the Politics of International Co-operation in the Realm of Science," in Patrick Petitjean (ed.), *Les Sciences colonials – figures et institutions*. Paris: Orstom e´ditions, pp. 163–202.

Finnemore, M. (1993) "International Organizations As Teachers of Norms: The United Nations Educational, Scientific and Cultural Organization and Science Policy," *International Organization*, Vol. 47, No. 4, pp. 565–597.

Frank, J. M. (1947) "Science and UNESCO" Address given before The Would Youth Festival, Prague, 16 August, Nat Sci./37, UNESCO Archive, Paris.

Gillett, C. R. E. (1957) "Science in Schools – Report on an international meeting of experts, 22–27 October, 1956", Hamburg, UNESCO Institute for Education.

Grant, Matthew (2009) *After the Bomb. Civil Defence and Nuclear War in Britain 1945–68*. Basingstoke: Palgrave Macmillan.

Hamblin, J. D. (2006) "Exorcising Ghosts in the Age of Automation: United Nations Experts and Atoms for Peace," *Technology and Culture*, Vol. 47, No. 4, pp. 734–756.

Heeren, J. (1971) "Karl Mannheim and the Intellectual Elite," *The British Journal of Sociology*, Vol. 22, No. 1, pp. 1–15.

Huxley, Julian (1947) *UNESCO: Its Purpose and Philosophy*. Washington DC: Public Affairs Press.

Huxley, J. (1949) "Freedom for Science: An Appeal for Action," in *Bulletin of the Atomic Scientists*, August,. pp. 209–210.

Joseph, E. D. (1953) *The Teaching of Science in Tropical Primary Schools – Being Volume I of the UNESCO Handbooks on the Teaching of Science in Tropical Countries* ed. F. Smithies. London: Oxford University Press.

Koselleck, Reinhart (2004) *Futures Past – On the Semantics of Historical Time*. New York: Columbia University Press.

Krige, John (2006) "Atoms for Peace, Scientific Internationalism, and Scientific Intelligence," History of Science Society, Vol. 21, Global Power Knowledge: Science and Technology in International Affairs, pp. 161–181.

Layton, D. (1995) "UNESCO and the Teaching of Science and Technology," UNESCO, Paris. Available at www.unesco.org/education/nfsunesco/pdf/LAYTON.PDF.

Petitjean, P., Zharov, V., Glaser, G., Richardson, J., de Padirac, B. and Archibald, G. (eds.) (2006). *Sixty Years of Science at UNESCO 1945–2005*. Paris: UNESCO.

Petitjean P. (2006) "Needham and UNESCO: Perspectives and Realizations," in P. Petitjean, V. Zharov, G. Glaser, J. Richardson, B. de Padirac, and G. Archibald (eds)., *Sixty Years of Science at Unesco, 1945–2005*. Paris: UNESCO, pp. 43–47.

Sluga, Glenda (2010), "UNESCO and the (One) World of Julian Huxley," *Journal of World History*, Vol. 21, No. 3, pp. 393–418.

Weart, S. (2012) *The Rise of Nuclear Fear*. Cambridge, MA: Harvard University Press.

5

The Right to Science and the Evolution of Scientific Integrity

Roberto Andorno

5.1 INTRODUCTION

As Aristotle famously claimed in the opening line of his *Metaphysics*, "all human beings, by nature, desire to know." In other words, the pursuit of knowledge is connatural to us. We cherish knowledge for its own sake, simply because we want to better understand the world in which we live, and ourselves, and not primarily for any practical utility or for the satisfaction of other human interests. We see knowledge as a good in itself, as an irreducible good, and one of the most important aspects of human flourishing. This is why the pursuit of knowledge deserves to be protected by legal norms and, in particular, by human rights norms.

The search for the "why" of things is one of the key features of the scientific enterprise. Indeed, science represents one of the highest expressions of human intellectual ability and contributes to a deeper and better understanding of both nature and ourselves. Besides its intrinsic, irreducible value, scientific research makes a crucial contribution to the well-being and progress of humankind by delivering new tools that help improve quality of life, and provide new diagnostic, preventive, and treatment measures for various diseases and conditions.

For these reasons, science should enjoy the greatest freedom to advance in the different fields in which it is carried out and to be promoted at all levels. This basic human interest is formally recognized by international law, which expressly protects the "freedom indispensable for scientific research and creative activity."[1] Although the freedom to conduct scientific research was not explicitly included in the founding instrument of the human rights movement, the Universal Declaration of Human Rights, it is generally regarded as implicit in the freedom of thought, and in the freedom of opinion and expression, protected by Articles 18 and 19 of the Declaration, respectively.

At the European level, the 2000 European Charter of Fundamental Rights expressly recognizes that "[t]he arts and scientific research shall be free of constraint" (Article 13). The Explanations Relating to the Charter specify that the freedom

---

[1] Art. 15, para. 2, International Covenant of Economic, Social and Cultural Rights, 1966.

enshrined in Article 13 "is deduced primarily from the right to freedom of thought and expression" and "is to be exercised having regard to Article 1 and may be subject to the limitations authorised by Article 10 of the ECHR."[2] This explanation is of great relevance as it makes clear that freedom of scientific research, like most freedoms, is not absolute, but may be subject to some limitations in the interests of other individuals and society. There is no doubt that scientific research, like any other activity in society, cannot operate at the margins of the ethical and legal principles that are basic to any democratic society, such as respect for human dignity and human rights, and other important societal values. The first limitation mentioned by the Explanations relates to Article 1 of the Charter, which enshrines the principle of *respect for human dignity*. Scientific research, even if motivated by the best of intentions, cannot be conducted in ways that involve the violation of people's dignity (for instance, medical research cannot be conducted without participants' free and informed consent). The second category of limitations is included in Article 10 of the ECHR, which stipulates that freedom of expression may be subject to such limitations as prescribed by law and "are necessary in a democratic society in the interests of public safety, for the protection of public order, health or morals, or for the protection of the rights and freedoms of others."

At this point, it should be emphasized that the right to science is a multifaceted notion, as it includes both the freedom to *do* science and the right to *enjoy* the benefits of science.[3] This right is therefore addressed to both *scientists*, whose efforts to conduct scientific research should not be hindered by the State, and to the *public* in general, who should have access to the results of scientific developments. Strangely, in spite of its enormous importance, especially in modern technological societies, the right to science has long been overlooked, with the consequence that its legal development is still rudimentary, and the scholarly literature around its meaning, scope, and practical implications is still relatively sparse.[4]

---

[2] "Explanations Relating to the Charter of Fundamental Rights" (2007/C 303/02), December 14, 2007. Available at: https://eur-lex.europa.eu/LexUriServ/LexUriServ.do?uri=OJ:C:2007:303:0017:0035: EN:PDF.

[3] Art. 15, para. 1b and para. 3, respectively, of the International Covenant of Economic, Social and Cultural Rights, 1966.

[4] See, for instance, Yvonne Donders, "The Right to Enjoy the Benefits of Scientific Progress: In Search of State Obligations in Relation to Health," *Medicine, Health Care and Philosophy*, 2011, 14: 371–381; William A. Schabas, "Study of the Right to Enjoy the Benefits of Scientific and Technological Progress and Its Application," in Yvonne Donders, and Vladimir Volodin (eds.), *Human Rights in Education Science and Culture–Legal Developments and Challenges*, Paris: UNESCO/Ashgate Publishing, 2007, pp. 273–308; Audrey R. Chapman, "Towards an Understanding of the Right to Enjoy the Benefits of Scientific Progress and Its Applications," *Journal of Human Rights*, 2009, 8(1): 1–36; Sebastian Porsdam Mann, Helle Porsdam, Christine Mitchell and Yvonne Donders , "The Human Right to Enjoy the Benefits of the Progress of Science and Its Applications," *The American Journal of Bioethics*, 2017, 17: 10, 34–36; Richard P. Claude, "Scientists Rights and the Human Right to the Benefits of Science," in Audrey Chapman and Sagel Russel (eds.), *Core Obligations: Building a Framework for ESCR*, Antwerp: Intersentia, 2002, pp. 249–278.

This chapter focuses on the first of the two components of the right to science mentioned above: the freedom to conduct scientific research, and discusses the limitations to that freedom that result from the rules generally recognized for the responsible conduct of research. The claim is that activities done by scientists that seriously violate the ethical requirements for conducting scientific research do not deserve to be awarded the label of "scientific." Practices involving, for instance, the fabrication or falsification of data and plagiarism contradict the very essence of science, as they encompass acts of deception intended to mislead the scientific community and society as a whole. Thus, these practices attack the very heart of scientific research, as they involve the manipulation of truth and thereby betray the purpose of science itself. This is especially clear if science is understood as "the quest for knowledge obtained through systematic study and thinking, observation and experimentation."[5]

Awareness of the importance of adhering to ethical standards in the conduct of science has increased significantly over the past few decades. Scientific misconduct became the subject of public attention beginning in the 1980s, which led to public statements and guidelines by academic and funding agencies, as well as the adoption of procedures for dealing with allegations of misconduct in science. After introducing the concept of scientific integrity, this chapter briefly presents the history of this development.

5.2 WHAT IS SCIENTIFIC INTEGRITY AND WHY DOES MISCONDUCT OCCUR?

The term "integrity" refers to the state of being whole and undivided, in the sense that the individual's behavior is not marked by duplicity, but is consistent with ethical principles. Integrity is, therefore, exactly the opposite of deceptive behavior; in a word, it is synonymous with *honesty*. What does this term imply when it is associated to scientific research? It means that "integrity is expected because science is built upon a foundation of trust and honesty."[6] Indeed, for researchers integrity embodies above all "a commitment to intellectual honesty and personal responsibility for one's actions and to a range of practices that characterize responsible research conduct."[7]

Science, which is often characterized as the "search for truth," is intrinsically incompatible with the manipulation of facts and data, and with the resort to falsehood and deception. The reputation of science in society is critically dependent upon adherence to the rules of good scientific practice, which have been developed

---

[5] All European Academies (ALLEA), *European Code of Conduct for Research Integrity*, 2017, Preamble.
[6] Francis L. Macrina, *Scientific Integrity. Text and Cases in Responsible Conduct of Research*. 4th ed. Washington DC: ASM Press, 2014, p. 1.
[7] US National Academy of Sciences. *Integrity in Scientific Research. Creating an Environment that Promotes Responsible Conduct*, Washington DC: National Academies Press, 2002.

by the scientific community itself. Therefore, it is unsurprising that, each time that a new case of scientific misconduct is reported, public trust in the work of scientists deteriorates. This also leads to broader skepticism in society about the scientific community's willingness and ability to self-regulate in order to ensure compliance with ethical principles.

Although misconduct occurs in all areas of science, it is interesting to note that the great majority of cases that surface take place in the field of medicine and closely related sciences (biology, for example). This can be explained primarily by two factors: firstly, the huge social expectations and enormous financial benefits that accompany scientific developments that could contribute to the prevention and treatment of diseases; and, secondly, the difficulty in reproducing experiments in the life sciences, due in large part to the biological variability that exists between organisms.[8] As Goodstein points out, "if two identical rats are treated with the same carcinogen, they are not expected to develop the same tumour in the same place at the same time."[9] These factors – the financial incentives coupled with the fact that actual fraud may be hard to even uncover let alone prove – make the manipulation of truth much more tempting in the life sciences than in other domains.

However, misconduct is not limited to the life sciences. Research activities in the social and human sciences are themselves not exempt from fraud, although how it manifests is slightly different. With the possible exceptions of sociology and psychology, social and human sciences generally use methods that are primarily not empirical, but rather analytical, critical, conceptual, hermeneutical, or normative. Dishonesty in these sciences often consists of the use of the ideas or words of others without proper acknowledgment (what is known as plagiarism), and in the violation of rules for authorship (for instance, the use of "honorary authorships"). Over the past decade in Europe, there have been a number of scandals concerning plagiarized doctoral dissertations in the legal field by high-level politicians. As a consequence, the topic of plagiarism in doctoral studies has received renewed attention from both the general public and the academic community, who have become more aware of the urgency in promoting scientific integrity also in the fields of social and human sciences.

The first and most obvious question that arises when discussing scientific misconduct is: Why does it happen? What strange attraction leads scientists to act in a way that so openly contradicts the goal of the scientific enterprise? The preliminary answer to this question is simple: scientific research, like any other human activity, is

---

[8] Reproducibility is generally regarded as an important marker of the scientific nature of a study, especially in natural sciences. It means that other scientists are able to repeat the experiment and obtain similar results. However, the difficulty to reproduce a study results does not automatically imply that there has been misconduct.

[9] David Goodstein, *On Facts and Fraud. Cautionary Tales from the Front Lines of Science*, Princeton: Princeton University Press, 2010, p. 4.

often exposed to temptations that call for dishonesty. After all, "scientists are not different from other people."[10] When they enter their office, laboratory, or research unit, scientists continue having the same negative passions and driving ambitions to which all human beings are vulnerable. They are tempted, like any other individual, to transgress the boundaries of ethical behavior in order to achieve their personal and professional goals more rapidly. This is to say that it is naïve to assume – as was traditionally thought until the 1970s – that scientists are necessarily honest and always comply with ethical standards simply because they have chosen to embark on the disinterested pursuit of knowledge.

In addition, it should be noted that in our increasingly globalized and competitive world, science is not just – or maybe it is no longer – a *vocation*, but primarily a *career*. Scientific research has become increasingly competitive, complex, and expensive, often demanding collaboration and leading to a diffusion of individual responsibility. Moreover, researchers are regularly under pressure from academic structures and funding agencies to be successful and produce quick results. They are expected to make original discoveries, publish as many articles as possible ("publish or perish"), obtain grants for research, receive awards, be appointed to scientific societies, and eventually become professors. Competition and the pressure to be successful at any price are sometimes too high and the temptation to pass over the rules of honesty is a great one.

David Goodstein, who has studied a number of cases of scientific misconduct, points out three underlying motives that are present in most cases: (1) scientists were under career pressure; (2) they believed they "knew" the answer to the problem they were considering, and that it was unnecessary to go to all the trouble of doing the work properly; (3) they were working in a field – such as life sciences – where experiments offer data that are not precisely reproducible, therefore, as the data manipulation is more difficult to detect, the temptation to cheat is greater.[11]

Besides the above-mentioned factors of misconduct in science, there is another element that should also be taken into account when approaching this phenomenon: there is not always a clear line between the accepted and the not-accepted practices that define what is called the "scientific method." According to most textbooks, scientists study existing information, formulate a hypothesis to explain certain facts, and then, through experimentation, try to test the hypothesis. The problem is that, as Bauer points out, the "scientific method" is, to some extent, a *myth*.[12] Scientific research rarely proceeds by the organized and systematic approach that is reflected in textbook presentations. The formulation itself of hypothesis is affected by the knowledge, opinions, biases, and resources of the

---

[10] William Broad and Nicholas Wade, *Betrayers of Truth: Fraud and Deceit in the Halls of Science*, New York: Simon & Schuster, 1982, p. 19.

[11] Goodstein, pp. 3–4.

[12] Henry H. Bauer, *Scientific Literacy and the Myth of the Scientific Method*, Chicago: University of Illinois Press, 1992.

scientist. Furthermore, hypotheses are subject to experimental testing by means of methods selected by scientists, who very often already have in mind a theory they want to prove. There is a more or less conscious self-deception in scientific research that paves the way for a deception of other colleagues and the public in general.[13] David Goodstein describes this myth of the scientific method very well when he notes:

> every scientific paper is written as if that particular investigation were a triumphant procession from one truth to another. All scientists who perform research, however, know that every scientific experiment is chaotic, like war. You never know what is going on; you cannot usually understand what the data mean. But in the end, you figure out what it was all about and then, with hindsight, you write it up describing it as one clear and certain step after the other. This is a kind of hypocrisy, but it is deeply embedded in the way we do science.[14]

The myth of entirely objective, impersonal, and disinterested scientific research leads the public to an unrealistic perception of science and scientists; it may also encourage scientists to be unrealistic about themselves and "to neglect the importance of cultivating consciously ethical behavior."[15] This is why, in order to avoid unrealistic expectations, it would be preferable to regard the "scientific method" as an *ideal* to strive for (even knowing that it is unattainable in its fullest form) and not as the description of an actual practice in scientific research.[16]

The preceding remarks do not amount, of course, to a denial of the fact that there are honest and dishonest, and acceptable and unacceptable, ways of doing science. However, the line between right and wrong in scientific research is not always crystal clear, and there can be many grey areas in between that deserve careful examination before assessing whether, in a particular case, the rules of the responsible conduct of research have been complied with or not.

5.3 A HISTORICAL PERSPECTIVE ON SCIENTIFIC MISCONDUCT

As a consequence of the scandals of scientific misconduct that have arisen in several countries in the past three or four decades, governments, funding agencies, scientific societies, and academic institutions began to recognize the need to do more to hold scientists accountable for their research practices. Since the mid-1980s in the USA, and since the end of the 1990s in Europe, governments and academic institutions have established specific bodies for dealing with allegations of scientific misconduct and developed guidelines and procedures to address these issues and to punish violations of codes of conduct.

---

[13] Macrina, p. 5.
[14] Goodstein, p. 5.
[15] Bauer, p. 40.
[16] Ibid., p. 39.

Scientific misconduct became a public issue in the USA in the 1980s, when several cases of fabricated research by high-profile scientists were discovered in prestigious academic institutions. These were publicly prosecuted and widely reported by the news media. However, it would be a mistake to think that questionable research behavior is confined to recent times and that scientists from previous decades and centuries have always acted honestly. The Piltdown Man forgery of the early twentieth century is perhaps the most famous fraud in the history of anthropology. In 1912, Charles Dawson, an English lawyer and amateur anthropologist, claimed to have found pieces of a skull and parts of an apelike jaw in a gravel pit in Sussex, England, which he said was the "missing link" between humans and apes. This allegation was controversial from the outset, as many claimed that the skull was inconsistent with other hominid fossils. It was only forty years later, when Dawson had already died, that physical and chemical tests proved that the purported missing link in human evolution was a complete hoax. The upper part of the skull was from a modern human being, the jaw came from an orangutan, and the teeth were from a chimpanzee. The pieces of the skull had been treated with chemicals to make them appear to be fossils.[17]

Science journalists William Broad and Nicolas Wade have closely examined the work done by famous scientists from the past and have shown that they were not always as honest as one might believe.[18] For instance, such scientists did not always obtain the experimental results they reported, or omitted data that were contrary to their hypothesis, or took ideas from others without proper acknowledgment: Isaac Newton, the founder of modern physics, "adjusted" his calculations on the velocity of sound and altered some data in order to make the predictive power of his theory seem much greater than it actually was; Charles Darwin took ideas on natural selection and evolution from another naturalist, Alfred Russell Wallace, without proper acknowledgment; Gregor Mendel, the founder of genetics, selected data from his experiments with peas so as to make them agree with his theory; Louis Pasteur, whose work led to the development of vaccines for anthrax and rabies, prepared his vaccine for anthrax using a chemical method developed by his competitor, Henri Toussaint, while publicly claiming that he had employed his own method; Robert Millikan, the American physicist who won the Nobel Prize in 1923 for determining the electric charge of the electron, extensively misrepresented his work in order to make his experimental results seem more convincing.

Although it is clear that scientific dishonesty has always existed, it was only in the 1980s that a number of high-profile cases of data fabrication and falsification by scientists in the USA started to be publicly prosecuted and covered by the media. Before that decade, public trust in science was very high. There was a naïve optimism that scientists always acted honestly and could perfectly self-regulate their own

---

[17] David B. Resnik, "Scientific Misconduct and Research Integrity," in Henk ten Have and Bert Gordijn (eds.), *Handbook of Global Bioethics*, Dordrecht: Springer, 2014, pp. 799–810.
[18] Broad and Wade.

activities. But these high-profile cases increased public awareness of this problem, opening eyes to the sad news that science could also fall victim to the unethical behavior of some of its practitioners.

In 1981, then Representative Albert Gore, Jr., chaired a US Congress committee that looked at the question of fraud in science and held the first hearings on the emerging problem. In the following years, several cases of data fabrication and falsification were directly investigated by Congress, as it was evident that research institutions were inadequately responding to allegations of misconduct, or were trying to protect their own researchers. In 1985, the Congress passed the *Health Research Extension Act*, which mandates that any research institution receiving financial support from the National Institutes of Health (NIH) must have an established administrative process to review reports of scientific fraud.

In 1986, the so-called Baltimore case became public and attracted attention for a decade.[19] The case had at its center Nobel Prize winner David Baltimore, immunologist and Professor of Biology at MIT. His name appeared on a paper published in the prestigious journal *Cell* and listed as first author Thereza Imanishi-Kari, a colleague at MIT. A junior scientist working in the same laboratory, Margaret O'Toole, became convinced that the paper contained fabricated data and reported her concern to several senior colleagues at the institution. As a consequence, an investigation was launched, first by MIT, then by an NIH panel and subsequently by the Office of Research Integrity (ORI). Even Congress and the Secret Service became involved in the investigation. In the end, in 1996, an appeals panel at the Department of Health and Human Services determined that there was not enough evidence to prove that Imanishi-Kari committed misconduct, but in the meantime the public was surprised to learn that the work done by serious scientists could be doubted, and that coauthors on scientific papers often have contributed very little to the actual work done.

In 1989, the Public Health Service (PHS) created the Office of Scientific Integrity (OSI), renamed in 1992 the Office of Research Integrity (ORI), as the government office charged with oversight of scientific integrity within biomedicine. The 1990s began with the articulation of definitions and rules about scientific misconduct, and institutions receiving federal funds had to have policies in place for pursuing allegations of misconduct. Political attention began to shift away from attaching blame to scientists and focused instead on improving the investigatory procedures for dealing with misconduct and on preventing it through the education of young scientists in the area.[20] The current situation in the US is that every institution and research center that receives federal funding has the primary responsibility for responding to allegations of scientific misconduct. The ORI conducts oversight

---

[19] Daniel J. Kevles, *The Baltimore Case: a Trial of Politics, Science, and Character*, New York: W.W. Norton, 1998.
[20] Marcel C. LaFollette, "The Evolution of the Scientific Misconduct Issue: An Historical Overview," *Proceedings of the Society for Experimental Biology and Medicine*, 2000, (4): 211–215.

reviews of all investigations. When the ORI receives a report of an institutional inquiry, it examines the institution's report to determine whether the findings are defensible, well supported by the evidence, and acceptable as a final resolution of the allegations. Then, on the basis of the ORI's recommendations, a final decision is made by the PHS, which may impose sanctions when research misconduct is found.

European concern about scientific misconduct only began in the 1990s in some countries, such as Germany and Denmark, and much later in others. In 1997, the German scientific community was shocked by a strong suspicion that a large number of papers published by two eminent cancer researchers, Friedhelm Hermann and Marion Brach, included fabricated data. Once this was confirmed by preliminary investigations, a scandal unfolded which marked a turning point in the history of scientific misconduct in Germany. In 2000, the German Research Foundation, Deutsche Forschungsgemeinschaft (DFG), created a task force to investigate the case, which found evidence of data manipulation in at least ninety-four papers coauthored by both researchers.[21] The Hermann and Brach case prompted the two major German research agencies (the DFG and the Max Planck Society) to develop guidelines defining the rules for good scientific practice and establishing procedures for dealing with allegations of scientific misconduct.[22]

In Denmark, scientific misconduct investigations began in 1992 with the establishment of the Danish Committees on Scientific Dishonesty (DCSD), which was a group of committees tasked with handling allegations of research misconduct based on complaints brought by individuals or institutions. This body was, and still is, the only centralized national authority in a European country for dealing with the violation of rules of good scientific practice. In 2017, the DCSD was replaced by the Danish Committee on Research Misconduct.[23] In the same year, the Danish Parliament passed the Research Misconduct Act, which distinguishes between *scientific misconduct* and *questionable research practice*. While the centralized committee continues to deal with allegations of scientific misconduct, cases of questionable research practice have to be handled internally at each research institution. Since 2014, a national Code of Conduct for Research Integrity defines the rules of good scientific practice. Although the Code is not legally binding in itself, researchers can adhere to it and research institutions can integrate the document into their own guidelines.

The former Danish Committees on Scientific Dishonesty became embroiled in controversy in 2003 after its decision concerning the book *The Skeptical Environmentalist* by political scientist Bjørn Lomborg. According to Lomborg,

---

[21] Annette Tuffs, "Fraud Investigation Concludes That Self-Regulation Has Failed," *British Medical Journal*, 2000, 321(7253): 72.

[22] DFG, *Proposals for Safeguarding Good Scientific Practice*. Bonn: Deutsche Forschungsgemeinschaft, 1998; Max-Planck-Society, *Rules of Good Scientific Practice & Rules of Procedure in Cases of Suspected Misconduct*. Munich: Max Planck Society, 2000 (revised in 2009).

[23] See https://ufm.dk/en/research-and-innovation/councils-and-commissions/The-Danish-Committee-on-Research-Misconduct.

claims by environmentalists about global warming, overpopulation, and deforestation, and other related matters, have not been scientifically proven. The DCSD considered that the book was "objectively speaking, deemed to fall within the concept of scientific dishonesty" due to the author's biased choice of data and arguments. However, the DCSD concluded that Lomborg could not be convicted of subjectively intentional misconduct or gross negligence.[24] This decision was heavily criticized by social scientists, who considered that Lomborg's book ought not to be judged by the same criteria used to assess dishonesty in the natural and medical sciences. They pointed out that the selection of information and arguments to develop a theory is an integral part of many social sciences.[25]

Since the end of the 1990s, a number of serious cases of scientific misconduct have taken place in various European countries. To take a few examples:

- Andrew Wakefield, a former physician at the Royal Free Hospital in London, published a paper in *The Lancet* in 1998, claiming a possible link between the measles, mumps, and rubella (MMR) vaccine and autism and other childhood diseases or conditions.[26] The British General Medical Council conducted an inquiry into the case and found Wakefield guilty of dishonesty in his research and banned him from practicing medicine. The British Medical Journal pointed out that "the MMR scare was based not on bad science but on a deliberate fraud" and that it was hard to find a parallel of a paper with such potential to damage public health in the history of medical science."[27] It is noteworthy that the 1998 paper was retracted only twelve years later by *The Lancet*. Wakefield's study has been linked to a steep decline in vaccination rates in the United Kingdom and a corresponding rise in measles cases, resulting in serious illness and fatalities.[28]
- Diederik Stapel is a Dutch social psychologist, former professor at Tilburg University in the Netherlands, and former Dean of the Social and Behavioural Sciences Faculty. In 2011, three of his junior researchers reported they suspected he had fabricated data for a large number of his papers. Stapel's most recent work at that time included one article published in *Science*, where he claimed that a dirty or messy environment may lead to racist behavior in individuals.[29] A few days earlier, he received media attention for a study (not published in a scientific journal) claiming that eating meat made people selfish

[24] Alison Abbott, "Ethics Panel Attacks Environment Book," *Nature*, 2003, vol. 421: 201.
[25] Alison Abbott, "Social Scientists Call for Abolition of Dishonesty Committee," *Nature*, 2003, vol. 421: 681.
[26] Wakefield A. et al. "Ileal-Lymphoid-Nodular Hyperplasia, Non-Specific Colitis, and Pervasive Developmental Disorder in Children," *Lancet*, 1998, 351 (9103): 637–641.
[27] Fiona Godlee, "The Fraud Behind the MMR Scare," *British Medical Journal*, 2011: 342.
[28] Sarah Boseley, "Young People in England Urged to Have MMR Vaccine Following Mumps Surge," *The Guardian*, February 14, 2020.
[29] Diederik Stapel and Siegwart Lindenberg, "Coping with Chaos: How Disordered Contexts Promote Stereotyping and Discrimination," *Science*, 2011, 332(6026): 251–253 (retracted).

and less social. Both studies, based entirely on faked data, are just a small sample of the kind of "scientific research" Stapel had conducted for over a decade. Three investigative committees that studied the case concluded that at least fifty-five of Stapel's publications included fabricated or manipulated data.[30] As a result of these findings, Tilburg University suspended him from his position as professor.

- Paolo Macchiarini, an Italian surgeon and former researcher at Karolinska Institute in Stockholm, was famous for transplanting synthetic tracheas coated with stem cells into more than a dozen patients. In 2014, following the death of two of the three patients operated on by Macchiarini at the Karolinska Institute, an investigation was opened. Two separate internal reports concluded that research results had been described in overly positive terms in Macchiarini's papers, which incorrectly describe the postoperative status of the patients and the functionality of the implants. An external investigation conducted one year later concluded that "there were data in the papers that could not be found in the medical records." The number of mismatches leads to the conclusion that there was "a systemic misrepresentation of the truth that lead the reader to have a completely false impression of the success of the technique."[31]
- In 2011, Karl-Theodor zu Guttenberg was German Defense Minister and a star politician, when a newspaper reported that his doctoral thesis from the University of Bayreuth's Faculty of Law included several passages that had been plagiarized, taken almost verbatim from various sources, mainly newspaper articles. The university began an investigation and concluded that Guttenberg had "grossly violated standard research practices and in so doing deliberately deceived." Based on the "extensive violations" of doctoral regulations by the omission of the source citations, his doctoral degree was revoked and he was forced to step down as Defense Minister.[32]

In an attempt to contribute to the prevention of such cases of misconduct and to promote the responsible conduct of research in Europe, a new *European Code of Conduct for Research Integrity* was developed in 2017 by the national academies of sciences and humanities through their umbrella organization, the All European Academies (ALLEA) federation, in close cooperation with the European Commission.[33] After specifying in its first section the principles that are relevant for guiding researchers in their work (reliability, honesty, respect for others, and

---

[30] Levelt, Noort and Drenth Committees, *Flawed Science: The Fraudulent Research Practices of Social Psychologist Diederik Stapel*. Tilburg: Commissioned by the Tilburg University, University of Amsterdam and the University of Groningen, 2012.
[31] Gretchen Vogel, "Report Finds Trachea Surgeon Committed Misconduct," *Science*, May 19, 2015.
[32] Helen Pidd, "German Defence Minister Resigns in PhD Plagiarism Row," *The Guardian*, March 1, 2011.
[33] See https://ec.europa.eu/research/participants/data/ref/h2020/other/hi/h2020-ethics_code-of-conduct_en.pdf. The Code is a revised and updated edition of the original version published in 2011.

accountability for the research), the Code goes on to describe, in its second section, good research practices in respect of various areas such as: research environment, training, supervision, and mentoring; research procedures; safeguards to prevent harm to public health and the environment; data management; collaborative working; publication and dissemination; and review process of publications. The Code's third section defines the various practices that are regarded as violations of research integrity and recommends some principles for handling allegations of scientific misconduct.

At the global level, the UNESCO *Recommendation on Science and Scientific Researchers*, adopted in 2017, also demonstrates this renewed concern for the ethical aspects of scientific research. The Recommendation, which is a revised, updated, and extended version of the 1974 *Recommendation on the Status of Scientific Researchers*, is more explicit than its predecessor about the need to ensure that scientific research is conducted with full respect for human rights and human dignity (for instance, the rights of research subjects and the confidentiality of personal data). It also strengthens the importance of honesty in data use and data sharing as well as the need to promote open access publications and dialogue science-society. After recognizing in the Preamble "the value of science as a common good" and that "academic freedom lies at the very heart of the scientific process, and provides the strongest guarantee of accuracy and objectivity of scientific results," the Recommendation stipulates that Member States, "in order to have sound science," should establish "suitable means to address the ethics of science and the use of scientific knowledge and its applications" (Article 5 c). It also draws attention to the fact that effective scientific research requires researchers' integrity and intellectual maturity, as well as respect for ethical principles (Article 12). For these reasons, educational initiatives should be designed "to incorporate or develop in each domain's curricula and courses the ethical dimensions of science and of research" and "intellectual integrity, sensitivity to conflict of interest, respect for ethical principles pertaining to research" (Article 13).

Even more so than the UNESCO Recommendation, and in a more succinct manner, the 2010 *Singapore Statement on Research Integrity* can be regarded as a global guide to the responsible conduct of research. This document addresses all the major themes relating to research integrity, including data integrity, data sharing, record keeping, authorship, publication, peer review, conflict of interest, reporting misconduct, communicating with the public, complying with regulations, and social responsibilities. The Statement also includes four ethical principles: honesty in all aspects of research, accountability in the conduct of research, professional courtesy and fairness in working with others, and good stewardship of scientific resources.[34]

---

[34] Second World Conference on Research Integrity, *Singapore Statement on Research Integrity*, 2010. Available at: https://wcrif.org/statement.

5.4 CONCLUSION

Science is an enterprise producing reliable knowledge which is based on the assumption of honesty on the part of scientists.[35] Today, there is a widespread international agreement that, on the one hand, scientists should enjoy freedom to conduct their studies, but also that, on the other, such a freedom presupposes that research is conducted in a way that conforms to principles of respect for human rights and human dignity, and according to the procedures generally established for good scientific practice. In other words, scientific freedom to advance knowledge is tied to a responsibility to act *honestly*. The scientific community has, over time, developed commonly agreed standards in the production and sharing of knowledge. All forms of dishonest science violate that agreement and therefore violate a defining characteristic of science.[36] Today, in our increasingly technological, globalized, and science-driven societies, there is a need to find an adequate balance between the freedom of scientific research, and other rights, interests and values that are also crucial for society. Honesty in the conduct and communication of scientific results is undoubtedly one of those values.

---

[35] US National Academy of Sciences, Engineering and Medicine, *Fostering Integrity in Research*, Washington DC: National Academies Press, 2017, p. 31.
[36] Ibid., p. 32.

PART II

The Right to Science, Now

6

On the Right to Science As a Cultural Human Right

*Farida Shaheed and Andrew Mazibrada**

6.1 INTRODUCTION

What is science, and what role should it play in the future mediation of our global society? Any discussion of the human right to science ought to begin by trying to answer those two foundational questions. As counterintuitive as it may seem in an age dominated by technology, consensus on how those questions might be answered has thus far proved elusive. More difficult still is elucidating the position of science within a framework of human rights.

It may seem strange at first to talk of science as mediation. Yet science pervades complex societal spaces in areas beyond innovation, technology, and access to their benefits. Science and culture intertwine and overlap, and contribute symbiotically to intellectual creativity and expression in complicated ways. These are best framed and analysed as mediations of complex, bidirectional relationships. This, we believe, offers more invaluable insights into the future role of science in our society.

6.2 SCIENCE AS GLOBAL KNOWLEDGE AND A PUBLIC GOOD

Several core themes must be appreciated before these questions can be addressed in the modern context, as global interconnectedness, human rights, and cultures have evolved in tandem with science and technology.

Science and culture are symbiotic. Freedom to engage in *creativity* is central to both and, perhaps more importantly, each informs and shapes the other in crucial ways. General Comment 25, published in April 2020, reinforces this view:

> Cultural life is an "inclusive concept encompassing all manifestations of human existence." Cultural life is therefore larger than science as it includes other aspects of human existence; it is however reasonable to include scientific activity in cultural

---

* This chapter had its origins in an interview conducted on March 5, 2020 between Farida Shaheed, Helle Porsdam, and Sebastian Porsdam-Mann whom the authors would like to thank for their insightful questions and contributions.

life. Thus, the right of everyone to take part in cultural life includes the right of every person to take part in scientific progress and in decisions concerning its direction.[1]

The indelible relationship between science and culture is also reflected in the intentions of the drafters of the Universal Declaration on Human Rights (UDHR). There was, at the time of its drafting shortly after World War II, an intention to promote universal access to both science and culture. Lea Bishop, to whom scholarship in this area owes a great debt, has also suggested that, when the UDHR was being signed, the United Nations had come to envisage the sharing of scientific and cultural *knowledge* as something that could unite an international community.[2] It would be a "task in common" that would bring people together, uniting them with a common journey of discovery. This would, in turn, help "promote cross-cultural understandings" and "yield a more secure world."[3] Understanding science as contributing to knowledge is holistic. Knowledge production is the intellectual and creative activity of engaging with the world around us, which necessitates translating the product of that activity into different forms, only one of which is what we traditionally see as science. Others include art, literature, philosophy, and the social sciences.

For this collaborative intent to truly succeed, knowledge must itself be seen as a public good, there to be shared across the world without exception.

It is not just a question of having access to what people produce, but to the whole process of creativity. It is the ability to fully explore the whole of one's own potential in all its diverse aspects, to benefit from the creativity of others, and the protection of the moral and material interests that result – as the Covenant stipulates, those which emanate from any scientific, literary, or artistic production.

6.3 PARTICIPATION IN SCIENCE, CULTURE, AND RIGHTS DISCOURSES

Human development is about participation, necessitating freedom to fully and actively contribute, and the right to science must also be interpreted from that perspective.[4] It cannot be just about access to the benefits, or the products, of scientific advances. Discourses about access to science are too often framed as exclusively concerning access to the end product, whether an idea or invention.

---

[1] Committee on Economic, Social and Cultural Rights, *General Comment No. 25 (2020) on Science and economic, social and cultural rights Art. 15.1.b, 15.2, 15.3 and 15.4*, (E/C.12/GC/25, 7 April 2020), para. 10
[2] Lea Bishop, "The Right to Science and Culture" (2010) *Wisconsin Law Review* 121, 141. Also see generally Lea Bishop, "The Right to Science: Ensuring that Everyone Benefits from Scientific and Technological Progress" (2014) 4 *European Journal of Human Rights* 411.
[3] Bishop, "The Right to Science and Culture," ibid.
[4] There is a great deal to be gained from a historical analysis of the way in which the right to science evolved, touched on by the chapters contributed to this volume by Aurora Plomer (Chapter 3) and Cesar Romano (Chapter 2).

Access also includes the participation of people affected by science, meaning everyone worldwide, as confirmed in General Comment 25.[5]

Participation includes the freedom to experiment and fully explore one's own creative potential, and informed engagement in the political decision-making processes concerning research prioritization. Participation in ethically significant and politically polarized areas and contexts, such as artificial intelligence and the modification of the human germline, raise several tensions and necessitate a reconceptualization of science's role in modern society. That role cannot be understood outside a cultural context.

One way of conceptualizing the influence science has on rights is through the emerging technologies it has created, and more specifically through of the problem of *meaningful consent*. This allows us to understand the role science will play in global society in several linked ways. Firstly, in scientific research, consent is the ethical ground zero. This fundamental principle sheds light on two related tensions explored in this chapter. The first concerns the tensions between publicly and privately funded research. The second considers what makes consent meaningful and explores what that means beyond the research context, into the application of such research.

Facebook has conducted at least two now well-known experiments in social manipulation.[6] No consent was obtained from participants in advance. Public outrage seemed not to deter Facebook at all. The second study, published in a prestigious scientific journal, the Proceedings of the National Academy of Sciences (PNAS), "manipulated the extent to which [689,003] people ... were exposed to emotional expressions in their News Feed."[7] Most interesting, however, was the debate between scientific professionals about the role of consent. On July 3, 2014, Inder M. Verma, the then PNAS editor-in-chief, published an "Editorial Note of Concern" responding to concerns "raised about the principles of informed consent and opportunity to opt out in connection with the research in this paper," and defending publication.[8]

---

[5] Committee on Economic, Social and Cultural Rights, *General comment No. 25 (2020) on Science and economic, social and cultural rights Art. 15.1.b, 15.2, 15.3 and 15.4*, (n 2), para. 10.

[6] Robert M. Bond, Christopher J. Fariss, Jason J. Jones, Adam D. I. Kramer, Cameron Marlow, Jaime E. Settle and James H. Fowler, "A 61-Million-Person Experiment in Social Influence and Political Mobilization" (2012) 489 *Nature* 295. In a controlled, randomized study conducted during the 2010 US congressional elections, Facebook researchers manipulated the content of "political mobilization messages" in the news feeds of nearly sixty-one million Facebook users while also establishing a control group. The results showed that "the messages directly influenced political self-expression, information seeking and real-world voting behaviour of millions of people"; Adam D. I. Kramer, Jamie E. Guillory, and Jeffrey T. Hancock, "Experimental Evidence of Massive-Scale Emotional Contagion Through Social Networks" (2014) 111(24) *Proceedings of the National Academy of Sciences* 8788.

[7] Kramer, Guillory, and Hancock (n. 7).

[8] Editorial Expression of Concern: Experimental evidence of massive-scale emotional contagion through social networks, PNAS July 22, 2014 111 (29) 10779; first published July 3, 2014 https://doi.org/10.1073/pnas.1412469111. This response remains attached to the paper: "Adherence to the Common Rule is PNAS policy, but as a private company Facebook was under no obligation to conform to the

A central issue in ethical discourses concerning emerging technology, and information and communication technology (ICT) in particular, regards Big Data: the collection, storage, and analyses of massive databases. The issue of consent is complex and extends beyond scientific research to use of the resulting products, for example in the Terms of Service offered to users of Internet platforms. Recent research demonstrates that reading all the agreements attached to the various applications we regularly use would take something in the order of weeks.[9] Nevertheless, we just click and go on. There is no interaction and certainly we are not *informed* in any meaningful way. There are few alternatives: in a recent US Supreme Court case, the view was expressed that foreclosing "access to social media altogether is to prevent the user from engaging in the legitimate exercise of [free speech] rights."[10]

The lack of genuine consent is of concern where platforms extract user data and then profile those users for marketing and manipulation.[11] They do so in a way that is opaque, not clearly understood, and unaccountable to a democratically elected

provisions of the Common Rule when it collected the data used by the authors, and the Common Rule does not preclude their use of the data. Based on the information provided by the authors, PNAS editors deemed it appropriate to publish the paper. It is nevertheless a matter of concern that the collection of the data by Facebook may have involved practices that were not fully consistent with the principles of obtaining informed consent and allowing participants to opt out." The study's editor, Susan Fiske from Princeton University's Department of Psychology, reportedly told *The Atlantic* that as a private company, Facebook did not have to conform to the legal standards for scientific research required of federally-funded researchers: Adrienne Lafrance, "Even the Editor of Facebook's Mood Study Thought It Was Creepy" *The Atlantic*, June 28, 2014, (www.theatlantic.com/technology/archive/2014/06/even-the-editor-of-facebooks-mood-study-thought-it-was-creepy/373649/). The legal standards are known as the Common Rule. It is a rule of ethics in biomedical and behavior research involving human subjects ratified in 1981 and later significantly revised in 2018. The Common Rule sets out procedures for informed consent and transparency generally, and protections for certain vulnerable subjects. It is administered by Institutional Review Boards, appointed within every research institution, the members of which must be "sufficiently qualified through the experience and expertise of its members (professional competence), and the diversity of its members, including race, gender, and cultural backgrounds and sensitivity to such issues as community attitudes, to promote respect for its advice and counsel in safeguarding the rights and welfare of human subjects." "Protection of Human Subjects", *Code for Federal Regulations*, Title 45, (2018), Part 46.107(a).

[9] See for example Aleecia M. McDonald, Lorrie Faith Cranor, "The Cost of Reading Privacy Policies" (2008) 4(3) *I/S: A Journal of Law and Policy for the Information Society* 543 (estimating that if an individual actually read privacy policies, this would require 244 hours per year) and more generally on consent in terms of privacy considerations, Daniel J. Solove, "Privacy Self-Management and the Consent Dilemma" (2013) 126 *Harv. L. Rev.* 1880.

[10] *Packingham v. North Carolina* 137 S. Ct. 1730 (2017) (describing internet platform and social media services as a "modern public square," Justice Kennedy acknowledged their essential nature to speech, calling them "perhaps the most powerful mechanisms available to a private citizen to make his or her voice heard"). See also Kate Klonick, "The New Governors: The People, Rules, and Processes Governing Online Speech" (2018) 131 *Harv. L. Rev.* 1598.

[11] Daniel Susser, Beate Roessler, and Helen Nissenbaum, "Online Manipulation: Hidden Influences in a Digital World" (2019) 4 *Geo. L. Tech. Rev.* 1; Karen Yeung "'Hypernudge': Big Data As a Mode of Regulation by Design" (2017) 20(1) *Information, Communication & Society* 118; Shoshana Zuboff, "Big Other: Surveillance Capitalism and the Prospects of an Information Civilization" (2015) 30 *Journal of Information Technology* 75.

body.[12] Users are simply not aware of how much data is being collected from their use of these technologies and to what use it has been or will be put. The long-term effects on the well-being of both individuals and communities is unknown to us, but is likely to be considerable. It will reshape cultures in an undemocratic way.

6.4 DATA NEUTRALITY

There are frameworks that address the way commercial entities should act in such circumstances: the UN Guiding Principles on Business and Human Rights,[13] for instance, or the Montréal Declaration on the Responsible Use of Artificial Intelligence.[14] These are areas in which UN Special rapporteurs are particularly active, drafting instruments and advice for the governing of that surveillance in order to protect our rights to free speech and privacy.[15] However, governing these sprawling, global commercial entities is challenging not only because of the transnational nature of their use and influence, but also because many are US-based organizations.

There is particular emphasis in the US context on protecting free speech and the free market, sometimes at the expense of protecting individual and collective rights.[16] These technologies and their derivatives, that is, AI and Big Data algorithms, demonstrate that science is fundamentally intertwined with culture and directly impacts how culture evolves. This has significant implications for the right to science and its relationship with other rights.

From a privacy perspective, for example, seeking the deletion of such data is challenging. Europe has recently adopted a different approach to the USA under the GDPR.[17] However, there is little consensus among scholars as to whether GDPR

---

[12] See generally Shoshana Zuboff, *The Age of Surveillance Capitalism: The Fight for a Human Future at the New Frontier of Power* (New York: Public Affairs, 2019) and Julie E. Cohen, *Between Truth and Power: The Legal Constructions of Informational Capitalism* (Oxford: Oxford University Press, 2019).

[13] United Nations, *Guiding principles on business and human rights: Implementing the United Nations "Protect, Respect and Remedy" framework* (United Nations, Office of the High Commissioner for Human Rights, 2011).

[14] www.montrealdeclaration-responsibleai.com/.

[15] See, for example, the work of David Kaye, Special Rapporteur on the promotion and protection of the right to freedom of opinion and expression, who has authored several reports on freedom of expression in the information and digital age, covering topics such as online hate speech (A/74/486, October 9, 2019), Artificial Intelligence technologies and implications for the information environment (A/73/348, August 29, 2018), online content regulation (A/HRC/38/35, April 6, 2018) and the role of digital access providers (A/HRC/35/22, March 30, 2017). David Kaye, *Speech Police: The Global Struggle to Govern the Internet* (Columbia Global Reports, 2019).

[16] See, for example, Julie E. Cohen, "The Zombie First Amendment" (2015) 56 Wm. & Mary L. Rev. 1119 and Jack M. Balkin, "Free Speech in the Algorithmic Society: Big Data, Private Governance, and New School Speech Regulation" (2018) 51 UCD L. Rev. 1149.

[17] Regulation (EU) 2016/679 of the European Parliament and of the Council of 27 April 2016 on the protection of natural persons with regard to the processing of personal data and on the free movement of such data, and repealing Directive 95/46/EC [2016] OJ L119/1 (GDPR).

will be effective.[18] We are faced with tools for our everyday lives that develop so rapidly that governance structures and legislative measures cannot hope to keep up. Fines imposed under regimes like GDPR are easily written off, for example as tax deductible expenses. To huge, wealthy platforms, such fines are merely another cost of doing business. This US emphasis on innovation highlights the tension between access to the benefits of science and its advancements, and intellectual property rights and innovation. There is a balance to be struck between these elements, but it must not be at the expense of other rights or natural justice.

There's a tendency to presume that data is neutral. It is not. Algorithms predict based on incomplete data in all kinds of areas, and their use will likely increase with time. There is wide consensus among scholars that this will exacerbate existing problems of discrimination.[19] This manifests in several ways. Firstly, those currently at the margins of society are also the furthest from access to such technology, exacerbating their inequality. Secondly, algorithms reflect the biases of their creators and training data: their use may further perpetuate societal biases in opaque ways. Further, exclusion leads to skewed or value-laden data.[20] For instance, if marginalized communities are excluded in some way or another from using various technologies, their data cannot be considered by the algorithms that otherwise govern them. People in authoritarian countries will experience this effect even more dramatically. Dissidents whose voices are violently silenced will have no place in this collected mega data, and it is voices like these, diverse and independent voices, whose data would reflect the true texture of the world we inhabit. Often it is in the margins where change begins, where debate and insight are catalysts for new awareness. There is, for instance, widely expressed concern regarding increased surveillance through smartphone technology as a consequence of the global emergency engendered by the COVID-19 pandemic and the state of that surveillance once the state of emergency has ended.[21]

There is, we suggest, no such thing as neutral data just as there is no such thing as neutral research. When investigative research parameters are set out, and questions

[18] See, for example, Tal Z. Zarsky, "Incompatible: The GDPR in the Age of Big Data" (2017) 47 *Seton Hall L. Rev.* 995; Lilian Edwards and Michael Veale, "Slave to the Algorithm: Why a Right to an Explanation Is Probably Not the Remedy You Are Looking for" (2017–2018) 16 *Duke L. & Tech. Rev.* 18; and Margot E. Kaminski, "The Right to Explanation, Explained" (2019) 34 *Berkeley Tech L.J.* 189.
[19] See for example, Frank Pasquale, *The Black Box Society* (Cambridge, MA: Harvard University Press, 2015); Cathy O'Neill, *Weapons of Math Destruction* (London: Penguin UK, 2017); Danielle Keats Citron and Frank Pasquale, "The Scored Society: Due Process for Automated Predictions" (2014) 89 *Wash. L. Rev.* 1; Sonia K. Katyal, "Private Accountability in the Age of Artificial Intelligence" (2019) 66 *UCLA L. Rev.* 54.
[20] See, for example, Chapter 9 in this volume authored by Valerie Bradley on the effect of such algorithms on people with disabilities who, it might be argued, are too often left out of such discourses on discriminatory algorithms.
[21] Yuval Noah Harari, "The World After Coronavirus," *The Financial Times*, March 20, 2020; Natasha Singer and Choe Sang-Hun, "As Coronavirus Surveillance Escalates, Personal Privacy Plummets," *The New York Times*, published March 23, 2020, updated April 17, 2020 (www.nytimes.com/2020/03/23/technology/coronavirus-surveillance-tracking-privacy.html).

framed, there is often a way of thinking about assumptions that can combine inherent and often subconscious prejudices. Culture and ideology affects the conduct even of good science. It is worth recalling General Comment 25: the expression, "to enjoy the benefits of scientific progress" is "not restricted to the material benefits or products of scientific advancement, but includes the development of the critical mind."[22]

In 2012, during the process of researching the special rapporteur's report for the UN on the right to science, the need of mobile phones for migrant women workers had become critical. For migrant workers to lose access to their phones – because they were taken from them by their employers – while alone and in unfamiliar parts of the world, in regions and cultures that might be alien to them, meant stripping them of access to any kind of support system. But now we see that telephones, in particular smart phones, also expose them to new kinds of risks – surveillance by private actors and by states, for different but no less potentially damaging reasons. There must always be a balance in terms of who has access to and use of such data, what it is ultimately used for, and what kind of informed consent has been obtained for those uses. Access must not be limited by income or background, and a realistic degree of privacy must always accompany access. When governments and organizations formulate policies and plans of data collection and use, we must acknowledge that it is potentially skewed in unpredictable ways and we must protect those who might be excluded or prejudiced as a consequence.

At a recent meeting on children's rights in the digital world, as part of the UN Committee on the Rights of the Child's endeavor to draft a General Comment, it was noted that the young see no difference between their online and offline lives. To them, it is simply one life. The UN takes the view that all the rights enjoyed offline, in the physical world, should also be enjoyed online, in cyberspace. That, we know, is not currently the reality. How we move from simply saying it should be this way, to ensuring those rights can be enjoyed in cyberspace, is one of the core challenges facing human rights in the digital era.

This raises an interesting question. For the moment, we can set scientific knowledge to one side and simply ask, what do we mean when we say "knowledge"? We live in a world where many young people believe that the only valid source of information and knowledge is mediated by ICT. But not all information of value is to be found online. This framing raises a key question on the nature of knowledge itself: Who populates knowledge? In developed states in the Global North, it is easy to forget that not everyone worldwide has the same access to ICT. Even in the digital age, we all contribute to what we consider our vast reservoir of knowledge, but not everyone does so in the same way. What we consider to be "knowledge" is distorted by the gap between those who have access to ICT, to digital means of populating knowledge, and those who do not. This affects how we define who is able to

---

[22] Committee on Economic, Social and Cultural Rights, *General Comment No. 25* (n. 2), para. 10.

participate in the production of knowledge. Language is another example of how the Global North biases this framing of what constitutes knowledge. It plays a substantial role in who can actually access, contribute to, and therefore participate in knowledge production. It doesn't matter how advanced a community's ICT technology is, if a community is unable to communicate in the right languages, very often English, it will not be able to access and participate in knowledge production, or share their own knowledge. In time, artificial intelligence may contribute solutions to this problem by offering translation affordances, but we must not allow participation in, access to, and production of knowledge to be delayed while we wait.

To take this one stage further, knowledge access, production, and participation cannot become monopolized as a consequence of information technology architecture. Regulation and governance structures to avoid the kind of monopolistic practices we are seeing with major Internet platforms and ICT companies must be explored. This inevitably involves an interdisciplinary approach, utilizing tools from other disciplines outside of international human rights law, such as antitrust and competition law. It means reconceptualizing governance structures and approaches that can react more quickly to changes in the landscape of the digital world than can international human rights law. It means, we believe, integrating the norms of international human rights law into governance and regulation structures that do not necessarily need to rely on courts to ensure compliance with States' obligations and duties. Here again we see the inexorable convergence of science with culture, and of the right to science with cultural rights. This is the value of the initiation of the commons era of knowledge, of "open source," where anyone can contribute and make access open to all kinds of knowledge production and participation.

6.5 THE TENSIONS BETWEEN PUBLICLY FUNDED AND PRIVATELY FUNDED RESEARCH

Part of this monopoly-based concern centers on scientific research, and research in general, in public institutions that is being increasingly driven by private sector funding. This channeling of scientific interrogation in certain directions is deeply instrumentalist. And as public funding is regularly reduced across the board, even in Europe and wealthy industrialized states, funding for pure research is decreasing.

There is a perception that research must be focused on a product, the need for something tangible at its conclusion, rather than simply the advancement of scholarship and knowledge. This is especially the case when such research is privately funded. Consequently there is little space for purely theoretical research. So much of our early scientific research, whether in the natural and physical sciences, or the social, economic, and political sciences and philosophy, focused on thinking theoretically about the world and the universe it inhabits. There was no demand for a product at the end of that process. Now, the market drives the areas into which research is able to go, and how it explores those areas. It leaves little room for serendipity and, we believe, stifles the very creativity it seeks to foster.

Scientists conducting research are concerned with negotiating patents for whatever it is that they have, before publishing and making their research available to others. The importance of these issues was highlighted in the two 2015 follow-up reports to the UN the right to science, on Patent policy and the right to science and culture,[23] and on Copyright policy and the right to science and culture[24] and has taken on an even greater significance since. Access to the most prestigious scientific journals can be very difficult. Here, the digital age affords great potential for the sharing of knowledge, and for working with published scientific research. However, the essence of scientific work cannot be usurped by commercial incentives, or hindered by the need to copyright that work before sharing it and inviting its analysis. The core idea of science is that other researchers should be able to freely access, and thereby replicate, test and, if necessary, refute, the theories advanced. This is a process of thinking that requires onward momentum. We know that scientific hypotheses are not intended to be permanent, but should be continually tested. We must be able to communicate freely with each other to share new ideas. Intellectual property ideals cannot hinder that process. Framing the right to science in terms of cultural rights lends that notion added weight.

The other side of the public/private dynamic concerns work carried out in the public sector, but which is then transferred to the private sector. In this, we refer to public sector institutions receiving public funding for research that, on completion, leads to a product or outcome that profits the private sector.

The 2012 report to the UN on scientific progress and its applications and subsequent reports related to intellectual property laws[25] were not received without comment, some of it strongly in opposition. The strongest opposition, unsurprisingly, came from highly developed countries and from country representatives in the World Intellectual Property Organization (WIPO). There were expressions of genuine concern about the unrest the report had created.[26] This highlights a problem of background: the attendees at conferences and symposiums involving commercially or business oriented organizations like the World Trade Organization (WTO) and WIPO have dramatically different perspectives to those attending similar events focused on human rights issues. Private sector companies are rarely seated at tables

[23] UNGA, "Report of the Special Rapporteur in the field of cultural rights on Patent policy and the right to science and culture" (2015) UN Doc. A/70/279. See also UNHRC, "Report of the Special Rapporteur in the field of cultural rights on The right to enjoy the benefits of scientific progress and its applications" (2012) UN Doc. A/HRC/20/26.
[24] UNHRC, "Report of the Special Rapporteur in the field of cultural rights on Copyright policy and the right to science and culture" (2014) UN Doc. A/HRC/28/57.
[25] See above n. 24 and 25.
[26] During the Interactive Dialogues around the first report on the right to scientific progress and its applications and subsequent reports in conversations at the time between one of the authors, Farida Shaheed, in her capacity as UN Special Rapporteur in the field of Cultural Rights, and members of the WIPO.

with human rights scholars and practitioners. The outcome of this division, which has been obvious for some time, is the perception, particularly among scientific practitioners and researchers, that the courts favor market-oriented resolutions rather than those predicated on human rights. There are rare exceptions, of course, where intellectual property rights take a back seat to human rights, both individually but also collectively. Often, however, it is only as a result of public pressure and media attention.[27]

In the consultations and expert group meetings leading to the drafting of the Copyright and Patent reports, there was little in the way of engagement from the private sector. Only when the discussions concerned food-related rights was interest shown by a few private sector people engaged in the agricultural industry. It is hard to overstate the importance of such a diversity of expert opinion on an issue like food-related rights. The future of scientific research in this area is certainly dominated at present by genetically modified food chains. However, the same could be said of almost any area of emergent technology and scientific research: diversity of engagement is key.

In 2009, the then special rapporteur on the right to food identified the increasing application of intellectual property regimes to plant varieties and seeds as a significant threat to food security, particularly for the poor.[28] Intellectual property regimes focus exclusively on the commercial seed system, overlooking farmers' informal systems. National rules frequently prohibit even small farmers and public institutions from sharing, replanting, and improving seeds covered by patents and plant varieties.[29] The "excessive protection of monopoly rights over genetic resources can stifle progress in the name of rewarding it." Such an approach "undermines the livelihoods of small farmers, traditional and not-for-profit crop innovation systems, agro-biodiversity as a global public good and the planetary food

[27] In 2001, the United States agreed to bring to an end a trade dispute that had endangered supplies of cheaper drugs for HIV/Aids treatment in Brazil. Brazilian law allowed its government to grant compulsory licenses in special circumstances, waiving the patent rights of foreign companies in return for cheaper, locally produced, generic drugs which was the cornerstone of Brazil's then widely praised national Aids policy. The dispute had been seen as attempts by the USA and pharmaceutical multinationals to intimidate developing countries trying to obtain cheaper, wider access to essential medication. Brazil asserted the provision "was an important instrument available to the government, in particular in its efforts to increase access of the population to medicines and to combat diseases such as Aids." Peter Capella, "Brazil wins HIV drug concession from US," *The Guardian*, June 26, 2001 (www.theguardian.com/business/2001/jun/26/internationaleducationnews.medicalscience). In a similar case concerning Aids, amid public outrage thirty-nine pharmaceutical companies terminated legal proceedings in South Africa which had sought to stop the South African government importing cheaper generic medicines from abroad. See generally: William W. Fisher III and Cyrill P. Rigamonti, "The South Africa AIDS Controversy: A Case Study in Patent Law and Policy," *The Law and Business of Patents, Harvard Business School* (February 10, 2005) (https://cyber.harvard.edu/people/tfisher/South%20Africa.pdf).
[28] UNGA, "The right to food: Seed policies and the right to food: enhancing agrobiodiversity and encouraging innovation" (2009) UN Doc. A/64/170. See also UN Doc. A/70/279 (n. 24), para. 52.
[29] UNDP, "Global Commission on HIV and the law: risks, rights and health" (New York, 2012), recommendation 6.1.

system as a whole."[30] The critical point to recognize is that (at least) two parallel agricultural systems exist, and should continue to exist together and in harmony: the commercial seed system and the farmers' seeds (landraces) or informal systems.[31] This is where the biodiversity emerges from.

Farmers working for generations with particular grains, and experts working in food technology, have valuable insight to offer. Wild seeds need to be mixed in with other varieties, for example, and the result then steeped in the chaotic complexity of nature, in order to draw out higher yielding seeds. Intellectual property regimes cause tension in other ways. Some new commercial patented seeds specifically block reproduction so cannot be replanted unless farmers pay again for the technology to release the reproductive part of the seed. Yet, and perhaps ironically, GMO patented seeds could not have been developed without the very same landraces seeds they threaten. Still commercial enterprises bring legal actions against farmers who harvest plants that include their patented seeds even if it is the wind that has carried them to adjacent fields.

Similar experiences can be gleaned from the perspective of indigenous peoples and small, local communities. The Small Island Developing States, for example, particularly those in the Pacific region, who do not consider themselves "indigenous" in the way developed States have tended to label them, possess considerable traditional knowledge, but they hold it communally. In such communities, knowledge is considered a common good. There are no individualized rights of property. When we consider the concept of moral and material interests of the author, for example, they respond that they are the collective authors, and the collective holders, of that knowledge. They are also its stewards and, as such, it is passed down from generation to generation.

Clearly, intellectual property law clashes violently with this normative system because it rejects the notion that such knowledge could be owned by any one individual or corporate entity. However, where such indigenous knowledge has been retained, cultivated, and improved over many generations, and in a way that is directly influenced by and sympathetic to the particular conditions of the region, it often becomes valuable to Global North commercial entities. In a situation where such intellectual property rights are simply unknown to such communities, it is easy to appropriate that knowledge for commercial purposes without the kind of compensation or recognition that would attach to researchers from the developed world doing similar work. Such appropriation has become widespread and is known as biopiracy, or in terms that are less politically charged, bioprospecting.[32] The neem

---

[30] UN Doc. A/70/279 (n 24), para. 52.
[31] Olivier De Schutter, "The Right of Everyone to Enjoy the Benefits of Scientific Progress and the Right to Food: From Conflict to Complementarity" (2011) 33(2) *Human Rights Quarterly* 304.
[32] See, for example, Janna Rose, "Biopiracy: When Indigenous Knowledge Is Patented for Profit', *The Conversation*, March 8, 2016 (https://theconversation.com/biopiracy-when-indigenous-knowledge-is-patented-for-profit-55589) who also links this practice to "scientific colonialism."

tree case,[33] which concluded a decade of litigation in 2005, provides a stark example of traditional knowledge becoming the subject of a prolonged patent battle and the tensions between different normative approaches in patent systems. It also offers a potential way forward to protect traditional knowledge. In the United States, prior knowledge or use which would deny a patent was recognized only if previously published in a printed publication[34] – not, for example, if it had been passed down through generations of oral tradition. The European Patent Office (EPO), who had initially granted a patent to develop antifungal products to the US Department of Agriculture and multinational WR Grace in 1995, eventually agreed that the neem had actually been in use in India for a very long time.[35] Since that case, India has bought about the cancellation or withdrawal of numerous patent applications relating to traditionally known medicinal formulations. Its Traditional Knowledge Digital Library (TKDL), a database containing millions of pages of formatted information on more than two million medicinal formulations in multiple languages, "bridges the linguistic gap between traditional knowledge expressed in languages such as Sanskrit, Arabic, Persian, Urdu and Tamil, and those used by patent examiners of major IP offices."[36]

If unchecked, privately funded research and intellectual property law can act to enclose[37] the products of creativity and access to knowledge, whether that research arises out of traditional scientific practices or the exploitation of indigenous or traditional knowledge.[38] As General Comment 25 observes:

> Local, traditional and indigenous knowledge, especially regarding nature, species (flora, fauna, seeds) and their properties, are precious and has an important role to play in the global scientific dialogue. States must take measures to protect such knowledge, through different means, including special regimes of intellectual

---

[33] T 0416/01 (Method for controlling fungi on plants/THERMO TRILOGY CORPORATION) of 8.3.2005, ECLI:EP:BA:2005:T041601.20050308 (www.epo.org/law-practice/case-law-appeals/recent/t010416eu1.html).

[34] Pre-AIA 35 U.S.C. 102, Conditions for patentability; novelty and loss of right to patent (www.uspto.gov/web/offices/pac/mpep/s2132.html).

[35] Ibid. See also Ulrike Hellerer and K. S. Jarayaman, "Greens Persuade Europe to Revoke Patent on Neem Tree" (2000) 405 Nature 266–267 (https://doi.org/10.1038/35012778) (concerning the first instance decision in 2000) and "India wins landmark patent battle" BBC News, March 9, 2005 (http://news.bbc.co.uk/2/hi/science/nature/4333627.stm) and Vandana Shiva, "The Neem Tree – A Case History of Biopiracy' (https://twn.my/title/pir-ch.htm).

[36] V. K. Gupta, 'Protecting India's Traditional Knowledge' WIPO Magazine, June 2011 (www.wipo.int/wipo_magazine/en/2011/03/article_0002.html#2).

[37] On the concept of enclosure used this way see Cohen, Between Truth and Power: The Legal Constructions of Informational Capitalism (n. 13) 8–12, 15–33.

[38] There are various measures being taken to protect these kinds of interests and prevent biopiracy. See for example the WIPO definition of "traditional knowledge" from the Intergovernmental Committee on Intellectual Property and Genetic Resources, Traditional Knowledge and Folklore, and the other WIPO resources available online: www.wipo.int/tk/en/tk/ including the WIPO Alternative Dispute Resolution (ADR) for Biodiversity (www.wipo.int/amc/en/center/specific-sectors/biodiversity/).

property, and measures to secure the ownership and control of this traditional knowledge by local and traditional communities and indigenous peoples.[39]

6.6 THE IMPORTANCE OF CRITICAL THINKING AND HUMAN RIGHTS IN KNOWLEDGE PRODUCTION

This chapter began by asking what science actually is and what role it should play in mediating our global society. In its concluding paragraphs, we hope to draw the preceding threads together to begin answering those questions. What then is the added value of a human rights approach to this idea of science and its role? Equality is key. A diversity of input is essential. Decolonization of knowledge is fundamental. What science's role in society should be cannot be answered without reference to who has control over it, who decides what is or is not "scientific" research, and how its best methodologies are determined.

We build an idea of the role science ought to play by drawing on international legal instruments such as General Comments, particularly the CESCR's General Comment 25, and other UN documents, in particular the 2017 UNESCO Recommendation on Science and Scientific Researchers.[40] That idea focuses mainly on empirical science, that which can be tested and refuted, but also includes knowledge from diverse sources, including traditional knowledge. It requires that we apply to knowledge a degree of critical thinking. It requires the understanding that such knowledge may one day be proved wrong, or no longer apply, and that this, in itself, is deeply valuable. Even local communities, who have stewarded traditional knowledge from one generation to the next, may benefit from a university or similar institution doing further research. Their own knowledge is then tested and refuted or confirmed, but in either case it is built upon. Traditional knowledge may not be derived from the same rigorous principles as those that govern the practice of scientific research, but it has an important place in our reservoir of knowledge. Such communities may have explanations for phenomena that may at first seem rooted in superstition or ritual but often are based on invaluable lived experimentation. We must accept that the conceptualization of knowledge derives from different perspectives on the world – and that nevertheless each can contribute precious knowledge.

The progress of science and access to its benefits means different things to different groups, cultures, and societies. An understanding of science and what it should do, will be very different for the agricultural industry than it will be for the individual farmer, although they may share concerns about seeds and productivity. It will be more different still for younger people in the digital age, than for those of us who remember a time before information and communication technology, or before the Internet and social media.

---

[39] Committee on Economic, Social and Cultural Rights, *General Comment No. 25* (n. 2) para. 39.
[40] Records of the General Conference, 39th session, Paris, October, 30–November 14, 2017, v. 1: Annex II (https://unesdoc.unesco.org/ark:/48223/pf0000260889.page=116).

We have highlighted the importance of participation in science, whether this relates to participation in research, or to access to the benefits of that research, be it through an end product or the furtherance of future research. But this also includes participation in decision-making about how science ought to contribute to society. Science has the capacity not just to contribute through end products and usages, but also through knowledge and education. It contributes a particular way of critical thinking which is valuable as a methodology for approaching all the vast and sometimes chaotic information we are confronted with in the digital age.[41] As the Committee puts it in General Comment 25: "doing science does not only concern scientific professionals but also includes 'citizen science' (ordinary people doing science) and the dissemination of scientific knowledge. State Parties should not only refrain from preventing citizen participation in scientific activities but should actively facilitate it."

However, in the digital age, as technology progresses at an ever-accelerating pace, expertise has become even more indispensable. It is impossible for ordinary people to be even reasonably cognizant of all the technological advancements taking place at a given moment in their own society, much less be knowledgeable enough to make informed decisions about economic, political, social, and ethical considerations concerning those developments. By definition, there is a necessity, when considering what participation in science actually means, and therefore in the decision-making processes that govern how it mediates our individual and collective societies, to take into account the wide diversity of contributions that individuals in a society are capable of making. We suggest viewing participation as a continuum on which all contributions can be seen, analyzed, and made use of.[42] Public consultations can be valuable, and are made easier by ICT in the networked, digital age, but the extent to which even a well-educated public can valuably contribute to informed policy and decision-making processes is debatable.[43] Yet, to discount such participation would be undemocratic and undermine the political ideologies of most developed States.

6.7 INTERDISCIPLINARY RELATIONSHIPS ALLOW DIVERSITY WITHIN DISCOURSES

A further complication exists among even those who are experts in a given field: specialism. Few experts in technology fields are experts in the entirety of that field. Gone are the days when science commentators could usefully comment on the detail of

---

[41] On which see, for example, Mark Andrejevic, *Infoglut: How Too Much Information Is Changing the Way We Think and Know* (Routledge, 2013).

[42] We are grateful to Sebastian Porsdam-Mann whose questions on this area during the original interview, and comments on this draft, have been instrumental in framing and driving this idea.

[43] An entire field has arisen that critically engages with the relationship between science and technology and society, led by scholars such as Bruno Latour, Langdon Winner, Donna Haraway, and Sheila Jasanoff. See Sheila Jasanoff, "A Field of Its Own: The Emergence of Science and Technology Studies," in Robert Froderman (ed.), *The Oxford Handbook of Interdisciplinarity* (Oxford University Press, 2017).

a given scientific or technological discipline. An expert in particle physics may have something useful to say on the generality of artificial intelligence and the ethics of its various applications, but this is quite probably where their contribution would end. That same expert might have even less to say on the issues relating to biomedical research. So, how do we ensure the opportunity for participation from everyone in a meaningful way?

It begins with transparency, and progresses to valuable contributions through education – popular and life-long education about what emergent technologies actually involve and what the ethical debates surrounding their use really mean. Only a small cadre of experts in a given field understand its applications, but even they are not experts in how those applications might impact society in the short, medium, and long terms. It is not only human rights scholars and practitioners who express concern about those in the technology industries dictating how human rights will apply to the myriad applications of their technological innovations – many in the technology industries themselves accept they should not be making those kinds of decisions. One key example is content moderation by Internet platforms. The frameworks applied by the platforms to govern speech on their networks only approximates human rights norms, and very often, given the US-centric approach, is informed only by the First Amendment to the US Constitution, rather than by regional and international human rights instruments and jurisprudence.[44] A framework already exists, but it is not the framework platforms are using to regulate speech in the principal environment in which speech now takes place.[45] This conflict cannot continue and can only be resolved through interdisciplinary approaches that necessitate conversations and cooperation between specialists in disparate areas.

Commercial incentives driving innovation, and therefore the practice of scientific research, must not ignore fundamental human rights principles. The right to science necessarily influences and supports in a cross-cutting way the application of science and technology, and discussion of the ethics of both, to many other human rights. Experimentation in the behavioral and neurosciences, for example, where consultation and consent are in issue because a private entity conducts the research rather than one is that is publicly funded and therefore subject to different legal scrutiny, identifies a lacuna that is becoming more pervasive and dangerous. Potential harms ought to be identified and debated, and here again transparency is key. Trade secrets have, for too long, made the products of scientific research opaque and unaccountable. This problem, as we have already identified, is significant in the area of bias in algorithms. Related to this, in the criminal law context, algorithms currently assist law enforcement and courts in ways that are almost entirely opaque and therefore unknowable to the subjects of those investigations and court

---

[44] Klonick, "The New Governors: The People, Rules, and Processes Governing Online Speech" (n. 10); Cohen, "The Zombie First Amendment," and Balkin, "Free Speech in the Algorithmic Society: Big Data, Private Governance, and New School Speech Regulation" (n. 16).
[45] David Kaye (n 15) and Evelyn Mary Aswad, "To Protect Freedom of Expression, Why Not Steal Victory from the Jaws of Defeat?" (2020) 77 Wash. & Lee L. Rev. 609.

proceedings.[46] Independent oversight structured so as to protect trade secrets is possible, but technology innovators resist it. The balance towards commercial interests at the expense of human rights and notions of natural justice and due process has leaned too heavily the wrong way for too long. Commercial entities have greater resources and influence and have used that to unbalance the field in their favor. They are not accountable to the human rights system, nor do they sufficiently participate or engage with it.[47] In fact, they are beginning to claim false legitimacy from the language of human rights without being properly bound by its norms. This must change.

Another way in which the difficulties inherent in participation as a result of barriers imposed by specialist expertise may be addressed is through the formation of interdisciplinary groups and organizations whose debates and cooperation take advantage of diverse viewpoints and expertise. These can be both formal and informally constituted, but they must include stakeholders for a wide variety of interested, but appropriately qualified groups; from private industry as well as the public sphere. In all of the consultations and meetings preceding the Patent and Copyright reports to the UN in 2015, where anything relevant to intellectual property was to be discussed or that might conceivably have relevant implications, WIPO was present. Yet those representatives from WIPO who attended seemed to be isolated within the wider organization. While they themselves were responsive, their institution did not necessarily speak with a unified voice or a unified narrative. Private law and public law conversations must overlap, particularly those having human rights implications. Here again, culture intersects with science and cultural rights inform how the right to science, and participation in science in all the guises we have discussed, must be interpreted.

In the ICT arena, given the transnational nature of Internet platforms and networked communication and interaction, such interdisciplinary and international collaboration gains greater significance. We have identified a problematic divide between the way human rights have traditionally mediated the relationship between the individual and the State, but not between the individual and private entities. Yet private entities, even those with purely commercial incentives, can and should play an important role in facilitating this relationship. Such actors have changed the appearance of the rights landscape, and human rights thinking will need to adapt as a consequence. Human rights scholars and practitioners must find like-minded allies in the private arena. Until we actually come together in discussions on issues that impact law and policy, it doesn't matter what guiding principles we may have for businesses. These are not binding instruments, so we must always be keen to have further conversations in order to actually make rights collaboration a reality on the ground. CESCR has said very clearly that the State where an individual is a citizen has responsibilities, duties, and obligations in respect of rights, but that in reality it doesn't always work that way. Private entities, particularly influential nonstate actors

---

[46] For an excellent summary and analysis of the key debates in this area, see Sonia K. Katyal, "Private Accountability in the Age of Artificial Intelligence" (2019) 66 UCLA L. Rev. 54.

[47] Evelyn Douek, "The Limits of International Law in Content Moderation" (2020) UCI Journal of International, Transnational, and Comparative Law (Forthcoming) (https://ssrn.com/abstract=3709566 or http://dx.doi.org/10.2139/ssrn.3709566).

like Internet platforms, actually have, we believe, a part to play in removing lacunae and ensuring compliance with rights.

6.8 CONCLUDING REMARKS

It remains to be seen what impact the CESCR's General Comment 25 will have, but it seems clear it is a stepping stone to something else; the opening of a door to a more complex, nuanced debate and, perhaps, a renewed importance for the right to science, and an evolving role in the protection of other human rights. It highlights, we believe, the need for (1) a broader perspective on the right to science, and (2) concrete mechanisms for giving effect to its core principles outside of human rights law. One clear statement it makes is to emphasize the symbiotic relationship between the right to science and cultural rights. We repeat the following: "Cultural life is an 'inclusive concept encompassing all manifestations of human existence' ... Thus, the right of everyone to take part in cultural life includes the right of every person to take part in scientific progress and in decisions concerning its direction."

For the justiciability of the right to science to become a reality, we must recognize that the modern landscape of rights and technology is complex and nuanced, and raises many unknowns. A useful approach might be to pick perhaps one or two discrete areas of concern in order to determine what it is that can really be done and which would allow a certain balance to be achieved, rather than attempting to solve the whole problem at once. Collaboration, as envisaged by the drafters of the UDHR and as required now in the interdisciplinary contexts we believe are necessary, involves steep learning curves for all involved, and a willingness to step out of comfort zones and be vulnerable. All involved will be characterized by their own compulsions and obligations, whether they are representatives of a State's executive organs and institutions, or human rights practitioners and scholars, or those with private commercial interests. We must attempt to understand each other's interests and obligations, and see the discourse from the perspective of those on the opposite side.

Science can and should be common ground; a way of thinking and approaching the problems critically, but also a means by which knowledge production and serendipity can be optimized. Academics from different disciplines, who are steeped in those scientific ideals of testing and refuting, are one way in which that interactive discourse can be facilitated. Perhaps most importantly, in the digital age, is the need for technology professionals and technology industry representatives, particularly those with some influence within their organizations as well as independent experts, to be present and to engage fully and openly. And while it would be valuable to have some of these groups formally discussing these areas under the auspices of international organizations like the UN and UNESCO, through the Office of the High Commissioner for Human Rights (OHCHR) and the principal treaty bodies, it is important given how swiftly technology moves, to have adaptable frameworks for discourse and informal policy advice that is truly interdisciplinary and diverse.

7

Mainstreaming Science and Human Rights in UNESCO

Yvonne Donders and Konstantinos Tararas

7.1 INTRODUCTION

The promotion of justice, the rule of law, and human rights as prerequisites for the consolidation of peace and security is common ground in the United Nations (UN) system. The uniqueness of the mandate of the United Nations Educational, Scientific and Cultural Organization (UNESCO) lies in the specificity of its pathway and its approach to peace. For UNESCO, the achievement of these goals is promoted through greater "collaboration among the nations through education, science and culture" (Article 1 UNESCO Constitution).[1] In addition to delineating the Organization's playing field, this proclamation carries a double symbolic value. Firstly, it presages the inclusion of a science-related human right in the Universal Declaration of Human Rights (UDHR). Secondly, it places emphasis on the significance of international cooperation and exchange if science is to fulfil its role in promoting human well-being. While education is a field where competition among UN agencies grew considerably over the years, the broad domains of science and culture are still mainly the prerogative of UNESCO.

By virtue of this mandate, UNESCO has adopted legal instruments and has developed programmes and activities in the field of science and human rights, most notably in the field of bioethics and the ethics of science. Its Member States have created several bodies to advise on issues and challenges relating to these topics: the Intergovernmental Bioethics Committee (IGBC)[2] composed of representatives of Member States; the International Bioethics Committee (IBC)[3] composed of

---

[1] UNESCO Constitution, adopted in London on November 16, 1945, entry into force November 1946. The authors are responsible for the choice and the presentation of the facts contained in this chapter and for the opinions expressed therein, which are not necessarily those of UNESCO and do not commit the Organization.

[2] The Intergovernmental Bioethics Committee (IGBC) was created in 1998, under Article 11 of the Statutes of the International Bioethics Committee (IBC). Comprised of thirty-six Member States, it examines the advice and recommendations of the IBC and recommends follow-up action. More information is available at: https://en.unesco.org/themes/ethics-science-and-technology/igbc.

[3] The International Bioethics Committee (IBC) is a body of thirty-six independent experts that since its creation in 1993 follows progress in the life sciences and its applications in order to ensure respect for

independent experts; and the World Commission on the Ethics of Scientific Knowledge and Technology (COMEST),[4] also composed of independent experts.

The articulation of human rights and science is interwoven with UNESCO's efforts to implement new global frameworks such as the 2030 Agenda for Sustainable Development and its Sustainable Development Goals (SDGs) and the New Urban Agenda. It was also an important dimension of the Organization's responses to the challenges of the COVID-19 pandemic. This approach builds on UNESCO's lead role in the Scientific Advisory Board, the UN expert body that was established in 2013 to bring science to the core of the sustainable development agenda.

This contribution discusses how UNESCO has worked on human rights in relation to science, and on science in relation to human rights with emphasis on standard-setting. It attempts to foreground the core approaches underpinning these efforts; to highlight the evolution in the Organization's thinking; and to show to what extent these are aligned with and promote the advancement of the right to enjoy the benefits of scientific progress as included in human rights instruments, in particular the dimensions of scientific freedom, protection against harm, benefit sharing, and international cooperation.

7.2 FOUNDATIONS OF UNESCO'S ACTION ON HUMAN RIGHTS

7.2.1 *Mandate*

The vision of an inextricable link between peace and the realization of human rights is the foundation of UNESCO's mandate and its work in this domain. The Organization's constitutional commitment was immediately translated into action. UNESCO contributed to the reflection underpinning the elaboration of the UDHR. Through a committee especially created in 1947, UNESCO studied the philosophical foundations of human rights in order to foreground convergences between various cultures and schools of thought.[5] UNESCO was also the first UN entity that undertook to disseminate information about the UDHR through mass communication programs and teaching materials in schools, and to incorporate it in its programs.[6] In the following decades, drawing on its normative action, UNESCO contributed to the promotion of human rights in its fields of competence through research, capacity development, advocacy, and agenda-setting.

---

human dignity and freedom. More information is available at: https://en.unesco.org/themes/ethics-science-and-technology/ibc.

[4] The World Commission on the Ethics of Scientific Knowledge and Technology COMEST is an eighteen-member advisory body and forum of reflection that was set up by UNESCO in 1998. More information is available at: https://en.unesco.org/themes/ethics-science-and-technology/comest.

[5] UNESCO, Report of the Meeting of the UNESCO Committee on the Philosophical Principles on the Rights of Man (1947); available at: http://unesdoc.unesco.org/images/0012/001243/124347Eb.pdf.

[6] Records of the General Conference of UNESCO, third session, Beirut, 1948, Volume II Resolutions (Miscellaneous Resolutions, 8 UDHR, page 118); available at: http://unesdoc.unesco.org/images/0011/001145/114593e.pdf.

While UNESCO's constitutional mandate is broad and covers the promotion of all human rights, its action focuses on the rights directly linked to its mandate. These include: the right to education; the right to freedom of opinion and expression, including the right to seek, receive, and impart information; the right to take part in cultural life and artistic freedom; the right to water and sanitation; and the right to enjoy the benefits of scientific progress and its applications.

UNESCO's general commitment to human rights mainstreaming was reaffirmed in the early 2000s. The Organization's 2003 Human Rights Strategy elevated the integration of a human rights-based approach (HRBA) in all its activities to a house-wide priority. This UN-wide approach, forged out of the momentum of the 1997 UN Reform, implies that the work of UN Agencies and Programmes, including that of UNESCO, is guided by human rights principles, as laid down in the UDHR and other international human rights instruments. These principles include: universality; indivisibility and interdependence of all human rights; equality and nondiscrimination; participation and inclusion; accountability; and the rule of law.[7] HRBA is a key programming principle in UNESCO's Medium-Term Strategy for 2014–2021, reaffirmed in the draft Medium-Term Strategy for 2022-2029[8], and a cornerstone for the implementation of gender equality, one of the Organization's two global priorities.[9]

The right to enjoy the benefits of scientific progress and its applications is included in Article 27 UDHR and in Article 15(1)(b) of the International Covenant on Economic, Social and Cultural Rights (ICESCR). These instruments recognize that this right includes the right of individuals to enjoy the benefits of scientific advancement and the rights of scientists to freely conduct science and to have the results of their work protected. Another inherent component of the right to enjoy the benefits of scientific progress and its applications is the protection from possible harmful effects of science. A cross-cutting dimension of this right, and of the Covenant, is international cooperation.

UNESCO has actively supported the elaboration of this right. Most importantly, it drew the right from its oblivion by initiating a series of experts' meetings that led to the adoption by a group of experts of the Venice Statement on the Right to Enjoy the Benefits of Scientific Progress and its

---

[7] According to the UN Statement of Common Understanding on Human Rights-Based Approache to Development Cooperation and Programming, adopted in 2003, the HRBA entails that: all programs of development cooperation, policies and technical assistance should further the realization of human rights; human rights standards and principles derived guide all development cooperation and programming in all sectors and in all phases of the programming process, and development cooperation contributes to the development of the capacities of "duty-bearers" to meet their obligations and/or of "rights-holders" to claim their rights.

[8] Medium-Term Strategy for 2014–2021, approved by the General Conference at its 37th session (General Conference resolution 37 C/Res.1), Document 37 C/4, paragraph 23; Executive Board, Draft Medium Term Strategy for 2022-2029 (41C/4), 10 March 2021, Document 211 EX/18.I.

[9] See the UNESCO Gender Equality Action Plan, available at: https://unesdoc.unesco.org/ark:/48223/pf0000227222/PDF/227222eng.pdf.multi.

Applications in July 2009.[10] This statement aimed to clarify the normative content of the right, as well as to generate discussion among all relevant stakeholders with a view to enhancing its implementation.

7.2.2 UN Global Frameworks

Being part of the UN family, UNESCO's work fits within a broader context defined by human rights-driven global action frameworks, most notably the 2030 Agenda for Sustainable Development and the SDGs, and the New Urban Agenda. Agenda 2030 and the SDGs embody an unprecedented universal consensus on key prerequisites for sustainable human development that are anchored in human rights. Guided by the commitment of "leaving no one behind," Agenda 2030 marks a paradigm shift towards an inclusive and transformative vision of human development that establishes clear imperatives for the UN system regarding respect for, protection of, and fulfilment of human rights. Moreover, acknowledging their close interconnection, Agenda 2030 endorses a holistic approach to the set of challenges at hand, significantly expanding the list prioritized by the Millennium Development Goals (MDGs) and making the elimination of inequalities a transversal thread. Contrary to previous political commitments, Agenda 2030 constitutes – to paraphrase the preamble of the UDHR – "a common standard of achievement for all peoples and all nations" towards which all efforts must converge. Interestingly, science is a cross-cutting thread of Agenda 2030. The preamble's acknowledgement of science, technology and innovation (STI) as a key driver for sustainable development, is mirrored by the inclusion of as many as twenty-three STI-related SDG targets.

The New Urban Agenda[11] localizes the commitments of Agenda 2030 and the content of the SDGs by acknowledging that local authorities are also responsible for protecting, respecting, and fulfilling the human rights of the inhabitants at the city level, in line with central governments.

UNESCO has placed the implementation of Agenda 2030 at the core of its action. The Organization focuses on and contributes significantly to nine SDGs, namely: SDG 4 (Quality Education); SGD 5 (Gender Equality); SDG 6 (Clean Water and Sanitation); SDG 9 (Industry, Innovation and Infrastructure); SDG 11 (Sustainable Cities and Communities); SDG 13 (Climate Action); SDG 14 (Life below Water); SDG 15 (Life on Land), and SDG 16 (Peace, Justice and Strong Institutions).[12] In

---

[10] Venice Statement on the Right to Enjoy the Benefits of Scientific Progress, adopted July 17, 2009, available at https://unesdoc.unesco.org/ark:/48223/pf0000185558. This statement was one of the inspirational sources of General Comment No. 25 (2020) on science and economic, social and cultural rights Art. 15.1.b, 15.2, 15.3 and 15.4, adopted by the Committee on Economic, Social and Cultural Rights in April 2020.

[11] The New Urban Agenda was adopted by all UN Member States in October 2016 at the United Nations Conference on Housing and Sustainable Urban Development (Habitat III) in Quito, Ecuador; available at: http://habitat3.org/wp-content/uploads/NUA-English.pdf.

[12] An overview of how UNESCO moves forward the Agenda 2030 is available at: https://unesdoc.unesco.org/ark:/48223/pf0000247785.

TABLE 7.1 *Science Technology and Innovation (STI) and Agenda 2030*

Areas explicitly mentioned in Agenda 2030	SDGs making explicit references to STI	SDG targets making specific references to STI
Science	4; 14	4.b ; 14.3 ; 14.4 ; 14.5
Technology	1; 2; 5; 6; 7; 9; 17	1.4 ; 2.a ; 5.b; 6.a ; 7.a; 7.b ; 9.4 ; 9.a ; 9.c; 17.7 ; 17.16
Innovation	8	8.2 ; 8.3
STI	9; 12; 14;17	9.5 ; 9.b; 12.a ; 14.a ; 17.6 ; 17.8

connection with these SDGs, UNESCO has the following key roles: internationally recognized global or shared leadership and coordination; monitoring and benchmarking; global advocacy to sustain political commitment; leading or co-leading global multi-stakeholder coalitions; normative mandate and provider of upstream policy support and capacity development. Furthermore, the Organization contributes to SDG 1 and 10, and is concerned with aspects of SDG 17.[13]

7.3 UNESCO'S APPROACH TO SCIENCE AND HUMAN RIGHTS

UNESCO's work in the field of science and human rights, and in particular the right to enjoy the benefits of scientific progress and its applications, has evolved significantly. The Organization has explicitly focused on promoting an ethical and rights-based approach to the advancement of science and technology, inter alia, by fostering the rights and freedoms of scientific researchers and an equitable sharing of the benefits of that research. It has also addressed the ethical challenges deriving from cutting-edge science, for instance in connection with bioengineering and biotechnology, and, more recently artificial intelligence, big data, and the Internet of Things. Its work has also supported a stronger interlinkage between scientific evidence and policy-making and it has fostered gender equality in sciences by strengthening the opportunities of women. A good example of the last is UNESCO's program For Women in Science, which it has hosted since 1998 in cooperation with L'Oréal. The motto of this program is "the world needs science, science needs women." It aims to reward excellent female scientists for their important contributions to the progress of science, either in life sciences or in the fields of physical sciences, mathematics, and computer science. In the last 20 years, more than 3100 scientists from 117 countries have been supported and more than 50 countries grant national and regional scholarships under the flag of this program.[14]

---

[13] Ibid
[14] More information on this programme can be found at: www.forwomeninscience.com/en/home.

7.3.1 Early Approaches: Do No Harm, Benefits Sharing, and International Cooperation

In the decades after the adoption of the ICESCR, States focused on three aspects of science. The first aspect was promoting "the optimum utilization of science and scientific methods for the benefit of mankind and for the preservation of peace and the reduction of international tensions."[15] The second was to address "dangers which constitute a threat, especially in cases where the results of scientific research are used against mankind's vital interests in order to prepare wars involving destruction on a massive scale or for purposes of the exploitation of one nation by another, and in any event give rise to complex ethical and legal problems."[16] Finally, States aimed to promote international cooperation so that the full potential of scientific and technological knowledge could be promptly geared to the benefit of all peoples.[17]

These dimensions were explicitly included in the *Recommendation on the Status of Scientific Researchers*, adopted by the Member States of UNESCO in 1974. The Recommendation calls upon States to foster an environment where scientific researchers can "contribute positively and constructively to the fabric of science, culture and education in their own country, as well as to the achievement of national goals, the enhancement of their fellow citizens' well-being, and the furtherance of the international ideals and objectives of the United Nations."[18] At the same time, the Recommendation allows States a considerable margin of appreciation. Deviations from the Recommendation are acceptable under the condition that the cases where these apply are specified "as explicitly and narrowly as possible."[19]

This three-pronged approach of States is also included the *Recommendation concerning Education for International Understanding, Co-operation and Peace and Education relating to Human Rights and Fundamental Freedoms* adopted at the same time. Specifically, the Recommendation recognizes as an integral part of human rights education the duty to promote "the inadmissibility of using science and technology for warlike purposes and their use for the purposes of peace and progress."[20] The Recommendation also underscores the role of education in harnessing the power of knowledge towards problem-solving and the critical role of international cooperation in this regard.[21]

---

[15] Preamble of the Recommendation on the Status of Scientific Researchers, UNESCO Gen. Conf. Res. 18 C/Res.40, 18th Sess. (1974).
[16] Ibid
[17] Ibid, Article 19.
[18] Recommendation on the Status of Scientific Researchers, UNESCO Gen. Conf. Res. 18 C/Res.40, 18th Sess. (1974), Article 14(d).
[19] Ibid., Article 14 (d).
[20] Recommendation concerning Education for International Understanding, Co-operation and Peace and Education relating to Human Rights and Fundamental Freedoms, UNESCO Gen. Conf. Res. 18 C/Res. 38, 18th Sess. (1974), Article 18 (b).
[21] Ibid, Articles 18, 19, and 26.

Another general feature of UNESCO's approach is the importance allocated to culture. In a reply to a survey by the UN Commission on Human Rights in 1976, the Organization's Director-General observed that science and technology "are merely the instruments for carving out decisions made elsewhere – what we find at the fountainhead of the long and complex chain of those decisions but the determining factor of culture?" Hence, "the use made of science and technology, like pure science itself, is a matter of culture."[22] The role of culture is underscored later on in the context of reflection about ethical considerations in relation to scientific discoveries and the progress of technology. A valuable dialogue between cultures is seen as crucial for bioethics, in the same way as the breaking down of barriers between disciplines.[23]

The approach and emphasis of the two Recommendations of 1974 actually underpin the several instruments related to science adopted around the same time in the broader context of the UN. Most of these concentrate on international cooperation in the field of science and on the possible harmful effects of science and technology with a focus on the duties of States and scientists to promote, conduct, and use science in a responsible way. For example, the *Charter of Economic Rights and Duties of States*, adopted by the UN General Assembly in 1974, recognizes a right of States – not of individuals – to benefit from scientific advancement and developments in science and technology. It also calls upon States to promote international scientific and technological cooperation and the transfer of technology to developing countries, as well as facilitate access of developing countries to the achievements of modern science and technology (Article 13).

Similarly, the *Declaration on the Use of Scientific and Technological Progress in the Interests of Peace and for the Benefit of Mankind*, adopted by the UN General Assembly in 1975, concentrates on the possible abusive use of science contrary to human rights. Its preamble acknowledges that scientific and technological achievements could improve the conditions of peoples and nations and, at the same time, cause social problems or threaten human rights and fundamental freedoms. Other issues in this Declaration include non-discrimination and international cooperation to ensure that the results of science and technology are used in the interests of peace and security, and for the economic and social development of peoples. It is further laid down that States should prevent the use of scientific and technological development to limit the enjoyment of human rights and protect the population from possible harmful effects of the misuse of science and technology (Article 2).

---

[22] Report of the Secretary-General, Human Rights and Scientific and Technological Developments, The balance which should be established between scientific and technological progress and the intellectual, spiritual, cultural and moral advancement of humanity, Commission on Human Rights, 32nd session, Document E/CN.4/1199/Add.1 of February 2, 1976, para. 196, available at: https://digitallibrary.un.org/record/720321?ln=en.

[23] Report by the Director-General on the possibility of drawing up an international instrument on the protection of the human genome, Document 28 C/38 of September 7, 1995, para. 7.

7.3.2 Emphasis on Science and (Bio-)Ethics

About two decades later, UNESCO initiated the adoption of several international instruments relating to science in relation to ethics and bioethics. The *Universal Declaration on the Human Genome and Human Rights*, adopted by UNESCO's General Conference in 1997 and endorsed by the UN General Assembly in 1998, focuses on the potential abuse of science and research. In this sense, it echoes a series of General Conference resolutions that express concern and call upon UNESCO to take initiatives around such abuse of science, such as the development of sophisticated weaponry.[24] The Declaration states, for instance, that researchers have special responsibilities in carrying out their research, including meticulousness, caution, intellectual honesty, and integrity (Article 13). It also states that persons have the right to be informed about research on their genome and that such research should in principle not be carried out without a person's consent. If such consent is not possible, research should be carried out only for the person's health benefit or the health benefit of others (Article 5). The Declaration also urges States to promote international dissemination of knowledge, in particular between industrialized and developing countries (Article 18).

The idea of *sharing* the benefits of science is more clearly present in the *International Declaration on Human Genetic Data*, adopted by the General Conference of UNESCO in 2003. According to this Declaration, the benefits of science, including access to medical care, the provision of new diagnostics, facilities for new treatments or drugs deriving from research, and support for health services, should be shared with society as a whole and with the international community (Article 19).

An explicit reference to the sharing of benefits of science can be found in the *Universal Declaration on Bioethics and Human Rights*, adopted by UNESCO's General Conference in 2005. Article 15 includes that "[b]enefits resulting from any scientific research and its applications should be shared with society as a whole and within the international community, in particular with developing countries." Part of such benefits could be access to scientific and technological knowledge (Article 15(1)e). This provision focuses more on the sharing of the results of science and less on the advancement of science or the freedom to conduct science. UNESCO's International Bioethics Committee (IBC) extensively elaborated on the concept of benefit sharing in a report issued in 2015.[25] It explicitly linked

---

[24] UNESCO's General Conference 29 C/Resolution 16, adopting the Declaration, recalled a series of resolutions of the 1980s and early 1990s (namely 22 C/Resolution 13.1, 23 C/Resolution 13.1, 24 C/Resolution 13.1, 25 C/Resolutions 5.2and 7.3, 27 C/Resolution 5.15 and 28 C/Resolutions 0.12, 2.1 and 2.2) that urged "UNESCO to promote and develop ethical studies, and the actions arising out of them, on the consequences of scientific and technological progress in the fields of biology and genetics, within the framework of respect for human rights and fundamental freedoms."

[25] International Bioethics Committee, Draft Report of the IBC on the principle of the sharing of benefits, UNESCO Doc. SHS/YES/IBC-22/15/3 REV.2, available at https://unesdoc.unesco.org/ark:/48223/pf0000233230.

Article 15 of the Declaration to Article 27 UDHR and Article 15 ICESCR. It reaffirmed the importance of sharing the benefits of science with society as a whole, and with the international community, while also addressing the possible tradeoff with the protection of intellectual property and patents. The IBC further maintained that sharing should be seen as participation and not as top-down beneficence, emphasizing the importance of capacity building and science education, open access to information, and empowerment and participation in the production of knowledge.

7.3.3 Broadening the Scope: Science-Based Decision Making

7.3.3.1 UNESCO Declaration of Ethical Principles in Relation to Climate Change

In recent years, UNESCO's work in the field of science and human rights was given a new impetus. Much influenced by the global discussions on sustainable development and climate change, Member States of UNESCO elaborated and adopted in 2017 the *UNESCO Declaration of Ethical Principles in relation to Climate Change*. This Declaration emphasizes the fundamental importance of science, technological innovation, relevant knowledge, and education for sustainable development in the response to climate change. Several of the human rights dimensions of science, such as prevention of harm and international cooperation, are reflected in the Declaration. The Declaration adds an important new dimension in relation to science and human rights, namely the promotion of decision-making based on science.

As regards the prevention of harm, the Declaration maintains in Article 2 that people should aim to "anticipate, avoid or minimize harm, wherever it might emerge, from climate change, as well as from climate mitigation and adaptation policies and actions." Science is also relevant in relation to another dimension of possible harm, namely the precautionary principle. Article 3 states that: "Where there are threats of serious or irreversible harm, a lack of full scientific certainty should not be used as a reason for postponing cost-effective measures to anticipate, prevent or minimize the causes of climate change and mitigate its adverse effects."

International cooperation is included in several parts of the Declaration. For instance, Article 2 states that States should "seek and promote transnational cooperation before deploying new technologies that may have negative transnational impacts." Article 7 includes that "scientific cooperation and capacity building should be strengthened in developing countries."

Scientific freedom is less present in the Declaration, but it is included in Article 7(4) that States should "take measures which help protect and maintain the independence of science and the integrity of the scientific process."

The Declaration adds explicit provisions on scientific knowledge and integrity in decision-making. Article 7(1) states that "decisions should be based on, and guided by, the best available knowledge from the natural and social sciences, including interdisciplinary and transdisciplinary science, and by taking into account, as appropriate, local, traditional and indigenous knowledge." States should therefore "build effective mechanisms to strengthen the interface between science and policy to ensure a strong knowledge base in decision-making" (Article 7(4)d).

7.3.3.2 UNESCO Recommendation on Science and Scientific Researchers

One of the most crucial instruments by UNESCO that connects science and human rights is the *Revised Recommendation on Science and Scientific Researchers*, also adopted in 2017. This document supersedes the Recommendation on the Status of Scientific Researchers of 1974. As the Director-General noted in her report on the revision, the Recommendation reflects a "conceptual paradigm shift toward systematically addressing risks and responsibilities in science, while recognizing that the freedom of expression and conscience of researchers and their professionalism is its backbone."[26] The idea driving the Recommendation was the establishment of closer links with the SDGs, and in particular Target 9.5 that aims to enhance scientific research. The Recommendation underscores the importance of another application of science, namely the use of scientific and technological knowledge in decision-making (paragraphs 5 (g), 7, 8, and 9).

The revised Recommendation sets out the operational standards for a contemporary and forward-looking vision for science. A main innovation of the Recommendation is the recognition that harnessing the transformative power of science requires a holistic approach, which is anchored unequivocally in human rights.

The Recommendation adopts a broad strategy, looking at the whole process of science as a departure point for determining the role of scientific researchers. In doing so, the Recommendation pays specific attention to new developments, such as the internationalization of science and mobility of scientists, the changing security and environmental concerns, the increased role of the private sector, the increased concern about the ethical aspects of the science enterprise, and the interdisciplinary nature of science, including social and human sciences. All these have led to an increased recognition that the responsibilities of scientists have widened and that a firm link with human rights is required.

Human rights is set as a cornerstone for building a sound science, technology, and innovation system indispensable for achieving sustainable development. In that spirit, the Recommendation incorporates human rights in multiple ways. By

---

[26] UNESCO Doc. SHS/BIO/SSR/2017/1, Revision of the Recommendation on the Status of Scientific Researchers (1974), May 17, 2017, p. 3, para. 8.

explicitly setting the human right to share in scientific advancement and its benefits (paragraph 21) as a reference point, the Recommendation broadly endorses its different elements, including the sharing of its benefits, academic freedom, protection from possible harm, and international cooperation. It also refers to the human rights of scientists, the rights of people to access knowledge produced by science, and the rights of people affected.

Among its many important principles, three deserve to be highlighted in this context. First of all, emphasis is placed on the responsibility of science towards UN ideals of human dignity, progress, justice, peace, welfare of humankind, and respect for the environment (paragraph 4) and the need to subject scientific conduct to universal human rights standards (paragraphs 18a,e, 20a,b,c, 21, 22, 42). As a result, science should be fully integrated into efforts to develop more humane, just, and inclusive societies. A second feature relates to the need for science to interact meaningfully with society and vice versa towards tackling global challenges (paragraphs 4, 5 c, 13d, 19, 20, 22). This calls for the active participation of society in science and research in a democratic and horizontal manner, through the identification of knowledge needs, the conduct of scientific research, and the use of results. Finally, the Recommendation promotes science as a common good (paragraphs 6, 13e, 16a–v, 18b,c,d, 21, 34e, 35, 36, 38). According to the text, this entails that public funding of research and development should be perceived as a form of public investment, the returns on which are long-term and serve the public interest. Likewise, States should facilitate and encourage open science, including the sharing of data, methods, results, and the knowledge derived from it, in view of its potential benefits. It also entails the removal of obstacles preventing women and other underrepresented groups from receiving, on an equal footing, basic education, training and, ultimately, access to employment in scientific fields.[27]

7.3.3.3 UNESCO and the UN Scientific Advisory Board (2013–2016)

The work of UNESCO in the UN Scientific Board is also worth brief exploration. The need to bring science to the core of the sustainable development agenda was acknowledged by the UN Secretary-General's High-level Panel on Global Sustainability in its report entitled "Resilient People, Resilient Planet: A Future Worth Choosing," adopted in January 2012.[28] Beyond addressing global challenges, the Panel insisted on the importance of a strengthened science policy interface as a necessary complement to efforts on economic and social aspects, and factors such as inequalities. The Panel considered that this objective could be best achieved either by "naming a chief scientific adviser or establishing a scientific advisory board with diverse knowledge and experience" (Recommendation 51, page 75).

[27] The annex to UNESCO's General Conference 39 C/Resolution 85 that adopted the Recommendation identifies a set of ten key related areas.
[28] The Report is available at: https://en.unesco.org/system/files/GSP_Report_web_final.pdf.

UNESCO played a decisive role in taking this Recommendation forward. It convened the Executive Heads of UN organizations with a science-related mandate and representatives of major scientific bodies into an ad hoc group mandated to provide advice to the SG and the UN system as a whole. Recognizing the strategic opportunity, the ad hoc group opted for the establishment of a representative body, the Scientific Advisory Board. This body came into being in September 2013. UNESCO hosted its secretariat and the UNESCO DG took the lead in establishing the body and taking up the function of its chair.[29]

The Scientific Advisory Board was given an ambitious mandate. Its areas of focus included improving coordination among UN entities having a mandate in science, technology, engineering, and humanities; avoiding mission creep and overlap and curbing counter-productive competition; advising on 2030 Agenda science priorities; and providing insights on the promotion of democratic global governance for a responsible and ethical development of science that reinforces sustainability.[30]

To fulfil its mandate, the Board was tasked to connect and mobilize all relevant scientific fields for the purpose of fostering coherence. And so it covered the basic sciences, engineering and technology, social science and humanities, ethics, health, economic, behavioral, environmental, and agricultural sciences.

Thus defined, the mandate given to the Scientific Advisory Board opened important avenues for connecting science with human rights considerations. The final report of the Scientific Advisory Board with its main findings and recommendations, submitted in September 2016, reveals that human rights-related considerations were on its radar. First of all, it explicitly recognized science as a public good, which deserves to be valued more highly, employed more widely, and used effectively by decision-makers at all levels.[31]

A corollary to considering science a public good was the emphasis on a society-policy-science interface. The science process should thus involve a diversity of stakeholders, including government, civil society, indigenous peoples and local communities, businesses, academia, and research organizations, each with their own accountabilities. This way, the Board considered, the diverse perspectives and priorities could be synthesized in a manner aligned with the evidence and serve the long-term interests of society and the planet.[32]

Another important aspect related to human rights is the advocacy for a holistic approach to science with emphasis placed both on knowledge production for innovation (basic research) and applied research, as well as on linking such factors as health, education, opportunity, incomes, social mobility, and nutrition. This

---

[29] More information available at: https://en.unesco.org/themes/science-sustainable-future/scientific-advisory-board-united-nations-secretary-general.
[30] Ibid
[31] The Future of Scientific Advice for the United Nations – a Summary Report to the Secretary-General of the United Nations from the Scientific Advisory Board, September 2016, available at https://unesdoc.unesco.org/ark:/48223/pf0000245801/PDF/245801eng.pdf.multi.
[32] Ibid, p. 17–21.

reaffirmed the close interlinkages between the right to enjoy the benefits of scientific progress and other human rights related to health, food, labor, and education.

Finally, the influence of human rights and the "leave no one behind" vision of Agenda 2030 is evident in its emphasis on inequalities. The report calls for co-designing and co-ownership by all as the basis for developing science, technology and innovation across the board. It stresses that the complexity of today's world and its challenges require the mobilization of resources and assets in all parts of the world, developing and developed, as it passes imperatively through the elimination of gender disparities.[33]

A full assessment of the work of the Scientific Advisory Board is outside the scope of this contribution. However, it is fair to say that the Board partially met the expectations surrounding its creation. Counted among its strengths and positive contributions are its call for a more central role for science in fostering sustainable development and also the emphasis on a holistic approach to science. Another is its echoing of fundamental principles of Agenda 2030, in particular transparency, participation, and inclusion, and the elimination of inequalities. It is probably no coincidence that these elements were key to the vision for science embodied in the 2017 Recommendation on Science and Scientific Researchers. Yet, the Board did not succeed in building the case for a holistic approach to human rights with the right to enjoy the benefits of scientific progress and its applications at its core, at least not using explicit terms. That was a missed opportunity. A strong recommendation towards such an orientation at the beginning of the SDG era could perhaps have helped integrate a human rights lens into the monitoring process of specific targets and indicators.

7.4 CONCLUDING REMARKS

The significant role of science in consolidating peace, fostering human well-being, and achieving sustainability cannot be overestimated. Hence, it is only natural that science, technology, and innovation were woven into the fabric of the 2030 Agenda for Sustainable Development, cutting across virtually all of the seventeen SDGs, including their targets and means of implementation.

This contribution shows that UNESCO, with its specific mandate in the field of science, has worked on human rights in relation to science, and on science in relation to human rights, in many different ways. Shifting over the years from a narrower to a more holistic approach, it has developed numerous instruments that connect the advancement of science to ethical and human rights standards and principles. These include academic freedom and protection of the rights of scientists, protection against harm, sharing benefits of scientific and technological advancements, including related knowledge and their applications, international cooperation and, more recently, science-based decision-making. In addition,

---

[33] Ibid, p. 22–24.

Mainstreaming Science and Human Rights in UNESCO

UNESCO embarked since November 2019 on the elaboration of two new instruments: on ethics of artificial intelligence[34] and on open science,[35] potentially enhancing the science-related normative arsenal. Standard-setting efforts have been reinforced by converging advocacy initiatives such as the Joint Appeal for Open Science, launched by the leadership of UNESCO, WHO and OHCHR in October 2020. The appeal acknowledged the right to enjoy the benefits of scientific progress and its applications as the cornerstone of efforts to promote open, inclusive and collaborative science. The idea of linking science to human rights has clearly underpinned UNESCO's position and advice during the COVID-19 pandemic. For example, it is a central tenet of the statements issued by the Organizations' ethics bodies, COMEST and IBC on global ethical considerations and on global vaccines equity and solidarity.[36]

It should be noted that all UNESCO science-related instruments – being declarations or recommendations and not treaties – are not legally binding upon States. Moreover, their monitoring is mostly State-driven[37] and therefore not comparable to that relating to UN human rights treaties and their expert bodies.

Yet, these instruments demonstrate a large degree of consensus among States on the need to promote science as a public good accessible to all and to integrate human rights norms and principles into the advancement and promotion of science and technology and related policies. At the same time, it is important that the articulation of the link between science and human rights goes beyond the realm of aspirations.

The General Comment on science and economic, social and cultural rights,[38] adopted by the Committee on Economic, Social and Cultural Rights, is a milestone in removing some of the normative ambiguity. The General Comment reserves an important place for the work of UNESCO. Further to reiterating the definition of science developed by UNESCO, the General Comment recognizes particularly the Universal Declaration on Bioethics and Human Rights and the Recommendation on Science and Scientific Researchers, as sources of inspiration for the elaboration of the relationship between science and human rights. The various dimensions of

---

[34] More information about this process is available at: https://en.unesco.org/artificial-intelligence/ethics.
[35] More information about this process is available at: https://en.unesco.org/science-sustainable-future/open-science/recommendation.
[36] Statement on COVID-19: ethical considerations from a global perspective, Document SHS/IBC-COMEST/COVID-19 REV, April 6, 2020; UNESCO's ethics commissions call for global vaccines equity and solidarity, Document SHS/BIO/IBC-COMEST/COVID-19 Vaccines, February 24, 2021.
[37] According to Article 18 of the *Rules of Procedure concerning recommendations to Member States and international conventions covered by the terms of Article IV, paragraph 4, of the Constitution* (adopted by the General Conference at its 5th session, and amended at its 7th, 17th, 25th, and 32nd sessions), "The General Conference shall entrust the examination of the reports on such conventions and recommendations received from Member States to the Executive Board."
[38] Committee on Economic, Social and Cultural Rights, General Comment No. 25 (2020) on Science and economic, social and cultural rights Art. 15.1.b, 15.2, 15.3, and 15.4, April 7, 2020, UN Doc. E/C.12/GC/25.

academic freedom,[39] protection against harm,[40] sharing benefits of scientific and technological advancements,[41] international cooperation,[42] and science-based decision-making[43] – that the Committee considers part of the core obligations of States in the implementation of the right to enjoy the benefits of scientific progress[44] – are prominent in those UNESCO instruments.

In light of this development, the emphasis now needs to be placed on developing appropriate tools, instruments, and guidance for States and other stakeholders to implement these ambitious standards through sustainable laws, policies, and practices. A large part of the challenge ahead derives from the breadth of the approach. Indeed, a comprehensive vision of science – going beyond benefits sharing, and the prevention of the negative effects of scientific development – emerges as the necessary point of departure for all related efforts. The UNESCO instruments actually build that case convincingly. However, while a comprehensive approach can respond more adequately to the complexity of the issues at stake, it also raises the difficulty of translating the vision into praxis. In the absence of clear guidance and extensive State practice, the numerous and broad principles contained in the 2017 Recommendation could hamper or discourage implementation and risk transforming the instrument into an empty shell. The first monitoring of the 2017 Recommendation, launched in 2020, offers an opportunity for addressing some of the many operational challenges. However, unless that process engenders the development of specific programs by UNESCO, its Member States, and other stakeholders, the hurdles will remain high if not insurmountable.

Clearly, a positive change also depends on the uptake of issues linked to the right to enjoy the benefits of scientific progress and its applications by the Committee in its examination of periodic reports. Current reporting and the related discussions with States Parties are insufficient. The recently adopted General Comment could be an excellent tool to promote such reporting and discussions before the CESCR. An ideal development would be that monitoring by the Committee and that of the UNESCO instruments evolve to be seen as mutually beneficial and reinforcing one another. The enhanced operational convergence resulting from such an approach is likely to spill over into other human rights monitoring processes, including the Universal Periodic Review of the UN Human Rights Council where broader science-related issues remain absent.

Investing further in strengthening coordination and coherence across the UN system towards a closer articulation between science and human rights should be a priority in the years to come. Integrated approaches are necessary in view of the

[39] Ibid, paras. 3, 14, 15, 46, and 86.
[40] Ibid, paras. 19 and 56.
[41] Ibid, paras. 61, 62, 80, 82, and 83.
[42] Ibid, Section VI, paras. 77–84.
[43] Ibid, paras. 54 and 75.
[44] Ibid, para. 54.

multitude of entities working in the vast realm of science. They become even more compelling given the interconnectedness between the different scientific fields at a time when the UN is expected to focus increasingly on accelerating the implementation of Agenda 2030 while coping with the consequences of the COVID-19 pandemic. The September 2019 SDG Summit addressed an urgent call for accelerated action, premised on human rights and the "leave no one behind" vision. It also reiterated the importance of science, technology and innovation for sustainable development, placing emphasis inter alia on promoting the use of scientific evidence from all fields, empowering all persons with relevant knowledge and skills and fostering international cooperation.[45] Furthermore, the UN General Assembly acknowledged the need for science-based comprehensive and coordinated responses to the COVID-19 pandemic.[46]

Given the frenetic pace of scientific innovation but also its critical role in addressing challenges to human well-being – the COVID-19 pandemic being a tragic reminder thereof – it is crucial that the discussion about operationalizing the link between science and human rights advances urgently and that it involves all concerned stakeholders. Their ownership of contemplated solutions will be a key success factor. The increasing focus of scientific and engineering communities on problem-solving in relation to development challenges presages that a call for cooperation will not remain unanswered.

---

[45] *Gearing up for a decade of action and delivery for sustainable development: political declaration of the Sustainable Development Goals Summit (24–25 September 2019)*, as endorsed by the UN General Assembly by virtue of Resolution 74/4 of October 15, 2019, para. 27 (g).

[46] General Assembly Resolution A/RES/74/306, Comprehensive and coordinated response to the coronavirus disease (COVID-19) pandemic, September 15, 2020.

8

Considering the Right to Enjoy the Benefits of Scientific Progress and Its Applications As a Cultural Right

A Change in Perspective

Mylène Bidault[*]

Whether the right to enjoy the benefits of scientific progress and its applications is a cultural right is a fundamental question and far from a matter of mere form.

A positive answer invites us to reconsider the meaning of, and to give full scope to, the "right to science" increasingly invoked today in academic and NGO circles, as well as by human rights mechanisms. Considering the right to enjoy the benefits of scientific progress and its applications as a cultural right means understanding it as an integral part of the rights that enable people to access and make use of the most diverse sources of knowledge and the cultural resources most meaningful for them. It also means enabling people to contribute to those resources, and to use them for the benefit of their own dignity and development.

Consequently, this right is more than simply a right to science. The time has come to speak of a much more substantial "right to participate in scientific life" and to see it as a component of the right to participate in cultural life. This right enables everyone to have access to, and contribute to, the development of science, and to exercise his or her critical and scientific spirit in everyday life.

This does not mean that everyone ought suddenly to become a high-level scientific researcher; but rather, that everyone can aspire to be a researcher in his or her own spheres of interest, using and deploying knowledge for the benefit of his or her own development. Herein lies the eminently human and emancipatory dimension of this right.

---

[*] This chapter is taken from a presentation made during the Day of General Discussion on the right to enjoy the benefits of scientific progress and its applications and the other provisions of article 15 of the International Covenant on Economic, Social and Cultural Rights, on the relationship between science and economic, social and cultural rights, organized on October 9, 2018 by the Committee on Economic, Social and Cultural Rights. I would like to thank Patrice Meyer-Bisch for our discussions on this topic, which were very helpful to me. The views expressed in this chapter are personal and do not necessarily reflect those of the Office of the High Commissioner for Human Rights.

8.1 PURE FORMAL REASONS

Several elements, both in international human rights treaties and declarations, as well as in the practice of monitoring mechanisms, call for the right to enjoy the benefits of scientific progress and its applications to be considered as a cultural right.

In the first place, the right to enjoy the benefits of scientific progress and its applications is often found juxtaposed with the right to take part in cultural life in universal and regional texts. In particular, it is to be found in Article 27 of the Universal Declaration of Human Rights (UDHR) and Article 15 of the International Covenant on Economic, Social and Cultural Rights (ICESCR), which are usually considered to set out cultural rights.[1]

Furthermore, the resolutions of the Human Rights Council establishing and subsequently renewing the mandate of the Special Rapporteur in the field of cultural rights expressly mention the right to enjoy the benefits of scientific progress and its applications as an integral part of the Rapporteur's mandate. The Special Rapporteur has devoted an entire thematic report to this right.[2] Member States of the Council seem to have naturally considered, by consensus, that the right to enjoy the benefits of scientific progress and its applications is a cultural right.

8.2 SUBSTANTIVE REASONS

But these elements are ultimately only formal indications. The argument that the right to enjoy the benefits of scientific progress and its applications should be considered as a cultural right is supported by far more substantial grounds. Its proximity in the texts to the right to take part in cultural life seems to be no coincidence. It appears, at least, to be the result of a particularly accurate intuition on the part of the authors of the founding texts. And, as will be explained below, it makes it possible today to deploy the scope of this right in a far more powerful and significant manner.

When one looks more closely at the structure of Article 15 of ICESCR, one understands that, when taken as a whole, it is the universal right of access to culture and science that is protected by this provision, as Farida Shaheed, the first Special Rapporteur in the field of cultural rights, has emphasized.[3] The right is accompanied by correlative obligations on States to respect and protect creative freedoms; to respect and protect the moral and material interests resulting from scientific, literary or artistic productions; to ensure the conservation, development and diffusion of science and culture; and to develop international contacts and cooperation in these fields.

---

[1] Many other provisions in international treaties do protect cultural rights. For an in-depth overview, see Mylène Bidault, *La protection internationale des droits culturels*, Brussels, Bruylant, 2009, 559 pages.
[2] A/HRC/20/26, The right to enjoy the benefits of scientific progress and its applications.
[3] A/HRC/20/26, § 17.

But there is an even more fundamental reason for considering the right to enjoy the benefits of scientific progress and its applications as a cultural right: *science is part of culture*.

8.2.1 *The Scientific Field As an Integral Part of the Cultural Field*

The right to take part in cultural life necessarily implies a right to take part in scientific life, which must be understood as legally based on both Article 15(1)(a) of the ICESCR (right to take part in cultural life) and Article 15(1)(b) (right to enjoy the benefits of scientific progress and its applications). The second element is in fact a specification of the first one.

Let me explain what is meant by "cultural field." The 2007 Fribourg Declaration on Cultural Rights proposes a definition of "culture" as covering "the values, beliefs, convictions, languages, knowledge and the arts, traditions, institutions and ways of life through which a person or group expresses their humanity and the meanings that they give to their existence and to their development" (Article 2).[4]

This definition has been a major source of inspiration for both the Committee on Economic, Social and Cultural Rights (hereinafter the Committee) and the Special Rapporteur in the field of cultural rights throughout her work.

The cultural field is therefore very broad, as reflected in the list inserted in the Fribourg Declaration: values, beliefs, convictions, languages, knowledge, arts, traditions, institutions and ways of life. In its General Comment No. 21 on the right to take part in cultural life, the Committee defined what was covered by "cultural life" and added elements to this list, including in particular "methods of production or technology" (§ 13). The Committee stressed that "culture is a broad, inclusive concept encompassing all manifestations of human existence" (§ 11). It is, again according to the Committee, "an interactive process whereby individuals and communities, while preserving their specificities and purposes, give expression to the culture of humanity" (§ 12).

The Committee has further clarified that science is a part of culture in its new General Comment 25 (2020) on science and economic, social and cultural rights.[5] A whole paragraph 10 is devoted to this aspect. Reiterating that culture is an inclusive

---

[4] The Fribourg Declaration on cultural rights is a civil society document adopted in 2007. It brings together and unfolds cultural rights scattered throughout international texts. It is the result of consultations and work carried out by the members of the Fribourg Group, inter alia with UNESCO, the Council of Europe and the International Organization of the Francophonie and has inspired much work at the international and national levels on cultural rights. It has been supported by more than fifty national and international experts, including members of the CESCR and Special Rapporteurs at that time. It has now been translated into more than ten languages. For more information, please see Patrice Meyer-Bisch and Mylène Bidault, *Déclarer les droits culturels, Commentaire de la Déclaration de Fribourg*, Schulthess, Bruxelles, Genève, Zurich, Bâle, Bruylant, 154 pages (freely available on Academia); https://droitsculturels.org/observatoire/la-declaration-de-fribourg/; or simply use an internet search engine to see the multiple uses of the Declaration by various actors.

[5] E/C.12/GC/25.

concept encompassing all manifestations of human existence, the Committee added that "Cultural life is therefore larger than science, as it includes other aspects of human existence; it is, however, reasonable to include scientific activity in cultural life. Thus, the right of everyone to take part in cultural life includes the right of every person to take part in scientific progress and in decisions concerning its direction."

This does not mean that the field of culture is a great pool of conceptual magma in which all human endeavors merge and agglomerate. The specificity of the scientific field, that is, what makes it an element apart from the other elements of culture, must be defined (see Section 8.3.2.below).

8.3 SIGNIFICANT IMPACTS

When considering why the question of whether the right to enjoy the benefits of scientific progress and its applications is a cultural right is important, one might be tempted to ask what difference such an understanding actually makes. Is this a purely theoretical discussion without practical implications, or are there important consequences to understanding the right to enjoy the benefits of scientific progress and its applications as a cultural right? Framing the question this way will help evolve our understanding of the content of the right.

8.3.1 What Is a Cultural Right?

Important elements of definition have been provided by the Special Rapporteur in the field of cultural rights, who has drawn inspiration from the work of the Committee and its General Comment No. 21, as well as from the work of the Fribourg Group. Several elements have been identified:

- Cultural rights are the rights of persons "to develop and freely express their humanity, their world view and the meaning they give to their existence and development."
- People do this "through, inter alia, values, beliefs, convictions, languages, knowledge and the arts, institutions and ways of life."
- Cultural rights also protect "access to cultural heritage as important resources enabling such identification and development processes."[6]

Cultural rights are therefore a broad set of freedoms and rights of access to and participation in resources. They protect:

- The freedom of persons, alone or in community with others, to choose and build their identity, world view and the meaning they give to their humanity;

---

[6] A/HRC/14/36, § 9; A/67/287 on the enjoyment of cultural rights by women on an equal basis with men, § 7; A/HRC/31/59 (2016), § 7.

- The freedom of persons, alone or in community with others, to participate in cultural life while expressing that identity, world view or humanity; and
- The rights of persons, alone or in community with others, to have access to the resources necessary for the development and fulfilment of their identities, world views and humanity, which implies the right to know, understand, discuss and transmit these resources, to make use of them and to participate in their development.

"Knowledge" in the broadest sense *enables* people in the same way as "beliefs" and "convictions" do. Knowledge enables individuals to build their identity, humanity and worldview, to forge their responses to adversity, to conceive of the world, and to conceive of themselves as part of this world.

It is sometimes difficult to separate beliefs from knowledge, whether these be individual or collective. Moreover, knowledge is not exclusively of a scientific nature – knowledge exists in the field of arts, for example, and there exist even more diverse forms of knowledge. It is from all these resources that individuals draw in order to develop themselves, arranging such resources at the individual level in a way that is very particular to them: to express their creativity, to influence their living conditions, or to overcome an ordeal such as an illness or a disaster. It is through these resources that people can "aspire" to a better future by identifying the elements they consider essential for a life with dignity.

Thus, as Farida Shaheed has strongly expressed:

> The link between the right to science and the right to culture can be further understood with regard to people's ability to "aspire." A growing body of literature suggests that the ability to aspire – namely, to conceive of a better future that is not only desirable but attainable – is an important cultural capability that needs to be supported and developed, especially among the marginalized and vulnerable. Aspirations embody people's conceptions of elements deemed essential for a life with dignity. Never a mere individual exercise, aspirations are informed by, and in turn inform, communities of shared cultural values and draw upon cultural heritage, including accessible, accumulated scientific knowledge. New scientific knowledge and innovations increase available options, thereby strengthening people's capacity to envisage a better future for which access to specific technologies may sometimes be pivotal.[7]

8.3.2 *The Specificity of the Scientific Field Within the Cultural Field*

One important question is to define the specificity of scientific resources within this set of essential resources: what makes them different from other cultural resources.

---

[7] A/HRC/20/26, § 20, in reference to Arjun Appadurai, "The Capacity to Aspire: Culture and the Terms of Recognition," in *Culture and Public Action*, Vijayendra Rao et Micheal Walton (eds.), Stanford University Press, 2004.

Article 15(1)(b) requires that this specificity be developed. Some elements of this are provided, again, in the report by Farida Shaheed:

> As for other cultural rights, a prerequisite for implementing the right to enjoy the benefits of scientific progress and its applications is ensuring the necessary conditions for everyone to continuously engage in critical thinking about themselves and the world they inhabit, and to have the opportunity and wherewithal to interrogate, investigate and contribute new knowledge with ideas, expressions and innovative applications, regardless of frontiers. More precisely, the right to participate in cultural life entails ensuring conditions that allow people to reconsider, create and contribute to cultural meanings and manifestations in a continuously developing manner. The right to enjoy the benefits of science and its applications entails the same possibilities in the field of science, understood as knowledge that is testable and refutable, including revisiting and refuting existing theorems and understandings.[8]

The Committee, in its General Comment, takes a similar approach, cautious to refer to the specificity of science, and referring to the definition offered in the 2017 UNESCO Recommendation on Science and Scientific Researchers.[9]

To develop themselves, therefore, people draw on cultural heritage, including "accessible scientific knowledge," which is extremely diverse; and thus we should not be afraid to speak of "scientific diversity" as an integral part of "cultural diversity." There is no such thing as science on the one hand and culture on the other. And since we talk about cultures today in the plural form, we must also talk about sciences, given the great diversity of scientific disciplines and traditions. All of them have their contribution to make in terms of the way in which we face our world.

For example, the various medical traditions are valuable, ranging from the very Cartesian vision, which understands the human person as a machine that can be examined and healed piece by piece, to the most holistic visions that understand the human person in its inseparable dimension body-mind, in permanent relationship with its environment. This is what many non-Western approaches teach us, or reteach us. To lose this diversity would be an appalling impoverishment.

We must also be careful not to restrict the scope of what we mean by scientific, at the risk of favoring some scientific traditions to the detriment of others and thereby preventing potentially valuable and culturally diverse contributions. We must not forget too that behind the scenes of debates on what is or is not science lie powerful political dynamics and asymmetries as well as significant economic stakes. There are fierce debates, for instance, over the question of which medical drugs will or will not be covered by medical insurances, a major economic issue for

---

[8] A/HRC/20/26, § 18.
[9] § 4.

pharmaceutical companies. Attacks on homeopathy do not seem to be unrelated to these issues.

8.4 FROM THE RIGHT TO ENJOY THE BENEFITS OF SCIENTIFIC PROGRESS AND ITS APPLICATIONS TO THE RIGHT TO PARTICIPATE IN SCIENTIFIC LIFE

One matter considered by the Committee during its discussions on the text of the General Comment concerned whether it would be appropriate to speak of a "right to science," rather than of a "right to enjoy the benefits of scientific progress and its applications." It is true that the expressions "right to culture" and "right to science" are often used to refer to the rights contained in Article 15 of the ICESCR.

These expressions, which are also sometimes used by the Special Rapporteur in the field of cultural rights, are intended to give full scope to the rights set out in Article 15, which, it should be recalled, enshrines a universal, fundamental right of participation in and access to culture, including science. This was the approach adopted by Farida Shaheed, who also found that "right to science" was a strong formula that was more striking.

A similar proposal had been made by the Committee in a Draft General Comment that it circulated for comments on January 20, 2020. A whole paragraph 89, at the end of the document, proposed to use a "single broad concept named the human right to science." However, that proposal was not retained in the final version of the General Comment.

Indeed, if we are not careful, these expressions ("right to culture," "right to science") can misrepresent the content of the rights and give a truncated and incomplete vision of them. On the one hand, with such expressions, culture remains separated from science. Science, understood as "verifiable and testable knowledge," must not be situated in opposition to "culture," but to "belief" (although there are some grey areas). Furthermore, we still speak of "culture" (which culture?) and "science" in the singular form, even though we are in front of what should be called "cultural" and "scientific diversity."

Finally, this risks reducing the right to the notion of access only (whether to culture or to science). While access to both culture and science is obviously extremely important, in its General Comment No. 21, the Committee considered the right to participate in cultural life as concerning rights to participate in, contribute to, *and* have access to cultural life. A reductionist access-based approach risks reducing the rights-holder conceptually to a "consumer" of rights, whereas the spirit of human rights demands that he or she should be understood as a citizen and actor, an agent of his or her own rights.

If these expressions are used, then they must be defined so as to avoid these pitfalls, emphasizing not only the crucial issue of access, but also participation and contribution, which are no less fundamental.

8.4.1 Towards a Right to Participate in Scientific Life

The Committee, in General Comment No. 25, has chosen not to refer to a "right to science." It underlined that "The right enshrined in article 15 (1) (b) encompasses not only a right to receive the benefits of the applications of scientific progress, but also a right to participate in scientific progress. Thus, it is the right to participate in and to enjoy the benefits of scientific progress and its applications." The latter expression is used by the Committee throughout General Comment No. 25.[10]

It is useful, as the Committee did, to read Article 15 of the ICESCR in conjunction with Article 27 of the UDHR, which wording better corresponds to the nature of the right as a cultural right. The Universal Declaration sets out a right to "share in scientific advancement and its benefits." The use of the phrase "share in" unveils the cultural element of the right, and gives context to its placement within a provision rooted in wider cultural considerations. Therefore, an ambitious approach is to understand the provision as protecting a right to participate in scientific "life," modeled on the right to participate in cultural life. This gives us a fresh and valuable perspective on what the right truly means.

Clearly there are surface-level criticisms that can be leveled against such formula. In particular, not everyone can be a scientific researcher. But that would be a restrictive, even reductionist, reading of the right if formulated this way. Life is complex and multi-faceted and we all participate in different ways. A right to participate in scientific life does, therefore, not imply that we all ought to become high-level researchers. Rather it means that we might become researchers in our own fields and in relation to our own concerns and aspirations; that we use knowledge and refine it for our own personal development.

Farmers who cultivate their land, for example, must have access to all relevant data and information in order to eke from that land the greatest possible yield. That data is collated, analyzed, tested, and applied; processes are improved. The cycle is iterated to meet new challenges or obstacles. Farmers are not mere performers implementing guidelines and instructions manuals. They are participants, in the fullest sense of the word: observing, being creative, practicing science, adapting it, improving it. Let us draw a parallel, this time, with the right to artistic freedom: the question is not for each person to develop into a locally or world-renowned artist, but to be able to enjoy the artistic experience, for his or her own development; to be creative and to contribute, in one's own ways, to cultural life.

[10] § 11.

There are many advantages to talking about participation in scientific life. It enables an understanding that cultural life is multifaceted, with religious, artistic, scientific and family dimensions, for example, which all are key to the development and fulfilment of people. These facets are interrelated. All cultural freedoms, including scientific freedoms, enable the emergence of a critical spirit, the imagining of possibilities, and individual and collective emancipation.

For here we find ourselves at the heart of individual freedoms. In many areas, for example in the field of the environment (think of global warming) or public health (think of sugar in food), it is a question of practicing critical thinking on a daily basis (I insist here on the term "practicing," which I will talk about later). Why do some people lie? Because there is a lack of scientific knowledge among the public. It is certainly not in the interest of those who dominate or manipulate to promote a right to participate in scientific life.

Thus, the meaning of this right is not limited to a right of access to material results or technologies (to a progress that would be a given, indisputable), but also includes a right of access to knowledge, and to conditions allowing the development of scientific and critical thinking. That is why there is a very strong link between the right to participate in cultural life and the rights to information and education. The issue is not only about teaching "scientific content." It is above all about providing references, knowledge and tools to enable people to make informed choices. It is about instilling curiosity and critical and scientific spirit, offering ways to develop one's thinking in order to be free and autonomous. It is about knowing that knowledge is verifiable and contestable. The right to education and the right to participate in scientific life both require that science education programs be systematically provided at all levels.

Participation in science also means emphasizing people's right and ability to access, use and improve cultural resources, including scientific resources, for their development and the implementation of their own rights.

Thus, for example, the person with a chronic illness needs to be able to access the best medical care available, while at the same time being put in a position to keep a critical mind, to decide for himself or herself on the care provided (understanding its side effects), to draw on knowledge to treat himself or herself, and to build his or her healing power on the basis of the traditions and beliefs that make sense to him or her. As underlined by the Committee, "States parties must guarantee everyone the right to choose or refuse the treatment they want with the full knowledge of the risks and benefits of the relevant treatment, subject to any limitations that meet the criteria of article 4 of the Covenant."[11]

This is why it would be useful to take up the triptych used in General Comment No. 21 to describe the content of the right to take part in cultural life: "participate, contribute, access." It could be improved and become "access, practice, contribute."

[11] General Comment 25, para. 44.

It is here that I return to the notion of "practice," which helps to emphasize that everyone participates by developing his or her daily practice.

8.5 CONCLUSION

The inclusion of the right to share in the benefits of science within the main provisions of the UDHR and the ICESCR devoted to cultural rights is fundamental. For culture is also science. This is not to level the playing field and consider science to be of the same nature as a philosophical or religious conviction, practice or way of life. No, it does have a specificity, and must be understood as "verifiable and contestable knowledge," with "the possibility of revising and rejecting existing conceptions and theorems."

However, science is not above culture either, it is part of it. And it is from a multitude of cultural resources, including scientific resources, that people build their identity, their world view and their humanity.

9

Implications of the Right to Science for People with Disabilities

Valerie J. Bradley

This chapter will explore the unique and critical importance of the right to science for people with intellectual, physical, and mental health disabilities. To put the subject in a global context, approximately one billion people, or 15 percent of the world's population, experience some form of disability, and disability prevalence is higher for developing countries. One-fifth of the global total, or between 110 million and 190 million people, experience significant disabilities (The World Bank, 2019). Science and the products of science are critical to the realization of the human rights of people with disabilities and to their inclusion in society. This is especially true in the time of the corona virus pandemic which has presented additional challenges for people with disabilities over and above those visited on the general population.

The right to science, this chapter will suggest, is a powerful tool to support and inform other rights as they relate to people with disabilities. In an age dominated by fast-paced technological advances, the right to science represents a meaningful way to protect the relationship between the scientific community and people with disabilities. It is vital that people with disabilities are not excluded from decisions about scientific priorities, the conduct of scientific research, and the design of technology that will impact their lives. Diversity in the development of new technology such as algorithms, for example, is essential in order to reflect the characteristics of those people who will ultimately be governed and affected by them. For example, informed consent policies for people with intellectual disabilities are required in order to ensure that they are neither exploited nor excluded from scientific studies.

The ensuing discussion in this chapter will include the history of the disability rights movement, the ways in which the Convention on the Rights of Persons With Disabilities reaffirms the right to science, the role of science in the lives of people with disabilities – both positive and negative, the importance of scientifically based treatment interventions, the importance of including people with disabilities in scientific research and the ability of people with disabilities to gain access to scientific findings. It will conclude with some recommendations for a more inclusive approach that embraces the views and needs of people with disabilities in the scientific enterprise, including access to science as part of international monitoring of the CRPD by the Special Rapporteur and the Committee on the Rights of People with Disabilities.

9.1 HISTORY OF THE DISABILITY RIGHTS MOVEMENT

The 1960s are remembered as a period of disruption. This disruption took the form of social protest against racial segregation, authoritarianism, colonialism, discrimination against women, and an unpopular war. In the United States, this period also saw the mobilization of people with disabilities and their families. In the mental health field, consumer groups like the Mental Patients Liberation Front took on involuntary treatment and forced medication. They argued for housing, jobs, and income supports in addition to psychiatric services (Chamberlin, 1990). In the developmental disabilities field, the fledgling Association for Retarded Children (now The Arc) organized families around the country to advocate for a more positive public perception of children with intellectual disabilities and their potential (The Arc, n.d.). They sought concrete reforms such as access to education, preschool, and jobs. In the physical disability community, important figures such as Ed Roberts – one of the founders of the historic Berkeley Center for Independent Living in 1972 – rallied people with physical disabilities to take charge of their own lives, to demand the support they needed to live independently, and to reject the medical model and the notion that they needed to be fixed (Anderson, 2013). Finally, activism among the elderly also burgeoned during this period, as groups like the Gray Panthers argued against forced retirement and in favor of better health care, housing, and income support (Sanjek, 2009).

The emergence of advocacy for the human and legal rights of people with disabilities was not limited to the USA. Similar movements were taking place around the world as people with disabilities and family members advocated access to education, income support, employment, and inclusion in their communities. In 1969, a group of parent-sponsored organizations from around the world formed The International League of Societies for the Mentally Handicapped (Dybwad, 1975). The group would later become known as Inclusion International. Subsequently, multiple groups representing specific disability organizations formed in multiple countries, but it wasn't until 1999 that an international pan-disability alliance was forged – The International Disability Alliance (International Disability Alliance, "Who We Are"). The Alliance brought together a global network of previously separate disability organizations under one umbrella. Some of the groups that joined forces were the World Blind Union, the World Federation of the Deaf, the World Network of Users and Survivors of Psychiatry, and the International Federation of Hard of Hearing People. Regional networks such as the Arab Organization of People with Disabilities and the Latin American Disabled Persons Organization were included in 2007, as well as regional organizations of persons with disabilities and their families.

The IDA was instrumental in establishing the International Disability Caucus (IDC) which was comprised of global, regional, and national organizations of persons with disabilities and allied non-governmental organizations (NGOs). The IDC became a critical player in negotiations regarding the provisions of the United Nations Convention on the Rights of Persons with Disabilities (CRPD) (UN General Assembly, 2007)).

According to an interview with Diana Samarasan of the Disability Rights Fund (Bell, 2014), the negotiations that preceded the passage of the CRPD were unique in that one-third of the seats in the working group that drafted the treaty were reserved for people with disabilities. Samarasan stressed that the process brought together people with disabilities from around the world and from different disability organizations including blind people, people with intellectual disabilities, people with psychosocial disabilities, people with physical disabilities, and little people. For the first time, they had a platform and a target for joint advocacy. The IDA now has a secretariat in New York and in Geneva. In addition to monitoring state compliance with the CRPD, the IDA is involved with all of the UN development organizations for inclusion of people of disabilities.

9.2 RIGHT TO SCIENCE AND THE CONVENTION ON THE RIGHTS OF PERSONS WITH DISABILITIES

9.2.1 *Background of the Right to Science*

The human rights of people with disabilities articulated in the Convention on the Rights of People with Disabilities directly connect to the principles and aspirations of another right grounded in affirmation of global human rights – the Right to Science (hereafter RtS). The RtS posits generally that all citizens have a human right to enjoy the benefits of scientific progress. The right can be traced to Article 27 of the United Nations 1948 Universal Declaration of Human Rights, which was adopted in the wake of the human carnage that resulted from World War II. In 1966, the UN adopted the International Covenant on Economic, Social and Cultural Rights which codified the provisions of the Declaration under international law. Article 15(1) of the Covenant states that:The States Parties to the present Covenant recognize the right of everyone:

(a) To take part in cultural life;
(b) To enjoy the benefits of scientific progress and its applications;
(c) To benefit from the protection of the moral and material interests resulting from any scientific, literary or artistic production of which he is the author.

According to Porsdam-Mann, et al., (2018), who conducted a methodical review of the scholarship on the RtS, the right has not received the attention needed to make it a force for scientific freedom, access, policy reform, and improvement of human rights. In order to elevate the RtS, it will be necessary for the scientific community as well as those who benefit from the fruits of scientific research to find ways of promoting the right. One of the communities with a direct interest in RtS is people with disabilities and their families.

9.2.2 *Provisions of the CRPD*

The Convention on the Rights of People with Disabilities asserted a broad range of rights and obligations on States consistent with the aspirations of the international disability rights movement. The provisions went well beyond traditional medical and clinical concerns to embrace the multiple aspects of a quality and valued life. That included the right to live a full life in the community. The CRPD definition of the beneficiaries of the provisions, stated in Article 1, is as follows: "People with disabilities include those who have long-term physical, mental, intellectual or sensory impairments which in interaction with various barriers may hinder their full and effective participation in society on an equal basis with others."

Prior to the CRPD, there were other declarations on the rights of people with disabilities, but they were not binding on States. During 1981, the International Year of Disabled Persons, there were activities geared towards bringing attention to the rights of people with disabilities including conferences, research projects, and policy initiatives. This included the First Founding Congress of Disabled People International, in Singapore from November 30 to December 6. In 1982, the UN General Assembly took a major step towards ensuring effective follow-up to the International Year by adopting, on December 3, 1982, the World Programme of Action concerning Disabled Persons. The Programme restructured disability policy into three distinct areas: prevention, rehabilitation, and equalization of opportunities.

The 1990s were deemed the Decade of Disabled People. In recognition of this, the United Nations passed Standard Rules on the Equalization of Opportunities for Persons with Disabilities in 1993. The twenty-two rules were arranged in four chapters – preconditions for equal participation, target areas for equal participation, implementation measures, and the monitoring mechanism – and cover all aspects of life of persons with disabilities.

The CRPD was an important advance on previous initiatives since it required compliance on the part of signatories. Unlike previous initiatives, the CRPD was both a development and human rights instrument as well as a policy instrument that was cross-disability and cross-sectoral. The UN convention has now been signed by 164 countries worldwide and ratified by 180; 94 countries have signed the Optional

Protocol to the Convention, and 95 have ratified it. It is therefore legally binding on those states who have ratified it.

The CRPD has taken on even more relevance during the coronavirus pandemic. The Council of Europe (2020) has noted:

> Although the ongoing crisis is unprecedented, respect for international human rights standards must be at the heart of state responses to it. In this connection, it is important to remember that Article 11 of the UN Convention on the Rights of Persons with Disabilities (CRPD), ratified by 46 of the 47 member states of the Council of Europe, provides that states shall take "all necessary measures to ensure the protection and safety of persons with disabilities in situations of risk, including situations of armed conflict, humanitarian emergencies and the occurrence of natural disasters."

The specific protections outlined above and the antidiscrimination provisions of the CRPD are particularly important during a pandemic given threats to the accessibility of needed supports concern as well among persons with disabilities and their advocates that they will be left behind in accessing lifesaving medical interventions.

9.2.3 *Implications of the CRPD for the Right to Science*

The Convention marks a "paradigm shift" in attitudes and approaches to persons with disabilities. Persons with disabilities are not viewed as "objects" of charity, medical treatment, or social protection; rather as "subjects" with rights, who are capable of claiming those rights and making decisions for their own lives based on their free and informed consent as well as being active members of society (United Nations. Convention on the Rights of Persons with Disabilities and Its Optional Protocol (PPT) (UN CRPD PPT)). The author argues that for people with disabilities to realize the expansive rights laid out in the CRPD they must rely heavily on the availability of both the products of scientific inquiry as well as scientific research that generates evidence-based practices and policies that lay out successful intervention strategies. Some of the technological and other innovations that have made it possible for individuals to live in communities, to be educated, to be employed, to communicate, and to generally lead lives of meaning include ("What Are Some Types of Assistive Devices" n.d.):

- GPS technology that assists people navigate their environment;
- Augmentative and alternative communication devices;
- Computer software and hardware, such as voice recognition programs, screen readers, and screen enlargement applications, to help people with mobility and sensory impairments use computers and mobile devices;
- Adaptive equipment for a range of functions including eating, bathing, etc.
- Remote monitoring by direct support professionals in order to augment staff;

- Tools such as automatic page turners, book holders, and adapted pencil grips to help children with disabilities to participate in educational activities;
- Smart homes that can control lighting, climate, entertainment systems, appliances, and security and alarm systems;
- Universal architectural design;
- Health monitoring and health aids and prompts;
- Adapted cell phones;
- Mobility aids (electric wheelchairs, prosthetic devices, etc.);
- Hearing aids;
- Cognitive aids, including computer or electrical assistive devices, to help people with memory, attention, or other challenges in their thinking skills.

RIGHTS IN THE CRPD

- Right to life, liberty and security of the person
- Equal recognition before the law and legal capacity
- Freedom from torture
- Freedom from exploitation, violence and abuse
- Right to respect physical and mental integrity
- Freedom of movement and nationality
- Right to live in the community
- Respect for privacy
- Respect for home and the family
- Right to education
- Right to health
- Right to work
- Right to adequate standard of living
- Right to participate in political and public life
- Right to participation in cultural life
- Freedom of expression and opinion

In addition to these assistive technologies, there are also rehabilitation technologies that aid people with other than congenital disabilities including ("What Are Some Types of Rehabilitation Technologies," n.d.):

- Specialized robots help people regain and improve function in arms or legs after a stroke.
- Virtual reality allows people recovering from injury to retrain themselves to perform motions within a virtual environment.
- Musculoskeletal modeling and simulations can help improve assistive aids or physical therapies.

- Transcranial magnetic stimulation (TMS) helps people who have had a stroke recover movement and brain function.
- Transcranial direct current stimulation helps patients to recover movement following a stroke or other conditions.
- Analysis of human motion to gives a detailed picture of a person's specific movement challenges to guide proper therapy.

The global importance of access to technology for people with disabilities internationally was memorialized at the 71st World Health Assembly (WHA, 2018) during which the Resolution on Improving Access to Assistive Technology was unanimously approved. The Resolution calls on Member States to develop, implement, and strengthen policies and programs to improve access to assistive technology (AT) within universal health coverage. The Resolution was sponsored by Pakistan and requires the World Health Organization (WHO) to prepare a global report by 2021 on access to AT in Member States. The Resolution makes specific mention of the Convention on the Rights of Persons with Disabilities as well as the 2030 Agenda for Sustainable Development as actions taken internationally that underpin and provide a rationale for AT access.

The resolution also recognizes the need to support the application of technology with trained personnel to ensure maintenance, and quality and safety. In addition, it requires Member states to develop national lists of priority products, to carry out research, to develop new products, and to invest in barrier-free environments so that all people who need assistive technology can make optimum use of it.

The provisions of the CRPD, when combined with the human right to science – and the move to establish a right to technology – provide a road map for understanding the ways in which the right can guarantee access to the technology and other scientific advances needed to support an enhanced quality of life for people with disabilities. In other words, taken together, the CRPD and the right science provide both the aspiration and the means for achieving lives of equality and inclusion.

9.3 EVIDENCE-BASED PRACTICES

In order to ensure that the treatments, therapies, rehabilitation techniques, technologies, and other interventions applied to maintain or improve functioning of individuals with disabilities are efficacious, scientific proof of such efficacy is considered the gold standard. Evidence is defined as (Singer, Agran, and Spooner, 2017, page 63):

> formal objectivist research that uses experimental control to make a case for a causal or functional relation between a practice and its outcomes, that is, to rule out plausible alternative explanations. It is this ruling out of plausible alternatives that is central to the requirement that evidence be drawn from controlled experiments (e.g., randomized control trials, single-case research.

Without the use of evidence to validate such interventions, people with disabilities have been subjected to approaches that are the product of poor science, fads, or wishful thinking and that have ultimately proven to be inefficacious. In some instances, the interventions have continued even after the evidence has proved their inefficaciousness conclusively.

Singer, et al. (2017) assert that the pursuit of unproven practices is the result of "the absence of well-established evidence and an effective interface between scientific researchers and family members and practitioners" (page 67). Examples of the persistence of practices proven over and over not to result in the presumed outcome include Facilitated Communication (FC). According to a review of research on FC, it does not elicit speech from those who previously did not use words to speak via a typing device (American Psychological Association, 2003). The Autism Science Foundation (2019) has denounced a range of unproven treatments for autism including chelation therapy, nutritional supplements, hyperbaric oxygen therapy, secretin injections, and nicotine patch therapy. Patterning is a series of exercises designed to improve the "neurologic organization" of a child's neurologic impairments and has been used on children with cerebral palsy, Down Syndrome, learning disabilities, and brain injuries. The treatment, according to the American Academy of Pediatrics (1999), is based on an outmoded and oversimplified theory of brain development. Research does not support the claims by proponents that this treatment is efficacious, and its continued use is unwarranted. All of these approaches, though discredited and wasteful, have advocates to this day. While these advocates by and large operate with the best of intentions, they are depriving people with disabilities and their families of the scientific research needed to help them make informed decisions.

9.4 PEOPLE WITH DISABILITIES AS UNWITTING SCIENTIFIC SUBJECTS

The use of unproven treatment interventions on people with disabilities seems benign when compared to the multiple instances over decades of people with disabilities being included in scientific experimentation without their knowledge. For instance, in 1949, at Fernald State School (previously the Massachusetts School for the Feeble Minded), seventy-four boys aged ten to seventeen were recruited to join the "Science Club." They were given special privileges but were also given oatmeal for breakfast with milk laced with radiative tracers. While health dangers were ultimately determined to be minimal (small increase in cancer risk), neither the residents nor their families were given the opportunity to make an informed decision. In another experiment, some of the boys were injected with radioactive calcium. These experiments were approved by the Atomic Energy Commission. Ironically, some of the boys enthusiastically joined the club thinking that the scientists themselves would expose the abuse that went on at the facility (Boissoneault, 2017).

Additional examples of unwitting victims of experimentation were described in an NBC health posting by Associated Press journalist Mike Stobbe (2011). He described one study that began in 1942 that targeted male subjects who were residents of a state mental hospital in Ypsilanti, Michigan. The study involved injecting the men with an experimental flu vaccine and then exposing them to the flu months later. One of the co-authors was Dr. Jonas Salk who later discovered the polio vaccine. Given their disabilities and lack of cognitive acuity, it was not clear that any of them understood what was being done to them. Stobbe also described a second federally funded study in the 1940s that exposed men from mental hospitals in Middletown and Norwich Connecticut to hepatitis. The scientist was Dr. W. Paul Havens Jr. who was a World Health Organization expert on viral diseases.

Finally, Eric Boodman writing for *Stat* (2015) described an experiment at a Staten Island School for students with intellectual disabilities. The study, which took place from 1963 to 1966 involved feeding the children human feces in milkshakes. The chief scientist argued that he obtained consent from families, but it was not clear whether the families understood what the experiment involved. The experiment eventually led to the discovery that there were at least two types of hepatitis – Type A and Type B.

Scientists involved in these and other studies that took advantage of vulnerable and cognitively compromised individuals argued that the experiments befitted the greater good. For people with disabilities, the RtS should include an assumption that scientific progress is not achieved at the expense of their human rights such as the right to be free from exploitation, the right to health, and the right to life, liberty, and security.

9.5 PEOPLE WITH DISABILITIES AS PARTICIPANTS IN SCIENTIFIC RESEARCH

With the slogan, "Nothing About Us Without Us," people with disabilities have increasingly pressed to be included in discussions about research topics and research methods, and to be included a participant in scientific research projects. This kind of involvement has been described as "participant action research" (PAR). This approach is not limited to people with disabilities but has currency with a range of marginalized groups including minorities, indigenous peoples, and LGBTQ+ communities. With respect to PAR for people with disabilities, Balcazar, Keys, Kaplan and Suarez Balcazar (2006) noted four characteristics of this research approach (page 1): (1) the active role individuals with disabilities to define, analyze, and solve identified problems; (2) the opportunities for more accurate and authentic analysis of the social reality of people with disabilities; (3) the resulting awareness among people with disabilities about their own resources and strengths; and (4) the opportunities for improving the quality of life of people with disabilities. Stack and MacDonald (2014), following their review of the PAR literature in developmental disabilities, concluded that: "action research with adults with developmental disabilities holds promise for people with developmental disabilities, their allies within and outside the research, community, and a more inclusive society" (page 90).

The Autism community has been particularly aggressive in advocating for inclusion in research efforts specifically aimed at people on the spectrum. They argue that research has traditionally focused on causes or cures for autism and have primarily targeted children, not adults; and men, to the exclusion of women. An analysis of the 2010 National Institutes of Health autism research agenda found that of $217 million devoted to autism research in that year, only 1.5 percent of the funds went towards research on the needs of autistic adults while only 2.45 percent went towards research on the service-needs of people on the autism spectrum across the lifespan (Autism Self Advocacy Network, 2012; Office of Autism Research Coordination IACC Portfolio Analysis Web Tool, 2012). The Autistic Self-Advocacy Network has argued that people with autism should be included in determining research priorities in order to ensure that topics of concern to the community are addressed including communication strategies, building relationships, employment support, and strategies to manage their support and services.

In addition to the importance of involving people with disabilities in determining research priorities that affect their lives, it is also important to ensure the people with disabilities are included as subjects in longitudinal health and drug trials. People with disabilities have historically been left out of such studies. Without their participation, the results of these important studies will not include important information about any idiosyncratic disease markers and drug interactions affecting people with disabilities. Maya Satabello (2018) makes the case that such inclusion is of particular importance to the growing field of precision medicine that involves treatment initiatives that target the particular genome of individuals or groups of individuals relative to specific health conditions. She makes that point that if people with disabilities are not intentionally included, any scientific advances may be limited and health disparities for this population will be exacerbated.

9.6 BIG DATA AND ARTIFICIAL INTELLIGENCE DIGITAL DIVIDE

9.6.1 *Big Data Applications*

Big data, or extremely large data sets that may be analyzed to reveal patterns, trends, and associations, especially relating to human behavior and interactions, can be a substantial boon to people with disabilities. In a recent blog by the Data-Pop Alliance (2016) seven areas of research in which big data could be employed to ameliorate specific challenges that they face:

- **Voting and Representation** – including whether people with disabilities are under-represented of disenfranchised;

- **Employment** – mapping the availability and location of employment opportunities, monitoring compliance with employment mandates, or assessing the variable that predict employment success;
- **Community and Social Media** – studying people with disabilities as a network with specific characteristics, using social media to gain access to others with similar challenges, medical issues;
- **Accessibility** – using data, including crowd-sourcing, to map locations of public places, businesses, lodging, and transportation that are accessible as well as a tool determine compliance with accessibility standards;
- **National and International Programs** – comparing countries based on their implementation of national and global targets, such as the CRPD;
- **Education** – There are a variety of descriptive uses of data, in particular relating to the proportion of children with disabilities who are included in the education system (either in specially designed programs or integrated into other programs), to observing what opportunities exist for them to receive education and identifying gaps and issues in the education system. Data can also be used for creating education material, such as using innovative approaches to digitize books or studying the effectiveness of various teaching tools and methods;
- **Awareness and Advocacy** – using big data on the topics above to raise awareness, to monitor progress toward global goals, and to influence disability policy reform.

With respect to using big data to monitor international progress, The Internet Governance Lab recently co-sponsored "Data, Disability and Development: Innovative Approaches to Monitoring and Evaluating CRPD Implementation and Disability-Inclusive Development using Big Data Analytics and Text Mining." This session took place at the 11th Conference of States Parties to the UN Convention on the Rights of Persons with Disabilities (CRPD) at the United Nations in New York, in 2018. Topics included international mapping of accessibility to political life, using smartphone and online applications to crowd-source data on accessibility to cities, and development a categorization model to automate the analysis of CRPD state party reports.

Big data can also pose challenges to people with disabilities. Specifically, many of the data sets used to develop a range of technologies, medical interventions, or to assess or evaluate quality of life and well-being of the general population, fail to include data from or regarding people with disabilities. Reasons for the absence of such data includes lack of access to people with disabilities, privacy concerns, communication issues, and lack of knowledge regarding the value this data can provide. Without representation in these data sets, the specific needs and rights of individuals with disabilities will be overlooked, or worse, directly contravened.

Sharona Hoffmann (2017) argues that big data may lead to employment discrimination in respect of people with disabilities. She argues that the Americans with

Disabilities Act (ADA) should be amended in response to the big data phenomenon "in order to protect individuals who are perceived as likely to develop physical or mental impairments in the future" (page 777). She suggests that employers can obtain medical data about employees not only through the traditional means of medical examinations and inquiries, but also through the nontraditional mechanisms of social media, wellness programs, and data brokers. "Information about workers' habits, behaviors, or attributes ... can be used to create profiles of undesirable employees ... to exclude healthy and qualified individuals" whose profiles suggest that they may be vulnerable to future disabilities or illnesses. Her argument could also extend to screening for insurance eligibility or bank loans if such screening shows certain markers for disease and disability as revealed through big data.

9.6.2 Artificial Intelligence

Like big data, artificial intelligence and machine learning promise enormous benefits for people with disabilities whether through GPS tracking, voice recognition, or products like digital personal assistants such as Alexa that can remotely control a range of household functions (e.g., lights, music, alarms, etc.). However, the algorithms that drive the machine learning behind such devices do not routinely include data on people with disabilities. As a consequence, voice recognition devices may not recognize deaf speakers, people with cerebral palsy, or people with cognitive limitations. Facial recognition programs may not recognize people with Down Syndrome or facial dysplasia. Trewin (2018), who is an accessibility analyst for IBM, argues that unless the data that underpins the algorithms behind elements of AI such as facial, speech, and gesture recognition, they will not be accessible to those left out of the data. There are several reasons why this data is not included in such algorithms including privacy concerns, legal restrictions, and lack of accessibility to accurate data. The possible discrimination that these algorithms may visit on a range of marginalized and disadvantaged groups is a growing and complicated issue and cannot be thoroughly examined here. However, suffice it to say that, as Trewin (2018, pages 6–7) asserts: "For systems that will make or influence decisions affecting human lives, it is critical that a broad range of user stakeholders are involved in development, including people with disabilities who can help developers to think through the possible implications of the technology, and to test the technology's performance on edge cases and under-represented populations."

9.6.3 Digital Divide

Being able to navigate the Internet is facilitated by a variety of devices including computers, tablets, and smart phones and is increasingly becoming critical to modern life. Being a part of social media, shopping, communicating with friends, getting directions, and ordering food are all increasingly being done online. However, a recent Pew poll conducted in 2016 (Anderson and Perrin, 2017), Americans with disabilities were about three times as likely as those without a disability to say they never go online (23 percent versus 8 percent). Further, adults with disabilities are roughly 20 percentage points less likely to say they subscribe to home broadband and own a traditional computer, a smartphone, or a tablet.

The survey also found that people with disabilities have fewer devices capable of connecting with the Internet. One-in-four respondents said they had high-speed Internet at home, a smartphone, a desktop or laptop computer and a tablet, compared with 42 percent of those who report not having a disability. For those able to get onto the Internet, respondents with disabilities said they spent less time connected than their nondisabled peers. Finally, people with disabilities indicated that they had less confidence in their ability to negotiate the Internet.

Unfortunately, many assistive technologies can be expensive. Screen readers, text-to-speech software, and Augmentative and Alternative Communication (AAC) devices can all cost more than $1,000 each, and not everyone knows how to find grants in their countries to secure such devices. These factors have prevented many people with disabilities from gaining access to technological advancements, leaving only a select population with the ability to take advantage of them. Digital exclusion "means fewer employment, educational, social and political opportunities, lack of access to confidential financial and health information, and a general inability to fully participate in all aspects of society" (Feingold, 2013, paragraph 3) Advocates for people with disabilities argue that digital inclusion is a civil right.

9.7 CONCLUSION

This discussion of the application of the right to science to people with disabilities is not meant to be exhaustive but hopefully highlights the complexity and interrelationship of the issues involved. Science and the products of science are critical to the realization of the human rights of people with disabilities and to their inclusion in society. However, the conduct of science also poses challenges and obstacles to people with disabilities when they are excluded from decisions about scientific priorities, the conduct of scientific research, and the design of technology. The following are some brief recommendations aimed at increasing awareness in the general public and the scientific community regarding the needs and aspirations of a critical segment of the global population:

- Introduce disability issues into engineering and other curricula to ensure that product development includes access considerations.

- Include people with disabilities in design decisions for products, equipment, clinical approaches and other scientific endeavors that will affect their inclusion in their communities and their ability to manage their own lives.
- Support evidence-based practices normed on disability populations.
- Include people with disabilities in data used to identify markers for specific illnesses.
- Explore informed consent policies for people with intellectual disabilities in order to ensure that they are neither exploited nor excluded from scientific studies.
- In developing nations with few resources, prioritize low cost solutions.
- Include access to science as part of international monitoring of the CRPD by the Special Rapporteur and the Committee on the Rights of People with Disabilities.
- Develop longitudinal surveys to track the well-being of people with disabilities and to identify gaps in their access to science-based supports.

REFERENCES

American Academy of Pediatrics, Committee on Children with Disabilities. (1999). *The Treatment of Neurologically Impaired Children Using Patterning.* www.srmhp.org/archives/patterning.html.

American Psychological Association. (2003). *Facilitated Communication: Sifting the Psychological Wheat from the Chaff.* www.apa.org/research/action/facilitated.

Anderson, A. (2013). *Ed Roberts: The father of independent living.* Retrieved from www.foundsf.org/index.php?title=Ed_Roberts:_The_Father_of_Independent_Living.

Anderson, M. and Perrin, A. (2017). *Disabled Americans are less likely to use technology.* Pew Research Center. d.docs.live.net/6274d2ed1c70cbeb/Desktop/Integra/Porsdam/normalised%20ms%20files-for%20copyediting/www.pewresearch.org/fact-tank/2017/04/07/disabled-americans-are-less-likely-to-use-technology.

Autism Science Foundation (2019). *Beware of non-evidence-based treatment.* https://autismsciencefoundation.org/what-is-autism/beware-of-non-evidence-based-treatments/nts.

Autistic Self-Advocacy Network (2012). *Update on November 29 Autism Hearing.* https://autisticadvocacy.org/2012/11/updated-statement-on-november-29-autism-hearing/.

Balcazar, F. E., Keys, C. B., Kaplan, D. L., and Suarez Balcazar, Y. (2006). *Participatory action research and people with disabilities: Principles and challenges.* Canadian Journal of Rehabilitation, Winter, 1998, Vol.12(2), 105–112.

Bell, B. (2014). The global disability rights movement: Winning power, participation, and access. *Huffington Post* www.huffpost.com/entry/the-global-disability-rig_b_5651235.

Boissoneault, L. (2017). A spoonful of sugar helps the radioactive oatmeal go down: When MIT and Quaker Oats paired up to conduct experiments on unsuspecting young boys. *Smithsonian.com.* d.docs.live.net/6274d2ed1c70cbeb/Desktop/Integra/Porsdam/normalised%20ms%20files-for%20copyediting/www.smithsonianmag.com/history/spoonful-sugar-helps-radioactive-oatmeal-go-down-180962424.

Chamberlin, J. (1990). The ex-patients' movement: Where we've been and where we're going. *The Journal of Mind and Behavior,* Vol. 11(3), 323–336.

Council of Europe. (2020). *Persons with disabilities must not be left behind in the response to the COVID -19 pandemic*. www.coe.int/en/web/commissioner/-/persons-with-disabilities-must-not-be-left-behind-in-the-response-to-the-covid-19-pandemic.

Data-Pop Alliance DataFeed (2016). *Big Data and Disability: Part 1*. https://datapopalliance.org/big-data-and-disability-part-1/.

Dybwad, R. F. (1975). *Mental handicap: The world scene*. Disability History Museum. https://disabilitymuseum.org/dhm/lib/detail.html?id=2010&&print=1&page=all.

Feingold, L. (2013). The digital divide and people with disabilities. www.lflegal.com/2013/08/digital-divide/.

Hoffman, S. (2017). Big data and the Americans with Disabilities Act. 68 *Hastings Law Journal* 777; Case Legal Studies Research Paper No. 2016–33. Available at SSRN: https://ssrn.com/abstract=2841431.

International Society for Orthotics and Prosthetics. (2018). Resolution to improve access to assistive technology adopted at World Health Assembly. www.ispoint.org/news/405719/Resolution-to-improve-access-to-assistive-technology-adopted-at-World-Health-Assembly.htm.

Internet Governance Lab. (2018). *Data, disability and development: innovative approaches to monitoring and evaluating CRPD implementation and disability-inclusive development using big data analytics and text mining*. https://internetgovernancelab.org/events/cosp-11-side-event.

Office of Autism Research Coordination. (2012). IACC Portfolio Analysis Web Tool. Retrieved from: https://iacc.hhs.gov/apps/portfolio-analysis-web-tool/funderdata?funderId=4010&fy=2010.

Porsdam Mann, S., Donders, Y., Mitchell, C., Bradley, V. J., Choug, M. F., M. Mann, Church, G., and Porsdam, H., (2018). Advocating for science progress as a human right. *Proceeding of the National Academy of Sciences of the United States*. https://www.pnas.org/content/115/43/10820.

Sabatello, M. (2018). Precision medicine, health disparities, and ethics: The case for disability inclusion. Commentary. *Genetics in Medicine*. Vol. 2(4), 397–399.

Sabatello, M., and Schulze, M. (2013). *Human Rights and Disability Advocacy*. Philadelphia: University of Pennsylvania Press. muse.jhu.edu/book/27609.

Sanjek, R. (2009). *Gray Panthers*. Philadelphia, PA: University of Pennsylvania Press.

Singer, H. S., Agran, Martin, and Spooner, Fred (2017). *Evidence-Based and Values-Based Practices for People With Severe Disabilities*. Research and Practice for Persons with Severe Disabilities. Vol. 42 (1), 62–72. http://web.a.ebscohost.com.ezp-prod1.hul.harvard.edu/ehost/pdfviewer/pdfviewer?vid=1&sid=40353ce4-2599-4fa4-ae09-ce8b3a29520b%40sessionmgr4007.

Stack,E. and McDonald, K. E. (2014). Nothing about us without us: Does action research in developmental disabilities research measure up? *Journal of Policy and Practice in Intellectual Disabilities*. Vol. 11 (2), 83–91.

Stobbe, M. (2011). *Ugly past of U.S. human experiments: Tests including exposing mental patients and prisoners to infectious diseases*. NBC News.com. www.nbcnews.com/id/41811750/ns/health-health_care/t/ugly-past-us-human-experiments-uncovered/#.Xcsynm5Fyat.

The Arc. (n.d.). *Our History*. www.thearc.org/about-us/history/.

The World Bank. (2019). *Disability inclusion*. www.worldbank.org/en/topic/disability.

Trewin, S. (2018). *AI fairness for people with disabilities: point of view*. https://arxiv.org/abs/1811.10670v1.

United Nations. (1993). Standard Rules on the Equalization of Opportunities for Persons with Disabilities. www.un.org/development/desa/disabilities/standard-rules-on-the-equalization-of-opportunities-for-persons-with-disabilities.html.

United Nations General Assembly. (2007). *Convention on the Rights of Persons with Disabilities: resolution / adopted by the General Assembly*, January 24, 2007, A/RES/61/106. www.refworld.org/docid/45f973632.html.

United Nations Department of Economic and Social Affairs Disability. (1981). The World Programme of Action Concerning Disabled Persons. www.un.org/development/desa/disabilities/history-of-united-nations-and-persons-with-disabilities-the-world-programme-of-action-concerning-disabled-persons.html.

United Nations Human Rights Office of the High Commissioner. (1966). International Covenant on Economic, Social and Cultural Rights. Available at www.ohchr.org/EN/ProfessionalInterest/Pages/CESCR.aspx.

United Nations. Convention on the Rights of Persons with Disabilities and Its Optional Protocol (PPT) www.un.org/disabilities/documents/ppt/crpdbasics.ppt.

"What are some types of assistive devices and how are they used?" (n.d.). Eunice Kennedy Shriver National Institute of Child Health and Human Development. www.nichd.nih.gov/health/topics/rehabtech/conditioninfo/device.

"What are some types of rehabilitation technologies." (n.d.). Eunice Kennedy Shriver National Institute of Child Health and Human Development. www.nichd.nih.gov/health/topics/rehabtech/conditioninfo/device.

10

Science in the Times of SARS-CoV-2

Stjepan Orešković and Sebastian Porsdam Mann

10.1 INTRODUCTION

The post–World War II world has seen huge progress in scientific research. The generators have been large-scale projects funded by national governments, big business and global corporations, individual talent, and initiatives creating thousands of technology spin-offs and innovative start-ups. The role of organized knowledge in society has never been more important and the impact of STEM (Science, Technologies, Engineering, Mathematics) on people's everyday lives is growing. New scientific and technological fields as diverse as biotechnology and nanotechnology, gene therapy and pharmacogenomics, membrane technology, neural computing, nanotechnology, and ICTs in general are creating a basis for a society in which the "creation, dissemination, and utilization of information and knowledge has become the most important factor of production."[1]

Consequently, the quantity and quality of scientific inputs and outputs, as measured by the Nature Science Index,[2] have increased. Applied science is flourishing. Its outputs are tangible and evident in the areas of science, technology development, and innovation (STDI), as measured by the Global Innovation Index.[3] IBM researchers estimate that 90 percent of the world's data have been created in the last two years: more data than was created in the entire previous history of the human race.[4]

For the first time in the history of science, including the history of data science itself, we are witnessing a paramount attempt to integrate all existing and possible sources of data, information, and knowledge, to confront a single phenomenon: the SARS-CoV-2 pandemic.

---

[1] Knowledge society. www.encyclopedia.com/social-sciences/applied-and-social-sciences-magazines/knowledge-society.
[2] Nature Index. www.natureindex.com/country-outputs/generate/All/global/All/score.
[3] Global Innovation Index. http://www.globalinnovationindex.org/gii-2019-report#.
[4] IBM Watson. Big data: Big Challenge or Big Opportunity. www.ibm.com/watson/infographic/discovery/big-data-challenge-opportunity/.

The long-lasting linear growth of science and its impact on societies beginning in the aftermath of WWII received a major structural blow on January 7, 2020, in the city of Wuhan. Public health authorities identified a novel coronavirus. Wuhan was placed under quarantine within days and, on January 31, the World Health Organization declared a public health emergency.

The figures[5] of more than 130 million cases and more than 2.8 million deaths globally convey neither the inevitable final death toll and suffering, nor the overall effect of COVID-19 on mortality. The Institute for Health Metrics and Evaluation (**IHME**) projection, that was based on current projections scenario, by July 1, 2021 we will see 4.4 millions COVID-19 deaths globally[6] The broader disruption caused by COVID-19 could result in many additional deaths that are not directly attributable to the spread of the virus. Declines in households' economic wellbeing and changes of prioritization in access to health services for non-COVID illnesses will cause many additional deaths yet to be recorded. Credible and reliable estimates of the overall effect of the COVID-19 epidemic on health outcomes will not be available before the end of the year 2021[7]. and long-lasting problems from COVID-19 make it even more important to reduce the spread of the disease[8].

As the SARS-CoV-2 virus started to spread in humans and the COVID-19 epidemics/pandemics emerged, global society rapidly experienced a deluge of controversial if not contradictory data concerning scientific facts, governmental evidence-based policies, as well as health and security intelligence.[9] In a global pandemic situation, data are an essential tool for making decisions concerning the allocation of resources as well as for measuring the effectiveness of interventions. Many significant and basic facts about COVID-19 are still missing, including the most important one: how many people have been infected so far? Without reliable virological testing data, we cannot develop epidemiological projections and models accurately.[10] Without having exact data on the total number of people infected we also cannot precisely calculate the

---

[5] All country-specific figures and numbers in the chapter are taken from the Johns Hopkins COVID-19 Dashboard, accurate as of June 14, 2020. Johns Hopkins University Medicine. COVID-19 Dashboard by the Center for Systemic Science and Engineering (CSSE) at Johns Hopkins University. https://coronavirus.jhu.edu/data/mortality. Figures for GDP are from World Bank Data, see 130 10.1 for sources.

[6] The Institute for Health Metrics and Evaluation. Covid-19 projections. https://covid19.healthdata.org/global?view=total-deaths&tab=trend

[7] World Health Organization. The true death toll of COVID-19: Estimating global excess mortality. Available at: https://www.who.int/data/stories/the-true-death-toll-of-covid-19-estimating-global-excess-mortality

[8] Mayo Clinic. Covid-19 (coronavirus): Long term effects. https://www.mayoclinic.org/diseases-conditions/coronavirus/in-depth/coronavirus-long-term-effects/art-20490351

[9] S. Herman and J. Seldin. Trump Contradicts US Intelligence; Says COVID-19 Came From Chinese Lab. Updated May 1, 2020 09:40 AM. Available at: www.voanews.com/covid-19-pandemic/trump-contradicts-us-intelligence-says-covid-19-came-chinese-lab.

[10] Without knowing how many people are being infected we cannot get a credible calculation of any other key epidemic parameters such as attack the rate/ratio, the reproduction rate (the average number of people an infectious person is expected to infect in an entirely susceptible population mathematically defined as follows: $R_0 = \beta * \kappa * D$ in which β is the risk of transmission per contact, K is the contact rate, and D is the duration of infectiousness).

case-fatality rate (CFR) (the percentage of patients with the disease (cases) who die from the condition), which likely ranges widely with covariates.

This is an important problem. Knowing the number of deaths during a period of the pandemic is not enough. Moreover, in many cases, we cannot even rely on simple and standard measures such as the mortality rate which countries are reporting to the World Health Organization. We need these measures to calculate excess deaths/excess mortality rates. These rates compare the number of deaths during a period of the pandemic with the average number of deaths during the same period in previous years, thus unmasking potential hidden effects.[11],[12] Thus, in the period between 26 January and 3 October 2020, the US registered 360,000 deaths in excess of the five-year average,[13] of which 209,000 cases were confirmed to be due to COVID-19. The same trend applied for all G-8 countries, although following a different cycles, different seasonal patterns and strong difference in intensity.

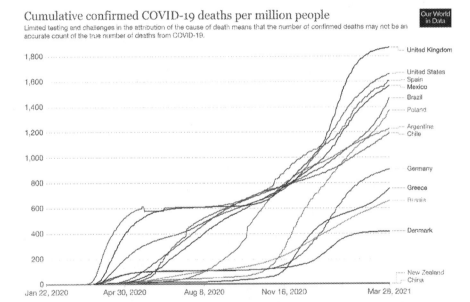

FIGURE 10.1 Excess mortality during COVID-19 Pandemic: Deaths from all causes compared to previous year, all ages in G-8 Countries

---

[11] The mortality rate is the number of people who died in a defined population for a given time interval expressed as number of deaths per 100,000 people.
[12] J. Wu, A. McCann, J. Katz, and A. Peltier, A. 87,000 Missing Deaths: Tracking the True Toll of the Coronavirus Outbreak. New York Times, Updated May 28, 2020, 12:30 P.M. E.T. available at: www.nytimes.com/interactive/2020/04/21/world/coronavirus-missing-deaths.html.
[13] Center for Disease Control and Prevention. Excess Deaths Associated with COVID-19, by Age and Race and Ethnicity – United States, January 26–October 3, 2020. Available at: https://www.cdc.gov/mmwr/volumes/69/wr/mm6942e2.htm

Not all excess deaths should be directly attributed to the COVID-19 pandemic. Lives will be lost because of interactions with other illnesses, the necessary reduction in the quality and magnitude of medical care for everyone else implied by the vast resource drain of COVID-19, as well as factors such as domestic violence. These facts stress the importance of the distinction between death "with" or "from" COVID-19.

Notwithstanding the profound uncertainty and questionable credibility of the available data, specific numbers and statistics are being presented by scientists, the media, and governments with the appearance of conviction and certitude. However, incomplete or incorrect data may create or contribute to false senses of security, or alternatively to anxiety and even social hysteria. Far-fetched, exaggerated or manipulated information derived from questionable data have already generated serious scientific and policy mistakes in relation to the appropriate separation and restriction of movement of individuals exposed to a contagious disease (sc. quarantine, self-quarantine, and isolation.) Such measures, as well as their society-wide analogues of lockdown and social distancing, are known from previous experience to be the single most effective set of public health measures. By "flattening the curve," these tried-and-tested methods reduce the burden incumbent on healthcare systems at any specific time point, thereby preventing the most serious collateral iatrogenic damage resulting from the pressure on overburdened and under-resourced medical staff and facilities. However, without reliable data specifically relevant to the COVID-19 pandemic, efficacious and evidence-based social distancing policies cannot be established, but must rather be approximated. The severity of the ethical implications of this lack of data integrity and availability may be appreciated by considering their direct translatability into lives not saved, avoidable illnesses, and unnecessary public resource drainage.

This chapter demonstrates the utility and validity of applying a human rights lens to topical and important issues in science and society through an in-depth case study of the current SARS-COVID-2 pandemic. After setting out the relevant background, recent developments in the scientific fight against the pandemic are considered in light of the provisions of Article 15 ICESCR and 27 UDHR, which enshrine the human right to enjoy the benefits of scientific progress and its applications. This right is relevant to several aspects of the scientific process, from funding, data acquisition, hypothesis selection and experimentation all the way through to publication, knowledge sharing and the implementation of resulting knowledge in the spheres of policy and technology.[14]

---

[14] On the right to science and its relevance to science and society, see S. Porsdam Mann, Y. Donders, C. Mitchell, V. J. Bradley, M. F. Chou, G. Church, H. Porsdam. "Advocating for science progress as a human right." PNAS 115(42), pp. 10820–23 and S. Porsdam Mann, H. Porsdam, Y. Donders "Sleeping Beauty: The right to science as a global ethical discourse." Human Rights Quarterly 42(2) 332–356.

The second half of the chapter focuses on a highly pertinent yet little-discussed dimension of scientific research: the speed at which it is conducted. The analysis proceeds by way of analogy to the central thesis of Nobel Laureate Daniel Kahneman's summary of decades of research into heuristics and biases, *Thinking, Fast and Slow*.[15] It is suggested that the dichotomy between a "fast," instinctive and affective cognitive process and its "slow," logical, and deliberative counterpart also accurately characterizes two idealized, diametrically opposed and extreme approaches to the scientific process. Nowhere is this distinction of greater practical significance than in the contemporary response to the SARS-CoV-2 pandemic.

The ongoing threat to human life and progress, the constant attention from the media and the public, as well as the possibility of glory for major advances, all affect scientists and their work. While this enables practical cooperation and reduces the timeframe for possible breakthroughs to such an extent as to offer hope to individuals currently suffering under the burden of the disease, these same factors likely introduce the very heuristics and biases that the scientific method is supposed to rule out or minimize. From an abstract, collective and long-term perspective, nothing beats "slow," curiosity-driven and methodologically unimpeachable research based on a rigorous understanding of the scientific method. Yet the price paid for greater certainty is greater latency, and in the case of the SARS-CoV-2 pandemic, time is already running short for hundreds of thousands of infected individuals.

Building on this discussion, the importance of trust in science and in evidence are underlined, and the argument advanced that the "right to science lens" provides a useful framework for identifying the elements necessary for such trust, and offers guidance as to how it is best achieved. We argue that this can be seen in practice through a comparison of the disparate impact of the virus in different countries. We suggest three broad factors which may account for much of this difference: the presence of scientifically informed leadership with respect for slow science and methodological rigor; societal trust in both science and in political and public health leadership; and a lower degree of income and wealth inequality. The RtS, as elucidated in the Committee on Economic, Social, and Cultural Rights' authoritative General Comment No. 25 (2020),[16] which in turn relies on relevant provisions of the 2017 UNESCO Statement on Science and Scientific Researchers,[17] and elsewhere in this volume, provides useful and workable guidance as to how the development of these factors can be encouraged.

---

[15] D. Kahneman. Thinking, Fast and Slow. Farrar, Strauss and Giroux. New York, 2011.
[16] United Nations. Economic and Social Council. Committee on Economic, Social and Cultural Rights General Comment No. 25 (2020) on science and economic, social and cultural rights (article 15 (1) (b), (2), (3) and (4) of the International Covenant on Economic, Social and Cultural Rights). https://undocs.org/E./C.12/GC/25.
[17] UNESCO General Conference, Recommendation on Science and Scientific Researchers, UNESCO Doc 39 C/Res 85.

10.2 SOCIETIES AND SCIENCE: THE GOOD, THE BAD, AND THE UGLY

In *Blueprint: The Evolutionary Origins of a Good Society*,[18] Nicholas M. Christakis has collected rich evidence from various disciplines to show that historically, whole scientific fields have focused on the dark side of our biological heritage. "In other words, we humans can be awful – prone to selfishness, tribalism, hatred, and violence," writes Christakis. "But, equally, we are good, prone to love, friendship, cooperation, and teaching ... we evolved these capacities, and the good must necessarily have outweighed the bad, in order for us to live as a social species."[19] It is therefore important not to forget the "human" in "human rights."

"Because [science] is a discipline given to objective fact-finding addressed by hypotheses and using inductive methodologies, it appears by its reliance on empiricism to exclude all consideration of value-laden issues," wrote Richard Pierre Claude, one of the first and foremost commentators on the right to science. "Whether this view stands up to scrutiny or not, it remains obvious that science is a discipline pursued by human beings."[20] One implication is that the mixed traits Christakis identifies as hallmarks of the human experience – selfishness and tribalism, but also cooperation, teaching and friendship – may influence the motivation and conduct of scientists and through their actions eventually shape the content, quality, and focus of scientific debate and progress.

In the second part of this chapter, we suggest this dynamic is visible in the context of scholarship on the SARS-CoV-2 pandemic. The desire to produce helpful and useful science, which falls squarely within the "good" part of human nature, motivates meticulous adherence to procedures and protocols designed to maximize scientific validity and minimizes any possibility of harm. Science carried out in this way may be termed "slow" science. The desire to help those who are suffering *now* may tempt less scrupulous scientists to rush publication and cut methodological corners, however. Likewise, the prospect of honor, fame and professional recognition that follow major breakthroughs, perhaps combined with a fear of being scooped, may subconsciously influence even the most methodical and meticulous scientists, editors, and commentators. Where these kinds of motivations significantly influence methodology, we might speak of "fast" science.

The choice or balance between fast and slow science has serious consequences for the fulfillment of the human right to enjoy the benefits of scientific progress and its applications. Indeed, much of the normative content of the right to science aims at

---

[18] N. A. Christakis. Blueprint: The Evolutionary Origins of a Good Society. Little Brown Spark, March, 2019.

[19] N. A. Christakis. Hope in a time of Trump and turbulent campus politics: Interview with Nicholas Christakis. US Today. Mastio, D. USA TODAY Updated 3:05 AM EST Dec 16, 2019. Available at: https://eu.usatoday.com/story/opinion/2019/04/12/interview-nicholas-a-christakis-blueprint-evolutionary-origins-good-society-column/3425958002/.

[20] J. P. Claude. Science in the Service of Human Rights. Philadelphia: University of Pennsylvania Press, 2002, 15.

preventing the kinds of extraneous influences on scientific method, which characterize fast science. The following section sets the stage for the analysis of fast and slow science by exploring the elements of the right to science in the context of ongoing efforts to combat the SARS-CoV-2 virus. It begins by examining several positive factors, including the high degree of international scientific cooperation, medical altruism, and funding available for scientific research, which represent the "good" in human nature and scientific conduct. In contrast, the disproportionate impact of the pandemic on the already disadvantaged, as well as the evidence of disparate treatment and outright racial discrimination, demonstrate the reality of "bad" factors. Finally, the worldwide reliance on data for scientific progress in general, and on location and contact tracing for COVID-19 positive individuals in particular, renders data science particularly susceptible to dual-use concerns. Where these concerns are warranted, the likely negative impacts are so widespread and so invasive that we may speak of truly repugnant or "ugly" effects.

10.3 THE GOOD: SCIENCE AS A PUBLIC GOOD

Human rights, and in particular the right to science, are not only a fundamental human value and a normative imperative for good society. As recognized in paragraph 8 of the CESCR's General Comment No. 25, the benefits of science extend beyond the "material results of the applications of scientific research" to include "the scientific knowledge and information directly deriving from scientific activity" as well as "science's role in forming critical and responsible citizens who are able to participate fully in a democratic society."[21]

When integrated into basic societal rules and principles, human rights are strong generators of economic development, social progress, and international cooperation and assistance. We visualize this relationship below using comparative data connecting human rights protection scores and GDP per capita. The countries included in the analysis are G-7 member states plus Russia, Brazil and the country with the lowest relative number of cases and 0 deaths – the best overall success in controlling the pandemic.

The "good" of state investment in human rights-relevant factors may be exemplified at the level of international governmental aid. The US State Department and USAID are the largest donors globally, providing nearly $274 million in annual emergency health and humanitarian assistance to countries in need, in addition to funding already provided to multilateral organizations such as the World Health Organization[22] and UNICEF.[23]

---

[21] Supra, n. 11, at para. 8.
[22] The USA donates in excess of $400 million per year to the WHO, more than any other country in the world. Nevertheless, US President Trump has accused the WHO of failing to properly respond to the disease, suggesting it was too closely allied to China and has threatened the withdrawal of US funding as a consequence.
[23] US Department of State. The United States Is Leading the Humanitarian and Health Assistance Response to COVID-19. March 27, 2020. www.state.gov/the-united-states-is-leading-the-humanitarian-and-health-assistance-response-to-covid-19/.

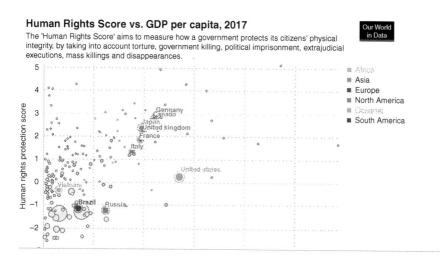

FIGURE 10.2 Human Rights Score vs. GDP per capita 1990–2017. "The 'Human Rights Score' aims to measure how a government protects its citizens' physical integrity, by taking into account torture, government killing, political imprisonment, extrajudicial executions, mass killings and disappearances". Sources: World Bank, Schnakenberg and Fariss (2014) Fariss (2019). OurWorldData.org/cascade-or-rights/

In the context of the current pandemic, there are several examples of collaborative and altruistic State behavior. For example, the German university hospital in Essen-Holsterhausen has admitted COVID-19 patients from France; Albania has issued a group of thirty doctors and nurses to neighboring Italy; and France has responded forcefully to the need for more blood donations. The Chinese corporation Alibaba has donated 500,000 test kits and one million face masks to the US, and several Japanese clothing manufacturers and retailers have donated another million protective face masks to American hospitals.[24]

---

[24] Human Rights Watch. COVID-19: A Human Rights Checklist April 14, 2020. "In Portugal, the government has announced that it will treat people with pending residency and asylum applications as if they were permanent residents until June 30, giving them equal access to health care under the national system. The Italian government extended until mid-June all existing residency permits due to expire, giving those people access to national health care. While the US has made testing for COVID-19 free, millions of people in the US are uninsured and unable to get state-funded health care, and medical treatment for the virus still costs more than many people – even those with health insurance – can afford, which forces them to choose between seeking care or risking bankruptcy". Positive examples or transnational intergovernmental collaboration include many governments or international organizations such as the "USA government, Government of Canada, the European Union, the World Bank, and the African Development Bank approved emergency funding for humanitarian assistance to support developing countries' response to COVID-19. Russia provided some medical supplies to the US at below-market cost. The Chinese government has been distributing testing supplies globally, although some recipients have been forced to recall defective tests and masks. Several multinational companies have announced aid efforts."

Such examples of altruistic and collaborative behavior cannot erase the fact, however, that most of the benefits of scientific progress and its applications are unequally distributed. As scientific knowledge has become a crucial factor in the production of wealth, its international distribution has become steadily more inequitable. This is due to structural asymmetries among countries, regions and social groups, and between races and the sexes. What distinguishes poor people or underdeveloped countries from their richer counterparts is not only that they control fewer assets, but also that they do not create, shape, and enjoy as many benefits of scientific knowledge.[25]

This reality demonstrates the importance of international cooperation, an essential element of the right to science. Article 15(4) ICESCR states that, "[t]he States Parties to the present Covenant recognize the benefits to be derived from the encouragement and development of international contacts and co-operation in the scientific and cultural fields".[26] Moreover, it illustrates importance of scientific freedom, another essential element recognized in Article 15(3). Without scientific freedom, the safe exchange of medical personnel, technological equipment, and scientific knowledge cannot be guaranteed.

Several steps have already been taken to curb the Coronavirus pandemic. These involve controlling and changing human behavior; searching for drugs and testing vaccines; stimulating the economy,; and creating datasets and collecting information from sources as diverse as those about population genetic and public health, traffic controls, and GPS signals, social media sites, purchase transaction records, as well as the climate. In the face of the pandemic, science has been recognized as the strongest and most legitimate instrument to pursue the ideals of a safer life and improved overall human conditions.

This promise of science is, however, conditional on the broad distribution of scientific information and the growth and dissemination of evidence-based knowledge (cf. ICESCR Article 15(2)).[27] Scientists are expected to search for drug therapies and vaccines and deliver solutions under unprecedented time pressure, potentially undermining these conditions.[28]

10.4 THE BAD: INEQUALITY AND ACCESS TO SCIENCE

As the ability to manipulate abstractions and data becomes ever more important for the attainment of societal ends, we should remember that a *knowledge* society is not

---

[25] World Conference on Science. Science for the 21st Century. Declaration on science and the use of scientific knowledge. www.unesco.org/science/wcs/eng/declaration_e.htm#top.
[26] United Nations Human Rights Office of the High Commissioner. International Covenant on Economic, Social and Cultural Rights. www.ohchr.org/en/professionalinterest/pages/cescr.aspx.
[27] Ibid.
[28] V. Rul. The most important application of science. EMBO Rep v.15(9); 2014 Sep PMC4198034.

necessarily a *good* society.[29] Neoclassical economic theory equates development with GDP growth that can be measured through the lens of an aggregate production function, relating "relates the total output of an economy to the aggregate amounts of labour, human capital and physical capital in the economy, and some simple measure of the level of technology in the economy as a whole."[30] This model fails to provide an adequate picture even of economic development, as it entirely ignores externalities including, but not limited to, social costs, environmental impacts, and income inequality.[31]

It is not surprising that such an approach to society at times creates fear and reluctance to adopt new technologies. Much of the current inequality both within and between societies can be traced to technical innovations introduced at first to benefit only a privileged minority.[32] These are partially to blame for the creation of a global society in which, according to a Pew Research Center analysis, the vast majority of the world's population (4.4 billion people – 71% of the global population of 6.2 billion) lives on a budget that falls well short of the poverty line in advanced economies[33].[34] The most recently available data analysis finds that the global middle class encompassed 54 million fewer people in 2020 than the number projected prior to the onset of the pandemic and the number of poor is estimated to have been 131 million higher because of the recession[35].

Since socioeconomic determinants such as education and poverty are deeply interrelated with health, this stark inequality will be exacerbated as the COVID-19 pandemic plunges the global economy into a synchronized recession the likes of which has not been witnessed since the Great Depression. The rise in the number of people infected by COVID-19 in Africa and South Asia, for example, is creating new economic and social shocks that threaten to deepen global inequalities, especially

---

[29] *The Good Society* is a journal published by Penn State University press. Articles in the journal respond to the premise that "current versions of socialism and democratic capitalism fail to offer workable visions of a good society and seem increasingly to contradict such basic values as liberty, democracy, equality, and environmental sustainability." The journal publishes outstanding dialectical articles on the pressing political, social, religious, and legal questions facing twenty-first-century society and aims to "create a theoretical basis for the eventual restructuring of real world political-economic systems." Project Muse. The Good Society. Available at: https://muse.jhu.edu/journal/69.

[30] A. V. Banerjee and E. Duflo. Growth Theory Through the Lens of Development Economics. MIT, March 2004. https://economics.mit.edu/files/798.

[31] R. Costanza, I. Kubiszewski, E. Giovannini, H. Lovins, J. McGlade, K. E. Pickett. Time to leave GDP behind. Nature. 2014; 505: 283–285.

[32] The Role of Science and Technology in Society and Governance Toward a New Contract between Science and Society. Executive Summary of the Report of the North American Meeting held in advance of the World Conference on Science. www.nature.com/wcs/mo5s.html.

[33] R. Kochhar. Seven-in-ten people globally live on $10 or less per day. Pew Research Center. https://www.pewresearch.org/fact-tank/2015/09/23/seven-in-ten-people-globally-live-on-10-or-less-per-day/

[34] M. Roser and E. Ortiz-Ospina. Global Extreme Poverty. The World Bank. March 2017. https://ourworldindata.org/extreme-poverty.

[35] R. Kochhar. The Pandemic Stalls Growth in the Global Middle Class, Pushes Poverty Up Sharply. Pew Research Center. https://www.pewresearch.org/global/2021/03/18/the-pandemic-stalls-growth-in-the-global-middle-class-pushes-poverty-up-sharply/

affecting the people living in rural areas or overcrowded megalopolises lacking access to basic health and social services.[36]

Where the obligations imposed on States under the right to science have been met, societies are better prepared for the type of emergency responses necessary in a global pandemic, including effective means of tracing, testing, and quarantining. Article 2 ICESCR provides that

> States Parties must take steps, to the maximum of their available resources, for the full realization of the [right to science]. While full realization of the right may be achieved progressively, steps towards it must be taken immediately or within a reasonably short period of time. Such steps should be deliberate, concrete and targeted, using all appropriate means, including the adoption of legislative and budgetary measures.[37]

Moreover, "maximum available resources"[38] should be understood to include resources available through international cooperation. Where countries have not met this standard despite good faith attempts to comply with their duty of progressive realization for reasons of resource scarcity, it is frequently the international community's failure to live up to their own obligations which is to blame.

Over the course of the last two decades, developmental economists have attempted to build alternative growth models responsive to the fact that some people are more favored by their legislators and governments than others are. Adherents of the "Unified Growth Theory," for example, have expounded important theoretical perspectives and breakthroughs by studying the interplay between growth and political[39] as well as social institutions.[40] The new conception of economy envisaged is a global view of systems of production that have fundamental implications for our everyday material and mental reality.[41] Unified Growth Theory was designed to resolve the conflict between growth designed to satisfy the interests of profit and the interests of the majority of the population.[42]

---

[36] P. Akiwumi and G. Valensisi. When it rains it pours: COVID-19 exacerbates poverty risks in the poorest countries. Division for Africa and Least Developed Countries, UNCTAD. May 4, 2020.
[37] Supra n. 21.
[38] Ibid.
[39] D. Acemoglu, S. Johnson, and J. Robinson. The colonial origins of comparative development: An empirical investigation. American Economic Review. 2001; 91(5): 1369–1401.
[40] G. Oded and J. Zeira. Income distribution and macroeconomics. Review of Economic Studies.1993; 60(1): 35–52.
[41] I. Tuomi. From Periphery to Center: Emerging Research Topics on Knowledge Society. Technology Review.2001; 116. http://staff.stir.ac.uk/w.m.thompson/Innocom/Library/Knowledge_Society.pdf.
[42] G. Oded. From Stagnation to Growth: Unified Growth Theory. Journal Handbook of Economic Growth. 2005; 171–293.

Science in the Times of SARS-CoV-2

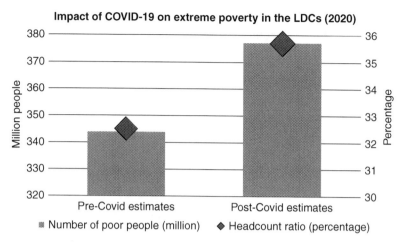

FIGURE 10.3 The worsening economic outlook following the emergence of COVID-19 entails an increase of over three percentage points in LDC poverty headcount, with more than 33 million additional people living in extreme poverty. Source: https://unctad.org/en/pages/newsdetails.aspx?OriginalVersionID=2356

10.5 THE BAD II: DISCRIMINATION

Human Rights Watch has identified forty questions to guide a rights-respecting response to the COVID-19 crisis. These principally target the needs of groups most at risk, including people living as ethnic minorities and/or refugees, religious groups, elderly and disabled people,[43] children and women, and members of the LGTBQ+ community.[44] Racially discriminatory treatments related to the COVID-19 pandemic have occurred repeatedly around the world. There have been reports of discrimination in employment and housing directed at Africans and people of African descent throughout China, and attempts were made to forcibly test Africans in the Guangdong province.[45] A significant increase of racist incidents against Asian Australians has been recorded in Australia, ranging from racial slurs to physical assault

---

[43] S. Orešković. No country for old men: five prevalent stereotypes affecting the life of the elderly. Croat Med J. 2020; 61: 184–188.
[44] Human Rights Watch. COVID-19: A Human Rights Checklist April 14, 2020. Government officials in many countries "have exhibited disturbing denialism about COVID-19, depriving their publics of accurate information on the pandemic. In India, authorities have done little to curb the spread of viral disinformation which claims that the minority Muslim community is deliberately spreading COVID-19. In contrast, United Kingdom police launched investigation into efforts to smear Muslims in UK. In China, outrage over the reprimand of a whistleblower led to a rare apology from the local police". www.hrw.org/news/2020/04/14/covid-19-human-rights-checklist.
[45] Human Rights Watch. China: Covid-19 Discrimination Against Africans Forced Quarantines, Evictions, Refused Services in Guangzhou May 5, 2020 12:00AM EDT. www.hrw.org/news/2020/05/05/china-covid-19-discrimination-against-africans.

committed against women (62 percent).[46] Racial discrimination also plays a part in the pattern of victim-blaming that occurs when inequality widens for communities of color. An exclusive focus on individuals' risky behavior is typically adopted, trivializing the importance of socioeconomic determinants of health in the interpretation of the high mortality rates among people of color.

Analysis of the death toll of COVID-19 furthermore reveals that the poor, uninsured, and members of minority groups are the most affected. The rate of COVID-19-related deaths among Black and Latino residents of Chicago and New York is more than twice the Caucasians rate. Similar highly disproportionate rates are measured in other densely populated cities and neighborhoods in the USA.[47] The need to take public transportation to get to work and/or the presence of pre-existing health problems radically increase exposure to the virus and are necessarily related to socioeconomic status. This is not specific to the USA. In the United Kingdom, black males are 4.2 times and black females 4.3 times more likely to die from a COVID-19-related death than Caucasians.[48]

These disproportionate burdens on already marginalized groups are a particularly egregious violation of the basic human rights principles which underlie the right to science. Unlike the duty of progressive realization, which applies to most obligations derived from this right, there are no excuses under international human rights law for allowing such discrimination to happen. Article 2(2) ICESCR is clear on this point: "The States Parties to the present Covenant undertake to guarantee that the rights enunciated in the present Covenant will be exercised without discrimination of any kind as to race, colour, sex, language, religion, political or other opinion, national or social origin, property, birth or other status."[49] The CESCR's General Comment No. 25 reminds us that "States Parties are under an immediate obligation to eliminate all forms of discrimination against individuals and groups in their enjoyment of ESCRs."[50] The obligation to remedy discrimination is absolute, cannot be limited, and obtains even in emergencies and situations involving the total destitution of the State.

One implication is that States Parties must address socioeconomic determinants of exposure. This can happen, for example, by establishing temporary, less crowded

[46] N. Zhou. Survey of Covid-19 racism against Asian Australians records 178 incidents in two weeks. The Guardian. Apr. 17, 2020 07:35 BST. Last modified on Apr. 17, 2020 07:36 BST. www.theguardian.com/world/2020/apr/17/survey-of-covid-19-racism-against-asian-australians-records-178-incidents-in-two-weeks.

[47] R. Elving. What Coronavirus Exposes About America's Political Divide. NPR. April 12, 2020, 7:00 AM ET.

[48] UK Office of National Statistics. Coronavirus (COVID-19) related deaths by ethnic group, England and Wales: 2 March 2020 to 10 April 2020. www.ons.gov.uk/peoplepopulationandcommunity/birthsdeathsandmarriages/deaths/articles/coronavirusrelateddeathsbyethnicgroupenglandandwales/2march2020to10april2020.

[49] Supra n. 21.

[50] Supra n. 11, at para. 25.

institutions (care homes, prisons, schools) or by providing financial incentives not to commute using public transportation (i.e. furlough programs and programs enabling those most in need to stay at home altogether without losing their jobs by subsiding their employers). States could disseminate evidence-based advice on social distancing, hygiene and personal protective equipment, especially among those most in need and least able to otherwise obtain it.

10.6 THE UGLY: DUAL USE, HARM, CORONAVIRUS CAPITALISM, AND THE DIGNITY OF THE INDIVIDUAL

A major menace to scientific freedom arises from the interaction between digital technologies and capitalism – specifically, the threat of "surveillance capitalism."[51] This mutant strain of capitalism works by providing free services to citizens in exchange for their personal data, enabling services providers to monitor users' online behaviour with or without their explicit consent.

> Although some of these data are applied to service improvement, the rest are declared as a proprietary behavioural surplus, fed into advanced manufacturing processes known as "machine intelligence," and fabricated into prediction products that anticipate what you will do now, soon, and later. Finally, these prediction products are traded in a new kind of marketplace that I call behavioural futures markets. Surveillance capitalists have grown immensely wealthy from these trading operations, for many companies are willing to lay bets on our future behavior.[52]

Why has surveillance capitalism been so successful over the last decade or so? In part, it is because we have lost support from our real-world institutions:

> whether it's health care, the educational system, the bank ... It's just a tale of woe wherever you go. The economic and political institutions right now leave us feeling so frustrated. We've all been driven in this way toward the internet, toward these services, because we need help. And no one else is helping us. That's how we got hooked.[53]

Coronavirus Capitalism is an even newer term coined to cover a broader set of structural changes resulting from the pandemic.[54] The analogy of "surveillance capitalism" is applicable to the role of digital technologies in the context of the COVID-19 pandemic: technologies employed by governments around the world are aimed at identifying how infected people behave, where they move, with whom they

---

[51] Zuboff, Shoshana. The Age of Surveillance Capitalism: The Fight for a Human Future at the New Frontier of Power. London, England: Profile Books. 2019.
[52] Ibid.
[53] S. Zuboff. A fundamentally illegitimate choice. Sam Biddle, The Intercept. February 2, 2019. https://theintercept.com/2019/02/02/shoshana-zuboff-age-of-surveillance-capitalism/.
[54] N. Taplin. Coronavirus Capitalism Has a Darker Side. Wall Street Journal. April 9, 2020 6:50 am ET. www.wsj.com/articles/coronavirus-capitalism-has-a-darker-side-11586429401.

socialize, but not only for the purpose of monitoring self-isolation or enforcing quarantines. Governments are demanding extraordinary new surveillance powers[55] intended to contain the virus' spread.

Significant problems related to data security may arise from private corporations storing large quantities of consumers' personal data. Instead of looking to invest their resources in boosting testing, unchecked power-seeking governments might end up using the COVID-19 surveillance technologies to normalize data gathering on individuals for the purpose of social and political control.[56] This prospect would not comply with the European Data Protection Board (EDPB)'s guidelines, which state that restrictions of freedom during the pandemic are acceptable only to the extent that they are consistent with narrowly defined purposes, limited timeframes, and the recommendation that "pseudonymisation, encryption, non-disclosure agreements and strict access role distribution, access role restrictions as well as access logs should be employed."[57]

For example, machine-readable QR codes, which are typically used to store URLs or other information to be scanned by smartphone cameras, have been used to monitor citizens and alert authorities about the movements and actions of individuals who have tested positive for SARS-CoV-2 in China, Russia, and Hong Kong. Closed-circuit television has been deployed to track such individuals in South Korea. In Israel, citizens' cell phone location data are used for quarantine control purposes by the government[58].

The EU currently proposes to track citizens using Bluetooth. Computer science and machine learning experts from eight European nations are developing the Pan-European Privacy-Preserving Proximity Tracing Project,[59] which aims to enable technologies to alert users to the presence of nearby individuals who have tested positive for the virus. Moreover, the Massachusetts Institute of Technology is

[55] Human Rights Watch reports that "China, Iran, and Russia are using digital surveillance measures that threaten individuals' right to privacy, free expression, and association. Armenia and Israel passed sweeping laws that threaten privacy by requiring telecommunications companies to turn over phone call histories and location data to authorities. In South Korea, new regulations allow authorities to send anonymized information about individuals' movements to the general public, but the updates have included enough detail that they left people wary of their private lives being exposed. While data protection guarantees vary in each context, France, Germany, India, Italy, Poland, Singapore, the UK, and the US are also exploring or already using cell phone location data or facial recognition." www.hrw.org/news/2020/04/14/covid-19-human-rights-checklist.
[56] S. Cunningham. Privacy nightmare or potential salvation? The new pan-European platform that aims to disrupt COVID-19 transmission chains. KCRW. Berlin. https://kcrwberlin.com/2020/04/privacy-nightmare-or-potential-salvation-the-new-pan-european-platform-that-aims-to-disrupt-covid-19-transmission-chains/.
[57] EDPB. Guidelines 03/2020 on the processing of data concerning health for the purpose of scientific research in the context of the COVID-19 outbreak. April 21, 2020. https://edpb.europa.eu/our-work-tools/our-documents/guidelines/guidelines-032020-processing-data-concerning-health-purpose_en.
[58] RS Surber. Corona pan(dem)ic: gateway to global surveillance. *Ethics Inf Technol*. 2020;1-10. doi:10.1007/s10676-020-09569-5
[59] Pan-European Privacy-Preserving Proximity Tracing. (PEPP-PT). www.pepp-pt.org/.

developing new platforms using existing mobile technologies to enable privacy-preserving contact tracing. The aim of these platforms is to enable health care providers to download the names of those who have been physically close to infected individuals. Algorithms developed by data scientists will furthermore be able to integrate data from different sources to forecast precise community-level infection risks.[60] All these examples are the result of the theory that the interest of public health prevails over privacy rights and interests when the demand for processing sensitive private information increases due to severe threats[61] to survival among the general population.

The *Joint Civil Society Statement*, issued by more than one hundred national and international civil society organizations, "urge[s] governments to show leadership in tackling the pandemic in a way that ensures that the use of digital technologies to track and monitor individuals and populations are carried out strictly in line with human rights."[62] Proposals that would invade privacy, deter free speech, and disparately burden vulnerable groups are not acceptable, the Electronic Frontier Foundation argues, and suggests three questions to be answered in every situation when decisions are being made to give greater surveillance powers to the government:

1) Would the proposal work?
2) Would it excessively intrude on privacy and freedoms?
3) Are there sufficient safeguards?[63]

These misgivings show that the kind of surveillance characterizing *Coronavirus Capitalism* is liable to misuse. The problem is familiar from pre-Corona contexts, but the emergency powers sought by governments to combat COVID-19 are more extensive and invasive. The problem arises from the fact that the same technologies – surveillance,

---

[60] J. Shah and N. Shah. Fighting Coronavirus with Big Data. Harvard Business Review. April 06, 2020. https://hbr.org/2020/04/fighting-coronavirus-with-big-data.

[61] A. Kharpal. Use of surveillance to fight coronavirus raises concerns about government power after pandemic ends. March 30, 2020,12:17 PM EDT. www.cnbc.com/2020/03/27/coronavirus-surveillance-used-by-governments-to-fight-pandemic-privacy-concerns.html.

[62] The Joint Civil Society Statement addresses the surveillance measures adopted to fight the pandemic. The Statement insists that "it must be lawful, necessary and proportionate, should only continue for as long as necessary to address the current pandemic, increased collection, retention, and aggregation of personal data, including health data, is only used for the purposes of responding to the COVID-19 pandemic, any claims that data is anonymous must be based on evidence how it has been anonymized. Surveillance should not facilitate discrimination against racial minorities, people living in poverty, and other marginalized populations., Data sharing agreements with other public or private sector entities must be based on law and publicly disclosed, should not fall under the domain of security or intelligence agencies, and should include means for free, active, and meaningful participation of relevant stakeholders, in particular experts in the public health sector and the most marginalized population groups." Human Rights Watch. Joint Civil Society Statement: States use of digital surveillance technologies to fight pandemic must respect human rights. www.hrw.org/news/2020/04/02/joint-civil-society-statement-states-use-digital-surveillance-technologies-fight.

[63] Electronic Frontier Foundation. COVID-19 and digital rights. www.eff.org/issues/covid-19.

tracking and tracing, identification, and contact using ICTs – which are capable of producing vast benefits (as the case of successful contact tracing in South Korea shows) are also capable of producing great harm through bad faith, selfish or even hostile uses. In the case of invasive individual surveillance, it is not hard to see that a wealth of information concerning individuals may be connected, amassed and analyzed. Nor is it difficult to appreciate that much of this information is likely to be sensitive and may give rise to neglect, discrimination, or even persecution, for data subjects, as well as unjust enrichment and undemocratic influence for those who wield the power of the resulting knowledge. Given the sheer scale of data involved, and the ease with which systems meant for emergencies may be repurposed for continued use, the danger of dual use may well be one of the ugliest problems currently facing societies.

The problem of dual-use surveillance also raises the issue of respect for human dignity. Dignity has a special meaning in international human rights law, where it serves as the foundational value from which human rights are derived.[64] Although a detailed definition is outside the scope of this chapter, dignity may be said to involve respect for individual autonomy and desires, balanced against interference with those of others, and entitlement to acknowledgement and respect as an agent whose life and interests have inherent value. Thus, dignity is violated whenever individuals are treated merely as tools or objects for the achievement of some purpose. Such treatment respects neither the equal rights of all humans nor their cognitive and affective capacities. The constellation of nonconsensual and exploitative practices which make up Coronavirus Capitalism not only undermine the interests of individuals to maintain the privacy necessary for self-development and the cultivation of relationships; they also fail to offer a reasonable degree of informational freedom.

10.7 THE UGLY II: EXECUTIVE DISTRUST OF SCIENCE

Not every country has reacted in the same manner during the pandemic, with the same level of ethical, social, and scientific responsibility, transparency, and evidence-based policies. Indeed, there are already indicators of significant differences in the transfer of knowledge and use of evidence-based policy between the highly developed EU countries as well as the USA. Whether members of high-risk groups, such as the elderly and people with preconditions, will live or die depends on the response of world leaders to the idea of evidence-based policy and the right to enjoy the benefits of scientific progress. Politics of denial and limited public access to evidence-based information and

---

[64] On dignity in ethics and human rights see Andorno, Roberto. "Human Dignity and Human Rights as a Common Ground for a Global Bioethics" (2009). Journal of Medicine and Philosophy, Vol. 34, Issue 3, pp. 223–240 and Porsdam Mann, S., Sun, R. and Hermerén, G. "A framework for the ethical assessment of chimeric animal research using human neural tissue" BMC medical ethics 20 (1), 1-9. https://doi.org/10.1186/s12910-019-0345-2.

independent scientific sources on the virus's spread have already contributed to the loss of hundreds of thousands of lives. In some countries, responses from heads of state have been marked by distrust of science, cover-ups, and *ad hominem* attacks on doctors who sounded the alarm at the beginning of the outbreak. There have been "predictions" that the virus would disappear like a miracle one day and dismissals of the disease as a hoax fantasy and a little flu.[65] Manipulation, exaggeration and conspiracy theories on the origins of SARS-Cov-2 are rampant, spreading faster than the virus and likewise producing deadly effects. Some of the most widespread are that:

- The virus has escaped from a Chinese laboratory in Wuhan
- The US military brought the virus to Wuhan
- 5G networks spread the virus
- The virus was created by Bill Gates who wants to make billions on the vaccine.

Social scientists are trying to chart the path of disinformation in the same way that epidemiologists are tracking the transmission of a new virus, with a special focus on so-called "superspreaders" whose actions cause significantly more viral dissemination than others.[66] Some politicians have held political rallies, kissing supporters and promoting an aversion to scientific inquiry and public health institutions. One aspect of populist manipulation of reports and official figures, which has puzzled researchers, is the reported mortality rate in many countries being far below those measured, expected, or projected for comparable economies, societies or health care systems. For example, Russia is positioned in upper tier of the Europe region in terms of number tests per million population(830 926 tests / 1 million people – 121 300 000 tests in total while Denmark leads the way with **4 476 378 tests / 1 million people – 25 996 859 tests in total**) However, Russia is standing, as of this writing, at 4,5 million reported cases and 99.000 deaths, resulting in relatively low **31,258 cases per million,**[67] and even lower level of deaths per million if compared to most of G-8 average, (Russia reports 683 deaths per million compared to UK reporting 1861 deaths per million, Italy, 1827, USA 1705, Germany 921)[68] . This is a country with an underfunded and vertically disconnected health care system, and in which no satisfactory explanations for such superior performance are obvious.

---

[65] Z. Rasheed. COVID-19 pandemic is testing world leaders. Who's stepping up? www.aljazeera.com/news/2020/04/covid-19-pandemic-testing-world-leaders-stepping-200402201221844.html.

[66] P. Ball and A. Maxel. The Epic Battle Against Coronavirus Misinformationa and Conspiracy Theories. Nature, May 27, 2020. www.nature.com/articles/d41586-020-01452-z.

[67] For example, The New York Times reports that a senior WHO official found Russia's figures "suspicious" on May 11, 2020. I. Necheporenko. "A Cornoravirus Mystery Explained: Moscow Has 1,700 Extra Deaths." New York Times, May 11, 2020. www.nytimes.com/2020/05/11/world/europe/coronavirus-deaths-moscow.html.

[68] Worldometer. **Reported Cases and Deaths by Country or Territory.** https://www.worldometers.info/coronavirus/?utm_campaign=homeAdvegas1?%20

Though fairly common, national responses aimed at obscuring the true extent of the virus's impact, constitute clear and fundamental violations of no less than three of the core minimal obligations of the right to science. The CESCR explicitly provides, in paragraph 52 of its General Comment No. 25, that the following obligations are "core," such that no government may be excused for failing to fulfil them unless they demonstrate exhaustion of available domestic and international resources in bona fide attempts at fulfillment (paragraph 51).

> Core obligations related to the [right to science] require States, inter alia, to:
> Adopt mechanisms aimed at aligning government policies and programs to the best available, generally accepted scientific evidence;
> Adopt mechanisms to protect people from the harmful consequences of false, misleading and pseudoscience-based practices, especially when other ESCRs are at risk;
> Promote accurate scientific information and refrain from disinformation, disparagement, or deliberate misinforming of the public, so as to erode citizen understanding and respect for science and scientific research.[69]

10.8 SCIENCE: FAST AND SLOW

Unfortunately, a rigorous approach to scientific method is a slow and ponderous process. Trials must adhere to strict safety and statistical standards. They have to obtain ethical review. Their results need to be confirmed by other trials and discussed in open scientific fora. Before they can be published, they typically undergo peer review. As a result, the scientific process operates on a temporal resolution of years and decades. Yet the Coronavirus cannot be persuaded to wait, and thousands need a cure, vaccine or treatment *now*. As a result, the natural, social and behavioral sciences are all under great pressure to answer difficult questions quickly. Whether consciously or subconsciously, methodological niceties and research credibility may be sacrificed or neglected in the process, leaving research or policy papers open to criticism.

A good example is the statistical bias which arises from attempts to understand the share of people who have contracted the coronavirus. Basic but fatal problems arise from the misinterpretation and miscalculation of epidemiological concepts. The second most important cause of bias is that a key metric, the number of deaths caused by coronaviruses, tends to lag. Although many regions publish daily death counts, these are typically underestimates and suffer from unrepresentative sampling and daily variability. The sampling-variability issue is exacerbated by the fact that polls or studies with extreme results are more likely to get reported on ("publication bias").[70]

---

[69] Supra n. 21.
[70] D. Kopf. Three concepts for interpreting data in the age of coronavirus. The Quartz. April 25, 2020.

Consequently, we cannot rely completely on the data that partly inform the 500+ research papers on COVID-19 published daily. The primary cause for this explosion in publications is the adoption of new scientific practices, stimulating scientists to share pre-print research directly online, without formal peer-review. These new practices have engendered a fair amount of skepticism. Like fast food, hastily compiled junk science[71] can be deleterious for health. Conflicts and mixed messages among scientists are symptomatic of a rushed approach and have stymied efforts to tackle the most pressing issues.[72]

The scientific knowledge and individual and collective experience we are amassing over the course of the SARS-CoV-2 pandemic will be the basis for the knowledge of tomorrow. Ideally, this knowledge and experience will inform the creation of new tools and techniques which in turn will help us collectively control future epidemics. Some will argue that the conduct of the scientific process – from generating hypotheses to designing research and evaluating hypotheses – should be a value-neutral exercise. However, conducting science in accordance with the requirements of the eponymous right means engaging with the concerns of the public, rather than shutting these out. In the words of Isabelle Stengers, scientists ought to behave like the

> "thinking, rational brain of humanity" and refuse to allow their expertise to be used to shut down the concerns of the public, or conversely, to spread the belief that scientific progress is inevitable and will resolve all of society's problems. Rather, science must engage openly and honestly with an intelligent public and be clear about the kind of knowledge it is capable of producing.[73]

The sometimes completely unrealistic societal expectations from science and technologies are vividly illustrated by the current pandemic.[74] The biomedical research pipeline begins with rigorous safety checks on small experimental groups during Phase 1; expands to groups of a few hundred in Phase 2; thousands in Phase 3; and only then may Phase 4 trials be initiated. Months normally pass between phases so that researchers can review the findings and obtain approval to proceed to subsequent phases; the process of bringing novel pharmaceuticals can thus extend over

---

[71] See bioRxiv. When citations come before peer-review – A new normal. 12 preprints on COVID-19 that have been supported or contradicted by subsequent research. https://medium.com/scite/12-preprints-on-covid-19-that-have-been-supported-or-contradicted-by-subsequent-research-2ef1738e01a2.

[72] The Slow Science Academy in Berlin has stood against such tendencies since its 2010 publication of a slow-science manifesto: "Slow science was pretty much the only science conceivable for hundreds of years; today, we argue, it deserves revival and needs protection. Society should give scientists the time they need, but more importantly, scientists must *take* their time. We do need time to think. We do need time to digest. We do need time to misunderstand each other, especially when fostering lost dialogue between humanities and natural sciences. We cannot continuously tell you what our science means; what it will be good for; because we simply don't know yet. Science needs time." Available at: http://slow-science.org/.

[73] I. Stengers. Another Science is Possible: A Manifesto for Slow Science. Polity: 2018.

[74] M. Borup, N. Brown, K. Konrad, and H. Van Lente. The sociology of expectations in science and technology. Technology Analysis & Strategic Management. 2006; 18:3–4: 285–298.

years or decades. Since 1992, the US Food and Drug Administration's development and drug approval standards and procedures include a track for the accelerated approval of antiretroviral drugs. Originating from the need to enable rapid access to HIV/AIDS medication, the FDA's accelerated approval track can be "applied to promising therapies that treat a serious or life-threatening condition and provide therapeutic benefit over available therapies."[75] The influence of the "fast" process can be illustrated by reference to the incredible statistic that nearly 30,000 of the COVID-19 articles published in 2020 were preprints — between 17% and 30% of total COVID-19 research papers Journals rushed to get COVID-19 articles through peer review. MedRxiv COVID-19 preprints appeared in peer-reviewed journals after a median review time of 72 days, twice as fast as preprints from the server on other topics[76]. The US National Library of Medicine's trial registry, ClinicalTrials.gov, presently records 5.248 ongoing or completed COVID-19 studies. The number of studies already recruiting patients is exceptional, at 2,562 current studies.[77] This pace is unprecedented in the history of science and medicine. Nevertheless, both the SARS-CoV-2 virus and the resultant COVID-19 disease are novel biological phenomena. Despite the fact that there only few vaccines for COVID-19 approved by either the FDA[78] or the European Medicines Agency (EMA),[79] unscrupulous companies are attempting to profit from the pandemic through illegally marketed and scientifically untested products falsely claimed to be efficacious against the disease.

A famous example of this phenomenon is hydroxychloroquine, a sometime antimalarial drug publicly promoted by US President Trump[80]. This drug was the subject of two major papers published in *The Lancet* and *New England Journal of Medicine*, the premier medical journals of the United Kingdom and US, respectively. The studies were both based on a database purportedly derived from the medical records of 96,000 COVID-19 patients. Their publication "had considerable impact, halting clinical trials of malaria drugs around the world and providing

---

[75] US Food & Drug Administration. Development & Approval Process | Drugs. www.fda.gov/drugs/development-approval-process-drugs.
[76] E. Holly. How torrent of COVID science changed research publishing – in seven charts. https://www.nature.com/articles/d41586-020-03564-y
[77] US National Library of Medicine. ClinicalTrials.gov. Updated 30 May, 2020. https://clinicaltrials.gov/ct2/results?cond=covid-19&term=&cntry=US&state=&city=&dist=&recrs=a.
[78] US Food and Drug Administration. Beware of Fraudulent Coronavirus Tests, Vaccines and Treatments. April 29, 2020. www.fda.gov/consumers/consumer-updates/beware-fraudulent-coronavirus-tests-vaccines-and-treatments.
[79] European Medicines Agency. Treatments and Vaccines for COVID-19. www.ema.europa.eu/en/human-regulatory/overview/public-health-threats/coronavirus-disease-covid-19/treatments-vaccines-covid-19#potential-treatments-under-investigation-section.
[80] A. Solender. All The Times Trump Has Promoted Hydroxychloroquine. Forbes, May 22, 2020. www.forbes.com/sites/andrewsolender/2020/05/22/all-the-times-trump-promoted-hydroxychloroquine/#2d336df64643.

reassurance about the risks of blood pressure medications taken by millions of patients."[81]

Based on suspicions about the source and accuracy of this database, more than a hundred academics signed an open letter to the editor of *The Lancet* requesting an independent validation of the study and details of the supporting evidence.[82] Both studies were subsequently retracted when it emerged that Surgisphere Corporation, the proprietors of the database, had refused access to its full contents to independent reviewers.[83] Under normal circumstances, the editorial and research standards in these journals is so high that retractions or allegations of serious mistakes or omissions are rare, especially in cases of studies, such as these two, authored by senior professionals from prestigious institutions. They would take months or years to conduct and go through multiple rounds of analysis and review. However, these studies went through the entire research pipeline from data analysis through submission to publication in little over five weeks. To the extent that such a hastily crafted paper would be unlikely to pass editorial and peer review in less pressured times, this story illustrates the impact that the "fast" process can exert, even in the best medical journals.

The difficult history of HIV treatment and the deployment of vaccines against the H1N1 outbreak in 2009 illustrate that even when tools have been available, they have not been equally available to all. In the long run, therapeutic drugs, together with vaccines, might change the fight against COVID-19 too.[84] One potential source of such optimistic and promising vaccine-development is that such "speculations" have caused the stocks of companies developing vaccines to surge and more than double since late February, despite some of these companies having never successfully brought a single product to market. For politicians, it is an attempt to invest in the potential surge of public support ahead of elections. Developing such huge expectations from science may be wreaking potentially serious damage to the

---

[81] R. Rabin. Scientists Question Medical Data Used in Second Coronavirus Study. The New York Times, June 2, 2020. www.nytimes.com/2020/06/02/health/coronavirus-study.html.

[82] "An Open Letter to [the authors] ... and Richard Horten (the Editor of *The Lancet*." https://zenodo.org/record/3862789#.Xu.

[83] In retracting the study, *The Lancet* stated that "several concerns were raised with respect to the veracity of the data and analyses conducted by Surgisphere Corporation and its founder and our co-author, Sapan Desai, in our publication ... As such, our reviewers were not able to conduct an independent and private peer review and therefore notified us of their withdrawal from the peer-review process. We always aspire to perform our research in accordance with the highest ethical and professional guidelines. We can never forget the responsibility we have as researchers to scrupulously ensure that we rely on data sources that adhere to our high standards. Based on this development, we can no longer vouch for the veracity of the primary data sources. Due to this unfortunate development, the authors request that the paper be retracted." The Lancet. Retraction – Hydroxychloroquine or chloroquine with or without a macrolide for treatment of COVID-19: a multinational registry analysis. www.thelancet.com/journals/lancet/article/PIIS0140-6736(20)31324-6/fulltext.

[84] S. A. Thompson. How Long Will a Vaccine Really Take? New York Times, April 30, 2020. www.nytimes.com/interactive/2020/04/30/opinion/coronavirus-covid-vaccine.html.

10.9 DISCUSSION: THE IMPORTANCE OF TRUST IN SCIENCE AND EVIDENCE AND HOW TO BUILD IT

The global spread of the SARS-CoV-2 virus and COVID-19 pandemic is an unexpected opportunity to see the principles of the right to science, and the effects of their absence, in action. It is also an opportunity to measure the quality and the pace of the implementation of scientific and applied science recommendations found in the ICESCR, General Comment No. 25, and the 2017 UNESCO Statement on Science and Scientific Researchers, which is the source of several of the normative definitions of terms used by the CESCR in its General Comment.

Figure 10.4 shows that only two countries among the most affected developed countries have experienced relatively positive outcomes of their attempts at prevention and viral control. Japan and Germany were well prepared, highly organized, and exceptionally effective with respect to prevention and tertiary intervention policies. Germany has since led the way in Europe with large-scale testing for COVID-19, collecting more than 50 million samples (600 per million) since the start of the crisis. Although the country as of the time of writing ranks seventh globally for the number of confirmed cases – exceeding 2.9, million infections (34.144 per million) – the fatality rate is much lower than those of other developed

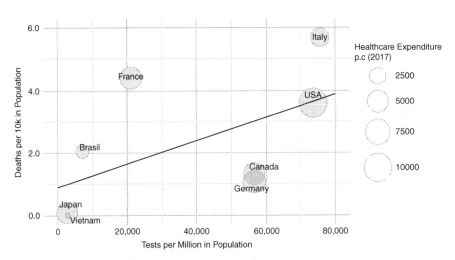

FIGURE 10.4 The relation between rate of deaths, SARS-CoV-2 testing frequency and expenditures on health per capita in the G-8 countries as compared to Vietnam – the most successful country in managing COVID/19 pandemics. Source: author's composite from various databases.

countries at 921 deaths per million. Japan represents an even more interesting and successful case with close to 500.000 infection cases (3.784 per million) and 9.195 deaths (73 deaths per million) so far recorded.

Among non-Western countries, success stories in handling the novel coronavirus outbreak include only highly developed countries such as South Korea, Taiwan and Hong Kong. However, there is one exception to this rule. Vietnam, a country of 97 million inhabitants, had not reported a single coronavirus-related death by June 9, 2020 and as of that time reported just 2.620 confirmed cases (27 per million!) and 0,4 deaths per million (total of 16 deaths!). Vietnam is a low–middle income country (2.185 USD per capita in 2017) with a low-spending healthcare system (130 USD per capita in 2017) and only 8 physicians per 10,000 population. However, unlike the case of Russia, there are several explanatory factors lending credence to Vietnam's claims. Fresh experience with the previous SARS and H5N1 epidemics allowed Vietnam to respond with immediacy, effectiveness, and transparency. The country relied on just four solutions, all of them cost-effective, to combat the virus: speedy implementation of a national lockdown; strategic testing (26.519 test per 1 million population)[85] using WHO-approved techniques and testing only those likely to be infected); contact tracing through apps; and effective public communication campaigns. Vietnam was also the first country in the world to be cleared of the SARS outbreak in 2003.

Based on these experiences, the most important factor influencing effectiveness of overall national policy appears to have been an educated approach to and respect for facts, evidence, and science from the national leadership as well as critical respect for international institutions.[86]

Learning from the scientific evidence and evidence-based practice in study of the effectiveness of non-pharmaceutical interventions against spread of SARS-CoV-2 is an imperative. Control of the pandemic while using combinations of movement restrictions, physical distancing, hygiene practices, and intensive case and contact detection and management proved effective in China, Singapore, and South Korea. However, the New Zealand government's strategy is unique because it represents the most effective strategy in high-income democratic setting, if measured by outcomes, while employing scientific evidence and technical expertise in controlling COVID-19 with total of 2501 cases and 25 cumulative deaths (500 cases and 5 deaths per 1 million population).

[85] Worldometer. **Reported Cases and Deaths by Country or Territory.** https://www.worldometers.info/coronavirus/?utm_campaign=homeAdvegas1?%20

[86] A video clip which has been shared hundreds of thousands of times on social media shows Merkel's explanation of the scientific basis behind her government's lockdown exit strategy. "She had all the calm confidence expected of a former research scientist with a doctorate in quantum chemistry who once co-authored a paper on the 'influence of spatial correlations on the rate of chemical reactions'." P. Olterman. Angela Merkel draws on science background in Covid-19 explainer. The Guardian. www.theguardian.com/world/2020/apr/16/angela-merkel-draws-on-science-background-in-covid-19-explainer-lockdown-exit.

Technical advisory group appointed by the Ministry of Health developed a strategy comprising of combination of intensive case and contact detection and management, physical distancing, movement restrictions, hygiene practices, and highlighting transmission hotspots and targeting community testing. It has been one of the keys to the success of its SARS-CoV-2 elimination and control strategy. It comprised of the following several science-led [87]sub-strategies as described in Nature Immunology paper:

- Quick and radical lockdowns. During the first wave of the pandemic (March 2020) the government implemented quick and radical lockdowns including travel restrictions and border closures. The speed and intensity of the New Zealand's governmental response to limit the epidemic is unprecedented internationally[88] representing the fastest trajectory to reach the highest country score in the Government Response Stringency Index[89].
- Timely and targeted testing. A key feature of the success in eliminating SARS-CoV-2 was moving early (January 31, 2020) to rapidly develop and implement in-house laboratory RT–PCR (PCR with reverse transcription) tests for SARS-CoV-2. The initiative was developed by regional diagnostic laboratories and academic scientists. Total number of 1.9 million people have been tested (380.000 per million population) significantly lower percentage of population tested as compared to the G-8 countries (UK 1.871.000 per million, USA 1.219.000 per million)
- Viral genomics. Viral genomics was also critical to New Zealand's successful public health response, with genomic sequencing being used as a key tool for understanding and limiting the spread of COVID-19
- Integrating genomics with epidemiological and modeling data. Local transmission chains and regional spread were able to be tracked and audited in real time
- Geographic information. When combined with geographic information, the pathways of viral spread, including from the global population, domestically and at the community level, were more easily revealed
- Superspreading events. A special focus of control was directed to identify superspreading events and trigger focused interventions.
- Transparent and credible governmental policy. Timely and decisive national leadership of New Zealand's by prime minister Jacinda Ardern was evidence-informed combining, rigorous case detection, isolation, contact tracing, and quarantine measures with population education and engagement.

These are the very qualities which national leaders are *obliged* to demonstrate, without excuses or qualifications, as a *bare minimum* to fulfill their duties under

---

[87] J. L. Geoghegan, N. J. Moreland, G. Le Gros, J. F. Ussher. New Zealand's science-led response to the SARS-CoV-2 pandemic. *Nat Immunol* 22, 262–263 (2021). https://doi.org/10.1038/s41590-021-00872-x

[88] S. Jefferies et al. COVID-19 in New Zealand and the impact of the national response: a descriptive epidemiological study. The Lancet Public Health, Volume 5, Issue 11, e612 - e623

[89] OXFORD COVID-19 Government Response Stringency index. https://data.humdata.org/dataset/oxford-covid-19-government-response-tracker

international human rights law. Thus General Comment No. 25 includes in its list of core minimal obligations (paragraph 52) the following:

- Ensure access to those applications of scientific progress that are critical to the enjoyment of the right to health and other ESCRs;
- Foster the development of international contacts and co-operation in the scientific field, without imposing restrictions on the movements of persons, goods and knowledge beyond those which are justifiable in accordance with article 4 of the Covenant.
- Develop a participatory national framework law on the RPEBSPA, which includes legal remedies in case of violations, and adopt and implement a participatory national strategy or an action plan for the realization of the RPEBSPA, which includes a strategy for the conservation, the development and diffusion of science;
- Adopt mechanisms aimed at aligning government policies and programs to the best available, generally accepted scientific evidence;
- Ensure that people have access to basic education and skills necessary for the comprehension and application of scientific knowledge and that scientific education in both public and private schools respect the best available scientific knowledge.[90]

Where individuals are informed and knowledgeable in scientific matters and methods, their trust in results derived from science is greater. Where government officials, and especially national leaders, are informed and knowledgeable, and act in accordance with scientific evidence and human rights, citizen trust in both their leadership and in science itself increases. This is explicitly recognized in paragraph 54 of General Comment No. 25:

> A clear benefit of scientific progress is that scientific knowledge is used in decision-making and policies, which should, as far as possible, be based on the best available scientific evidence. States should endeavor to align their policies to the best scientific evidence available. They should, furthermore, promote public trust and support for sciences throughout society and a culture of active citizen engagement with science, in particular through a vigorous and informed democratic debate on the production and use of scientific knowledge, and a dialogue between the scientific community and society.[91]

10.10 CONCLUSION

Trust in evidence-based policy and the right to science is a significant explanatory factor of the sharp contrast in the figures for deaths per 100,000 persons and case-fatality

---
[90] Supra n. 11, at para. 52.
[91] Ibid., at para. 54.

between Japan Japan (7.25/1,9%), Canada (62.06/2.3%), Russia (67,55/2,2%)[92], Germany (92.64/2.7%), France (143.47/2.0%), the US (169.07./1.8%), Italy (181.87/3.0%) and the United Kingdom (191,02/2.9%) respectively attributed to the SARS-CoV-2 virus.[93] . That helps us better understanding the governmental policies and social behavior determining not only the number of number of cumulative cases[94] but also in some cases capacity to organize effective vaccination policy[95] The extent of such trust is not only a question of how educated leaders are or how many scientists are directly involved in government or administrations.[96] It is also a question of the scientific organizational and social experience with epidemics, behavioral habits, cultural values, and respect for the institutional setup within and between nations.

This suggests and illustrates the significance of whether or not policy in general, and scientific policy in particular, follows the facts, data, and guidelines, as well as how much we adhere to the idea of a right to science. Given the general acknowledgement of the necessity and importance of science in the fight against COVID-19, it is an interesting question whether the respect for science generated by the episode is enough to counter the much-maligned pre-pandemic rise of "alternative facts" and "fake news" in the aftermath of the pandemic. Whatever the eventual outcome, the case of the SARS-CoV-2 virus pandemic clearly demonstrates that the right to science is equally challenging to implement and just as important for nations of the world as the idea of science itself. However, this chapter's analysis of the elements of the right to science and their ability to enhance societal trust in science indicate that attempting to meet that challenge is a good idea.

---

[92] The official figures coming from Russia, as well as from several other countries in EU and developing countries including Mexico, Belarus and India are contradictory.

[93] Johns Hopkins University Medicine. COVID-19 Dashboard by the Center for Systemic Science and Engineering (CSSE) at Johns Hopkins University. https://coronavirus.jhu.edu/data/mortality.

[94] Johns Hopkins University Medicine. Cumulative cases by days since 50th confirmed case. COVID-19 Dashboard by the Center for Systemic Science and Engineering (CSSE) at Johns Hopkins University. https://coronavirus.jhu.edu/data/cumulative-cases.

[95] According to data collected by Bloomberg vaccine tracker as of April 3, 2021, more than 628 millon doses The latest rate was roughly 16.3 million doses a day have been administered across 150 countries. It's the biggest vaccination campaign in history. https://www.bloomberg.com/graphics/covid-vaccine-tracker-global-distribution/

[96] In his first set of presidential appointments, Obama brought into his administration five science Nobel prize winners and twenty-five members of the National Academies of Science, Engineering and Medicine.

PART III

Disseminating, Implementing, and Putting into Practice the Right to Science

11

"Fight the Fear with the Facts!"

Ranga Yogeshwar[*]

"We hold these truths to be self-evident, that all men are created equal." These words mark the beginning of the Declaration of Independence of the United States of America. What is remarkable here is the formulation of "self-evidence" as an invitation to a social consensus that should be accepted by all parties. It is the basis of our democracy and a central element of the Enlightenment. Science has also firmly adopted this element within its own universe. In a complex system of peer reviewing, transparent reproducibility of results, and disclosure of its methods, a resilient process for scientific knowledge has emerged. Today, facts are based on countless tests and critical arguments within the scientific community and mark the result of an immense distillation process in the common search for truth. This well-established approach is self-evident to all participants. Within our scientific world there is consensus on the grammar of this methodology.

However, the dissemination of alternative facts has significantly grown as an increasing number of people have access to multimedia channels and the opportunity to post and broadcast their views. Therefore, we are currently experiencing a growing disregard for established scientific facts and even face questioning of the scientific system itself. The climate debate is a particularly powerful example of this. In their *Consensus Handbook* published in 2018, the authors note a remarkable gap:

> Despite many studies confirming the overwhelming scientific consensus on climate change, there is a large gap between the 97% consensus within science and the public's perception of the consensus. On average, people assume that only about 67% of climate scientists see humans as the cause of global warming. Even more worrying: only 13% of Americans know that the consensus is over 90%. This misjudgment is not only true for the general public. Even many science teachers are not aware of the consensus. The unfortunate consequence of this is that many

---

[*] The author would like to thank his youngest daughter Selina for her critical reviewing of the text and for her charming help to improve his language skills. I would also like to thank Andrew Mazibrada for his helpful and critical review.

teachers are equally opposed to current climate research when it comes to climate change.[1]

Thus, while the right of all people to benefit from scientific progress and its applications is recognized both in the Universal Declaration of Human Rights and in Article 15 of the International Covenant on Economic, Social and Cultural Rights (ICESCR), a broad questioning of scientific unity has emerged in several societies. Science itself is the focus of criticism and is confronted in many places with doubt – from climate sceptics to vaccination opponents, and from conspiracy supporters of chemtrails to citizens who turn their backs on classical medicine and follow obscure miracle healers.

The vehemence of this rejection of science has increased to such an extent that even scientists themselves are now actively raising their voices: On April 22, 2017, I engaged in the March for Science in Berlin. Similar demonstrations also took place in other cities. Some 11,000 people, including several presidents of German science organizations, the Mayor of Berlin, and many impassioned students, spoke out against alternative facts and in favour of a fact-based policy. As we walked along the avenue *Unter den Linden* towards the Brandenburg Gate, I realized how absurd the scenery was: in the midst of an enlightened industrial nation embracing the fruits of science, we had to demonstrate for the most elementary principles of evidence through scientific facts!

But how could this discrepancy occur? What factors led to this growing scientific scepticism? What role does the media play and is science itself partly to blame for this development? In this chapter, I would like to highlight some aspects of this apparently disturbed science communication within a greater context.

11.1 OUR PERCEPTIONS DO NOT CORRESPOND TO REALITY, BUT ARE INCREASINGLY SHAPED BY THE MEDIA

In 2017, Sinan Aral and his colleagues from the Massachusetts Institute of Technology (MIT) conducted a study[2] that analyzed how news spread on Twitter between 2006 and 2017. Their findings were worrying: on average, news that had been verified[3] as true took six times as long to reach 1,500 users than news verified to be false, and furthermore, false claims were shared 70 percent more often than correct information. "Falsehood diffused significantly farther, faster, deeper, and more broadly than the truth in all categories." The most striking thing was that the conventional wisdom that bots accelerated the spread of falsehood more than

---

[1] J. Cook, S. van der Linden, E. Maibach, and S. Lewandowsky The Consensus Handbook (2018). (www.climatechangecommunication.org/all/consensus-handbook), p. 4.
[2] http://ide.mit.edu/sites/default/files/publications/2017%20IDE%20Research%20Brief%20False%20News.pdf.
[3] News items used in the study were verified as true or false using information from six independent fact-checking organizations that exhibited 95 percent to 98 percent agreement on the classifications.

humans was wrong: "humans, not robots, are more likely responsible for the dramatic spread of false news." "Fake news" generates higher instances of emotional response, for example surprise or the perception of novelty, and thus substantially boosts click rates. In an interview with Sinan Aral, he explained to me that online portals financed by advertising in particular intensify this process, as they directly profit from the higher click rates induced by this cognitive effect.

The visibility of the respective content depends on the economic rules of a platform: while Facebook, Google, YouTube or Twitter may appear to be free of charge for the user, their business model focuses on their monetization as advertising platforms. The users themselves are the products as their data provides the basis for targeted advertising. The primary intention of social networks is therefore not mutual exchange and "connecting the world" as is often claimed, but rather to maximize the interaction of the user with tailored advertisements. Content that is frequently shared and viewed is automatically prioritized by algorithms and thus becomes even more visible.

Click rates, along with viewing duration and other parameters such as interactivity, flow into an algorithm and thereby determines the placement of the respective content. For YouTubers and Influencers, posted videos are even classified into different lucrative categories by algorithms. Depending on the content, you earn different amounts for the same number of clicks.

This focus on click-through rates automatically becomes an information filter. The focus is not on the content itself or its social relevance, but on a setup optimized for the algorithm, with the goal of maximizing advertising reach and thus the generation of higher income for the influencer. The grammar of these platforms determines the content. What began years ago in classic television media with an optimization of the audience flow has now developed into an art in its own right: search engine optimization (SEO), channel optimization, traffic control and keyword selection determine the reach on the net and thus the visibility of the information. All this has as its central purpose the maximization of user loyalty and retention time, since this forms the basis of the underlying business model of these platforms. The intensity of content-generation also plays an important role: Those who post only sporadically are downgraded by the algorithm and eventually end up in digital obscurity. Continuous activity, on the other hand, increases the reach of posted material. Out of this constraint, the content profile changes. The user does not post because they have something specific to say, but rather because the algorithm demands they be active. Through automatic reminders, the user is constantly encouraged by the platform to update their posts. The numerical recording and evaluation of page views, likes, reach, and responsiveness further fuels a spiral of excitement. Everything needs to be fast hence there is no time for pausing, questioning, and reflecting.

Interestingly, all this lacks any trace of transparency: companies like Google, Facebook, and Twitter do not disclose their internal modus operandi and so, even famous YouTubers and Influencers operate within a space that is digitally opaque. Instead of working with clear criteria and facts as a basis for the decision processes concerning the classification and evaluation of their videos, decisions are communicated to them as a result of the "almighty algorithm." No outsider knows the underlying mechanisms of these algorithms. This means that the world's largest video network lacks a culture of responsibility, openness, and accountability. There is no true communication with responsible "editors" and it is remarkable that the scene has not yet publicly protested, although a large number of YouTubers criticize this "algorithmic" handling. What would happen in the real working world, if employees without transparent criteria and rules were paid differently according to almost arbitrary arguments?

11.2 THE INSCRUTABLE ALGORITHMS INCREASINGLY DETERMINE THE CONTENT, BUT SO FAR, WE HAVE DEALT TOO LITTLE WITH THE CONSEQUENCES OF THIS CHANGED GRAMMAR

Even in the classical media world, content has been used as bait for advertising, but this interaction has thus far been subject to clear rules: Advertisements had to be labelled as such and journalistic work followed a clearly formulated code, rooted in principles such as truthfulness, due diligence, and the clear separation of advertising and editorial work. This agreement provided the freedom for journalistic independence despite the commercial basis of a newspaper. Although advertising revenue indirectly financed journalistic research, the editorial part remained largely unaffected.

In the new digital world of communication, these protected information spaces have disappeared. The celebrated Influencers are essentially masters of surreptitious advertising, for this is precisely where their business model lies. The world of colorful irrelevance is soaked in advertising impulses. What matters are the number of followers, and the larger the community, the more potent the advertising effect in the selected target group. In order for this to work, the algorithm has to be fed as optimally as possible. The medium shapes the content as only such content that fulfils the logic of the algorithms has a chance of reaching a wide audience. Therefore, content is determined by the commercial objectives of the algorithm's coders and not by any journalistic criteria such as social relevance. Modern media focus on a new kind of business based on excitement.

Players such as Google took over the classical advertising business and professionalized it. The precise crystallization and addressing of target groups, the numerical accuracy of campaigns, the integration and targeted forwarding of buying impulses, the timely evaluation of advertising activities – all of these are not commonly offered by classic media. The user reveals their activities and interests and their data influences the information streams they get to see. This feedback automatically leads to the isolation and profiling of the individual. How far we have come in terms of targeting has been recently shown in a revealing experiment: As part of its "Privacy Project," the *New York Times* bought targeted Internet advertising.[4] The newspaper "picked 16 categories (like registered Democrats or people trying to lose weight) and targeted ads at people in them." However, instead of trying to sell products or services, they "used the ads to reveal the invisible information itself." For example: "This ad believes that you are male, currently paying off your debts, but often shop in luxury shops." The fine granularity of data captured allows, when combined with predictive algorithms, the ever more precise addressing of the individual, despite promised anonymity.[5] This "surveillance capitalism"[6] is the core business of digital platforms. The prediction of the user's coming consumer desire becomes more and more accurate through better models and what, at the moment, still appears to be pure observation can easily degenerate into active manipulation through interspersed information.

11.3 THESE INTELLIGENT MEDIA DO NOT INFORM, BUT CHANGE AND SHAPE THE BEHAVIOR OF THEIR USERS

What emerges here is a widespread attack on free will. The consistent application of these tools within the political arena could end any hope of free democracies. Internet platforms are becoming more and more powerful and at the same time their traditional media opponents, the free press, are dissolving. The newspaper and magazine industries are facing a dramatic decline in revenues and circulation figures. Larger publishers are securing their own survival with new digital business models, decoupling the old advertising business and setting up separate commercial platforms, job exchanges, real estate portals, or news aggregators whose algorithms reflect the individual interests of users. This change threatens not only the existence of the traditional media industry, but also that of critical journalism itself as the digital world currently lacks resilient business models for independent journalism.

11.4 JOURNALISM IS REDUCED TO A COMMERCIAL EXCITATION BUSINESS

In the current transition phase between old and new media worlds, the categories of the digital platforms also infect the working basis of traditional media. We can all follow the fierce struggle for existence through circulation and quotas, which results in an increasingly hysterical press. The endless scandal-mongering and

---

[4] www.nytimes.com/interactive/2019/04/30/opinion/privacy-targeted-advertising.html.
[5] Data providers claim the information stored and shared is anonymous, but that doesn't mean it remains that way. Specific facets of the data, and patterns within it, can learn to the identification of individuals.
[6] Shoshana Zuboff, *The Age of Surveillance Capitalism: The Fight for a Human Future at the New Frontier of Power* (PublicAffairs, 2019).

sensationalist headlines are like a last-ditch attempt to make oneself heard within the media noise. Once a theme becomes viral, it is taken up by everyone in a reactive cycle and drama-fueled feedback-loop. Editors break with the norms of classical journalism: In news programs, reports are accompanied by music and artificial moods are created through the use of slow motion. The former president of the German Bundestag, Wolfgang Thierse, put it aptly: "The talk shows are an essential part of the hysterical political communication in Germany. The focus not only on topicality, which is correct and understandable, but also on the aggravation in the title and in the moderation – fear, negative expectations, anxiety. That doesn't promote and alleviate anxiety and fear, that doesn't promote and fight populism."[7]

A study of the 141 German political talk shows in 2016, where German media constantly talked about refugees, showed that other relevant topics such as climate change or renewable energy concepts were not taken up in a single round.[8] However, now, only three years later, the climate debate is vigorously discussed across all forms of media following the global "Fridays for Future" protests.

The focus is no longer on content, but on attention. The guiding principles are not facts or social relevance, but reach, hit rates, and aggressive click-baiting.

11.5 WE UNDERESTIMATE THE EFFECT OF THIS EXCITATION BUSINESS ON OUR PERCEPTION

One well known example from science is the media coverage of animal experiments.[9] Emotions always win. The British market research company Ipsos MORI conducted a survey compromising 25,000 people from 33 countries in order to find out how the perceived reality of citizens differs from the actual facts in the country.[10] People in Germany, for example, estimated the percentage of migrants living in their own country to be twice as high as it actually was, whereas, in contrast, they underestimated the proportion of overweight people. When asked what proportion of children and young people under the age of fourteen were overweight, the answer was half that of the actual figure.

The open social networks are a tempting invitation to populists and conspiracy theorists. The Polish sociologist and philosopher Zygmunt Bauman describes this historical transformation process as *liquid modernity*:

---

[7] www1.wdr.de/daserste/monitor/sendungen/talkshows-102.html.
[8] Ibid.
[9] Tipu Aziz, John Stein and Ranga Yogeshwar, "Animal testing: TV or not TV?," Nature, volume 470, 457–459 (2011).
[10] Ipsos MORI, Perils of Perception 2015; www.ipsos.com/ipsos-mori/en-uk/perils-perception-2015; Folien unter www.ipsos.com/sites/default/files/migrations/en-uk/files/Assets/Docs/Polls/ipsos-perils-of-perception-charts-2015.pdf. Ashley Kirk, "What are the world's most ignorant countries?", The Telegraph, 12 December, 2015; www.telegraph.co.uk/news/worldnews/12043708/What-are-the-worlds-most-ignorant-countries.html).

Social media do not promote our capacity for dialogue because it is so easy to avoid controversies ... Most do not use the social media to promote community, not to broaden their horizons, but on the contrary to hide in a comfort zone where they only hear the echoes of their own voice, and where everything they see is reflections of their own faces.[11]

This shift in priorities leads to a decoupling between the media world and reality. The perceived truth is more important than actual facts; the perceived will of the voter wins, even if this is perhaps only a wish far away from reality. When politicians intend to put a topic on the agenda, its media effect is explored first. Subsequently, we observe how the political agenda is increasingly dictated primarily by its media impact and not by the necessity of its content. How dramatic this situation has become can be seen, for example, in the absurd buckling of the Japanese government in the context of cervical cancer vaccination. The media power of the Japanese vaccination opponents led to a decline in the vaccination coverage from 70 percent to less than 1 percent.[12]

11.6 "DIGITALITY" AND REALITY START TO MIX

The appeal of the digital Eldorado lies in its latency-free response time, the complete dissolution of geographical distances, and its promise of abundance and augmented reality. Here, one moves from one impulse to another and the digital space turns out to be the breeding ground of a new world dynamic demanding constant innovations and surprises. This unprecedented attraction leads to a novel kind of global migration to a "digital continent." Some see this migration into the digital world as running away from reality; an escapism from a real world replete with shortcomings and threats. Our attitude toward our personal lives is increasingly determined by the digital world. It is not only communication and information gathering that are organized by search engines and platforms. The net is increasingly becoming the kernel of our lives and the cosmos of our dreams. The focus of our consciousness is shifting into the digital world where profiles are the emerging substitute for the actual human and likes are becoming a barometer for one's attitude to life.

The current German public television (ARD-ZDF) online study states in its 2018 report that the average daily Internet usage time of 14-year-olds and older has now grown to 196 minutes per day. In the younger age group of 14- to 29-year-olds, the average daily Internet usage is just under six hours.[13] In this group alone, the daily time for individual communication – chatting, emailing, WhatsApp or other messenger activities – adds up to 152 minutes.

[11] http://elpais.com/elpais/2017/01/10/inenglish/1484037730_759492.html.
[12] www.spektrum.de/news/impfgegner-gewinnen-in-japan-mit-falschmeldungen-und-fake-experimenten/1635488.
[13] www.ard-zdf-onlinestudie.de/files/2018/ARD-ZDF-Onlinestudie_Infografik_2018.pdf.

As you are reading this sentence, over 200,000 Facebook posts and 22,800 new tweets are streaming online.[14] Facebook users watch one billion videos per day. Every second, 28,000 Instagram images are liked and on WhatsApp alone, more than 27 billion new messages are exchanged every day. These figures reflect the global intensity of this shift – no other medium has achieved such a high level of social penetration in such a short time.

In addition to communication, more and more processes are shifting from physical space to the digital universe: shopping, partner selection, booking travel, paying bills, and medical analyses, digital images of our reality are being created everywhere. This digital migration subsequently leads to changes in behavior, as "digitality" and reality mix. One example is the change in physicality: the portraits we see on Instagram or Facebook are often embellished by apps such as Facetune[15] which can smooth wrinkles and skin spots, retouch body shapes, and bleach teeth using algorithms. The posted images are thus beautified artefacts that unfold their normative power over time. Here, too, the flow direction is reversed: real people attempt to emulate and correspond to their digital alter egos. We want to look like digital avatars. Actresses eliminate their wrinkles, politicians straighten their teeth, and newscasters dye their hair, because the visual impression is becoming increasingly important. If we compare the political campaigning of the seventies with today's electoral campaigns, this change is obvious as the portraits of the candidates are now being retouched and smoothed in such a way that they look completely artificial. Here, a new culture of artefacts is established, which unconsciously extends to other areas as well.

While classical media still have to select their published content rigorously due to limited broadcasting space or newspaper pages, the digital world is free of these restrictions. The media space seems to be boundless and holds space for everything from potato cultivation, quantum physics, UFO sightings to political statements. Curation is almost completely eliminated, making the digital media space a gathering place for everything and everyone, superimposed by the dissolution of authenticity. Through the use of modern AI techniques, the production of "Deep Fakes" are now possible: artificial images and videos are already produced in such a perfect way that distinguishing between real and fake is almost impossible.

11.7 FAKE SCIENCE

The increasing use of the word "authentic" is ultimately a sign of this emerging culture of artificiality. Over time, we become accustomed to transforming reality to our taste. So why not also adjust the universe of scientific knowledge according to our needs? Tobacco companies present studies minimizing the risks of smoking in

---

[14] www.webfx.com/internet-real-time/ also: www.internetlivestats.com/watch/internet-users/.
[15] www.facetuneapp.com.

pseudo-journals; pharmaceutical companies praise the effectiveness of their medicines; climate "experts" provide alternative explanations for global warming; and scientific institutes present a novel "dual-fluid reactor" that supposedly meets high safety standards as well as economic goals.[16] There are numerous specialist conferences, institutes, and purported experts whose publications and websites are characterized by the same patterns that are also used within "serious" science: they quote each other, use complicated technical terms, and list their merits. A genuine expert may notice the bluff, but to the layman there is no comprehensible difference and so what we experience is a questionable fusion of fake and real science.

In 2018, research by journalists from Westdeutscher Rundfunk, Norddeutscher Rundfunk, and Süddeutsche Zeitung (WDR, NDR, and SZ) revealed how dubious journals are diluting quality standards of scientific publications such as anonymous peer reviews.[17] Open access procedures and a large number of *predatory journals*, as the librarian Jeffrey Beall calls them, have changed the current fee model of scientific journalism.[18] Traditionally, readers financed printed journals through their subscriptions. With electronic publishing, an increasing number of journals are asking authors to pay and posting their articles on the Internet free of charge for the reader. The open access model has its advantages, because in principle it makes research accessible to everyone. Poorer nations in particular benefit from open access to up-to-date research. Most open access publications are no less trustworthy than the average of their printed predecessors, but a questionable business model has emerged from this reversal of the flow direction: In the life sciences alone, some 30,000 journals vie for paying authors. Under the general pressure to publish and the struggle for attention, junk journals are created that wave through the articles of their customers without serious peer reviewing. This system is fueled by additional drivers such as "impact factors."

There is a remarkable parallel between the media and science landscapes, because in both cases traditional structures are being replaced by corresponding digital publication models. Editorial rigor begins to fade out and, in both cases, underlying commercial criteria become the driving force. As a result, the citizen is wrapped in a fog of questionable information and not in a position to distinguish between the relevant and the irrelevant or to classify news-streams accordingly. While for a long time, the procurement of information was an important criterion for responsible participation, we are now confronted with an ocean of information such that sorting and classifying becomes the essential skill, instead of critical analysis. But how is this possible, in an environment where algorithms and commercial platforms are taking over?

---

[16] https://festkoerper-kernphysik.de/dfr.
[17] www.ndr.de/nachrichten/investigation/Dossier-Das-Geschaeft-mit-der-Wissenschaft,fakesciencedossier100.html.
[18] www.zeit.de/2017/11/fachzeitschriften-fake-forschung-wissenschaft-betrug-publikationen/komplettansicht.

On the occasion of the 70th anniversary of the Universal Declaration of Human Rights, UNESCO expressed a desire to reaffirm its commitment, mandate, and role in the promotion and protection of human rights, but when the authors of the former declaration spoke of the merits of scientific progress in 1948, there was probably still more of a consensus on what it meant. In today's world, the term has become blurred and one would almost have to ask whether universal declarations still matter, as our frames of orientation seem to have changed. Large political parties are dissolving, classical leading media are on the retreat, privacy is being commercialized. The balance between public and privately financed research has shifted and the border between the two has become blurred.

The application of intelligent commercial algorithms leads to a social de-solidarization effect. Within the insurance industry, for example, behavioral policy pricing models have been introduced. The former "we" is shifting to "I" and fragmented societies are beginning to lose their common denominator.

11.8 WE UNDERESTIMATE THE EFFECT OF COMPLEXITY

Thus far, many science communicators – including myself – have been convinced that scientific literacy would automatically lead to more responsible decision-making among citizens. However, we seem to have underestimated the impact of growing complexity.

Medicine, for example, so essential to our continued health, is becoming inscrutable for most people, but so are the worlds of technology, the media, and finance. The virus of complexity has spread everywhere. No politician truly understands the details of a free trade agreement and bankers are ignorant about nonlinear derivative algorithms. Car mechanics no longer diagnose what is wrong with a car by the sound its engine makes, but instead connect its internal systems to a computerized interface. Complexity has taken on such proportions that even the most everyday items are beyond our understanding. What is hidden under the smooth user interfaces of our touchscreens is far beyond our ken. When we proclaim the necessity of public understanding of science, we ignore the simple fact that the inherent complexity of science in the modern world makes this level of widespread understanding impossible.

In our technological world of wonders, we have to trust computer scientists, chemists, climate researchers, and medical professionals. Every farmer fertilizes his fields in total ignorance of the deeper mechanisms of the expensive granulates and pellets he distributes. He, who ploughs the same soil as his fathers and grandfathers once did, suddenly falters, confronted with the incomprehensibility of his surroundings. For most people, the explosion of knowledge and innovation is felt like an act of incapacitation. Progress pushes them out of their comfort zones into a world that is deeply unfamiliar. Uncertainty and mistrust spread, and the gleam of the Enlightenment is dimming. Some desire a simple world backed by clear answers and, in their voices, we can perceive the fear-driven anger of incomprehension. They fight against their incapacitation, terrified that the future will snatch their world from them. The former rulers of the clear and comprehensible are now the slaves of complexity, the guardians of tradition have become the driven ones of a disruptive progress. The phenomenal changes wrought by science and technology have generated a growing posture of resistance within societies. Suddenly, the voices of doubters, climate sceptics and vaccination opponents increase. People yearn for simple answers and in a complex world they will believe those who promise simplicity and plausible pseudo-rationality above those who tend towards a more complex explanation even if that is the truth.

11.9 HOW TRUSTWORTHY IS SCIENCE?

When researchers examined the immune system of bacteria a few years ago, they came across strange, repetitive gene sequences. Over time, it became understood that similar structures existed in the genomes of many different prokaryotes, and gradually researchers began to understand how bacteria, for example, protect themselves against viral infections. But then it became clear that this system, known as CRISPR-Cas, also poses a revolutionary and simple method for gene modification.[19] And with this promising potential application, the entire branch of research was poisoned overnight by economic incentives. The ongoing patent dispute over CRISPR between the Broad Institute of MIT and Harvard, UC Berkeley, and other players is a shameful example of how the scientific joy of a promising discovery can quickly lead to a bitter battle for economic exploitability. Now, attorneys, patent judges, and venture capitalists run wild with a scepter snatched from scientists.

Similar observations can also be made in other disciplines. Recently, the *New York Times* published an illuminating article about the salaries of researchers in the field of artificial intelligence research.[20] At Google DeepMind in London, for example, the annual personnel cost for 400 employees amounted to USD 138 million in 2016. That is an average salary of $345,000 per employee. Consequence: Outstanding scientists leave public research institutes and universities in order to enter the service of large and well-paid private companies. These salaries siphon talent from the well of expertise that would normally feed independent, public institutions and universities. Independent expertise is lacking from discourses considering the medium- and long-term impacts of social networks and artificial intelligence. The questioning of Marc Zuckerberg by the US Congress in 2018 was a demonstration of political ignorance in the field of social media. The questions asked revealed a shameful paucity of knowledge about a fundamental influencer of global society and a relevant and necessary debate on the application of

---

[19] Martin Jinek et al., "A Programmable Dual-RNA-Guided DNA Endonuclease in Adaptive Bacterial Immunity," Science 337, Issue 6096: S. 816–82 (2012).
[20] www.nytimes.com/2018/04/19/technology/artificial-intelligence-salaries-openai.html.

basic democratic principles to social media platforms was ultimately derailed due to a lack of independent competence.

It is time for science, with confidence and passion, to set a counterpoint to one-dimensional economic perspectives. Scientists must insist that their findings serve the common good. If algorithms increasingly destabilize our financial world, or perpetrate inequality and discrimination, then it is for the scientific community to critically question their conduct and permissiveness and rethink the consequences of their actions. If the findings of the psychology and neuroscience disciplines are irresponsibly misused by companies for the manipulative targeting of voters, as in the case of Cambridge Analytica, then we ought to hear a clear voice of dissent and opposition from the ranks of scientific professionals and researchers. But where, within computer science, do we hear critical discussions about algorithms or the growing evaluation of big data? In these fields, it is critical that risks are examined by coalitions with interdisciplinary expertise and a social perspective.

We urgently need more reflected progress. In some areas we are confronted with questions of dual use and unfortunately, there are not only "benefits of scientific progress and its applications."[21] In the dawn of a new arms race, scientists could simply refuse to engage in any further research on autonomous weapons. Data scientists could question the goals of the commercial data collection frenzy, even if these questions could lead to restrictions within their own discipline. With the growing impact of science on all areas of our lives, societies must critically question the benefits and the objectives of scientific research. When science speaks of the "public understanding" of its disciplines, we should not conflate this with "public acceptance." The right for everyone to enjoy the benefits of scientific progress and its application contains within its normative framework a right to clearly define wherein those true benefits lie.

11.10 DOES SCIENCE REALLY WANT CRITICAL DIALOGUE AND IF SO, WHAT IS IT PREPARED TO DO ABOUT IT?

When research budgets are cut or funding falters, science likes to raise its voice. In June 2018, German astronaut Alexander Gerst started his mission on the International Space Station (ISS) and during each press event, the strictly "scientific" nature of his mission was repeatedly stressed. Here, "scientific knowledge" was used as an excuse, although there was no reliable basis for it.

Interestingly, criticism of space research is missing from the scientific world. But how different things are when people's own research budgets are up for grabs. This was the case in 1990, for example, when the Federal Republic of Germany's opulent space budget led to savings having to be made in other fields of research. Suddenly, there was an outcry: in November 1990, the German Physical Society published

---

[21] www.ohchr.org/EN/ProfessionalInterest/Pages/CESCR.aspx.

a sharp criticism of the benefits of manned space flight. At that time, there was a whole catalogue of plausible arguments against the promotion of expensive manned space flight. But was the underlying motive really a reasonable, critical discussion about the benefits of manned space flight? Did people want to set the priorities for funding according to scientific criteria in an advisory capacity? Or was it merely a matter of securing their own benefits? In the meantime, the physicists probably have enough money, and although the factual arguments against expensive manned space travel from that time are still valid, the critical voices seem to have faded. Thus, astronaut Alexander Gerst floated off on his "scientific" mission without any counterarguments.

If scientists want to argue credibly, they must demonstrate a degree of balance and rigor. They must take the floor to debate critically – also when their own interests are not the only consideration. Scientists ought to consider the misuse of the product of their own research a reason to raise their voices. Scientific knowledge shapes our technical progress, but its direction is currently set by private interests that do not always coincide with the interests of societies as a whole, and this is precisely where we need our scientific professionals to find the courage of their convictions.

The majority of digital innovations in Silicon Valley are based on lucrative business models. If these fail to materialize, usually no research will be conducted. However, there are some exceptions: In the early 1990s, Tim Berners-Lee invented the World Wide Web at the European research center CERN. On April 30, 1993, the directors of CERN declared that the technology should be freely available to everyone, without any patent claims.[22] Without this remarkable openness, marked by a decisive focus on sharing knowledge and foregoing profit, the overwhelming growth of the Internet may never have been possible.

Scientists ought not to orient themselves towards the market, but instead position themselves to offer the reasonable and independent guidance now much needed by an insecure society. This important dialogue between science and society, however, also requires appropriate financial support. So far, the scientific community has seemed disinclined to do so, apart from a handful of initiatives and projects whose paltry funding is at best measured alongside the purchase price of a somewhat more expensive piece of laboratory equipment.

11.11 COMMUNICATION WITH CITIZENS HAS PLAYED A SUBORDINATE ROLE IN SCIENCE SO FAR

Although there are good initiatives and some notable individual efforts, there is still a general lack of systematic dialogue focused on reliable processes for scientists and citizens jointly to discuss critical issues, even though they seem to have common goals. The Science Barometer 2018, a representative survey of science organizations in Germany, shows that for three-quarters of the respondents, consideration for the

---

[22] https://home.cern/science/computing/birth-web.

common good is among the most important qualities that a good scientist must possess. However, less than half of those surveyed (40 percent), believe that scientists actually work for the good of society.[23] According to the respondents, the principal explanation for distrust of modern science is its dependence on financial backers. Furthermore, more than two thirds of the respondents felt that the influence of industry on science was too great. If, in this context, we demand the right of all people to benefit from the advantages of scientific progress and its applications, then it is not only the ability of science to communicate and engage in dialogue that is of central importance, but also its independence.

Until now, young scientists have completed their studies without any obligatory education on the importance of, and techniques for, communication with lay people. There are no academic credits for the kind of dialogue with the public, which is frequently demanded of them. Education of new scientists simply does not focus on these issues. As a science journalist, I have spoken out for many years in favour of opening up science and, over the past twenty years, numerous initiatives have been launched in Germany. Since 2000, the *Communicator Prize* has been awarded to scientists in Germany who have rendered outstanding services to communicating their work or scientific issues in general to the public.[24] The prize was intended to encourage scientists to engage more extensively in dialogue beyond their own community. The vast majority of scientists are unknown to those who benefit from their work and rarely enter the public arena. This applies equally to young talents who now shine in scientific circles. Even wonderful public lectures by scientists ask too much of the lay person and are often aimed at the science community and not at the general public. Scientists are too rarely seen on political talk shows, for example, and thus still lack a formative impact on broad cross-sections of the population. As a science journalist, over the course of thirty years, I have had to learn how difficult it is for most scientists to communicate with the general public. Most scientists, when interviewed, fail to break down their exciting research in comprehensible words or to explain complex concepts in terms intelligible to the lay person. A developmental biologist, who was a Nobel Prize winner, was once asked by students during a public event whether it was possible to revive dinosaurs, as in the film Jurassic Park. She looked at the student and asked what Jurassic Park was.[25]

11.12 BOTTOM UP

In the summer of 2004, twenty-eight-year-old Salman Khan helped his cousin Nadia[26] who lived in New Orleans and had problems understanding mathematics. Salman

---

[23] www.wissenschaft-im-dialog.de/projekte/wissenschaftsbarometer/wissenschaftsbarometer-2018/.
[24] www.dfg.de/gefoerderte_projekte/wissenschaftliche_preise/communicator-preis/index.jsp.
[25] www.wissenschaft.de/allgemein/das-leben-zwischen-gott-und-genen/.
[26] Bryant Urstadt: "Salman Khan: The Messiah of Math", Bloomberg Businessweek, 19 May, 2011; www.bloomberg.com/news/articles/2011-05-19/salman-khan-the-messiah-of-math.

Kahn, who had recently completed his master's degree in computer science and electrical engineering at MIT and worked for the hedge fund Wohl Capital Management in Boston, designed a small website for his cousin. Nadia was then able to enjoy a special tutoring course despite a distance of more than two thousand kilometers. Salman has a great didactic talent. Using a simple messenger program, he first produced small online sequences with explanations and tasks for Nadia. He calmly taught her how to calculate fractions, guided her through the murky depths of the search for the lowest common denominator, and explained little tricks for shortening fractions and the secret of prime factor decomposition.[27]

As Nadia's performance dramatically improved, her younger brothers Arman and Ali also followed their cousin's online tutorials. Sal Khan expanded his website, bought a tablet and turned the screen into a lively blackboard where he gradually explained the mathematics curriculum to a growing crowd of students. He posted his first video on the internet on November 16, 2006. When he realized just how many people were avidly watching his lessons, he quit his job and created an informative world of online tutorials. Ten million students worldwide now use his free tutoring and can access over three thousand videos on the website of the Khan Academy. Yet Khan and his team continue to develop their learning platform. Personalized learning plans with tasks and tests make completely individual learning possible. In contrast to rigid, frontal teaching, the learning pace of the individual is also considered. Khan proved that even weak students can significantly improve their performance through the tutorials.

The Khan Academy is now one of the most successful free online learning platforms in the world.[28] Influential individuals like Bill Gates, as well as many well-known multinationals, have supported the expansion of Khan's online school with generous donations. With its staff of programmers, teachers, and data analysts still growing, every lesson is evaluated and optimized. This lively site represents a revolution in the education system. In addition, there is now an abundance of excellent YouTube channels that explain scientific connections in accessible and clear ways, often beautifully, artfully, and engagingly. Grant Sanderson's outstanding mathematics blog on YouTube, "3blue1brown," is an excellent example.[29] While communication within institutional science is progressing slowly, individual talents on the Internet have uploaded or established great tutorial systems. Some of these sites have several million subscribers and demonstrate the potential for good science education.

In 2012, Harvard and MIT founded the online platform edX.[30] A MOOC (Massive Open Online Course), it combines lecture videos with reading materials and open

---

[27] www.khanacademy.org/math/pre-algebra/pre-algebra-factors-multiples/pre-algebra-prime-factorization-prealg/v/prime-factorization.
[28] www.khanacademy.org.
[29] www.youtube.com/channel/UCYO_jab_esuFRV4b17AJtAw/channels.
[30] www.edx.org.

forums in which learners can exchange ideas. In the first year of edX, 155,000 students enrolled, more than have enrolled at MIT itself in the university's 150-year history. Renowned universities are contributing to the platform in greater numbers: The University of California, Berkeley, for example, as well as the TU Delft, the Sorbonne in Paris, the ETH Zurich and the RWTH Aachen.

The curriculum of edX covers over 1,300 courses and, in the virtual classrooms, students from as disparate places as Brazil, the United States, India, and South Korea exchange knowledge, form study groups, and discuss teaching materials in Skype conferences. In this the largest virtual university in human history, world-renowned experts teach. Online education is now global and tens of thousands of students from every continent take part in a single virtual course on genetics, macroeconomics, or the history of the 1854 London cholera epidemic. For developing countries in particular, platforms like edX offer tremendous opportunities as they enable poorer students to gain access to education that might otherwise be beyond their reach. Other virtual universities have emerged, such as Coursera, Udacity, and NovoEd, and it is inevitable that many more will follow.

11.13 A NEW SCIENTIFIC SELF-IMAGE

Although the teaching of science has improved considerably over the years, a resilient and professional dialogue is still missing when it comes to the goals of research, for example, or to ethical aspects of the research itself or its uses, or to questioning scientific progress in a broader, social context. In a world characterized by wide, fast-paced, and dramatic change, science must learn to deal with the social consequences of its actions much more intensively than in the past. Ethical questions and the meaningfulness of progress will come to play an increasingly important role. The same can be said of the independence of science from economic demands. This presents an opportunity, because citizens are increasingly looking for orientation and science should be the way in which they find that orientation. Open, professional communication between science and the public should become part of a new scientific self-image.

12

The Right to Science

From Principle to Practice and the Role of National Science Academies

*Jessica M. Wyndham, Margaret W. Vitullo, Rebecca Everly, Teresa M. Stoepler, and Nathaniel Weisenberg**

12.1 INTRODUCTION

It is not primarily in the articulation of a human right that it is given life, but in its implementation. With the adoption by the United Nations (UN) of an authoritative statement on the meaning of the right to science,[1] the time is now to shift the focus of attention from conceptualization to implementation. To that end, this study moves beyond the previous work of the scientific, engineering, and health communities aimed at defining the right to science. The question at the heart of this study is whether there is potential for national academies to adopt a central role in the implementation of the right to science, serving as intermediaries to distill and frame key priorities regarding the right within their national context, and providing locally relevant and feasible recommendations for how their governments might fulfill their obligations under the right.

The "right to science" is a shorthand used to describe Article 15 of the International Covenant on Economic, Social and Cultural Rights (ICESCR). According to the text of Article 15, countries that are a party to the treaty (171 in total as of July 2021)[2] are obligated to recognize the right of everyone to "enjoy the benefits of scientific progress and its applications," to ensure the "conservation, development and diffusion of science," to protect "the freedom indispensable for

---

* The authors are grateful to Mina Mortchev and Julia Ziaee, interns at AAAS, who contributed to the preliminary analysis of the questionnaire data and conducted interviews as part of this study. The authors also acknowledge the IAP and GYA for distributing the questionnaire, and all the academies and their members and staff who responded to the questionnaire and participated in interviews. Any opinions, findings, and conclusions or recommendations expressed in this material are those of the authors and do not necessarily reflect the views of the US National Academies of Sciences, Engineering and Medicine, the International Human Rights Network of Academies and Scholarly Societies, or the InterAcademy Partnership.

[1] We use the term "science" to refer to the pursuit and application of knowledge and understanding of the natural, social, engineering, and medical worlds following an iterative and systematic methodology based on evidence.

[2] The current list of countries party to the treaty can be found here: https://indicators.ohchr.org/. The United States of America has signed but not ratified the treaty.

scientific research," and to encourage "international contacts and cooperation" in science.[3] Although the language of the right specifically addresses "science," the provision is intended to be inclusive of all sciences, engineering and health.[4]

This study represents the third stage in a decade-long research endeavor led by the American Association for the Advancement of Science (AAAS) and AAAS Science and Human Rights Coalition. The first stage involved seventeen disciplinary-specific focus groups of United States-based scientists who were the first to explore what the right to science means from the perspectives of scientists.[5] The second stage involved a global questionnaire of scientists, engineers, and health professionals to identify regional variations in scientists' views regarding the actions necessary to ensure realization of the right to science, as well as targeted interviews of public health professionals about the value of the right to practice.[6] This third stage involved a questionnaire of national academies of sciences and medicine, including national young academies, in countries that have ratified the ICESCR (and for senior academies, that are members of the InterAcademy Partnership), followed by interviews with a subsample of respondents to the questionnaire.

Multiple voices and perspectives are needed in the work to realize the right to science, including not only those of scientists, but also those particularly impacted by scientific progress or its absence, such as those affected by neglected diseases, those denied the benefits of scientific progress on religious or political grounds, and all children who stand to benefit from a quality science education. The focus of this study and decade of inquiry has been the engagement of the scientific community because, as the world's largest multidisciplinary scientific membership organization, AAAS's primary constituents, networks, and interlocutors consist of scientists. In addition, that engagement was explicitly encouraged by the UNESCO Venice Statement of 2009 which called on "scientists and their professional organizations to manifest their commitment to the right by ... participating in the elucidation of the right."[7] That said, for the right to have meaning in practice, all relevant

---

[3] UN General Assembly, International Covenant on Economic, Social and Cultural Rights, December 16, 1966, United Nations, Treaty Series, vol. 993, p. 3.

[4] Farida Shaheed, "The right to enjoy the benefits of scientific progress and its applications," May 14, 2012 (A/HRC/20/26, HRC, Geneva), p. 24.

[5] AAAS Science and Human Rights Coalition, "Defining the Right to Enjoy the Benefits of Scientific Progress and Its Applications: American Scientists' Perspectives" (Report prepared by Margaret Weigers Vitullo and Jessica Wyndham), October 2013. Note: we use the term "scientists" in the most inclusive sense, to include those who apply scientific methods within the natural, social, and physical sciences, engineering, and health fields.

[6] J. M. Wyndham, M. W. Vitullo, K. Kraska, N. Sianko, P. Carbajales, C. Nuñez-Eddy, E. Platts. 2017."Giving Meaning to the Right to Science: A Global and Multidisciplinary Approach." (Report prepared under the auspices of the AAAS Scientific Responsibility, Human Rights and Law Program and the AAAS Science and Human Rights Coalition).

[7] Venice Statement on the Right to Enjoy the Benefits of Scientific Progress and Its Applications (2009), UNESCO Experts' Meeting on the Right to Enjoy the Benefits of Scientific Progress and its Applications, 3rd Meeting, Venice, Italy, July 16–17, 2009.

communities, institutions, and authorities must be engaged to ensure the right, in its detail and nuance, is implemented and enjoyed by all.

12.2 LITERATURE REVIEW

The right to science was described by eminent international lawyer William A. Schabas as "tucked away at the tail end of the Universal Declaration of Human Rights," occupying "a similarly neglected and obscure position" in the International Covenant on Economic, Social and Cultural Rights, and as a right that "has received little attention" even taking into account "the more general marginalization of economic, social and cultural rights."[8] The relegated importance of the right within the human rights framework is reflected in the fact that not until March 2020 was a General Comment defining the right adopted by the UN treaty body responsible for monitoring its implementation, that is three decades after the first General Comment was adopted by the same treaty body. It is also reflected in the relative lack of literature on the right to science, although an upward trend in scholarly consideration of the right is discernible as of the last decade.

In 2015, Wyndham and Vitullo identified four stages in the evolution of the literature on the right to science: passing mention of the right as it related to other rights; consideration of the right as a whole as it related to the interests of the scientific community; exploration of the right as it relates to other human rights; and "a cautious coinciding of concerns among both human rights practitioners and scientists."[9] In the past several years, that final strand has expanded to explore the practical significance of the right as a tool to affect change in law and practice, and to encourage and measure implementation of the right.

Building on and contributing to this final strand in the literature, collaborations with the scientific, engineering and health communities have made five substantive contributions. The first was in recognizing that the right to science "is not only a right to benefit from material products of science and technology. It is also a right to benefit from the scientific method and scientific knowledge."[10] As such, the right to science is more than a general restatement, for example, of the right to health, to water, or to the Internet, as suggested in the early literature.[11] Rather, science – its methods and the knowledge it generates – holds inherent value including by

---

[8] W. A. Schabas, "Study of the Right to Enjoy the Benefits of Scientific and Technological Progress and Its Applications," in Y. Donders and V. Volodin, *Human Rights in Education, Science and Culture: Legal Developments and Challenges*, UNESCO, 2007, pp. 273–274.

[9] J. M. Wyndham and M. W. Vitullo, "The Right to Science – Whose Right? To What?," *European Journal of Human Rights*, 2015, vol. 4, p. 433.

[10] J. M. Wyndham and M. W. Vitullo, "Define the Human Right to Science," *Science*, 2018, vol. 362, Issue 6418, p. 975.

[11] See, for example, Stephen P. Marks, "The Evolving Field of Health and Human Rights: Issues and Methods," The Journal of Law, Medicine & Ethics, 2002, 30(4): 739–754; Martin R. Hilbert, "Latin America on its path to the digital age: where are we?" UN Doc. LC/L.1555-P, 1 June 2001.

providing an empirical basis for laws and policies, by providing understanding of personal behaviors, and as the basis for economic growth.[12] This point is specifically acknowledged in the General Comment.[13]

The second major contribution was in the development of a conceptual framework for understanding "access" in the context of the right to science. That framework was presented as a "continuum of access," defined at one end as "access for general public" and at the other as "access for scientists." "A person's position on this continuum can change over time, depending on his/her social context, interests, ability, and training."[14] To move along the continuum of access from the general public to a scientist involves not only greater participation in the production of science, but also greater risks and responsibilities, and should depend on interest, ability, motivation, and training and the judgement of scientific peers, rather than socioeconomic position or government preselection. As such, support for the notion that the right to science includes a right to participate in science is another contribution of this preliminary body of work.[15]

The third contribution of the preceding work is that the right to science, though only using the language of "benefits" and of "freedoms," must be "exercised in a manner consistent with scientific responsibility."[16] Such responsibilities are both internal in nature and align closely with ethical standards of practice as defined in most scientific disciplines, but also include responsibilities aimed at the larger community, or the "social responsibilities" of scientists, as recognized in the UNESCO Recommendation on Science and Scientific Researchers (2017) and by leading scholars in the field.[17]

Finally, previous research engaging the scientific community globally has demonstrated that the evolving meaning of the right to science, particularly the benefits of science to society and the government actions required to support the advancement of science, are generally shared by scientists across all regions of

[12] AAAS Science and Human Rights Coalition, "Defining the Right to Enjoy the Benefits of Scientific Progress and Its Applications: American Scientists' Perspectives" (Report prepared by Margaret Weigers Vitullo and Jessica Wyndham), October 2013, p. 2.
[13] UN Committee on Economic, Social and Cultural Rights (CESCR), *General Comment No. 25: On Science and Economic, Social and Cultural Rights*, April 7, 2020, E/C.12/GC/25, paragraphs 4–7.
[14] Ibid. p.6.
[15] J. M. Wyndham and M. W. Vitullo, "The Right to Science – Whose Right? To What?," *European Journal of Human Rights*, 2015, vol. 4, p. 451. See also L. Shaver, "The Right to Science and Culture," *Wisconsin Law Review*, 2010, p. 121; UNESCO, "The Right to Enjoy the Benefits of Scientific Progress and Its Applications," 2009, p. 17.
[16] J. M. Wyndham and M. W. Vitullo, "Define the Human Right to Science," *Science*, 2018, vol. 362, Issue 6418, p. 975.
[17] United Nations Educational, Scientific and Cultural Organization (UNESCO) Recommendation on Science and Scientific Researchers. In: United Nations Educational, Scientific and Cultural Organization. Report of the Social and Human Sciences Commission, 39C, November 11, 2017. Paris: UNESCO; 2017, pp. 31–47. See also M. S. Frankel, "Science as a Socially Responsibility Community," Paper adapted from an address presented at a Conference on Scientific (Mis)Conduct and Social (Ir)Responsibility, Indiana University, Bloomington, May 27, 1994, p. 1.

the world.[18] However, there is global variation across disciplines about the benefits of science to society, and the government actions that scientists in industry consider to be of most value are distinct from scientists in other sectors.[19]

Although the UN process to define the right has only just come to an end, literature on implementation of the right – how it could be achieved in specific domains, and how to measure implementation – is growing. For example, since 2016 the Luca Coscioni Association, together with the International Human Rights Clinic of the Loyola Law School, has developed reports on specific legislation and judicial measures that could be taken to implement the right. Topics of focus include access to in vitro fertilization,[20] and abortion and contraception.[21] In addition, the Association has developed a set of preliminary indicators by which to measure realization of the right along five dimensions: access to benefits; opportunities to participate; scientific freedom; enabling environment; and international cooperation.[22]

The shifting emphasis in the literature from conceptualization to implementation suggests growing consensus around foundational concepts at the core of the right. It also suggests that a pragmatic realization is emerging that only through testing the receptivity of domestic legislative bodies, national and regional judicial bodies, and UN treaty bodies to certain interpretations of the right will progress in its implementation in practice occur. It is to that end that this study examined the actual and potential role of academies in helping to realize the right to science.

12.3 NATIONAL ACADEMIES

National academies are merit-based organizations that champion the advancement of science, scientific exchange, and evidence-based decision-making.[23] They are

[18] J. M. Wyndham, M. W. Vitullo, et al., "Giving Meaning to the Right to Science: A Global and Multidisciplinary Approach" (Report prepared under the auspices of the AAAS Scientific Responsibility, Human Rights and Law Program and the AAAS Science and Human Rights Coalition, 2017), pp. 3–4.
[19] Ibid., p.4.
[20] "NGO Report on Costa Rica's Implementation of the International Covenant on Economic, Social and Cultural Rights," Submitted to the UN Committee on Economic, Social and Cultural Rights for consideration in the formulation of the List of Issues during the 57th Pre-Sessional Working Group (March 7–11, 2016) (submitted by International Human Rights Clinic, Loyola Law School Los Angeles and and Associazione Luca Coscioni per la libertà di ricerca scientifica).
[21] "NGO Parallel Report on the Republic of Estonia's Third Report on the Implementation of the Covenant on Economic, Social and Cultural Rights," submitted to the UN Committee on Economic, Social and Cultural Rights for consideration in the formulation of the List of Issues during the 62nd Pre-Sessional Working Group (April 3–6, 2018) (submitted by International Human Rights Clinic, Loyola Law School Los Angeles and and Associazione Luca Coscioni per la libertà di ricerca scientifica).
[22] A. Boggio, "Right to Science Indicators: Methodological Notes" (May 28, 2018).
[23] We use the umbrella term "academies" to encompass a wide variety of arrangements of merit-based organizations that focus on the sciences, social sciences, technology, health, and medicine, and sometimes also include the arts and humanities.

typically independent of government and are found in most countries of the world. Building on the foundations of Plato's academy (387 BC),[24] the oldest existing science academies originated in Europe in the 1600s, while academies in the Americas, Asia, and Africa emerged later, beginning in the mid-1800s up until today.[25] The newest academies have emerged just in the last few years, especially within Africa, including for example the Rwanda Academy of Sciences (2016),[26] the Burundi Academy of Science and Technology (2017),[27] and the Eswatini Academy of Sciences (KEAS, 2018)[28] among others.

In addition to large differences in the number of years they have been in existence, academies vary significantly in terms of their national role(s) and visibility/recognition, their relationship with their government, their size (i.e., number of members and staff), and their resourcing level and source. National academies of science can broadly serve any number of four primary functions in their countries:

(1) **Recognition:** members are typically elected by current members in recognition for their scholarship and achievements in their field.[29] In many countries, academy membership is among the highest honors a scientist can achieve in their career.

(2) **Science programs and outreach:** through various grant and fellowship programs and school/public outreach, many academies deliver science programs for young scholars and the broader community, including science diplomacy programs.

(3) **Independent science advice:** many academies provide high quality, independent advice to their governments on issues of policy importance through mechanisms such as consensus reports, statements, and other products.

(4) **Research funding:** some academies have research funding or laboratory institutions under their jurisdiction (e.g., many of the academies of the former Soviet Union and those in China).

Common challenges include reliance on project-based grant funding for many of their activities, and poor gender balance and diversity (the Global Young Academy and many of the National Young Academies, described below, being exceptions in terms of gender balance and diversity). The first women were elected to national

[24] A. Bevan, "A Modern State Academy of Science," *The Scientific Monthly*, 1951, 73(4): 255–260.
[25] M. Clegg and J. Boright, "Adapting to the Future: The Role of Science Academies in Capacity Building," *Int. J. Technology Management*, 2009, 46(1/2).
[26] M. Waruru, 'World Academy of Sciences Grows, Launches New Network,' *University World News* (November 18, 2016). Available at: www.universityworldnews.com/post.php?story=20161118070128525.
[27] Academy of Science of South Africa Newsletter, 4th Quarter, "AMASA 13 Held in Nigeria" (December 5, 2017). Available at: http://www.assaf.co.za/newsletter/?p=1837.
[28] The InterAcademy Partnership Annual Report (2018), Available at: www.interacademies.org/57875/IAP-Annual-Report-2018?source=generalSearch.
[29] M. Hassan, V. ter Meulen, P. F. McGrath, and R. Fears, "Academies of Science as Key Instruments of Science Diplomacy," *Science & Diplomacy*, 2015, 4 [online]. Available at: http://sciencediplomacy.org/perspective/2015/academies-science-key-instruments-science-diplomacy.

academies beginning in the 1920s. A 2015 survey of sixty-nine academies found that, on average, women made up 12 percent of total membership, although this gender imbalance is beginning to shift.[30] Some academies are not completely independent from their governments, due to their national structure.

Serving a coordinating function across academies, the InterAcademy Partnership (IAP) is a global network of 145 academies, including 25 medical academies and three engineering academies. Founded in 1993, the IAP's vision is for the world's academies to play a vital role in ensuring that science serves society inclusively and equitably and underpins global sustainable development. Among its activities, the IAP supports the Global Young Academy,[31] which, in turn, serves as a liaison among the independent National Young Academies (NYAs). In contrast to their "senior" academy counterparts, NYAs are made up of early- to mid-career scholars, often from a wider range of disciplines. Members apply and are competitively selected by their peers, often not only for their excellent scholarship and scientific achievement but for their commitment to serve society. Many NYAs are affiliated with and may receive funding or in-kind support from their country's senior academy, with various degrees of independence. Today there are more than forty NYAs, the majority having been established in the last ten years.[32]

12.3.1 *Academies and Human Rights*

Historically, national academy engagement with international human rights has tended to focus on advocacy for individual scientific colleagues whose rights have been threatened or violated. In the latter half of the twentieth century, concern about the persecution of colleagues – including certain prominent scientists such as Soviet physicist and dissident Andrei Sakharov – led some national academies to create human rights committees charged with supporting colleagues under threat. The French National Academy of Sciences' Committee for the Defence of Scientists' Rights, created in 1978, is among the earliest of these bodies.[33]

---

[30] G. Noordenboos, "Women in Academies of Sciences: From Exclusion to Exception," *Women's Studies International Forum*, 2002, 125(1): 127–137. Available at: www.sciencedirect.com/science/article/abs/pii/S0277539502002157; M. Galvin, "Historic Number of Women Elected to National Academy of Sciences," National Academies of Sciences Engineering and Medicine Press Release (April 30, 2019). Available at: www.eurekalert.org/pub_releases/2019-04/naos-hn0043019.php; M. Enserink, "In Bold New Step, Dutch Science Academy Holds Women-Only Elections," *Science* (November 15, 2016). Available at: www.sciencemag.org/news/2016/11/bold-new-step-dutch-science-academy-holds-women-only-elections.

[31] More information about the Global Young Academy can be found at: www.globalyoungacademy.net.

[32] A listing of the current National Young Academies can be found at: https://globalyoungacademy.net/national-young-academies/.

[33] *Standing Committee for the Defence of Scientists' Rights, French Academy of Sciences* [Online]. Available at: www.academie-sciences.fr/en/Experts-Committees/standing-committee-for-the-defence-of-scientists-rights-codhos-protecting-scientists-throughout-the-world.html.

In 1993, three Nobel Laureates in the sciences, Max Perutz (UK), Torsten Wiesel (USA/Sweden), and Francois Jacob (France), together with Dutch jurist Pieter van Dijk, established an international consortium of academies – the International Human Rights Network of Academies and Scholarly Societies (HR Network) – to enhance cooperation among national academies working on human rights.[34] The HR Network, which is not a formal membership body, has a mandate to "put into practice the professional duty of scientists and scholars to assist those colleagues whose human rights have been – or are threatened to be – infringed and to promote and protect the independence of academies and scholarly societies worldwide."[35]

The HR Network's Secretariat, based at the Committee on Human Rights of the US National Academies of Sciences, Engineering, and Medicine, shares information with national academies participating in the HR Network concerning rights abuses involving scientists, engineers, and health professionals. The HR Network also has an Executive Committee (EC) composed of national academy members – including some former academy presidents – that issues public statements concerning threats to the rights of scientific colleagues and the autonomy of academic institutions. Such statements are issued in the name of the Executive Committee, rather than on behalf of the academies of EC members. To date, the outreach of the HR Network Secretariat has focused on senior academies, which respond to rights abuses largely through private actions, for example, sending appeals/private petitions to government officials and making confidential submissions to UN and other human rights complaint bodies.

Since its first formal meeting in 1995, the HR Network has held biennial meetings on science and human rights, which are open to all interested national academies. Violations of colleagues' rights and freedoms is the major focus of these events, but increasingly – in response to interest from participating academies – they have also explored topical science and human rights themes, such as the relationship between sustainable development, climate change, and rights. More than ninety academies have attended at least one of the HR Network's biennial meetings or participated in another HR Network activity. Broader engagement of these academies with human rights, however, is highly varied, as revealed by a review of the HR Network's operations over time and described below.

12.3.1.1 Growing Number of Academy Structures for Human Rights Engagement

When the HR Network was established in 1993, half a dozen national academies had human rights committees. In response to a questionnaire distributed in June 2017 to

---

[34] *International Human Rights Network of Academies and Scholarly Societies* [Online]. Available at: www.internationalhrnetwork.org/. One of the authors of this study, Rebecca Everly, currently serves as Executive Director of the HR Network.

[35] International Human Rights Network of Academies and Scholarly Societies, *Proceedings – Symposium and Fifth Biennial Meeting, Paris, May 10–11, 2011*. Washington, DC: The National Academies Press, 2003.

The Right to Science

more than eighty academies, nine academies reported having such a committee and fourteen others reported "sharing" a human rights committee with other national academies in their countries.[36] Others, such as the Swiss Academies of Arts and Sciences, reported that they have formally designated a member with overall responsibility for addressing human rights issues. Academies without such structures tend to engage with international human rights and the HR Network on an ad hoc basis.

Most academies with formal, internal human rights structures are based in Europe, with exceptions including the national academies in Korea and Costa Rica. Yet, the academies involved in hosting and attending recent biennial meetings indicate increased interest on the part of academies in the Global South in exploring human rights issues.

While, for the most part, the HR Network continues to focus on responding to violations of the civil and political rights of colleagues and threats to the autonomy of academic institutions, outside the HR Network some academies have explored topics related to economic, social, and cultural rights. As an example, in 2016, the Academy of Science of South Africa (ASSAf) joined with the country's Department of Science and Technology to host a conference for young scientists that addressed the relationship between rights and genomics and the relevance of human rights for protection of indigenous knowledge systems.[37] A 2015 consensus study led by ASSAf, in collaboration with the Uganda National Academy of Sciences, considered both scientific evidence and human rights standards in assessing arguments used to make same-sex relationships illegal.[38] The Human Rights Committee of the German National Academy of Sciences Leopoldina[39] since 2010 has organized human rights symposia for the European scientific community, in cooperation with other European academies. Notably, a 2015 symposium held by the Leopoldina and the Swiss Academies of Arts and Sciences examined the right to science.[40]

Though the trend for academy engagement with economic, social, and cultural rights is upward, at present, national academies more frequently report undertaking activities on scientific topics that have *implications* for such rights (e.g., issues related to education, the environment) without explicitly using an international human rights lens.

---

[36] The questionnaire was administered by the HR Network's Secretariat.
[37] Academy of Science of South Africa, *Annual South African Young Scientists' Conference 2016*. Pretoria: Academy of Science of South Africa, 2016.
[38] Academy of Science of South Africa, *Diversity in Human Sexuality: Implications for Policy in Africa*. Pretoria: Academy of Science of South Africa, 2015.
[39] *Human Rights Committee of the Leopoldina* [Online]. Available at: www.leopoldina.org/en/international-issues/human-rights-committee/.
[40] Swiss Academies of Arts and Sciences and Leopoldina, *The Human Right to Science: New Directions for Human Rights in Science, International Conference*, 22 May 2015.

12.4 METHODOLOGY

As the first step in determining academies' views on how the right to science could be used to address core concerns at the intersection of science and society, the project team developed a fifteen-item questionnaire that was sent to all IAP member academies and National Young Academies in countries that have ratified the ICESCR. The questionnaire, deployed using the SurveyGizmo online platform, was sent by IAP to 128 senior national academies and by the Global Young Academy to 44 NYAs. Responses were received over approximately three weeks in June and July of 2019. Representatives of ninety-two academies total responded to the questionnaire, a response rate of 53 percent. Questionnaire responses were entered into SPSS for analysis.

Questionnaire respondents were asked if they would be willing to participate in a follow up interview. In total, fifty-three of the ninety-two respondents volunteered to be interviewed. Of the fifty-three, twenty senior and young academy respondents were selected. The selection was made to ensure diversity across multiple factors: region, academy size, the degree to which the academy did or did not already engage in human rights activities, and the respondents' opinion about whether the right to science may or may not be relevant to their work. Of these twenty, fourteen interviews were conducted. The remaining six respondents were either unavailable during the study timeframe or could not be reached. The interviews varied in length from approximately fifteen to sixty minutes, although most took about thirty minutes. The interviews were divided among several project team members and conducted by phone, Skype, or web conference. Interviewers took detailed notes during the conversations. Audio recordings made during the conversations were used to verify notes, as needed. The research team reviewed and verified interviewer notes before three members (M. Vitullo, N. Weisenberg, J. Wyndham) participated in the process of coding the interview notes. Excerpts from the interviewers' notes (with occasional quotations from the interviewees themselves) are included in the "Results" section.

The interview data analysis process had several stages. First, three members of the research team each closely read a subset of interview notes and used an inductive process[41] to identify concepts that appeared in those interviews. The results were then compiled into a single list of codes. Next, the interview notes were uploaded to the qualitative analysis software package Dedoose. The codes became the basis for an iterative coding process in which one member of the team (M. Vitullo) read and coded all of the interviews, including those from the first stage of the analysis, comparing the compiled list of codes with additional concepts and themes that emerged subsequently. As themes emerged, codes were

---

[41] K. Charmaz, *Constructing Grounded Theory* (2nd ed.) London: SAGE.. 2014.

added or removed. Finally, results from the coding process were then shared with the entire team for further discussion and refinement.

12.5 RESULTS

12.5.1 Characteristics of Responding National Academies

As indicated previously, there is wide variation in the characteristics of national academies, including the number of years in which they have been in existence, the size of their membership as well as the size of their staff. The characteristics of the responding senior and young national academies for this study reflected those same patterns (see Table 12.1):

- the number of academies per region ranged from a low of seven academies in the Middle East and North Africa to thirty-seven academies in Europe;
- the 19 African academies averaged 16 years of existence, while the 37 European academies, on average, were founded more than 150 years ago; and

TABLE 12.1 *Characteristics of Responding National Academies*

	Africa	Americas	Asia-Pacific	Europe	Middle East & North Africa
Number of Academies					
Senior	13	14	10	33	6
Young	6	1	4	4	1
Total	19	15	14	37	7
Average Years Since Founded	16	92	45	151	30
Members*					
0–50	42%	27%	29%	11%	0%
51–100	21%	20%	21%	8%	29%
101–200	11%	7%	14%	19%	29%
201+	21%	40%	29%	54%	29%
Staff*					
0–50	89%	87%	64%	43%	57%
51–100	0%	7%	21%	8%	29%
101–200	0%	0%	0%	19%	0%
201+	5%	0%	7%	22%	0%

*Due to missing data, regional percentages do not total 100.

- among the 37 European academies that participated in the study, more than half have 200 or more distinguished scientists as members. Similarly, 40 percent of the academies in the Americas reported having 200 or more members. In the other regions, less than one-third of responding academies are that large.
- Less variation in staff size is visible across the regions, with the vast majority reporting 100 or fewer staff. Again, European academies are the outliers, where 41 percent report having staffs that are larger. These differences have implications for the academies' potential role in working toward the fulfillment of the right to science, as will be explored below.

12.5.2 *Academies' Prior Engagement with Human Rights*

One indicator of academies' potential for serving as central actors in the implementation of the right to science may be their prior engagement on human rights issues. The questionnaire asked respondents how frequently their academy engaged in six possible activities related to human rights: (1) organizing panels or inviting speakers; (2) hosting a full program of activities; (3) referencing human rights in publications; (4) referencing human rights when trying to inform government policy; (5) referencing human rights when trying to inform public discussion; and (6) referencing human rights in an official statement.

The results from the prior engagement question were used to calculate an index score indicating the level of human rights engagement within each academy. Scores could range from zero (indicating no engagement with any of the activities) to six (indicating the academy often engaged in all six activities). Across all the academies the average human rights activity score was 2.1 (see Table 12.2). Given that respondents were answering these questions within the limits of their own personal knowledge as well as their own subjective evaluation of the frequency of activities, and acknowledging that within the HR Network there have been discussions regarding the imperfect nature of communication within academies, it is reasonable to assume that some respondents were not fully informed about all aspects of their academy's human rights engagement. Their responses nonetheless provide a window into academies' prior engagement with human rights activities, and how levels of activity vary across regions.

During the follow up interviews, respondents were asked to elaborate on their academy's engagement with human rights. Those discussions provide insight on at least part of the reason human rights activity was described as minimal: respondents were more likely to equate human rights activity with private actions in response to violations of civil and political rights rather than

TABLE 12.2 *National Academies Engagement with Human Rights and Article 15*

	Africa	Americas	Asia-Pacific	Europe	Middle East & North Africa	Mean	Standard Deviation
Human Rights Activity – average score							
Possible Range = 0 to 6	1.1	2.4	1.3	3.1[1]	1.0	2.1	1.2
Right to Science-Prior Awareness							
Percent that had prior awareness	33%	36%	15%	62%	43%	44%[2]	50%
Influence on gov policy – average score							
None=0; Significant=3	1.4	1.6	1.2	1.5	1.1	1.4	.77
Influence on public discourse – average score							
None=0; Significant=3	1.6	1.7	1.4	1.6	1.4	1.6	.77
Potential role in Article 15 fulfillment – average score							
None=0; Significant=3	2.8[3,4]	2.1	1.5[1]	1.8[1]	2.0[3]	2.0	.91

1. Across region difference significant at .005 in 1-way ANOVA tests. Due to unequal variances within groups, Welch tests of the equality of means were employed. For the same reason, in post-hoc analysis, Africa was used as the reference category and between group differences were tested using the Dunnett (2-sided) method.
2. Across region differences significant at .005. Tested using Chi Square.
3. Within region difference significant at .005 between "Influence on Government Policy" and "Potential Role in Article 15 fulfillment". Tested using Wilcoxon Signed-Rank Test for non-parametric samples.
4. Within region difference significant at .005 between "Influence on Public Discourse" and "Potential Role in Article 15 fulfillment". Tested using Wilcoxon Signed-Rank Test for non-parametric samples

with public actions taken to advance economic, social and cultural rights. As discussed above, the HR Network exists to encourage and help coordinate academies' human rights activities. To date, those activities most frequently focus on violations of civil and political rights and take the form of private appeals and submissions to human rights complaint bodies, in contrast to the six categories of public-facing human rights activity measured in the questionnaire. For example, when discussing their efforts on behalf of persecuted scientists, including those targeted, detained, or jailed for their scientific activities, respondents almost always described these efforts in the context of human rights. However, when describing work related to science education, advancing women in science, working toward socioeconomic development, the eradication and control of disease, or scientifically informed policies, respondents were less likely to frame that work explicitly in terms of human rights. An excerpt from a project interviewer's notes illustrate this point.

> He gave the example of a workshop that [the academy] helped to organize in 2017 concerning challenges facing female scientists and the impact of these challenges on career progression. He was on the organizing committee for this event, which provided an opportunity for female scientists (members of the academy and others) to share their experiences, hear the experiences of their colleagues, and discuss how challenges might be addressed. The academy also brought a resource person from the United States for this activity. He said that, in thinking further about our questionnaire, he sees this as an activity with a connection to human rights.

12.6 THE RIGHT TO SCIENCE IS LITTLE KNOWN YET PERCEIVED BY MANY AS CORE TO THE ACADEMIES' MISSIONS

Academies possessed limited prior knowledge of the right to science. Fewer than half of the ninety-two questionnaire respondents had heard of the right prior to receiving the questionnaire. There were, however, significant differences across regions. Academies in the Asia-Pacific region were the least likely to be aware of the right, where 33 percent reported prior knowledge. Academies in Europe were the most likely to report prior awareness, with 62 percent reporting having heard of the right before receiving the questionnaire.

After learning about the right to science, respondents described the ways the concept captured their attention. One respondent immediately sent the information to his academy's Executive Council. Other respondents asked for more information about the right, how it was defined, and what other countries were doing on the topic. One respondent told the project interviewer that she thought that there was a tacit understanding of the right to science within her academy, but that it had never been directly expressed as such.

> She mentioned that, when she viewed our questionnaire, this was the first time she had thought about a human right to science. She indicated that she has thought about scientific advancement almost as a privilege but would like to learn about the notion of science as a right. She mentioned that there is something powerful about this idea.

Although in most cases the academies had not engaged in activities explicitly tied to the right to science, many respondents viewed the concept as central to their missions and seemed to believe that future activity on this topic would be fully in alignment with their priorities.

> I think in many respects the academies are ideally placed to [work on the fulfillment of the right to science]. For two reasons. The one is that, most academies see themselves as offering policy advice to a range of role players who may in the first instance be legislators of some kind. But [they] may also be the general public, or business, or whatever. I think academies, by the reports that they produce, have the opportunity to influence people in these matters, and influence them to think of having a right to science. Second aspect of it, is that individual members of academies have expertise, and can use that expertise to highlight these issues and make them more available to the broader public.

On a scale of 0 to 3 (with 0 representing no influence, and 3 representing significant influence), academies across the globe reported an average government influence level of 1.4, and an average public discourse influence of 1.6. Regional variations in these two influence scores were not significant in one-way ANOVA tests of difference in means. The questionnaire respondents in Africa and in the Middle East evaluated their academies' potential role in the fulfillment of the right to science more positively than their ability to influence government policy generally. Academies in Africa also saw their potential role in the fulfillment of the right to science as greater than their potential to influence public discourse. Compared to the academies in Africa, academies in Asia-Pacific and Europe saw significantly less of a role for themselves in the fulfillment of the right to science.

12.7 BARRIERS

While the right to science resonated with the interview respondents once they were aware of it, and in many cases, it was concordant with the activities of their academy, that does not suggest a simple or easy path from nascent interest to meaningful engagement. Other parts of the interviews brought to light a variety of challenges that would have to be addressed in any such efforts.

12.7.1 *Lack of Knowledge*

While both the questionnaire responses and the interviews provided evidence that there was interest in the right to science, as noted above there was little basic understanding of its history, meaning, or implications. Interviewer notes reveal a variety of basic questions: What precisely is the right to science? Is it the right to human knowledge that has already been discovered? How could an academy go about taking action on the right to science? Who are the key stakeholders?

> He mentioned that it would be useful for the academy to have a better understanding of the right to science, particularly as many people are not conversant on this topic. It would, for instance, be useful ... to know what is being done in other countries on this issue.

One respondent thought that some of her academy's members might not have a strong interest in the right to science initially because of their lack of familiarity with the topic. But she thought others would be interested in learning more about the right and exploring its implications. She said that additional information, perhaps in the form of seminars and workshops, was needed to help members better understand the right.

12.7.2 *Organizational Structure*

Academies' ability to work toward the fulfillment of the right to science will be influenced by their organizational structures. The question of whether the right most appropriately fell within the purview of the physical sciences, the social sciences, or even philosophy and the humanities arose in several interviews. In one academy, the respondent was concerned that working on the right to science would seem to be too focused on the physical sciences and not sufficiently applicable to the other parts of the academy's mission. In another case, where the respondent's academy was focused exclusively on the physical sciences, the respondent was concerned that other academies in that country would see the right as more appropriately within their purview.

A few academies reported having standing committees on human rights with high-level members. In those academies, human rights activities were prioritized and acted upon. The fact that few academies have such a committee or office represents another potential organizational barrier to academies' engagement on the right to science. Still, the above-mentioned example of the South African

Academy of Science demonstrates that human rights committees are not a requirement for meaningful academy human rights engagement.[42]

Available resources can also be a barrier to engagement on the right to science. While the academies in Africa saw themselves as having the most potential for working toward the fulfillment of the right, nearly 90 percent of them had fifty or fewer staff and on average they had existed for the shortest time. And in a variety of cases from across the globe, relatively newly formed academies were in a very tenuous state of existence, with limited capacity to take on activities beyond their own actualization as a viable organization.

> This is a very "young" academy; it was created [about 20 years ago], and government only recognized the academy by presidential decree [a few years ago]. The first 10 years of the academy are primarily devoted to anchoring the foundations of the academy, to be recognized and establish the pillars.

Any effort to engage national academies in the right to science will need to consider the wide disparities in organizational structures and resources available across nations and between senior and young academies.

12.7.3 Government Relations

Ninety-five percent of respondents to the questionnaire said that informing policy at the national level was within the scope of their mission. Yet, in the interviews, lines of communication with government actors were often described as missing and, in some cases, openly hostile. Lack of government funding was an issue that was raised by several respondents, whose academies struggled to establish a program of activities without financial resources. The respondents also discussed political constraints on the academies related to both civil and political rights and economic, social, and cultural rights. When speaking out on behalf of persecuted scientists, some respondents mentioned experiencing pressure from the government not to endanger relationships with other offending countries by speaking out on human rights. One respondent mentioned receiving pressure from the government because the academy's recommendations regarding a major international development project were in contradiction to the government's plans.

12.8 APPROACHES TO OVERCOMING BARRIERS

While the data discussed here points to a variety of potential barriers to academies' engagement in the fulfillment of the right to science, it also provided insights on possible approaches to overcoming those barriers.

---

[42] See Section 12.3.1.3 above.

12.8.1 *Working with Partners in Collaborative Efforts*

When academies engaged in human rights-related activities, they often did so in partnership with other organizations and the value of collaboration was mentioned by respondents from a wide range of academies. Respondents spoke of collaborations with entities within their own countries, including their counterparts in government departments of science and technology as well as other government ministries, national museums, foreign offices, and embassies. They spoke of partnerships with other academies within their own countries. Creating partnerships with senior academies was seen as essential for young academies with fewer resources and less supporting infrastructure. One member of a young academy described its relationship with the country's senior academy as "symbiotic." Partnerships with other organizations were also commonly mentioned, including the ALLEA (European Federation of Academies for the Sciences and Humanities), the GYA, the HR Network, the IAP, Scholars at Risk, The World Academy of Sciences (TWAS), and the UN/UNESCO.

12.8.2 *Identifying Strong Shared Interests across Regions*

The questionnaire asked whether, over the past three years, the academy had engaged in activities related to any of eight specific topics: science education, health care, climate change, sustainable development, emerging technologies, ethics, scientific freedom, and open access. We were interested to see if there was regional variation in levels of interest in these topics. Within each region, the activity engaged in by the highest proportion of academies in that region was ranked first. The activity engaged in by the next highest proportion of academies was ranked second, and the one following third. If two activities enjoyed engagement in the same proportion of academies in a region, multiple activities could have the same rank. We then examined areas of overlap across regions.

The results of this analysis are presented in Table 12.3. Science education and sustainable development appeared among the first or second ranked topical activities for academies in every region examined. Conversely, open access was ranked just third in Europe, and scientific freedom did not rank in the top three for any region. This suggests that introducing the right to science as a tool for working on the areas of science education and sustainable development might be widely perceived as important and useful. On the other hand, focusing on the right to science as applied to open access and scientific freedom are topics that would be less likely to receive broad support.

TABLE 12.3 *Ranking and Overlap in Academy Activities by Region*

	Africa	Americas	Asia-Pacific	Europe	Middle East & North Africa
Rank 1	Africa	Americas	Asia-Pacific	Europe	Middle East & North Africa
Top three ranked activities by region	Science Education	Science Education	Science Education	Science Education	Scientific Ethics
			Sustainable Development	Climate Change	
	Sustainable Development	Climate Change	Climate Change	Sustainable Development	Sustainable Development
			Emerging Tech		Science Education
	Health Care	Sustainable Development	Scientific Ethics	Open Access	Climate Change
					Scientific Ethics
Rank 2 Rank 3					

Note: If within a region, the proportion of academies engaging in a specific activity were equal, this could result in two activities being "tied" within a rank.

12.9 CONCLUSION

The central question at the core of this study was whether, and to what extent, there existed the potential for national academies to adopt a central role in the implementation of the right to science. The right has been recognized as lying at the "heart of the mission" of the world's largest scientific membership organization[43] and it is a right that all countries that are a party to the International Covenant on Economic, Social, and Cultural Rights are bound to respect, to protect, and to fulfill. The UN General Comment on the right to science reveals conceptual agreement around the general scope of the right. Building on the growing literature on the right, and the

---

[43] AAAS Board of Directors, "On the human right to the benefits of scientific progress," Statement, April 16, 2010.

nascent UN efforts, the imperative now is to give the right life by applying it in practice.

The results of this study reveal that, to the extent that academies engage in activities adopting an explicit human rights frame, they are most often focused on civil and political rights, and particularly the rights of scientists. Yet, there is considerable work being undertaken by academies that addresses policy concerns directly related to the full scope of human rights, and a recognition that the right to science in particular is relevant, if not even core, to the work of the academies.

Although academies identified several actual and perceived barriers to greater engagement in human rights, they also provided examples of ways such barriers can be overcome, suggesting a roadmap for future engagement by academies with the right to science. The first and most vital step will be the provision of resources, including training and opportunities for dialogue about the right to science among academies, their staff, and their members to lay the groundwork for future engagement.

The findings also make clear that building upon existing partnerships and collaborative efforts on human rights would be the appropriate approach for any effort to engage academies in activities related to the fulfillment of the right to science. Moreover, such an approach has the benefit of leveraging the greater resources of some academies in ways that empower action on the part of those that are less robust organizationally. In addition to the HR Network, another specific mechanism that was mentioned in the interviews was for IAP to consider issuing a statement on the right to science; such a statement could be issued jointly with the GYA and the National Young Academies.

The right to science is articulated in an international treaty that binds states, and those states are required periodically to report to the UN about their efforts toward the fulfillment of their obligations. In that context, if national academies initiate new activities and frame existing activities in terms of the right to science, this could provide a unique benefit to states party, helping foster the progressive realization of the right in ways that could be documented to the United Nations but also building more positive relationships between academies and governments.

As such, the right to science could be a valuable tool to assist national academies in strengthening their current activities and furthering their overall goals. As multiple academies recognized the right to science as relevant to, if not central to, their activities, the opportunity exists for academies to explore how the framework of the right could be used to inform the cultivation of relationships with relevant interlocutors at the national level. Academies could also build bridges regionally and internationally with academies in countries bound by the right and potentially facilitate prioritization of organizational policy goals. Furthermore, as one respondent from a young academy said, connecting the activities of the academy to human rights might provide a way to respond to the interest of members to connect with something larger than themselves. Indeed, implementation of the right to science would be of great benefit not only to scientific enterprise, but also to all of society.

13

The Right to Science in Practice

A Proposed Test in Four Stages

Sebastian Porsdam Mann, Yvonne Donders, and Helle Porsdam

13.1 INTRODUCTION

The human right to enjoy the benefits of the progress of science and its applications (the right to science, or RtS), enshrined in Article 27(2) of the Universal Declaration of Human Rights (UDHR) and Article 15(1)b of the International Covenant on Economic, Social, and Cultural Rights (ICESCR) "adds a legal and moral dimension to a range of fundamental issues, including scientific freedom, funding, and policy, as well as access to data, materials, and knowledge" (Porsdam Mann et al., 2018). Part of the promise is that the RtS, as it becomes more developed, may be used as a legally binding and normatively weighty framework for the assessment of the ethical and human-rights related aspects of science and scientific policy.

This chapter introduces the four-step test, a framework developed as a means to assess whether a policy complies with the obligations imposed by the right to science under international human rights law. In doing so we, like the Committee on Economic, Social and Cultural Rights in its new General Comment (CESCR, 2020), adopt an "internal perspective" for the purposes of this sketch. This means that we have drawn extensively on scholarship, guidance, and interpretation of the ICESCR itself.

Unfortunately, there has not been space here to fully explore the "external perspective," in which the relations between rights across treaties and other human rights instruments are factored into the desiderata that make up our proposed test in four stages. We will explore this in subsequent work. We hope, however, that the sketch presented here will engender fruitful discussion so that it may be made into a useful judicial and policy framework.

13.2 BACKGROUND

We take as our points of departure several general approaches to the interpretation of State obligations under international human rights law (Donders, 2011), including the provisions laid out in the Vienna Convention on the Law of Treaties (Vienna Convention).[1] Article 31(1) of the Vienna Convention stipulates that, "[a] treaty shall be interpreted in good faith in accordance with the ordinary meaning to be given to the terms of the treaty in their context and in the light of its object and purpose." This context is defined in Article 31(2) as including general rules of international law as well as further applicable agreements and treaties. More importantly, since there are few[2] agreements and treaties between countries with regards to the RtS, Article 31(3) b states that also to be taken into account is "[a]ny subsequent practice in the application of the treaty which establishes the agreement of the parties regarding its interpretation." This includes statements of official treaty bodies, in particular General Comments, which are authoritative interpretations. In our case, the General Comments by the Committee on Economic, Social and Cultural Rights (the Committee) are especially relevant.

As a human right, the RtS places obligations on States which have signed and ratified the ICESCR. According to the tripartite typology (Eide, 1987), an analytical device much used by the UN and human right scholars to interpret the nature of State obligations under human rights law, these obligations can be conceptually stratified into three: the obligation to *respect* the right, to *protect* it and, finally, to *fulfil* it. Paragraph 41 of General Comment No. 25 adopts this language: "States Parties have an obligation to respect, protect and fulfil the [RtS]."

The first refers to the obligation of States not themselves to violate a right or unjustifiably interfere in its enjoyment. The obligation to protect is somewhat more burdensome, requiring that the State must prevent third parties from violating a right. Finally, to fulfil a right, a State must ensure (facilitate and provide) that the various resources, infrastructure, and necessary funding are available to fully realize its enjoyment, also for noncitizens.

As of this writing, 174 countries have signed the ICESCR. Of these, 170 are full States Parties; however, Palau, Comoros, Cuba, and the United States of America have signed but not ratified the Convention. As Cesare Romano points out in his contribution to this volume, the USA is, however, bound by the UDHR[3] and the American Declaration of the Rights and Duties of Man, the latter of which contains the first instance of the right to science in international law (see Chapter 2).

---

[1] Vienna Convention on the Law of Treaties (adopted May 23, 1969, entered into force January 27, 1980) 1155 UNTS 331.

[2] The 2017 UNESCO Recommendation on Science and Scientific Researchers may be seen as an important example.

[3] Although the Universal Declaration of Human Rights is a political document, not a legally-binding treaty, it has been viewed by the International Court of Justice, and States, as forming part of customary international law which means it is binding even on those States not a party to it. See, for example, Hurst Hannum. (2018). The Status of the Universal Declaration of Human Rights in National and International Law. GA. J. INT'L & COMP. L., 25, 287–397.

Moreover, a country which has signed but not ratified the ICESCR is still bound by Article 19 of the Vienna Convention not to act in a way that would defeat the object and purpose of that treaty. In other words, the USA is still bound to respect the RtS. This in contrast to the 170 countries that have signed and ratified the ICESCR, which are in theory bound by all three levels of obligations.

These obligations must, however, compete for scarce resources with other human rights and policy goals. For this reason, the obligations that States are under vis-à-vis the ICESCR are subject to the requirement of progressive realization, laid out in Article 2(1): States must "undertake to take steps, individually and through international assistance and cooperation, especially economic and technical, to the maximum of its available resources, with a view to achieving progressively the full realization of the rights recognized in the present Covenant by all appropriate means, including particularly the adoption of legislative measures."

In its General Comment on Article 2, the Committee has made clear that States are under an obligation to take these progressive steps within a "reasonable, short period of time" and that this obligation "implies not only legislative measures, but also administrative, financial, educational, social and other measures, including judicial remedies" (Donders, 2011). The Committee also states that these obligations are proportional to the resources available to a State, such that the more resources are available, the greater the obligations under the ICESCR.

Paragraph 24 of the General Comment closely follows this phrasing:

> States Parties must take steps, to the maximum of their available resources, for the full realization of the [RtS]. While full realization of the right may be achieved progressively, steps towards it must be taken immediately or within a reasonably short period of time. Such steps should be deliberate, concrete and targeted, using all appropriate means, including the adoption of legislative and budgetary measures.

Some obligations, however, are so important that they form an exception to this rule and must be observed immediately, regardless of resources. This includes the obligation under Article 2(2) ICESCR for the rights in that document to be enjoyed without discrimination. Thus, paragraph 25 of the General Comment reminds us that "States Parties are under an immediate obligation to eliminate all forms of discrimination against individuals and groups in their enjoyment of ESCRs."

Finally, both Articles 2(1) and 15(4) ICESCR mention the importance of international cooperation and assistance. In the General Comment on Article 2, the Committee makes clear that, for the purposes of obligations under the ICESCR, "available resources" should be interpreted to include those resources available from international cooperation, and that wealthier countries are under a special obligation to assist the less prosperous (CESCR, 1991). The General Comment on Science, in devoting its sixth section wholly to international cooperation and assistance, stresses the importance of these obligations.

13.3 NORMATIVE CONTENT

The normative content of the RtS has been treated in detail by the General Comment, which draws heavily on the 2017 UNESCO Recommendation on Science and Scientific Research. Section II of the General Comment is titled "Normative Content" and contains several provisions, laid out in paragraphs four to fifteen, which define key terms.

13.3.1 *Science*

Paragraph four of the General Comment quotes the 2017 UNESCO Recommendation's definition of science. Science is:

> the enterprise whereby humankind, acting individually or in small or large groups, makes an organized attempt, by means of the objective study of observed phenomena and its validation through sharing of findings and data and through peer review, to discover and master the chain of causalities, relations or interactions; brings together in a coordinated form subsystems of knowledge by means of systematic reflection and conceptualization; and thereby furnishes itself with the opportunity of using, to its own advantage, understanding of the processes and phenomena occurring in nature and society.

As clarified by paragraph six,

> science, which encompasses natural and social sciences, [thus] refers both to a process following a certain methodology ("doing science") and to the results of this process (knowledge, applications). Though other forms of knowledge may claim protection and promotion as a cultural right, knowledge should only be considered as science if it is based on critical inquiry and open to falsifiability and testability.

13.3.2 *Scientific Advancement and Scientific Progress*

Paragraph seven defines the terms "scientific advancement" (used in the UDHR) and "scientific progress" (used in the ICESCR): "these expressions emphasize the capacity of science to contribute to the well-being of persons and humankind. Thus, development of science in the service of peace and human rights should be prioritized by States over other uses."

13.3.3 *The Applications of Scientific Progress*

The RtS explicitly recognizes the rights of everyone to enjoy the benefits of science *and its applications*. The meaning of this latter phrase is defined in paragraph eight of the new General Comment:

Applications refer to the particular implementation of science to the specific concerns and needs of the population. Applied science also include the technology deriving from scientific knowledge, such as the medical applications, the industrial or agricultural applications, or the information and communication technologies.

13.3.4 *The Benefits*

The General Comment, in paragraph nine, also makes clear that the *benefits* of scientific progress and its applications extend beyond material gains such as "vaccination, fertilizers, technological instruments and the like." Benefits also refer to

> the scientific knowledge and information directly deriving from scientific activity, as science provides benefits through the development and dissemination of the knowledge itself. Finally, benefits refer also to science's role in forming critical and responsible citizens who are able to participate fully in a democratic society.

These definitions will be important resources as we sketch the four-step test framework below.

13.4 FOUR-STEP TEST

13.4.1 *Step One: Does a Given Policy, Product, or Aspect of Science Constitute a "Benefit of Scientific Progress" or "Its Applications"?*

The first step involves determining whether the RtS is applicable to a given situation or issue.

The legal subjectivity of the RtS – the question of who enjoys or is entitled to the right – is every individual human; in other words, all humans are a legal subject of this right. This is a feature of the human rights framework in which the RtS is nested. Secondly, the right applies equally to every human, so it is not the case that some have more or less of a RtS due to, for example, their education or income. These values of inclusion, equality, and universality are fundamental human rights principles, and are included in the Preamble and Article 2 ICESCR.

The scope of the RtS centers on the benefits of scientific progress or its applications. The definitions of these are laid out according to the General Comment in the section above.

Here it should be noted that the RtS grants all individuals the right to *share in* the benefits of the products of scientific progress, which implies a participatory aspect of the right. As paragraph 54 of the General Comment on Science states, "the principles of transparency and participation are essential to [making] science objective and reliable, and not subject to interests that are not scientific or are against human rights and the welfare of society."

Although this kind of inclusion is a fundamental human rights principle, the corresponding principle of participation takes on additional nuances in the present context. At one extreme, active participation by the citizenship in a dialogue with science and scientists can "promote public trust and support for sciences," as recognized in paragraphs 54 and 55, and "in particular through a vigorous and informed democratic debate on the production and use of scientific knowledge."

The General Comment acknowledges, however, that the level of participation in science will vary according to the interests and capacities of individuals. Thus, according to paragraph 65 "States parties should ... ensure [the active participation of peasants and other people working in rural areas] in the determination of priorities and the undertaking of research and development, *taking into account their experience and respecting their cultures*" (emphasis added).

Whereas there are some areas of science in which truly everyone can participate (such as data donation), much of science requires too much specialized knowledge and equipment for even trained scientists to participate in science outside their immediate expertise. There will necessarily be degrees between these extremes.

Thus, the first step in our framework is to ask whether the issue in question meets the definitions laid out in the General Comment and is therefore within the scope of the RtS.

13.4.2 *Step Two: Does the Policy Facilitate or Limit the Enjoyment of the RtS?*

Once it has been determined that an issue is within the scope of the RtS, the next step is categorizing the issue or policy according to whether it fulfills the RtS or meets criteria for legitimate *limitations, retrogressive measures*, or *derogations*. It is important to distinguish between these, because although all three involve a lower, or lowering of, the level of enjoyment of the RtS, they have widely different criteria for legitimacy (Donders, 2015).

A **derogation** is a full or partial elimination of an obligation under international human rights law invoked in exceptional circumstances, such as epidemics, civil unrest, or war. Derogations may be invoked where there is an exceptional threat to the functioning of the State, where a lesser restriction in the form of a limitation does not suffice, where the primary objective of the State in derogating from a right is the fast and full return to a situation in which the enjoyment of human rights can be restored, and where they are used as a last resort (Müller 2009). In addition, not all rights are derogable, although the list of non-derogable rights varies from treaty to treaty.

The ICESCR, unlike the ICCPR, does not contain a derogation clause specifying the circumstances under which a derogation may be legitimately made. Müller (2009) points out that there is not much interpretation by the Committee on Economic, Social and Cultural Rights on the topic of derogations to economic, social and cultural rights, and that their position as to the legal basis of any such derogations is unclear. Indeed, the new General Comment does not contain the word "derogation."

The Committee, has, however, in its Statement on Poverty and the ICESCR, stated that certain core minimal obligations are non-derogable: "if a national or international anti-poverty strategy does not reflect this minimum threshold [core obligations], it is inconsistent with the legally binding obligations of a state party" (CESCR, 2001, para. 17). This might be interpreted as implying that some obligations beyond the minimal core are indeed derogable.

A **retrogressive measure**, on the other hand, is an act which reduces the enjoyment of a human right relative to its previous level of enjoyment, and which thus interferes with the duty of progressive realization of human rights under Article 2(1) ICESCR. "As with all other rights in the Covenant," provides paragraph 24 of the General Comment, "there is a strong presumption that retrogressive measures taken in relation to the RPEBPSA are not permissible." It goes on to list several examples of retrogressive measures:

> the removal of programs or policies necessary for the conservation, the development and the diffusion of science; the imposition of barriers to education and information on science; the imposition of barriers to citizen participation in scientific activities, including misinformation, intended to erode citizen understanding and respect for science and scientific research; the adoption of legal and policy changes that reduce the extent of international collaboration on science, etc.

Retrogressive measures may, however, be necessary in exceptional circumstances such as those mentioned above for derogations (where their extent is not such as to require a derogation), but may also be justified by less extreme exigencies, such as severe recessions or natural disasters. The Committee has, in its Statement on the drafting of the Optional Protocol to the ICESCR, given guidelines as to how it will evaluate retrogressive measures in a case-by-case and country-by-country approach according to the following criteria:

(i) The country's level of development;
(ii) The severity of the alleged breach, in particular whether the situation concerned the enjoyment of the minimum core content of the Covenant;
(iii) The country's current economic situation, in particular whether the country was undergoing a period of economic recession;
(iv) The existence of other serious claims on the State party's limited resources; for example, resulting from a recent natural disaster or from recent internal or international armed conflict;
(v) Whether the State party had sought to identify low-cost options; and
(vi) Whether the State party had sought cooperation and assistance or rejected offers of resources from the international community for the purposes of implementing the provisions of the Covenant without sufficient reason.

To this, the Committee adds, in paragraph 24:

> In the exceptional circumstances under which retrogressive measures may be inevitable, States must ensure that such measures are necessary and proportionate. They should remain in place only insofar as they are necessary; they should mitigate inequalities that can grow in times of crisis and ensure that the rights of disadvantaged and marginalized individuals and groups are not disproportionately affected; and in addition guarantee the minimum core obligations.

The fact that retrogressive measures are justified by criteria such as these distinguishes them from **limitations**. Limitations reflect the fact that the enjoyment of most human rights is not absolute. The human rights of individuals compete with other legitimate goals such as the general welfare and State interests, and individual rights compete with each other for their realization; to reflect the fact that compromises between other projects and other human rights must be made to avoid stalemate, limitations may be imposed.

Of special relevance in the context of the RtS, paragraph 22 of General Comment No. 25 recognizes with regard to limitations that, "[some] limits on the [right] might be necessary, as science and its applications can, in certain contexts, affect [other economic, social and cultural rights]." As we shall see below, there are three elements highlighted in the Committee's understanding: respect for core obligations, proportionality, and the expectation that benefits outweigh burdens.

Policies or issues meeting the criteria for a derogation or retrogressive measure are unlikely to respect the RtS. Such policies will, except in exceptional circumstances, fail to be justified and should not be adopted. However, policies that do not meet the criteria for derogations or retrogressive measures may still infringe on the enjoyment of the RtS to a lesser extent, or two or more policy options may differ in the extent to which they are likely to facilitate enjoyment of the RtS. Whether such limitations are legitimate, and how to choose between competing policy options, is assessed in the next two steps.

13.4.3 Step Three: Does the Policy Form a Legitimate/Acceptable Limitation on the Enjoyment of the RtS?

A policy, regulation or law, which is not compatible with the RtS, is one that goes directly against the object and purpose of the RtS (especially its core normative content) or its associated foundational human rights structure. Paragraph 52 of the new General Comment recognizes this in the context of scientific freedom: "core obligations related to the right to participate in and to enjoy the benefits of scientific progress and its applications require States parties to … remove limitations to the freedom of scientific research that are incompatible with article 4 of the Covenant."

The third step involves evaluation of the options not ruled out by step two as unjustified derogations or retrogressive measures according to the criteria for legitimate limitations contained in Article 4 ICESCR.

In paragraph 21, the Committee refers to three relevant and important elements of ICESCR Article 4. These are that limitations must be *determined by law*, they must be *compatible with the nature of these rights*, and must be enacted *solely for the purpose of promoting the general welfare in a democratic society*. We comment below on the first and second of these and discuss the third in step four.

To be legitimate, limitations on the RtS must be **determined by law**. This means that such limitations must, as a minimum, observe the rule of law and be issued through the proper channels. According to the Limburg principles, this means that no limitations may occur unless "provided for by national law of general application which is consistent with the Covenant and is in force at the time the limitation is applied" (paragraph 48); that such laws shall not be "arbitrary or unreasonable or discriminatory" (paragraph 49); that they shall be "clear and accessible to everyone" (paragraph 50); and that adequate "safeguards and effective remedies shall be provided by law against illegal or abusive imposition on application of limitations on economic, social and cultural rights" (paragraph 51). These last safeguards may include vetting by the national judiciary in some national contexts.

For limitations which are proposed but not yet active, the equivalent of this criterion is that such limitations be determinable by law, for example, be of a form that can reasonably be expected to pass through the regular channels of the rule of law.

The requirement that a limitation be **compatible with the nature of the rights contained in the ICESCR** is an important but somewhat complex aspect of Article 4.

Firstly, this requires limitations to be compatible with the general and fundamental human rights principles that underlie all of human rights law. Originally set out in the UDHR, these include dignity, the rule of law, equality and nondiscrimination, and universality. Nondiscrimination in particular is mentioned prominently in the ICESCR and UDHR and is considered a core obligation of RtS with respect to science-related policy, both according to existing scholarship and to the new General Comment (paragraphs 26–28; (Donders, 2011)).

Most importantly, this means that everyone enjoys the RtS in equal measure, and thus that *ceteris paribus* no one's interests can be weightier than their fellow human's. Anything which is contrary to these fundamental principles cannot be compatible with the nature of the rights which are derived from them. Most of these are relatively easy to assess and understand.

Dignity, however, is not so easily defined. It is perhaps the most important, and certainly the most fundamental, human rights principle. At the same time, it is the least well characterized. Philosophers and legal scholars have defined dignity as reflecting, and respecting, the capacity of humans to act as moral agents and to choose for themselves worthwhile projects, goals and expressions of their character in their own life (Beyleveld and Brownsword, 2001). In the human rights system, however, the definition of dignity is not based on capacities, but rather on species membership: all humans possess human dignity.

Secondly, as briefly touched upon above, the provision, "compatible with the nature of [ICESCR] rights," has been defined by the Committee in its General Comment No. 25 with regard to the RtS:

> As understood by the Committee, this implies that limitations must respect the minimum core obligations of the right, and must be proportionate to the aim pursued, which means that where there are several means reasonably capable of achieving the legitimate aim of the limitation, the one least restrictive to ESCRs must be selected and the burdens imposed on the enjoyment of the RPEBSPA should not outweigh the benefits of the limitation.

This definition is complex in that it is a composite of several more or less easily defined elements. After stressing the respect for minimum core obligations, the Committee goes on to unpack the issue of proportionality into two specifications. The first concerns the selection of the limitation that is the one least restrictive to ESCRs; the second the burdens imposed that should not outweigh the benefits of such a limitation.

In paragraph 51 of General Comment No. 25, the Committee makes clear that "States parties have to implement, as a matter of priority, core obligations." Proposed limitations involving the dereliction of a core obligation are by definition not compatible with the nature of the ESCR rights.

It is extremely significant that the Committee has explicitly declared these to be minimum core obligations. Minimum core obligations are treated differently than other human rights obligations. As explained by Donders (2015):

> The CESCR ... has determined that, notwithstanding the concept of progressive realization laid down in Article 2 ICESCR, " ... a minimum core obligation to ensure the satisfaction of, at the very least, minimum essential levels of each of the rights is incumbent upon every State party" ... " ... in order for a State party to be able to attribute its failure to meet at least its minimum core obligations to a lack of available resources it must demonstrate that every effort has been made to use all resources that are at its disposition in an effort to satisfy, as a matter of priority, those minimum obligations". In other words, in principle, retrogressive measures may not affect the minimum core of the rights, *since the core should be implemented irrespectively of the availability of resources.* (emphasis added).

The requirement that any limitations be appropriate and proportionate can be derived from statements by the Human Rights Council and General Comments by the Human Rights Committee on the International Covenant on Civil and Political Rights, and, given their general nature and high importance, it is plausible to argue that they are also applicable in the context of ICESCR rights (Müller, 2009). As we saw, the understanding of 'proportionate' offered by the new General Comment in paragraph 22 encompasses two things: choosing the option least restrictive to other economic, social and cultural rights and only imposing burdens that do not outweigh the benefits of such a limitation.

Similarly, General Comment No. 27 on the ICCPR, paragraph 14, states that any limitations must be appropriate to achieving the suggested aim, and must be the least restrictive of the possible options. In the context of the ICESCR, the only legitimate aim of limitations is the general welfare. The requirement of proportionality here serves as a constraint on the choice of a limitation. Out of the set of possible limitations, only that limitation may be chosen which is appropriate for the aim *and* the least restrictive (on its impact on other human rights).

In practice this will mean that the stronger and more pressing a social need is – in terms of, for example, furthering the general welfare – the more likely it is that a given human right may be limited. Conversely, those rights that are arguably less important for the general welfare require less of a pressing social need to be legitimately limited.

13.4.4 Step Four: Which is the Best Remaining Option for Promoting the General Welfare in a Democratic Society?

Finally, once a list of options consistent with the requirements in the preceding three steps has been drawn up, the fourth step provides a few additional tools to narrow down the set of acceptable choices.

According to the final limitation criteria of ICESCR Article 4, "the State may subject such rights [to limitations] . . . solely for the purpose of promoting the general welfare in a democratic society." Importantly, it is not just the welfare in a society that is mentioned, but the *general* welfare. This reflects the human rights principle of inclusiveness and the premise, common to many consequentialist normative theories, that the preferences, interests and welfare of an individual is of the highest importance, but no more so for any one individual than for another.

It is worth stressing this point because it has so many important consequences. First, it makes it much harder to justify a limitation on the RtS which would benefit only a select group of individuals, rather than everyone in the society. Second, and related, this provision forces policymakers and policy evaluators to include all of a society's individual interests in their deliberations *before* issuing policy. This shift in perspective is likely to be a great boon in itself. It is also likely to increase public confidence in policy.

The "general welfare" is not defined in any greater detail. However, the requirement that any limitations be "solely" for the purpose of the general welfare may be interpreted to imply that limitations cannot be imposed for reasons of public order, public morality, national security, and so on. This essentially leaves only the social and economic wellbeing and happiness of each individual as a legitimate basis for limitations (Müller, 2009). It could however also be argued that public order, public morality, and national security serve the general welfare and are thereby included in this concept. Exceptions may also arise due to the close link between the RtS and other human rights that may be limited for some of the aforementioned reasons, such as freedom of expression and freedom of association (Donders, 2015). Moreover, restrictions due to fundamental human rights principles such as dignity and the interdependence of human rights still apply; legitimate limitations must meet all of these standards.

One concrete example where the human rights principle of inclusiveness comes into play is intellectual property (IP). Rights of authors and inventors are important to help assure the public "of the credibility of their claims of innovation," as well as offering "assurance to the public of the authenticity of the works presented to it," wrote Richard Pierre Claude, one of the earliest and most astute commentators on the RtS (Claude, 2002, p. 52). Should these rights clash with people's right to science and culture, however, "the burden of demonstrating priority lies with property rights claimants" (Claude, 2002, p. 53). From a human rights-based perspective, there exists a presumption against property rights because "the use of scientific achievements should promote the fullest realization of human rights without discrimination, including that which follows from the advantages enjoyed by those asserting property rights" (Claude 2002, p. 53).

This radically different baseline assumption, which puts the effects of scientific advances on individuals, rather than the inventor, at the center of analysis, is one of the most important features of the RtS framework. Under it, the default is that everyone should be able to benefit from scientific advances, and only if certain, well-described conditions are met, may this presumption in favor of individual access rights be limited. Similarly, the starting point for any conversation concerning the intersection between science and society based on the RtS must be its effects on all citizens equally, and not only those able to pay or otherwise to advance their interests.

That this is necessary is seen by simple statistics such as the 10/90 gap, whose name derives from the fact that less than 10 percent of the worlds medical expenditures are spent on the diseases and conditions which make up 90 percent of the disease burden. Typically this is because the majority of the disease burden is in countries less able to pay for medications; roughly a third of all deaths occur from diseases where a cure or prevention is already known, but is not undertaken or provided for reasons related to resources (Hesketh, 2005): Thus, "[the] issue, however, is not the unavailability of medicines in the world market. The problem in their view is that the poor are unable to access these medicines largely because of poverty, inadequate health infrastructure, and overbearing governments. These barriers need to be removed to make the drugs available to poor people" (Vidyasagar, 2006).

In contrast, access to medicines as a benefit of scientific progress would be the default option under the RtS. The point is that everybody has such a right unless clear, pre-defined criteria are met.

The inclusion of the qualifier, "in a democratic society", was, during the drafting process, considered to be of "vital importance ... since in its absence ... [the limitation clause] might very well serve the ends of dictatorship" (quoted in Müller, 2009). One way this might happen would be for an authoritarian or other nonrepresentative government to define the general welfare in a way that does not correspond to the aggregate welfare of each individual in society, for example by declaring the welfare of some class of political opponents to be irrelevant, or by focusing on elements of welfare that only benefit some rather than, or at the expense of, others, such as reductions in the maximal income tax brackets, or subsidies for farms or churches. Thus what really matters here is not necessarily that the government form be a pure democracy, but rather that it be a kind of governance structure that truly and equally values the interests of each member of society, rather than the ruling or some other class.

Of relevance here is also Section III: Elements of the right and its limitations of the General Comment, in its Section A, which lays out the elements of the right using the commonly utilized four-A (here AAQA) scheme. Paragraph 19, which defines acceptable science, includes a maximizing principle:

> Acceptability implies also that scientific research has to incorporate ethical standards ... Some of these standards are: benefits to research participants and other affected individuals *should be maximized* and any possible harm minimized with reasonable protections and safeguards [emphasis added].

It can be argued that a maximizing principle is implied generally. Just as proportionality means that the least restrictive option should be chosen, so the importance of the general welfare – the *only* aim for which limitations may be set – implies that the option most likely to provide the most overall general welfare *should* be chosen. We submit on our own authority that, *ceteris paribus*, the operative word *must* be preferred over the weaker *should*.

Thus, step four asks which of the policy options that have cleared steps one through three, as well as being appropriate, proportionate, and necessary in a democratic society, are likely to add to the general welfare of society, and requires that we choose the one out of these *most* likely to lead to the *greatest* increase in general welfare.

13.5 CONCLUDING REMARKS

One section of the new General Comment is dedicated to the interdependence of the RtS with other rights. Thus, paragraph 63 acknowledges that, "the REBSP is a human right with an intrinsic value, but it also has an instrumental value, as it constitutes an essential tool for the realization of other ESCRs, in particular for the right to food and the right to health."

In a systematic review conducted of the literature on the RtS, the most commonly stressed themes found were access and the connection to other human rights, with other highly cited themes including intellectual property protection, participation in science, and dual use (Porsdam Mann et al., 2018; Porsdam Mann, Donders, and Porsdam, 2020). Thus, it was acknowledged that science is important for the fulfilment of other human rights duties, but also that it has value of its own.

The RtS has wide applicability across themes at the intersection between science, society and the individual. Part of its promise lies in its universal nature: since the RtS is a human right, everyone is, in theory, equally entitled to enjoy it. The idea is that, barring good reasons to the contrary, everyone should be able to enjoy access to the benefits of the progress of science and its applications. By comparison, the standard framework for regulating access to scientific materials and output today is based on intellectual property protection, which is exclusionary in nature. Here, the idea is that, barring good reasons to the contrary, no one should be allowed access to the benefits of scientific progress unless they are willing and able to pay.

Our aim has been to provide a sketch of a framework for the assessment of policies according to their compliancy or otherwise with the obligations imposed by the RtS. One of the strengths of our model is that it has been developed using only pre-existing concepts and instruments, which should be largely uncontroversial, and should facilitate the evaluation of human rights implications by those familiar with these tools.

In the first step, general definitions are brought to bear to determine whether an issue or policy proposal falls within the scope of the RtS. The second step involves figuring out whether any of a set of proposals fulfils the RtS, and if it does not, whether the options are best classified as derogations, retrogressive measures, or limitations. In step three, commonly accepted human rights instruments and concepts are used to determine the legitimacy of proposed policy options. The fourth and final step then simply requires the choice of the best possible remaining option.

A policy option that makes it all the way through the four-step test fulfils the following criteria: it is enacted according to the rule of law; and it is the option which produces the greatest amount of general welfare in a democratic society out of the set of options which are based on science, compatible with the nature of economic, social and cultural rights, respect fundamental human rights principles, and are balanced according to their impact on the enjoyment of all human rights. Beholden to the general and individual interest, it is our contention that any such outcomes are likely to be superior to the criteria according to which current science policy is determined.

Our hope is that by bringing together different schemes, including the General Comment No. 25 and academic reflections, this sketch has contributed toward building a useable framework that may help activate the RtS in practice.

REFERENCES

Beyleveld, D., and Brownsword, R. (2001). *Human Dignity in Bioethics and Biolaw*. Oxford; New York: Oxford University Press.

CESCR. (1991). *CESCR General Comment No. 3: The Nature of States Parties' Obligations (Art. 2, Para. 1, of the Covenant).* (UN Doc E/1991/23).
CESCR. (2001). *Statement on Poverty and the ICESCR.* (E/C.12/2001/10). Retrieved from https://digitallibrary.un.org/record/452397?ln=en.
CESCR. (2020). *General comment No. 25 on science and economic, social and cultural rights (article 15 (1) (b), (2), (3) and (4) of the International Covenant on Economic, Social and Cultural Rights).* (UN Doc E/C.12/GC/25).
Claude, R. P. (2002). *Science in the Service of Human Rights.* Philadelphia: University of Pennsylvania Press.
Donders, Y. (2011). The Right to Enjoy the Benefits of Scientific Progress: In Search of State Obligations in Relation to Health. *Medicine, Health Care, and Philosophy,* 14(4), 371–381.
Donders, Y. (2015). Balancing Interests: Limitations to the Right to Enjoy the Benefits of Scientific Progress and Its Applications. *European Journal of Human Rights,* 4, 486–503.
Eide, A. (1987). *The Right to Adequate Food as a Human Right.* (E/CN.4/Sub.2/1987/23). Retrieved from https://digitallibrary.un.org/record/139080?ln=en.
Hesketh, T. (2005). The 10/90 Report on Health Research 2003–2004 Global Forum for Health Research. *Transactions of The Royal Society of Tropical Medicine and Hygiene,* 99(8), 638–638.
Müller, A., "Limitations to and Derogations from Economic, Social and Cultural Rights," *Human Rights Law Review,* Volume 9, Issue 4, 2009, Pages 557–601.
Porsdam Mann, S., Donders, Y., Mitchell, C., Bradley, V. J., Chou, M. F., Mann, M., Porsdam, H. (2018). Opinion: Advocating for Science Progress As a Human Right. *Proceedings of the National Academy of Sciences,* 115(43), 10820–10823.
Porsdam Mann, S., Donders, Y., and Porsdam, H. (2020). Sleeping Beauty: The Right to Science As a Global Ethical Discourse. *Human Rights Quarterly,* 42.
Vidyasagar, D. (2006). Global Notes: The 10/90 Gap Disparities in Global Health Research. *Journal of Perinatology,* 26(1), 55–56.

14

The Right to Science

A Practical Tool for Advancing Global Health Equity and Promoting the Human Rights of People with Tuberculosis

Mike Frick and Gisa Dang

"We need research, not hysteria!" – Banner at New York City Gay Pride, June 1983[1]

"We need good science like we need clean water." – Glenda Gray, president, South African Medical Research Council, 2016[2]

Human rights play a tremendous role in successfully tackling communicable diseases worldwide. The application of the right to health with the rights to nondiscrimination and participation has created pathways for civil society involvement in the design, implementation, and oversight of health programs, and has created space to grow social movements in the global health sphere. Activists in the HIV/AIDS movement, such as the ACT-UP members quoted in the above epigraph, realized early in the course of the HIV epidemic that science, health, and human rights are inextricably linked; and that, in fact, the combination of scientific progress and respect for human rights will be essential for achieving an AIDS-free generation. Scientists working on infectious diseases have themselves voiced the intrinsic human rights dimensions of science, exemplified by South African Medical Research Council president Glenda Gray's comparison of good science to clean water; both are public goods and basic requirements of a life with dignity.

Given the deep connections between science and rights, one might assume that the right to science has provided a rallying point for social movements tackling health and human rights issues. The right to science – established by Article 27 of the Universal Declaration of Human Rights (UDHR) and Article 15 of the International Covenant on Economic, Social, and Cultural Rights (ICESCR) – speaks to many of the freedoms and entitlements at the heart of

---

[1] As depicted in a photograph taken by Barbara Alper for Getty Images.
[2] Glenda Gray. State of the Field and Future Direction of Research and Development for TB and HIV/AIDS Vaccines. Presentation at: Vaccines are Needed to Conclusively End HIV/AIDS and TB. 21st International AIDS Conference. Durban, South Africa. July 18, 2016. http://programme.aids2016.org/Programme/Session/1069.

global health movements.[3] [4] Yet, the size and success of the HIV/AIDS movement remains exceptional; similar movements have not coalesced around other infectious diseases to the same extent. (The COVID-19 pandemic may yet spark social mobilizations rivaling the size and durability of those against HIV/AIDS, a potential explored in an addendum ending this chapter.) Nor has the right to science been analyzed in any form that comes close to matching analyses of the right to health advanced by civil society, scholars, and the United Nation (UN) system.

Consistent with the interrelation of human rights, the right to science cannot be entirely separated from the right to health and other rights, but is in fact a complementary right. Yet, global health advocates have so far not claimed the right to science as a practical tool for securing health and human rights. In this chapter, we show the importance of undertaking a detailed, applied analysis of the right to science for the elimination of tuberculosis (TB) as the world's deadliest infectious disease. We analyze the access and participation dimensions of the right to science, departing from a traditional right to health analysis to supply a workable entry point for advocacy for the global TB response. The discussion of two ethical pillars of participation – inclusion and reciprocity – illustrates how promoting the meaningful involvement of marginalized communities in TB research is a prerequisite for states' abilities to fulfil their obligation to ensure all people can enjoy the benefits and applications of scientific progress. The final section presents examples illustrating how activists have begun to invoke the right to science as a basic human right. These cases demonstrate the importance of disentangling the right to science from the right to health, even while acknowledging their interrelation, in order for this right to become a truly powerful avenue for advancing global health equity.

14.1 TB RESEARCH: IN SEARCH OF STATE ATTENTION

TB has killed more people than any other infectious disease in human history and remains the leading cause of death from a single infectious agent globally.[5] [6] In 2018, 10 million people developed TB and 1.3 million died from the disease. The deadly persistence of TB stems, in part, from the failure of scientific advances to keep pace with an epidemic that has evolved both in response to and away from last century's medical interventions. Over time, TB has grown more difficult to treat and formed syndemics (i.e., epidemics that occur together and magnify each other's effects) with other global health threats such as HIV and diabetes. A review of TB research investments by the World Health Organization (WHO) concluded: "The present and future threat TB

---

[3] Universal Declaration of Human Rights. New York, NY: United Nations. United Nations General Assembly Resolution 217 A (III) (1948).
[4] International Covenant on Economic, Social and Cultural Rights. New York, NY: United Nations. A/6316 (1966).
[5] T. Paulson. Epidemiology: a mortal foe. Nature. 2013; 502(7470): S2–3.
[6] World Health Organization. Global TB report 2019. Geneva: World Health Organization; 2019. www.who.int/tb/publications/global_report/en/.

poses to human health is mainly a consequence of the enormous neglect the TB research field has experienced over the past several decades."[7]

This neglect reflects chronic underinvestment in research and development (R&D). There is a lack of scientific innovation in TB due to insufficient funding by the public sector and limited and diminishing activity by the pharmaceutical industry.

At the 2018 United Nations High-Level Meeting on TB, UN member states committed "to mobilize sufficient and sustainable financing for research, with the aim of increasing overall global investments to US $2 billion [per year] ... ensuring that all countries contribute appropriately to R&D."[8] (The $2 billion annual target was first set by the Stop TB Partnership in 2006.) An annual survey of TB expenditures by public, philanthropic, private, and multilateral institutions conducted by Treatment Action Group (TAG) over the last fourteen years shows that annual investments in TB R&D have fallen far short of this $2 billion target, never exceeding $900 million in any given year.[9] This points to states' failure to support science, either by failing to directly fund TB research, or by not putting in place legislative, regulatory, and policy frameworks able to attract investment by other sectors.

In 2017, less than 0.1 percent of the estimated $97.2 billion spent on R&D by the pharmaceutical industry went to TB.[10] This is the consequence of a biomedical innovation system driven by market returns rather than public health need; any system focused on commercializing innovation for profit will direct few resources to TB and other diseases of poverty.[11][12] TAG's data document a clear decline in this already limited TB research spending by pharmaceutical companies and an increasing reliance on the public sector to fund TB R&D.[13]

[7] World Health Organization. Global investments in tuberculosis research and development: past, present, and future. Geneva: World Health Organization; 2017. https://apps.who.int/iris/bitstream/handle/10665/259412/9789241513326-eng.pdf;jsessionid=1187DBC99A85BB654C1C19CF2B638535?sequence=1.

[8] UN General Assembly. Political Declaration of the UN High Level Meeting on the Fight against Tuberculosis A/RES/73/3 (October 10, 2018). www.who.int/tb/unhlmonTBDeclaration.pdf.

[9] M. Low. 2018 report on tuberculosis research funding trends. New York: Treatment Action Group; 2018. www.treatmentactiongroup.org/content/tbrd2018.

[10] Combined, private-sector companies spent less than $100 million on TB research in 2017. This is less than 0.1 percent of the $97.2 billion EvaluatePharma estimates the pharmaceutical industry spent on R&D in the same year. See: M. Low. 2018 report on tuberculosis research funding trends. New York: Treatment Action Group; 2018. www.treatmentactiongroup.org/content/tbrd2018.

[11] Despite accounting for 2 percent of healthy life-years lost to disability, TB only receives 0.25 percent of the money spent on medical research annually. See: World Health Organization. Global investments in tuberculosis research and development: past, present, and future. Geneva: World Health Organization; 2017. https://apps.who.int/iris/bitstream/handle/10665/259412/9789241513326-eng.pdf;jsessionid=1187DBC99A85BB654C1C19CF2B638535?sequence=1.

[12] P. Farmer. Infections and inequalities: the modern plagues. Berkeley: University of California Press; 1999.

[13] In 2017, 66 percent of TB research funding came from the public sector compared to 11 percent from private-sector companies (with the remainder made up by philanthropic and multilateral organizations). While governments accounted for 60 percent or more of TB research expenditures in any

Although public money underwrites most TB research projects, pharmaceutical companies often retain control over research outputs. Responding to this, activists have demonstrated how the public pays three times for TB innovation.[14] First, to fund the research itself. Second, to purchase resulting technologies at prices set by pharmaceutical companies, which hold intellectual property on publicly funded innovations. And then again when these same companies that benefit from public research dollars deplete public budgets through tax evasion schemes.[15] When research produces breakthroughs, these tools are priced out of reach or otherwise remain unattainable for most people with TB. This reveals the importance of recognizing access as a cornerstone of the right to science.

14.2 "THE RIGHT TO SCIENCE CONNOTES, FIRST OF ALL, A RIGHT OF ACCESS"

Thus wrote former Special Rapporteur (SR) in the field of cultural rights, Farida Shaheed, in her 2012 report to the Human Rights Council.[16] Legal scholars such as Lea Shaver have similarly described access as "the touchstone concept of the right," inherent in its earliest formulations, and visible in the way UDHR Article 27 speaks of the right of everyone *"to participate* in cultural life," *"to enjoy* the arts," and *"to share* in scientific advancement and its benefits."[17]

Determining what constitutes access under the right to science is critical to turning this right into an entitlement that individuals can claim, and into a tool that activists can use to hold states accountable for meeting their attendant obligations. Under international human rights law, access is composed of multiple dimensions, and "the dimensions of access require some adaptability from right to right."[18] General Comment No. 14 of the Committee on Economic, Social and Cultural Rights (CESCR) describes access under the right to health as encompassing four domains: nondiscrimination, physical accessibility, economic accessibility

given year over the last decade, there was a steep decline in spending by the pharmaceutical industry during the same period. Industry investments in TB research dropped from a peak of $145 million in 2011 to less than $90 million in 2018. One company – the Japan-based Otsuka Pharmaceuticals – accounted for 60 percent of industry expenditures over this period. See: M. Low. 2018 report on tuberculosis research funding trends. New York: Treatment Action Group; 2018. www.treatmentactiongroup.org/content/tbrd2018.

[14] M. Balasegaram. Drugs for the poor, drugs for the rich: why the current R&D model doesn't deliver. PLoS Speaking of Medicine. February 14, 2014. https://blogs.plos.org/speakingofmedicine/2014/02/14/drugs-poor-drugs-rich-current-rd-model-doesnt-deliver/.
[15] See, for example: Oxfam. Prescriptions for poverty: drug companies as tax dodgers, price gougers, and influence peddlers. London: Oxfam; 2018. www.oxfam.org/en/research/prescription-poverty.
[16] United Nations, General Assembly. Report of the Special Rapporteur in the field of cultural rights, Farida Shaheed: The right to benefit from scientific applications and its progress. A/HRC/20/26 (May 14, 2012). www.ohchr.org/EN/Issues/CulturalRights/Pages/benefitfromscientificprogress.aspx.
[17] L. Shaver. The right to science and culture. Wisconsin Law Review. 2010; 121: 122–184 (emphases added).
[18] Ibid.

(affordability), and access to information.[19] In the 3AQ framework, accessibility sits alongside the availability, acceptability, and quality of health facilities, goods, and services as an essential element of the right to health in all its forms and at all levels.

In General Comment No. 25, CESCR related the 3AQ framework to the right to science and added a fifth element: the protection of freedom of scientific research.[20] The application of the 3AQ framework to the right to health has greatly clarified the nature of state obligations with respect to access. The analysis of access in General Comment No. 25 also reflects the work of scholars and activists to sketch the dimensions of access under the right in the lead up to CESCR issuing this authoritative legal interpretation. In keeping with one of the foundational principles of international human rights law, access must satisfy the requirement of nondiscrimination (e.g., ICESCR Article 2.2). The treaty language in Article 15 describes scientific progress in terms of both its "benefits" and "applications." This strongly suggests that access extends beyond general knowledge to encompass tangible applications of science.[21] Similarly, Audrey Chapman has said that the term "benefits" should be understood as including "material benefits," and that a human rights approach requires attention to how these benefits are distributed to disadvantaged communities.[22] Shaheed condensed these ideas into the powerful statement that "innovations essential for a life with dignity" must be accessible to everyone.[23]

This idea has provided a powerful hook for TB activists seeking to connect people affected by TB to the tangible outputs of science in the form of new drugs, diagnostics, and vaccines. This is familiar territory. The phrase "innovations essential for a life with dignity" contains echoes of the term "essential drugs," provision of which is a core obligation under the right to health.[24]

TB activists have intuited the importance of not narrowly defining access as meaning only material benefits. Just as people with TB need new drugs, scientists need access to data, samples, and compounds. The right, therefore, must encompass the ability of scientists to access the means, methods, and tools of discovery. And both scientists and the public need access to intangible forms of knowledge and

[19] Committee on Economic, Social and Cultural Rights. General Comment No. 14, The right to the highest attainable standard of health. E/C.12/2000/4 (August 11, 2000). https://digitallibrary.un.org/record/425041?ln=en.
[20] Committee on Economic, Social and Cultural Rights. General comment No. 25 (2020) on Science and economic, social and cultural rights Art. 15.1.b, 15.2, 15.3 and 15.4. E/C.12/GC/25 (April 7, 2020). www.ohchr.org/en/hrbodies/cescr/pages/cescrindex.aspx.
[21] L. Shaver. The right to science and culture. Wisconsin Law Review. 2010;121: 122–184.
[22] A. Chapman. Towards an understanding of the right to enjoy the benefits of scientific progress and its applications. Journal of Human Rights. 2009;8: 1–36.
[23] United Nations, General Assembly. Report of the Special Rapporteur in the field of cultural rights, Farida Shaheed: The right to benefit from scientific applications and its progress. A/HRC/20/26 (May 14, 2012). www.ohchr.org/EN/Issues/CulturalRights/Pages/benefitfromscientificprogress.aspx.
[24] Committee on Economic, Social and Cultural Rights. General Comment No. 14, The right to the highest attainable standard of health. E/C.12/2000/4 (August 11, 2000). https://digitallibrary.un.org/record/425041?ln=en.

information. This idea is represented by the "continuum of access" developed by the American Association for the Advancement of Science (AAAS), which depicts access as stretching from the public on one side to scientists on the other.[25]

Accordingly, TAG has previously framed state obligations to address TB under the right to science in line with Article 15.2 of ICESCR,[26] which establishes the conservation, development, and diffusion of science as state obligations. By combining all three, Article 15.2 lays out a concept of access that connects state support for science (development) with the equitable distribution of the benefits and applications of scientific progress (diffusion) and efforts to ensure that these benefits are lasting (conservation). In this context, we understand conservation as meaning that the benefits of science are available not only to people alive today, but also to future generations.[27] We argue that a state that satisfies its obligation to develop science without supporting diffusion and conservation has not created the conditions necessary for access.

14.3 PARTICIPATION IN SCIENCE IS A PREREQUISITE TO ACCESSING THE BENEFITS OF SCIENTIFIC PROGRESS

Participation is one of the animating values of the right to science and is directly linked to access. Most obviously, participation in relation to science refers to the ability of scientists to engage in the scientific endeavor. But it also speaks to the ability of nonscientists – including research participants and the intended beneficiaries of science – to have a voice in decision-making about science.[28] In her 2012 report, Shaheed identifies the participation of individuals and communities in decision-making about science as a key element of the right's normative content.[29] Participation is so central to the right to science that in General Comment No. 25 CESCR added the word participation to the longform name of the right itself: "Thus, it is the *right to participate* and to enjoy the benefits from scientific progress and its applications."[30]

[25] AAAS Science and Human Rights Coalition. Defining the right to enjoy the benefits of scientific progress and its applications: American scientists' perspectives. Washington, DC: American Association for the Advancement of Science; 2013. www.aaas.org/sites/default/files/content_files/UNReportAAAS.pdf.
[26] M. Frick, I. Henry, and E. Lessem. Falling short of the rights to health and scientific progress: inadequate TB drug research and access. Health and Human Rights. 2016; 18(1): 9–23.
[27] Ibid.
[28] For example, General Comment No. 25 para. 9 states that "The right ... cannot be interpreted as establishing a rigid distinction between the scientist who produces science and the general population entitled only to enjoy benefits derived from research conducted by scientists."
[29] United Nations, General Assembly. Report of the Special Rapporteur in the field of cultural rights, Farida Shaheed: The right to benefit from scientific applications and its progress. A/HRC/20/26 (May 14, 2012). www.ohchr.org/EN/Issues/CulturalRights/Pages/benefitfromscientificprogress.aspx.
[30] Emphasis added, see para. 11 of Committee on Economic, Social and Cultural Rights. General comment No. 25 (2020) on Science and economic, social and cultural rights Art. 15.1.b, 15.2, 15.3 and 15.4. E/C.12/GC/25 (April 7, 2020). www.ohchr.org/en/hrbodies/cescr/pages/cescrindex.aspx.

Participation protects people, especially marginalized populations, against scientific misconduct and the possible harms of technological development. It also creates opportunities for communities to advocate for research that addresses their needs and priorities. In order for this advocacy to be successful, communities must first find firm footing and representation among the many actors involved in doing science. In TB research, modeling the HIV approach, this representation has often advanced through community advisory boards (CABs). These groups are comprised of research-literate community members including people with TB, survivors of TB, affected family, local health activists, religious leaders, and other stakeholders.[31] CABs operate in an advisory capacity to research networks and sponsors of clinical trials and seek to raise community perspectives within funding bodies and scientific fora. These perspectives span issues of trial design, study conduct, results dissemination, and concerns about access to investigational technologies.[32]

When a CAB proposes a new study, objects to the exclusion of a particular population from a trial, questions the utility of a study procedure, or poses a research question to be examined, it is performing an important act of translational advocacy. This connects the objectives of scientists with interests vital to the communities for whom, and in which, research is conducted. If done well, the result is a dialogue between scientists and community representatives that produces value for both sides. For this dialogue to unfold, scientists themselves must recognize community expertise for what it is: a different way of approaching knowledge production, but one with equal legitimacy. More often, TB researchers have treated CABs either instrumentally (one common misconception is that community advisors exist only to promote the enrollment of participants into clinical trials), or have viewed them as stakeholders to placate before the real work of science can get underway. Confronting this dynamic has required CAB members to build their own knowledge of research in order to effectively advocate for community priorities with scientists on their own terms.

The experiences of two CABs coordinated by TAG – the Global TB Community Advisory Board (Global TB CAB) and the Community Research Advisors Group (CRAG) – illustrate how community participation has changed the direction of TB research. The Global TB CAB is a group of community-based activists from HIV and TB networks around the world that engages product developers, pharmaceutical companies, and public institutions conducting clinical trials of TB drug regimens, diagnostics, and vaccines.[33] The CRAG advises TB research conducted by the U.S. Centers for Disease Control and Prevention (CDC). Both groups have employed the early review of clinical trial protocols to influence studies before they begin. In

---

[31] A. DeLuca, E. Lessem, D. Wegener, L. Ruiz Mingote, M. Frick, D. Von Delft. The evolving role of advocacy in tuberculosis. Lancet Respir Med. 2014; 2(4): 258–259.
[32] Ibid.
[33] For more about the Global Tuberculosis Community Advisory Board, see: TBonline.info. http://tbonline.info/tbcab/.

2016, the Global TB CAB and CRAG examined their feedback on protocols for thirteen late-stage TB drug trials to identify common areas of concern and document the impact of community review. They found that study protocols routinely failed to address the following scientific and ethical concerns of high priority to communities: plans for results dissemination; post-trial access to investigational products; adequate composition (or even presence) of control arms; use of non-stigmatizing language in study documents; and the appropriate inclusion of key populations disproportionately impacted by TB, including people living with HIV (PLHIV), children, adolescents, and pregnant women.[34]

Community activists have made partial, but significant, progress on all of these fronts. For example, the CRAG successfully advocated with investigators planning a phase III trial of a shorter TB regimen to broaden the eligibility criteria to include PLHIV and adolescents.[35] The CRAG argued that since TB incidence is higher in young people and in PLHIV, it is important to assess new drug regimens in these populations. In another instance, the Global TB CAB won changes to the protocol of the STREAM study – at the time the largest drug-resistant TB treatment trial in history – by sharing concerns about the choice of the control arm in relation to the global standard of care.[36] Following this interaction, the study's investigators launched a robust program of community engagement at trial sites and supported the start-up of several local CABs.[37]

What motivates the work of the Global TB CAB, CRAG, and other TB community advisory structures is the hard-earned knowledge that participation in science is a prerequisite to accessing the benefits of scientific progress. The link between participation and access is rooted in two fundamental components of participation: inclusion and reciprocity.

14.3.1 Inclusion: Nothing About Us without Us

In global health movements, inclusion is often expressed through the organizing slogan "nothing about us without us!" The right of people affected by a disease to participate in all decisions concerning their lives has been a core tenant of global health advocacy since the formulation of the 1983 Denver Principles. Rejecting the

---

[34] L. McKenna, M. Frick, and D. Namutamba, et al. Community advisory boards on repeat: what's missing from TB clinical trials protocols. Paper presented at: 21st International AIDS Conference; Durban, South Africa; July 18–22, 2016.

[35] S. Dorman, P. Nahid, E. Kurbatova, et al. High-dose rifapentine with or without moxifloxacin for shortening treatment of pulmonary tuberculosis: study protocol for TBTC Study 31/ACTG A5349 phase 3 clinical trial. Contemp Clin Trials. 2020; 80: 105938.

[36] M. Frick. Sound science of redesigned STREAM trial (originally published as "Fool's errand: the sloppy science of the MDR-TB STREAM trial"). Tagline. 2014; 21(1): 14–15. www.treatmentactiongroup.org/tagline.

[37] See reflections by Ezio Tavora in M. Frick and L. McKenna. Sound off: three activists reflect on community victories and priorities in TB research, an interview with Sarah Mulera, Ezio Tavora, and Wim Vandevelde. Tagline. 2019; 26(1): 9–11. www.treatmentactiongroup.org/tagline.

passivity of labels such as "victims," "patients," or "subjects," a coalition calling itself People with AIDS laid out a foundational vision of self-determination, autonomy, and empowerment.[38] This vision included the right of people with AIDS to "be involved at every level of decision-making;" to "be included in all AIDS forums with equal credibility as other participants;" and to receive "full explanations of all medical procedures and risks, to choose or refuse their treatment modalities, to refuse to participate in research without jeopardizing their treatment, and to make informed decisions about their lives."[39]

The standard of inclusion articulated in the Denver Principles has become the guide star for an epistemic community working to ensure that global health centers people affected by HIV, TB, and other illnesses. In the context of HIV/AIDS programs, this philosophy is called the "greater involvement of people with AIDS" (GIPA).[40] In the setting of research, an odd kinship of grassroots activists, CABs, funders, scientists, and clinical trial participants has sought to enshrine "good participatory practice" (GPP) as an essential part of ethical medical research. Today, there are guidelines on GPP for HIV prevention research, TB drug trials, TB vaccine research, and trials on emerging pathogens.[41] [42] [43] [44] These guidelines provide researchers with a roadmap for meaningfully engaging communities at each stage of a clinical trial. GPP complements existing regulatory standards such as Good Clinical Practice. It sits alongside – though does not replace – other participatory research methods, including participatory action research and community-based participatory research.[45]

Participation in science also functions as a prerequisite for accessing the benefits and applications of scientific progress. While the Denver Principles articulated the right of People with AIDS to decline research participation – recalling the bioethical precepts of autonomy, and free and informed consent – just as often the fight is about

[38] Advisory Committee of the People with AIDS. The Denver Principles. Denver: People with AIDS; 1983. http://data.unaids.org/pub/externaldocument/2007/gipa1983denverprinciples_en.pdf.
[39] Ibid.
[40] UNAIDS. The Greater Involvement of People Living with HIV (GIPA): UNAIDS Policy Brief. Geneva: UNAIDS; 2007. http://data.unaids.org/pub/briefingnote/2007/jc1299_policy_brief_gipa.pdf.
[41] AVAC. Good participatory practice: guidelines for biomedical HIV prevention trials, 2nd edition. New York: AVAC; 2011. https://www.avac.org/good-participatory-practice
[42] Critical Path to TB Drug Regimens. Good participatory practice guidelines for TB drug trials. Washington, DC: Critical Path to TB Drug Regimens; 2012. www.cptrinitiative.org/downloads/resources/GPP-TB%20Oct1%202012%20FINAL.pdf.
[43] Aeras. Good participatory practice guidelines for TB vaccine research. Washington, D.C.: Aeras; 2017. www.avac.org/resource/good-participatory-practice-guidelines-tb-vaccine-research-2017.
[44] World Health Organization. Good participatory practice guidelines for trials of emerging (and re-emerging) pathogens that are likely to cause severe outbreaks in the near future and for which few or no medical countermeasures exist. Geneva: World Health Organization; 2016. www.avac.org/resource/good-participatory-practice-guidelines-trials-emerging-and-re-emerging-pathogens%C2%A0-are.
[45] K. MacQueen and J. Auerbach. It is not just about "the trial": the critical role of effective engagement and participatory practices for moving the HIV research field forward. J Int AIDS Soc. 2018; 21(S7): e25179.

gaining inclusion in the scientific agenda. The systematic exclusion of certain groups from research is a form of marginalization that reinforces disparities in which some populations shoulder a greater burden of TB than others. Activists have shown how TB clinical trials favor enrollment of "typical" TB patients with easier-to-treat forms of disease.[46] As a result, people with complicating comorbidities (e.g., HIV, diabetes) or severe disease manifestations (e.g., TB meningitis) are left out of trials. Other groups such as children, adolescents, and pregnant women are excluded out of a misplaced desire to protect vulnerable populations from harm.

In actuality, research protection interpreted as exclusion amplifies TB-related harms. Evidence-based guidelines cannot be made in the absence of evidence that an intervention works in a particular population. Some of the populations most vulnerable to TB are either not represented in normative guidance produced by WHO, or must wait years for well-established interventions to be recommended for their use. The CRAG and TB CAB mobilized to increase the inclusion of pregnant women in TB research, arguing that the risks inherent to research must be weighed against potential benefits as well as the predictable harms of *not* conducting research in pregnant women. "In the absence of research, each pregnant woman treated for TB becomes an individual experiment," CAB members argued. "Approaching each pregnant woman with TB as an experiment with a sample size of one precludes conducting the systematic research needed to produce the generalizable knowledge necessary to improve clinical care for all pregnant women with TB."[47] Rather than policies of blanket exclusion, the TB CAB and CRAG argued that researchers should presume pregnant women eligible for research participation and then provide specific ethical and scientific justification to support ineligibility. Thus, participation as inclusion constitutes an essential condition by which states can deliver on their obligation to provide all people with access to innovations essential for a life with dignity.

TB activists are not alone in confronting the unfairness through which exclusion from research results in the benefits of science accruing to some groups over others. AIDS activists have pointed out that HIV treatment and cure trials enroll more white gay men than women, transgender people, or people of color.[48] [49] That HIV and TB activists framed research inclusion as an issue of justice is thanks to the work of feminists and communities of color in the United States to secure policies from the

---

[46] Stillo, Jonathan, Mike Frick, and Yali Cong. "Upholding Ethical Values and Human Rights on New Frontiers of TB Care and Control". The International Journal of Tuberculosis and Lung Disease. 2020. 24(1) pp. 48-56.

[47] L. McKenna, M. Frick, D. Namutamba, et al. Community advisory boards on repeat: what's missing from TB clinical trials protocols. Paper presented at: 21st International AIDS Conference; Durban, South Africa; July 18–22, 2016.

[48] M. Curno, S. Rossi, I. Hodges-Mameletzis, et al. A systematic review of the inclusion (or exclusion) of women in HIV research. J Acquir Immune Defic Snydr. 2016; 71(2): 181–188.

[49] J. Castillo-Mancilla, S. Cohn, S. Krishnan, et al. Minorities remain underrepresented in HIV/AIDS research despite access to clinical trials. HIV Clin Trials. 2014; 15(1): 14–26.

National Institutes of Health and Food and Drug Administration (FDA) requiring the inclusion of women and racial minorities in clinical trials, and the analysis of data by gender and race.[50]

14.3.2 Reciprocity: From "Do No Harm" to Repairing Harm

Alongside inclusion, the concept of reciprocity is important for understanding state obligations with respect to participation under the right to science. Bioethicists have defined reciprocity as "returning goods in proportion to those received and compensating those who have been harmed."[51] Diego Silva and colleagues have used this notion of reciprocity to examine state obligations to people with TB who must endure periods of involuntary isolation or detention to limit the risk of transmission to others. They argue that reciprocity is more than a "thank you;" it is "a means of society and the state accepting responsibility for the conditions that have led to infection and disease from TB."[52],[53] To the extent TB is a disease of poverty, the state has an obligation to compensate people with TB for harm caused by the state's failure to ameliorate the conditions that give rise to TB and disproportionately distribute its harms.

In the context of research, that is, development under the right to science, the concept of reciprocity helps elucidate rights and responsibilities. Individuals who enroll in clinical trials assume real risk in exchange for benefits that are by definition unknown and not guaranteed. Communities that host research provide a valuable social good to scientific endeavors that are often led by scientists or pharmaceutical companies in the Global North. Through such participation, these individuals and communities create the conditions under which science advances. Recognizing a right to enjoy the benefits of scientific progress creates the possibility of reciprocity in this exchange.

To borrow Silva's reasoning that reciprocity creates the grounds for acknowledging state responsibility to repair harm: the clear connection between the lack of support for TB R&D and the continued toll that TB exacts further compels states to support the conservation, development, and diffusion of science and its benefits. Supporting the purposive development of science and technology for TB is a way for states to address harms arising from the inadequate tools and lack of innovation underlying the TB epidemic. This responsibility is shared by all states. As Cristian Timmermann points out, it is hardly forward-thinking to treat one part of the world

---

[50] K. Baird. The new NIH and FDA medical research policies: targeting gender, promoting justice. J Health Polit Policy Law. 1999; 24(3): 531–565.
[51] D. Silva, A. Dawson, and R. Upshur. Reciprocity and ethical tuberculosis treatment and control. Bioethical Inquiry. 2016; 13: 75–86. See also: L. Becker. Reciprocity. New York: Routledge & Kegan Paul Ltd.; 1986.
[52] D. Silva, A. Dawson, and R. Upshur. Reciprocity and ethical tuberculosis treatment and control. Bioethical Inquiry. 2016; 13: 75–86.
[53] A. Viens, C. Bensimon, R. Upshur. Your liberty or your life: reciprocity in the use of restrictive measures in contexts of contagion. Bioethical Inquiry. 2009; 6(2): 207–217.

as that which does science and another as that which receives it: "There is a huge amount of unacknowledged reciprocity for inventions placed in technology-dependent societies. Developers of technologies gain many insights from their users."[54] An ethic of reciprocity arises from the participation of individuals in research; this contribution creates an obligation by states to ensure that the benefits of research are equitably shared, again linking participation and access.

14.4 CREATING ACCOUNTABILITY THROUGH ADVOCACY

How have TB advocates used the above framework to hold governments accountable to meeting their obligations under the right to science? Over the past three years, TAG has sought opportunities to promote knowledge of the right to science within the UN system and among fellow advocates. As is clear from the above analyses of participation and access, the right holds tremendous potential for giving new impetus to the global TB response by focusing state attention on the development of new tools and interventions with meaningful community participation and through means that ensure the equitable diffusion of these advancements. Since human rights are interrelated, interdependent, and indivisible, the right to science also provides a new lens through which activists can frame issues they have been trying to change for decades.

14.4.1 *Working with United Nations Mechanisms*

One immediate barrier to realizing this potential is the absence of writing that analyzes specific issues using a right to science lens or attempts to take such analyses from international law into the realm of domestic law and local health policy. Therefore, TAG identified several UN mechanisms that would provide the opportunity to analyze TB as a human rights issue under the right to science.

The UN system provides several channels through which human rights violations can be brought to light. One mechanism is the Universal Periodic Review (UPR), which regularly reviews the human rights record of each member state and which allows for parallel submissions by civil society that feed into the official UPR documentation for each country. TAG wrote submissions for the third cycle UPR of three countries: China (2018),[55] Mexico (2018),[56] and the United Arab Emirates (2017).[57]

[54] C. Timmermann. Sharing in or benefitting from scientific advancement? *Sci Eng Ethics*. 2014; 20(1): 111133.
[55] Treatment Action Group. Submission to Human Rights Council Universal Periodic Review (Third Cycle) of the People's Republic of China. New York: Treatment Action Group; 2018. http://treatmentactiongroup.org/content/tb-human-rights-and-universal-periodic-review.
[56] Treatment Action Group. Submission to Human Rights Council Universal Periodic Review (Third Cycle) of Mexico. New York: Treatment Action Group; 2018. http://treatmentactiongroup.org/content/tb-human-rights-and-universal-periodic-review.
[57] Treatment Action Group. Submission to Human Rights Council Universal Periodic Review (Third Cycle) of the United Arab Emirates. New York: Treatment Action Group; 2018. http://treatmentactiongroup.org/content/tb-human-rights-and-universal-periodic-review.

TAG's United Arab Emirates (UAE) UPR submission grew from statements by migrant workers deported from the UAE for signs of TB based on a flawed diagnostic algorithm deployed in mandatory medical exams for work permit applications. We wrote a succinct analysis of how the public health policies governing TB screening and the laws directing its application in immigration proceedings failed to meet international scientific and human rights standards. TAG delivered an oral intervention at the UPR pre-session in Geneva, and has since engaged with the special procedures mechanisms to push for legal protections against deportation on the basis of TB or other health status. The issue of TB and migrant health screening in the UAE lent itself well to an analysis spanning the diffusion of scientific progress (i.e. TB screening according to global scientific standards) and related rights such as health, information, and nondiscrimination. Through this analysis, TAG hoped to showcase how the right to science contributes to an understanding of the rights of migrants with the explicit goal of influencing UN bodies that may not recognize the right to science as relevant to their missions.

For the UPR of China, TAG's submission analyzed China's response to drug-resistant TB (DR-TB), showing how in responding to its DR-TB epidemic, China had failed to both diffuse existing tools for confronting DR-TB to all people in need and develop improved tools through investments in research. As a country that heavily restricts civil society activities nationally, and aims to limit the activity of global civil society with regards to its human rights record and conduct, China exemplified the connection of the right to science to the right to participation, as well as to freedoms of association and assembly.

TAG's experience raising right to science issues in the third-cycle UPR has led to the realization that even within the UN system there remains a great distance to travel before the right to science gains wide recognition and acceptance. In particular, TAG has faced challenges disentangling the right to science from the right to health, which many observers may find more immediately applicable to the context of TB. One case in point: despite TAG's UPR submission for China supplying a right to science analysis, in the summary of stakeholder submissions, TAG's submission was mentioned under the subheading of right to health, without any mention of the right to science.

14.4.2 Linking Conservation, Development, and Diffusion

TAG has called out insufficient funding for TB research as a failure of governments to live up to their obligation to develop science.[58][59] One concrete solution activists have proposed to increase state attention to TB R&D is the Life Prize. The initiative

---

[58] M. Frick. Funding for tuberculosis research – an urgent crisis of political will, human rights, and global solidarity. *Int J Infect Dis.* 2017; 56: 21–24.

[59] M. Frick, I. Henry, E. Lessem. Falling short of the rights to health and scientific progress: inadequate TB drug research and access. Health and Human Rights. 2016; 18(1): 9–23.

seeks to foster open collaboration among different companies, drug developers, and governments to develop a one-month regimen for treating TB that is affordable and available to all. To accomplish this, the Life Prize would deploy three mechanisms: pull incentives that reward early-stage research on compounds through milestone-based prize funds; a pool for data and intellectual property so that compounds held by different companies can be developed together without patent barriers; and push incentives (e.g., grant funding) for the clinical development of candidate regimens.[60] Money for the prize funds and grants would come from governments, a form of international collaboration encouraged by Article 15.4 of ICESCR.[61]

By combining push, pool, and pull mechanisms, the Life Prize seeks to separate the costs of research and development from the prices and sales volumes of final products.[62] In doing so, it would promote the affordability of medicines by eliminating the need of manufacturers to recoup R&D investments with high prices and patent-protected monopolies. In spurring R&D without relying on market-based incentives, the Life Prize creates the conditions for a more equitable approach to innovation, one that sees scientific development and widespread diffusion as equal, complementary goals.

The Life Prize also provides a useful framework for thinking through the conservation of science in the context of infectious diseases. One pernicious debate circulating in the TB field pits antibiotic stewardship aimed at preventing drug resistance against universal access to medicines. This framing arises from the real urgency of confronting DR-TB and the well-intentioned desire to stem drug-resistance by limiting the improper use of TB medicines. In effect, however, this stance frames conservation not in terms of access, but exclusion. In doing so, it loses sight of the pressing reality that only one in four people who develop DR-TB in any given year have access to treatment.[63] It also obscures the roots of DR-TB, blaming patients for nonadherence to regimens or prescribers for antibiotic misuse. Scientific evidence points in another direction. Sequencing of clinical isolates from DR-TB outbreaks suggests "drug-resistant strains circulating today reflect not only

[60] G. Brigden, J. Castro, L. Ditiu, et al. Tuberculosis and antimicrobial resistance – new models of research and development needed. Bull World Health Organ. 2017; 95(5): 315.

[61] "The States Parties to the present Covenant recognize the benefits to be derived from the encouragement and development of international contacts and co-operation in the scientific and cultural fields." Article 15.4 of the International Covenant on Economic, Social and Cultural Rights. New York, NY: United Nations. A/6316 (1966).

[62] It is interesting to note that the concepts behind the Life Prize – namely, separating R&D incentives from sales volumes and prices – are contained in para. 62 of General Comment No. 25: "Firstly, to counter distortions of funding associated with intellectual property, States should provide adequate financial support for research that is important for the enjoyment of economic, social and cultural rights, either through national efforts or, if necessary, by resorting to international and technical cooperation. States could also resort to other incentives, such as so-called market entry rewards, which delink remuneration of successful research from future sales, thus fostering research by private actors in these otherwise neglected fields."

[63] World Health Organization. Global TB report 2019. Geneva: World Health Organization; 2019. www.who.int/tb/publications/global_report/en/.

vulnerabilities of current TB control efforts but also those that date back 50 years."[64] Instead of recognizing this historical legacy, when treatment fails, as it often does in TB, the assumption is that patients are nonadherent while medicines are always efficacious. In actuality, many existing TB drugs have little efficacy, and many adherence challenges stem from the toxic side effects of the medicines themselves or the long duration of treatment.[65] TB activists have tried to shift this narrative of individual blame by keeping the onus on governments to plug the glaring treatment access gaps that deny so many people with DR-TB effective therapy.

TB researchers and clinicians Jennifer Furin and Madhukar Pai have called out the "tension between wanting to 'protect the new drugs' as opposed to protecting the lives of patients, with the drugs being restricted in order to purportedly preserve their efficacy."[66] This perverse logic is so endemic in the TB field that within hours of the FDA approving a new regimen with novel antibiotic pretomanid to treat the most resistant strains of TB in 2019 there was talk of "saving" pretomanid from resistance. Heralding the FDA approval, the director of the largest NGO provider of TB technical assistance globally said: "Responsible use of pretomanid-based regimens needs to be ensured. After all, we have to protect our new medicines!"[67] TB activists responded differently. They pointed out that pretomanid was developed with public and philanthropic funding and was therefore a "public good." In addition, while acknowledging critical research gaps precluding wide use of pretomanid, activists called for its evidence-based introduction for patients in need according to a set of minimum terms.[68] Activists also called for additional research on the drug, particularly regarding its safety profile and use in special populations such as children.

The example of pretomanid, and other newer TB drugs, underscores the need for a new model of R&D, one able to link scientific development with equitable diffusion. One in which access is understood as part of conservation rather than anathema to it. The Life Prize would address the real need to safeguard the efficacy of news drugs against the development of drug-resistance without trading access for conservation. Regimens developed by the Life Prize would be licensed to

[64] K. Cohen, T. Abeel, and A. McGuire, et al. Evolution of extensively drug-resistant tuberculosis over four decades: whole genome sequencing and dating analysis of Mycobacterium tuberculosis isolates from KwaZulu-Natal. PLoS Medicine. 2015; 12(9) :d1001880.

[65] M. Frick, I. Henry, and E. Lessem. Falling short of the rights to health and scientific progress: inadequate TB drug research and access. Health and Human Rights. 2016; 18(1): 9–23.

[66] M. Pai and J. Furin. Tuberculosis innovations mean little if they cannot save lives. eLife. 2017; 6: e25956.

[67] KNCV Tuberculosis Foundation. FDA approval of BPaL regimen an important breakthrough in TB control. August 14, 2019. www.kncvtbc.org/en/2019/08/14/fda-approval-of-bpal-regimen-an-important-breakthrough-in-tb-control/.

[68] These terms included full transparency in the licensing agreement between the developer (TB Alliance) and the manufacturer (Mylan), broad registration in countries, pre-approval access for patients without alternative treatment regimens, and a low global access price of $1/day. See: Treatment Action Group. Statement from Treatment Action Group on US FDA approval of pretomanid. August 14, 2019. www.treatmentactiongroup.org/content/statement-treatment-action-group-us-fda-approval-pretomanid.

manufacturers, on a nonexclusive basis, with the terms of the license setting quality standards and expectations for pharmacovigilance.[69] Unfortunately, governments have not yet stepped forward to fund this proposed model.

14.4.3 Upholding the Right to Science through Strategic Litigation

One accountability tactic that has not been tried in TB is litigation on behalf of an individual claiming the state has failed to uphold their right to enjoy the benefits of scientific progress. Citing the lack of court cases in which individual petitioners invoke the right to science, Leslie London et al. argue that the right "does not entitle individuals to direct enforceable benefits of scientific progress" by, for example, compelling a state to develop a new drug to treat DR-TB.[70] In their view, the right to science is realized collectively: people are entitled to the adoption of legislative and policy frameworks aimed at making the benefits of scientific progress available and accessible.[71]

It may be premature to conclude that the right to science is not individually actionable when the justiciability of the right has not been thoroughly tried and tested. As normative consensus on the meaning of the right builds, and as activists, lawyers, and governments become more familiar with entitlements and obligations under Article 15, its potential use in individual litigation will only grow. Even now, it does not require a great deal of imagination to envision how petitioners could make claims under the right to science to argue that states have failed to meet their obligations to conserve, develop, and diffuse the benefits of scientific progress in the context of specific public health emergencies.

As an illustrative exercise, one can read the right to science into existing cases that cite the rights to health or life to argue that an individual or group has a right to access prevention or treatment. Two examples concerning TB come from recent court cases in India. In the first, the Indian Supreme Court directed the government's national TB program to replace the prevailing thrice-weekly administration of TB medicines with daily administration of fixed-dose combination tablets.[72] [73] The ruling followed a public interest litigation filed by physician Raman Kakkar, who had documented that giving TB treatment three times a week (a practice that

---

[69] G. Bridgen. Innovative funding mechanisms for TB R&D: the 3P project. Presentation at: World Health Organization Global Taskforce on TB Research and Development. Geneva, Switzerland; December 2019.

[70] L. London, H. Cox, and F. Coomans. Multidrug-resistant TB: implementing the right to health through the right to enjoy the benefits of scientific progress. Health and Human Rights. 2016; 18(1): 25–41.

[71] Ibid.

[72] Dr. Raman Kakar v. Union of India And Anr., Writ Petition (Civil) No. 604 of 2016, Supreme Court of India, Order dated January 23, 2017.

[73] V. Dhivan, V. Johari, K. Bhardwaj. Legal environment assessment for TB in India. Chennai: REACH; 2018. www.reachtbnetwork.org/wp-content/uploads/2018/09/REACH-CRG-LEA-2018-Full-Version.pdf.

set apart India from global guidelines recommending daily pill taking) resulted in higher rates of treatment failure by making it difficult for patients to adhere to treatment.[74] In his complaint to the court, Kakkar described the thrice-weekly protocol as "unscientific" and linked it to deaths among TB patients in his district of Faridabad.[75] Through a combination of his own systematic research and an appeal to international scientific standards, Kakkar argued that the Government of India had failed to keep its TB treatment policies aligned with evolving evidence on what constitutes the highest attainable standard of care.

The second example is one of the most prominent court cases concerning TB in recent years. Kaushal Tripathi, the father of a young woman with extensively drug-resistant tuberculosis (XDR-TB), sued a public hospital so that his daughter, Shreya Tripathi, could access a new TB drug, bedaquiline.[76] First diagnosed with TB in 2013, Shreya likely developed XDR-TB after years of ineffective treatment following a series of incorrect diagnoses. By 2017, the TB strain threatening Shreya's life was resistant to almost every available drug. Facing the end of her life, Shreya and her father traveled from their home in Patna to the Lal Ram Sarup TB Hospital (LRS) in New Delhi, where bedaquiline was available under a conditional access program run by the Indian government at six public hospitals throughout the country. The hospital declined to treat Shreya with bedaquiline, citing a condition of the program: that patients demonstrate legal domicile in the location of the clinic.[77] With her official residence registered as Patna, Shreya was ineligible to receive bedaquiline in Delhi.

Represented by the Lawyers Collective, Kaushal Tripathi sued LRS for access to bedaquiline for his daughter, arguing that denial of treatment was unconstitutional based on Shreya's fundamental rights to health and life. LRS authorities argued that the TB sickening Shreya was so resistant that it was impossible to construct a sufficiently strong regimen of other TB drugs.[78] Under these circumstances, giving Shreya bedaquiline would create the opportunity for her strain of TB to develop resistance to the drug – resistance that could spread to others in the community. The efficacy of bedaquiline for other people would thus be "lost." Amicus curiae

[74] Press Trust of India. SC asks government to implement new TB protocol. Press Trust of India. January 9, 2017. www.ptinews.com/news/8272011_SC-asks-Centre-to-implement-new-TB-protocol-.html.

[75] R. Kakar. SC abolishes thrice weekly dose; restores daily dose protocol in TB across India. Journal of Research in Medical Education and Ethics. 2017; 7(1): 1–2.

[76] V. Dhivan, V. Johari, and K. Bhardwaj. Legal environment assessment for TB in India. Chennai: REACH; 2018. www.reachtbnetwork.org/wp-content/uploads/2018/09/REACH-CRG-LEA-2018-Full-Version.pdf.

[77] Menaka Rao. A domicile rule is preventing an 18-year-old girl from getting a life-saving TB drug. Scroll.in. January 6, 2017. https://scroll.in/pulse/826005/a-domicile-rule-is-preventing-an-18-year-old-girl-from-getting-a-life-saving-tb-drug.

[78] Affidavit on behalf of respondent no. 1 (Lal Ram Sarup TB Hospital) to the Delhi High Court re. the case of *Kaushal Kishore Tripathi* v. *Lal Ram Sarup Hospital & Ors.*, Writ Petition (Civil) No. 11879 of 2016. (Electronic copy on file with authors).

submitted by a prominent TB doctor argued the opposite: that the dilemma between saving drugs versus saving lives is a false choice.[79] In order to protect the public from XDR-TB, the hospital needed to give Shreya bedaquiline as a matter of urgency. The most effective way to stop the spread of TB is to provide treatment, since once someone starts effective therapy the bacterial count in the body drops and onward transmission is less likely.

In a settlement between parties, the government agreed to grant Shreya access to bedaquiline and "to make clear that domicile or residence of the patient is not a criterion for the eligibility of bedaquiline for its administration."[80]

Shreya's XDR-TB was cured, but the access delays proved fatal. By the time Shreya received bedaquiline, her lungs were irreparably damaged; she passed away in October 2018 at the age of nineteen. The loss of Shreya's life is a painful demonstration of how restrictive government access policies turn people with treatable XDR-TB into terminally ill patients by denying them access to new drugs saved for use by future others. The public health goal of sparing drugs from resistance becomes an imperative setting conservation against access. Recognizing a right to science would shift this frame by positioning conservation as one obligation of governments on the same plane of concern as other dimensions of access, including the development and diffusion of scientific progress and its benefits.

14.5 THE RIGHT TO SCIENCE: FUTURE PROMISE AND POTENTIAL

If everyone has the right to enjoy the benefits of scientific progress and its applications then this enjoyment must ultimately be fought for, not just in courts but also in communities. Advancing the critical community education and mobilization required to turn the right to science from an underappreciated normative framework into a genuine tool for accountability will not be easy. Looking back at the quotes opening this chapter, and considering the above analyses, we are surprised that this right remains so under-utilized in global health advocacy. While still largely unreferenced in global public health, the right to science is slowly shrugging off its label of being a "forgotten human right," as described by Audrey Chapman in 2009.[81] However, this emergent awareness has traveled farther in academic circles than among civil society and human rights practitioners.

In part, this may reflect the structure of the international human rights system. While the international covenants and UN bodies offer many entry points for

---

[79] Amicus curiae submitted by Dr. Jennifer Furin (Harvard Medical School, Boston, USA) to the Delhi High Court re. the case of *Kaushal Kishore Tripathi v. Lal Ram Sarup Hospital & Ors.*, Writ Petition (Civil) No. 11879 of 2016. (Electronic copy on file with authors).

[80] *Kaushal Kishore Tripathi v. Lal Ram Sarup TB Hospital & Ors.*, Delhi High Court, Writ Petition (Civil) No. 11879 of 2016, Order dated January 20, 2017. http://delhihighcourt.nic.in/dhcqrydisp_o.asp?pn=11539&yr=2017.

[81] A. Chapman. Towards an understanding of the right to enjoy the benefits of scientific progress and its applications. *Journal of Human Rights*. 2009; 8: 1–36.

advocating for human rights, the nature of the system can encourage specialization. Thus advocates fluent in the right to health rarely connect these issues to the right to science. Many may have never heard about the right to science before; even among scientists whose work incorporates human rights analysis, the right to science is not well-known. This is one reason why the right to health remains the trusted analytical framework for advocacy in the realm of global health, even though the right to science may be able to make more direct claims regarding the accessibility of innovations. CESCR's issuance of General Comment No. 25 will draw greater attention by states and civil society to the right to science. We hope that it will, like General Comment No. 14 on the right to health (2000), yield new avenues for action and accountability, while enabling scholars and practitioners to begin to disentangle the right to science from the right to health.

Whether this attention leads to litigation, and whether the right to science joins the right to health as a tool for increasing access to medicines and other innovations essential for a life with dignity, will depend on mobilizing communities around the human rights dimensions of science. This will require dedicated efforts to raise awareness of the right among communities and translate its entitlements into actionable rights claims. Through efforts by TAG and other civil society actors, the right is slowly gaining more recognition in the TB response. For instance, the 2018 *Declaration of the Rights of People Affected by Tuberculosis* includes the right to science.[82] Yet even this community document, in its aim to appeal to an international audience and maintain broad applicability, uses high-level language that will require the development of additional resources to bring the concepts into local contexts so that the right to science may become a tangible form of knowledge and thus community power. Herein lies the responsibility of scholars to translate academic work on the right to science into persuasive arguments and accessible language that activists can use to create tools to turn the right from a set of promises on paper into entitlements claimed, contested, and fulfilled.

The idea of promises – which can be broken or fulfilled, pursued or abandoned – is an instructive angle from which to think about the future conjoining of science, human rights, and TB. Bharat Venkat has said that the always-present possibility of drug-resistance, relapse, or reinfection after TB treatment means that cures for TB "might be better conceived of as endings lacking finality ... a promise rather than a rupture ... a promise that, like all promises, can be broken."[83] Understanding TB cure as contingent rather than assured acknowledges that scientific progress cannot be taken for granted. The TB of today is different from the TB of yesterday. The scientific advances ushered in by germ theory, the microscope, the antibiotic revolution, the mapping of the human and *Mycobacterium tuberculosis* genomes,

[82] TB People. Declaration of the rights on people affected by tuberculosis. Geneva: Stop TB Partnership: May 2019. www.stoptb.org/assets/documents/communities/FINAL%20Declaration%20on%20the%20Right%20of%20People%20Affected%20by%20TB%2013.05.2019.pdf.

[83] B. Venkat. Cures. Public Culture. 2016; 28(3): 475–497.

and other leaps forward in knowledge have given us new tools and vantage points from which to fight TB.

Our tools will need to keep evolving. Keeping the promise of cure alive will always depend on science progressing. Writing nearly twenty years ago, Paul Farmer observed: "even as our biomedical interventions become more effective, our capacity to distribute them equitably is further eroded."[84] If we can share the fruits of scientific advancement more equitably in the future than we have in the past, then we may move closer to fulfilling the promise of lasting cure. Promises can be broken, but human rights must be fulfilled. The right to science has given individuals confronting TB a way to bring together the development, diffusion, and conservation of scientific progress in a unified vision for ending this deadly epidemic.

14.6 ADDENDUM – THE RIGHT TO SCIENCE AND COVID-19 – APRIL 2020

We began revising this chapter as the COVID-19 pandemic reached its staggering scale, shutting down societies across the globe. Writing under lockdown from our homes in New York City and the California Bay Area, we are struck by how the right to science provides a uniquely clarifying framework for thinking through a human rights-based response to this new global pandemic. This moment in late April 2020 is likely to be remembered as the ferocious opening chapter of an epidemic of unknown length. Against this indeterminate time horizon, TB advocacy provides instructive lessons on what it will take to sustain scientific progress against COVID-19 – not over months, but years.

Past experiences from TB and HIV advocacy illuminate possible paths for translating scientific advances against COVID-19 into an effective, evidence-based, and equitable public health response. Presently, the weight of advocacy has settled on the equity proposition of COVID-19 research, or the extent to which scientific advances will be accessible to all who need them. Activists from diverse health movements have jointly called on governments to commit to making the benefits of COVID-19 research available to all without discrimination.[85] For example, recalling that Jonas Salk refused to patent the world's first polio vaccine or grant exclusive rights to any single company, students and artists have formed "Salk teams" to devise creative ways to pressure universities, governments, and

---

[84] P. Farmer. Pathologies of power: rethinking health and human rights. American Journal of Public Health. 1999; 89(10): 1486–1496.

[85] For example, over 500 organizations signed the COVID-19 Principles for Global Access, Innovation and Cooperation urging governments and corporations to share medical advances and "promote access for all." See: Public Citizen [on behalf of over 500 signatories]. COVID-19: principles for global access, innovation, and cooperation. April 23, 2020. www.citizen.org/article/covid-19-principles-for-global-access-innovation-and-cooperation/

pharmaceutical companies to make tools against COVID-19 universally available at affordable prices.[86]

Advocacy to promote the development, diffusion, and conservation of science in the TB space has prepared activists to play a watchdog role over the repurposing of existing medical technologies for COVID-19. Activists decried the high price of a SARS-CoV-2 diagnostic cartridge run on a decades-old platform developed for TB through mostly public funding.[87] Pointing out that the innovation race against COVID-19 has proceeded without robust community engagement, over 200 organizations issued a call for greater participation in COVID-19 R&D.[88] Several groups are now partnering to establish a global CAB to advise COVID-19 research endeavors.[89] Based on their experience with other epidemics, these activists understand the centrality of participation for global health equity.

Right to science principles are latent within many of these initiatives. Yet, most commentaries on human rights and Covid-19 available at the point of writing – including statements by UNAIDS,[90] scientists and academics,[91] and activists – do not name the right. Thus, COVID-19 also presents an opportunity to raise awareness of the right to science as an analytical and organizing tool. Notably, a UNDP analysis applying lessons learned from the TB and HIV responses to COVID-19 explicitly points to the right to science, particularly its underlying value of transparency "as a critical enabler of both innovation of and access to health technology."[92]

COVID-19 has revealed the imperative of fostering greater international cooperation in science, of which transparency is one essential component. ICESCR Article 15.4 speaks of "international contacts and co-operation," and General Comment No.

[86] In 1955, Jonas Salk, in reply to a question from Edward Murrow about the ownership of the polio vaccine, said: "Well, the people, I would say. There is no patent. Could you patent the sun?" (See: C. DeCroes Jacobs. Jonas Salk: a life. Oxford: Oxford University Press; 2015.) In this spirit, the Salk teams "to free the COVID-19 vaccine" are a joint effort of the Center for Artistic Activism and Universities Allied for Essential Medicines.
[87] Treatment Action Group. Statement on the high price of Cepheid's Xpert test for COVID-19. March 27, 2020. www.treatmentactiongroup.org/statement/treatment-action-group-statement-on-the-high-price-of-cepheids-xpert-test-for-covid-19/.
[88] AVAC [on behalf of over 200 signatories]. Advocates call for ethical research for COVID-19 solutions. April 8, 2020. www.avac.org/blog/advocates-call-ethical-research-covid19.
[89] Treatment Action Group and AVAC. Statement on Ethical Conduct of SARS-CoV-2 Vaccine Challenge Studies. May 8, 2020. www.treatmentactiongroup.org/statement/avac-and-tag-statement-on-ethical-conduct-of-sars-cov-2-vaccine-challenge-studies/.
[90] UNAIDS. Rights in the Time of COVID-19: lessons from HIV for an effective, community-based response. March 20, 2020. www.unaids.org/en/resources/documents/2020/human-rights-and-covid-19.
[91] See, for example, Achieving A Fair and Effective COVID-19 Response: An Open Letter to Vice-President Mike Pence, and Other Federal, State, and Local Leaders from Public Health and Legal Experts in the United States. March 6, 2020. https://law.yale.edu/sites/default/files/area/center/ghjp/documents/march6_2020_final_covid-19_letter_from_public_health_and_legal_experts_2.pdf.
[92] T. Avafia, et al. A rights-based response to COVID-19: lessons learned from HIV and TB epidemics. Health and Human Rights. March 24, 2020. www.hhrjournal.org/2020/03/a-rights-based-response-to-covid-19-lessons-learned-from-hiv-and-tb-epidemics/#_edn3.

25 paragraph 82 explicitly references pandemics because, as we are currently witnessing, "a local epidemic can become very quickly a pandemic with devastating consequences." States therefore should respond with transparency by "sharing the best scientific knowledge and its applications..."[93] States and global agencies have put forward several concrete proposals to facilitate greater information sharing and research collaboration (though these stand against rights-denying actions by other states to control information, privatize knowledge, trade collaboration for competition, and undermine global solidarity). To take one positive example, UNESCO held a meeting in March 2020 on international cooperation in the face of COVID-19 to discuss the potential of sharing knowledge – building on its two-year process to develop a Recommendation on Open Science.[94] [95] Another promising example is the proposal by the government of Costa Rica – endorsed by the WHO – to establish a voluntary pool of COVID-19 patents, data, and technology that could be shared for developing drugs, vaccines, and diagnostics.[96] We cannot help but hear echoes of the Life Prize concept for TB drug development in this proposal and hope that governments step forward to support it.

With no tests, treatments, or vaccines available at the outset of the pandemic, and with country after country struggling with similar dire situations (e.g., shortages of personal protective equipment, ventilators, testing reagents) within weeks of each other, it is clear that societies must rally around scientific progress as a fundamental human right. The future will depend on states working in collaboration with each other, the private sector, and civil society to ensure that the fruits of scientific innovation – be it medicines, diagnostics, or vaccines developed for COVID-19, TB, or other diseases – are affordable and accessible for all across the globe, just as the right to science demands.

---

[93] See para. 82 of Committee on Economic, Social and Cultural Rights. General comment No. 25 (2020) on Science and economic, social and cultural rights Art. 15.1.b, 15.2, 15.3 and 15.4. E/C.12/GC/25 (April 7, 2020). www.ohchr.org/en/hrbodies/cescr/pages/cescrindex.aspx.
[94] UNESCO. Open Science. https://en.unesco.org/science-sustainable-future/open-science.
[95] UNESCO. UNESCO mobilizes 122 countries to promote open science and reinforced cooperation in the face of COVID-19. March 30, 2020. https://en.unesco.org/news/unesco-mobilizes-122-countries-promote-open-science-and-reinforced-cooperation-face-covid-19.
[96] Ed Silverman. WHO director endorses a voluntary intellectual property pool to develop Covid-19 products. STAT. April 6, 2020. www.statnews.com/pharmalot/2020/04/06/covid19-coronavirus-patents-voluntary-pool-world-health/.

15

A Proposal for Indicators of the Human Right to Science

Andrea Boggio and Brian Gran

15.1 INTRODUCTION

The human right to science has a long history. First recognized through Article 27 of the Universal Declaration of Human Rights, this right was codified in Article 15 of the International Covenant on Economic, Social and Cultural Rights (ICESCR) in 1966. However, until recently, international bodies and scholars have not paid the requisite attention to this right. As a result, our understanding of its normative content is relatively underdeveloped. We do not yet fully apprehend its potential to bring about positive change to individuals' lives and the communities in which they live. This right has the potential to bolster freedoms indispensable to science and culture, for example through education and through creative work. It may strengthen the freedom for scientists to collaborate and disseminate their research while protecting everyone from scientific harms.

As more scholarly attention is paid to this right, evidenced by the chapters collected in this volume, efforts must include the development of indicators to measure State Parties' compliance with the obligations set by the ICESCR. A call to "identify appropriate indicators and benchmarks, including disaggregated statistics and time frames" is also included in General comment No. 25 on Science and economic, social and cultural rights.[1] According to the document, State parties must develop indicators and benchmarks that will "allow them to monitor effectively the implementation" of the right to science. In general, indicators are useful in assessing whether improvements are made over time, as well as how units, such as nation states, are performing in comparison to each other. Hunt contends that human rights indicators can enable a state to assess its progress toward implementation of a particular human right.[2] This is valuable, Hunt notes, to officials who can then adjust regulations and policies. Such assessments can be important when structures

---

[1] UN Committee on Economic, Social and Cultural Rights, "General Comment No. 25 on Science and Economic, Social and Cultural Rights Art. 15.1.b, 15.2, 15.3 and 15.4, E/C.12/GC/25," 2020 [hereinafter, General Comment No. 25].

[2] Paul Hunt, Report of the Special Rapporteur on the right of everyone to the enjoyment of the highest attainable standard of physical and mental health. E/CN.4/2006/48, March 3, 2006.

A Proposal for Indicators of the Human Right to Science 269

and processes are changed in the hopes of producing superior outcomes. People want to know whether modifications to laws and policies lead to improved outcomes. They want to know whether the application of additional resources leads to improved outcomes.

Indicators may provide evidence that changes are working, and also when they are not. Yet it is possible to place undue reliance on indicators, even to become "seduced" by indicators.[3] Experts have raised questions about the use of indicators, particularly when examining human rights. They have criticized the potential for infatuation with indicators, as well as ignorance of valuable information that can shed light on and provide evidence of compliance with human rights obligations.

This chapter contributes to this movement by proposing a set of compliance indicators in respect of the human right to science. Developing these indicators is useful given that responsibilities and duties that State Parties bear in relation to the right to science are still relatively underdeveloped. The indicators we propose are an effort to better articulate these responsibilities and duties. They contribute to advancing the discussion of the normative content of the right and potentially to how State Parties report their compliance with their treaty obligations to the CESCR. This chapter therefore seeks to contribute to the volume's overarching objective of investigating the human right to science. Considering the right's importance, and that it has often been overlooked by scholars and policymakers, including the United Nations, the time has come to examine it more deeply and critically.

Following a review of the emergence of human rights indicators, this chapter examines utility of, and types of, indicators for economic, social, and cultural rights. It then examines indicators in relation to the human right to science, proposing a matrix of indicators of this innovative right (see Appendix A). The chapter concludes with a discussion of the utility of such indicators. What can indicators accomplish? What are downsides to establishing indicators for the human right to science?

15.2 THE EMERGENCE OF HUMAN RIGHTS INDICATORS

Human rights monitoring bodies have been recommending the use of indicators to monitor compliance with and progress towards the realization of economic, social, and cultural rights for over thirty years. In its General Comment No. 1 (1989) on reporting by States parties, the UN Committee on Economic, Social and Cultural Rights (CESCR) called on States "to identify specific benchmarks or goals against which their performance in a given area can be assessed" and "communicate them as part of their reporting duties."[4] The goal of this exercise, according to the CESCR, was "to effectively evaluate the extent to which progress has been made towards the

---

[3] Sally Engle Merry, *The Seductions of Quantification: Global Governance, Human Rights, and the Rise of Indicator Culture* (Chicago, London: University of Chicago, 2016).

[4] UN Committee on Economic, Social and Cultural Rights, *General Comment No. 1: Reporting by States Parties*, July 27, 1981, E/1989/22.

realization of the obligations contained in the Covenant."[5] Similar objectives appear in the work of other UN treaty bodies, human rights special procedures such as special rapporteurs, the Universal Periodic Review of the UN Human Rights Council, and in the recommendations of these bodies to the State Parties.

The emergence of human rights indicators is part of broader interest in indicators as tools for policymaking and political decision-making. Human rights indicators belong to a particular subset of indicators, legal governance indicators, which purport "to measure practices or perceptions of good governance rules of law, corruption, regulatory quality, and related measures."[6] The UNDP World Development Report, Freedom House's Freedom in the World, the World Justice Report's measurement of the rule of law, and the World Bank's Doing Business Index are examples of well-known efforts to measure governance outcomes using legal indicators. Indicators of legal governance are used to measure the "implementation of human rights standards and commitments, to support policy formulation, impact assessment and transparency."[7] Measuring the gap between universally acknowledged standards and implementation efforts of national governments will contribute to the realization of the human right to science. Further, because indicators can measure such gaps for different countries over various time points, researchers can employ indicators to draw geographical and chronological comparisons of efforts to realize the human right to science.

The popularity of indicators has generated interest among social scientists.[8] This literature describes indicators as the "technology of global governance."[9] Global governance is defined as "the means used to influence behavior, the production of resources and the distribution of resources" beyond a single state.[10] According to Miller and Rose, "technologies" are mechanisms that constitute the process of governance. Indicators, scholars contend, have surged to the status of "technology" of global governance, and are used to set standards and to make decisions concerning governance matters that transcend a single state. Indicators have acquired this status for two reasons: they are efficient and consistent tools,[11] and appear, at least on

---

[5] Ibid. at para. 6.
[6] Kevin E. Davis, Benedict Kingsbury, and Sally Engle Merry, "Introduction: The Local-Global Life of Indicators: Law, Power, and Resistance," in *The Quiet Power of Indicators: Measuring Governance, Corruption, and Rule of Law*, ed. Sally Engle Merry, Kevin E. Davis, and Benedict Kingsbury, Cambridge Studies in Law and Society (Cambridge: Cambridge University Press, 2015), 1.
[7] United Nations, Office of the High Commissioner for Human Rights, "Human Rights Indicators," www.ohchr.org/EN/Issues/Indicators/Pages/HRIndicatorsIndex.aspx.
[8] Merry, *The Seductions of Quantification: Global Governance, Human Rights, and the Rise of Indicator Culture*; Kevin E. Davis et al., *Governance by Indicators: Global Power Through Classification and Rankings, Law And Global Governance* (Oxford University Press, 2012).
[9] Kevin E. Davis, Benedict Kingsbury, and Sally Engle Merry, "Introduction: Global Governance by Indicators," in *Governance by Indicators: Global Power through Quantification and Rankings*, ed. Kevin E. Davis et al. (Oxford: Oxford University Press, 2012), 10–18.
[10] Davis, Kingsbury, and Merry, 10–12.
[11] Ibid., 17. The authors note that "[t]he striking increase over the decades since 1990 in the creation and use of indicators as forms of knowledge for global governance arguably reflects the greater demand for

their face, to be inherently bureaucratic rather than political, and thus devoid of the problems and contestations typically associated with political decisions in the global arena. These two reasons explain the success of indicators, a phenomenon captured effectively by Sally Engle Merry with the expression "seductions of quantification."[12] Insights arising from Merry's and others' work[13] are important to place human rights indicators in historical context and assess their role in human rights discourses. However, before we turn to human rights indicators, we want to first define what indicators are.

15.3 DEFINING INDICATORS

The Office of the United Nations High Commissioner for Human Rights (OHCHR) has defined indicators as "specific information on the state or condition of an object, event, activity or outcome that can be related to human rights norms and standards; that addresses and reflects human rights principles and concerns; and that can be used to assess and monitor the promotion and implementation of human rights."[14] An influential definition comes from Paul Hunt, former UN Special Rapporteur on the Right to Health: "a human rights indicator derives from, reflects and is designed to monitor realization or otherwise of a specific human rights norm, usually with a view to holding a duty-bearer to account."[15]

More generally, Davis, Kingsbury, and Merry, propose that an indicator can be defined as follows:

> A named collection of rank-ordered data that purports to represent the past and projected performance of different units. The data are generated through a process that simplifies raw data about a complex social phenomenon. The data, in this simplified and processed form, are capable of being used to compare particular units of analysis . . ., synchronically or over time, and to evaluate their performance by reference to one or more standards.[16]

> readily available and easily used comparative knowledge to inform decision-making as well as the increasing supply of information."

[12] Merry, *The Seductions of Quantification: Global Governance, Human Rights, and the Rise of Indicator Culture*.

[13] Markku Lehtonen, Léa Sébastien, and Tom Bauler, "The Multiple Roles of Sustainability Indicators in Informational Governance: Between Intended Use and Unanticipated Influence," *Sustainability Governance and Transformation 2016: Informational Governance and Environmental Sustainability* 18 (February 1, 2016): 1–9, https://doi.org/10.1016/j.cosust.2015.05.009.

[14] United Nations, Office of the High Commissioner for Human Rights, *Human Rights Indicators: A Guide to Measurement and Implementation* (New York; United Nations Human Rights, Office of the High Commissioner, 2012), 16 (hereinafter "OHCHR Guide").

[15] Paul Hunt, WHO Workshop on Indicators for the Right to Health, A Background Note (2003), cited in AnnJanette Rosga and Margaret L. Satterthwaite, , "The Trust in Indicators: Measuring Human Rights," *Berkeley Journal of International Law* 27, no. 2 (2009): 254. Hunt was one of the early proponents of indicators of human rights; his work concentrated on the right to health.

[16] Davis, Kingsbury, and Merry, "Introduction: The Local-Global Life of Indicators: Law, Power, and Resistance," 4.

This definition captures two important aspects of indicators: they are constructs and they simplify complex phenomena. Indicators are constructs in the sense that they do not exist in nature but are designed by human beings for a specific purpose, namely, to measure performance of units of analysis in reference to certain standards. A human right can be the unit of analysis, its realization the performance to be measured.

Further, indicators try to simplify complex phenomena. Human rights are multi-dimensional legal artefacts for which realization depends upon the activation of various institutional domains. Indicators are tools used to reduce the inherent complexity of each human right into "units" that lend themselves to measurement. Simplification is thus instrumental to measurement. However, indicators also enable analyses of human rights that add new dimensions of the reading of legal instruments, UN bodies' reports, case law, and related sources. This analytical level is located midway between a general notion of the normative content of human rights and how such rights operate in specific cases. Compared to doctrinal analyses, such as how human rights are codified and interpreted, indicators open the door to analyses that consider human rights less formalistically, but look at how rights are realized at a level that is closer to the rights holders and authority responsible for implementing the rights. Compared to data documenting specific violations of human rights, indicators operationalize data to permit the assessment of human rights at a more holistic level than that of specific violations. Still, experts attempt to disaggregate data to identify discrimination across suspect categories, such as by gender, skin color, or age. Such discrimination, of course, runs contrary to the quality of universalism characterizing human rights.

15.4 HUMAN RIGHTS INDICATORS AND THE CESCR

Although indicators have been part of the human rights reporting discourse for thirty years, their conceptualization and use with reference to economic, social, and cultural (ESC) rights is recent and relatively unsettled. This is the result of history.[17] The CESCR turned to indicators in the 1980s on realizing that ESC rights were not as developed as civil and political rights. The CESCR imagined that developing universally applicable, rights-specific indicators might bridge that gap and facilitate the development of the core content of ESC rights.[18] Consequently, throughout the 1990s, the CESCR led efforts to develop universally applicable,

---

[17] For a thorough account of this history, see, Rosga and Satterthwaite, "The Trust in Indicators: Measuring Human Rights"; AnnJanette Rosga and Margaret L. Satterthwaite, "Measuring Human Rights: U.N. Indicators in Critical Perspective," in *Governance by Indicators: Global Power through Quantification and Rankings*, ed. Kevin E. Davis et al. (Oxford University Press, 2012), 297–316.

[18] Rosga and Satterthwaite, "Measuring Human Rights: U.N. Indicators in Critical Perspective," 299–301.

rights-specific indicators. At that time, the Committee envisioned its role as the producer of such indicators.

After a decade of unsuccessful attempts to develop indicators, the CESCR abandoned their goal of producing them and repositioned itself as the auditor of state-produced indicators.[19] This change in position is documented in General Comment 14, in which the CESCR stated that, as part of their treaty obligations, State Parties were required to monitor the realization of ESC rights on their own. To do so, they were required to create and use their own indicators, with the CESCR acting as the reviewer and auditor of those indicators. At the same time, the CESCR engaged the OHCHR as the expert body responsible for developing compliance indicators. After extensive consultation with international experts, the OHCHR reached a more limited goal and, in 2012, published *Human Rights Indicators: A Guide to Measurement and Implementation* (hereinafter "OHCHR Guide"), laying out the conceptual framework and a set of illustrative indicators with the idea that States would use them in reporting to the CESCR.[20] Indicators for the right to science are not among the illustrative indicators produced by the OHCHR.

Engaging the OHCHR resulted in the transformation of indicators from political constructs to technical ones.[21] Based on its expertise, the OHCHR clearly indicated that ESC rights indicators must be designed and used primarily to monitor compliance with treaty provisions. Further, it distilled technical standards to which producers of indicators, such as State Parties and civil society organizations, should adhere. However, the OHCHR did not settle all questions regarding human rights indicators. The OHCHR Guide navigates with some difficulty the unsettled questions of whether human rights indicators should be universally available or state-generated and context specific. In fact, it suggests that both are true. However, this conclusion generates confusion when it comes to applying the OHCHR principles and standards to developing new indicators, as we attempt to do in this chapter. Should indicators focus on compliance measurements along dimensions that apply to all State Parties? Or should they reflect the different level of progressive realization of the right? Science is a field particularly fraught with imbalances because differences among countries' abilities to produce scientific knowledge, partly due to variation in availability of resources that can be allocated to research and development, are staggering. We will come back to this challenge later in the chapter.

15.5 DESIGNING INDICATORS OF THE RIGHT TO SCIENCE

According to the case study analysis conducted by Davis, Kingsbury, and Merry, indicators are developed following a three-step trajectory: conceptualization,

---

[19] Rosga and Satterthwaite, 307–311.
[20] OHCHR Guide, 88–101.
[21] Rosga and Satterthwaite, "Measuring Human Rights: U.N. Indicators in Critical Perspective," 310–311.

production, and use.[22] Conceptualization requires outlining a theory underpinning the indicator followed by developing categories for measurement and modes of analyzing the data.[23] At this stage, important choices are made that will define what is measured and how. Actors, institutions, expertise, temporality, and resources all influence these choices.[24] Production entails collecting data and promulgating indicators. According to Davis, Kingsbury and Merry, promulgation is comprised of presenting, packaging, and disseminating indicators.[25] Through promulgation, indicators accomplish one of their essential tasks: to represent the performance of what is measured. To perform this task, raw data must be organized and then operationalized to provide representations of the implications of that organization.[26] Operationalization is the process of connecting concepts to observations of a phenomenon, which includes a case's value on a variable.[27] Finally, use occurs when indicators are accessed, consumed, and deployed by the nonproducers of indicators.

Fortunately, the OHCHR Guide facilitates the design of human rights indicators as it addresses the three stages of development of indicators (conceptualization, production, and use). Our proposal of indicators of the right to science builds upon the conceptual framework and illustrative indicators presented in the Guide.

15.5.1 Conceptualization

The OHCHR Guide conceptualizes human rights indicators as compliance monitoring tools. They are therefore designed to measure the adherence by State Parties to a legal standard. For measurement to be possible, the particular human right's legal standard must be translated into a limited number (up to four or five) of tangible characteristics called "attributes," which must be at the same time comprehensive ("based on an exhaustive reading of the standard")[28] and selective ("[t]o the extent feasible, the attributes of the human right should collectively reflect the essence of its normative content.")[29] Compliance is then assessed through indicators that measure the State Party's commitment, effort, and achievements in relation to each attribute. Based on Hunt's work on the human right to health,[30] the OHCHR

---

[22] Davis, Kingsbury, and Merry, "Introduction: The Local-Global Life of Indicators: Law, Power, and Resistance," 10–16.
[23] Ibid., 10.
[24] Ibid., 11.
[25] Ibid., 12.
[26] Ibid., 12–14. Aspects of promulgation include the presentation of data in buckets so that specific measurements become evident, presentation of a data in the form of time-series analysis, and aggregation by country to allow cross-country comparison.
[27] Russell K. Schutt, *Investigating the Social World: The Process and Practice of Research*, 5th ed. (Thousand Oaks, Calif.: SAGE Publications, Inc., 2006), 98.
[28] OHCHR Guide, 31.
[29] Ibid.
[30] Paul Hunt, The right of everyone to enjoy the highest attainable standard of physical and mental health. A/C.3/58/SR.41.

Guide identifies three types of indicators: structural, process, and outcome. Structural indicators "help in capturing the acceptance, intent and commitment of the State to undertake measures in keeping with its human rights obligations."[31] Process indicators "help in assessing a State's efforts, through its implementation of policy measures and programmes of action, to transform its human rights commitments into the desired results."[32] Outcome indicators "help in assessing the results of State efforts in furthering the enjoyment of human rights."[33]

15.5.2 Production

Production involves data collection and promulgation. Data collection entails identifying sources for human rights indicators and, if needed, setting up data-generating mechanisms. The OHCHR identifies sources and methods to collect data, which include qualitative and quantitative information describing "acts of human rights violations and identif[ing]victims and perpetrators," socioeconomic and administrative statistics, perception and opinion surveys, and expert judgments. This list is typical of other governance indicators. Limitations on data availability and access to resources to collect new data may restrict the choice of indicators. As the OHCHR points out, this dilemma has implications for the choice of indicators because "[t]he use of indicators as a human rights assessment tool depends critically on the availability of relevant and reliable data."[34]

The OHCHR Guide lays out prescriptions that producers of indicators must follow in identifying sources of data or setting data-generating mechanisms. First, data collection must be reliable, transparent, and independent. Data sources and generating-mechanisms must be chosen to produce reliable indicators.[35] Indicators are reliable if the same mechanisms used over time produce consistent values, all things remaining equal. Second, transparent methods that a third party can verify lead to acceptable indicators that can be employed to study human rights. Third, when conducting data collection, individuals and organizations producing indicators should be independent of the subjects being monitored.

The OHCHR also prescribes that indicators be "global and universally meaningful but also amenable to contextualization and disaggregation by prohibited grounds of discrimination ... and by vulnerable or marginalized population group at country level."[36] Disaggregation is defined in terms of "sex, age, region (e.g., urban/rural) or administrative unit, economic wealth (e.g., quintile or decile of income or expenditure), socioeconomic status (e.g., employment status) or

---

[31] OHCHR Guide, 34.
[32] Ibid., 36.
[33] Ibid., 38.
[34] Ibid., 21.
[35] Ibid., 51. ("The reliability of an indicator refers to its consistency in the estimate or the value of an indicator if the data-generating mechanism employed for devising it is repeated.")
[36] Ibid., 51.

educational attainment."[37] Disaggregation permits analyses of discrimination according to categories that typically are socially unacceptable.

Indicators must also be "human rights standards-centric; anchored in the normative framework of rights." To ensure this requirement is met, three principles must be followed. First, when an indicator's unit is the individual, and the individual is the source of the indicator's data, that individual "should have the option of self-identifying when confronted with a question seeking sensitive personal information related to them" (the principle of self-identification). These include identification with a particular racial or ethnic group. Second, "all data-collection activities must respect robust guarantees to prevent abuse of sensitive data" and be regulated by law (the principle of data protection). Third, when feasible, data must be disaggregated at the desired level (the principle of disaggregation).

Finally, indicators must be developed employing a transparent and verifiable methodology, be timely, and be time-bound.[38] The "structural, process, and outcome indicators" framework helps achieve this objective.[39] In fact, structural indicators tend to be stable because legal reform and policy change occur relatively infrequently. Outcomes do not change momentarily but capture trends that develop over time. Conversely, process indicators are "more sensitive to changes ... therefore more effective in capturing the progressive realization of the right or in reflecting the efforts of the state parties in protecting the rights." To this list of prescriptions, we add validity and importance. Simply put, validity is actually measuring what we intend to measure.[40] An indicator may be reliable, but not valid. For instance, an indicator may measure a phenomenon repeatedly over time, but that measure may be incorrect, or invalid. Importance concerns whether the indicator is valuable and important for studying and assessing human rights.[41] The properties of being valuable and important are related to being meaningful, centered around human rights, and transparent, but merit distinct attention because of their utility to establishing human rights indicators.

Regarding promulgation, that is the presentation, packaging, and dissemination of indicators, the OHCHR Guide instructs readers to organize and visualize indicators in the form of a matrix in which the attributes that capture the normative standard of a right are placed on the horizontal axis and the indicators on the vertical axis. A matrix approach offers a bird's-eye view of the normative content of the right being monitored. "[T]he tabular format shows the range of indicators that are relevant to capturing the normative content and the corresponding obligations of human rights standards." It offers a reader a clear overview of the normative content

---

[37] Ibid., 68.
[38] Ibid., 50.
[39] Siobhan McInerney-Lankford and Hans-Otto Sano, *Human Rights Indicators in Development: An Introduction*, World Bank Studies (World Bank Publications, 2010), 19–20.
[40] Schutt, *Investigating the Social World: The Process and Practice of Research*, 129.
[41] UN Women, www.endvawnow.org/en/articles/336-indicators.html.

of a right just by looking at the one-page template laying out the indictors and the attributes of the right. Additionally, a matrix approach also offers readers the opportunity to focus solely on certain sections of the matrix. Focus may thus be restricted to indicators of a single attribute (a single column) or one a single indicator cutting across multiple attributes (a single row). This strategy may be useful to civil society organizations interesting in monitoring only certain indicators or certain attributes. This approach, the OHCHR argues, leads to "the selection of a few indicators, at any given point in time, to monitor the implementation of human rights is more informed and likely to be more meaningful than would otherwise be the case."[42]

15.5.3 Use

According to the OHCHR Guide, compliance monitoring is the most critical use of indicators. This use is at the core of the monitoring mechanism set up by the ICESCR, which focuses on State Parties' compliance with their treaty obligations and progress towards securing the universal realization of human rights. Indicators facilitate monitoring by offering a "structured and transparent approach to applying standardized information ... to national human rights assessments."[43] This is not the only use that the OHCHR Guide envisions though. In fact, four additional uses are possible: performance monitoring; human rights advocacy and people empowerment; national human rights plans and development plans; and human rights budgeting.[44]

Performance monitoring measures the extent to which development interventions achieve the intended results, relative to what was planned.[45] Indicators can be used in human rights advocacy to make "human rights more concrete and tangible in the eyes of policymakers," to contextualize efforts to realized human rights thus "encouraging national ownership of the advocacy strategy," and to capture the range of issues involved in the realization of specific rights.[46] Indicators can also be used in the design and implementation of national human rights plans and development plans. Introduced at the World Conference on Human Rights, national action plans are instruments in which a state identifies the steps necessary to improve the promotion and protection of human rights.[47] Commitment-effort-results indicators can be used to frame these plans and guide their implementation. Finally, indicators can be used by states to draft budgets that are aligned with their human rights

---

[42] OHCHR Guide, 73.
[43] Ibid., 104.
[44] Ibid., 104–126.
[45] Organisation for Economic Co-operation and Development, Glossary of Key Terms in Evaluation and Results Based Management (Paris, 2002).
[46] OHCHR Guide, 112.
[47] Vienna Declaration and Programme of Action (Adopted by the World Conference on Human Rights in Vienna on June 25, 1993), para. 71.

obligations and prioritize spending resources likely to result in improved development and governance.[48]

While adequate indicators can be used for any of these purposes, it is important to note that the intended use has an impact on the design of indicators. To reiterate, what indicators measure can become goals that guide nation states in their efforts to implement human rights. One significant concern is that if no indicator of a given component of a human right exists, a national government may fail to implement that particular component. This is particularly relevant to the work we present in the chapter as we are proposing newly designed indicators. If the goal is to monitor compliance, which is the case of the indicators we propose here, indicators must be anchored to human rights standards. If the goal is to measure the effectiveness of development programs or national human rights plans, indicators are better anchored to the objectives of those programs, which are to support the measurement of inputs, outputs, outcomes, and impact.[49]

15.6 BUILDING THE RIGHT TO SCIENCE INDICATORS

Before getting to the proposed indicators, it is important to state certain key assumptions of our proposal.

First, we had to define the intended use of the indicators because different uses call for different designs of the indicators concerned. We chose to propose indicators to be used primarily for compliance monitoring rather than performance monitoring. The implication for indicator design is that we follow the "structural, process, outcome" model of indicators rather than the "input, output, outcomes, impact" model.[50] Our choice is in line with how the CESCR and the OHCHR have engaged with human rights indicators for more than two decades. We envision the proposed indicators being referenced by the CESCR when instructing states as to what they must address in their periodical reports, by States parties when reporting their progress, and by civil society organizations when drafting parallel reports. We focus on compliance monitoring because we believe this is an important function in achieving progress towards the realization of the right to science.

Envisioning indicators for compliance monitoring does not exclude their use, directly or indirectly, to achieve other objectives discussed in the OHCHR Guide. In addition to referencing them in parallel reports, human rights advocates can use indicators *directly* to advocate for the realization of the right at the state level and in shaping the science policy discourse.[51] Monitoring indicators can also be used

---

[48] OHCHR Guide, 121–122.
[49] Ibid., 110.
[50] Ibid., 110. See the discussion of "uses" in above in Section 15.5.3.
[51] Andrea Boggio and Cesare P. R. Romano, "Freedom of Research and the Right to Science," in *The Freedom of Scientific Research* (Manchester, England: Manchester University Press, 2018), 170–172, www.manchesterhive.com/view/9781526127686/9781526127686.00023.xml.

directly in human rights budgeting as they identify areas (process indicators) that measure allocation of research funding. Monitoring indicators can also be used *indirectly* in performance evaluation to identify the inputs, outputs, outcomes, and impacts to be measured when a national human rights plan or a development program is assessed.

Second, we sought to clarify the human right standard expressed in Article 15 of the ICESCR because indicators must be grounded in, and drawn from, this standard. The challenge for us was that, as the essays in this volume amply demonstrate, the normative content of the right is underdeveloped compared to other rights – even other cultural rights.[52] Consequently, identifying attributes under these conditions was inherently difficult as the human rights standards that underpin the right are unsettled.[53] Keeping in mind that this is, for the most part, uncharted territory, we have identified attributes and indicators based on various sources. The most important is General comment No. 25 on Science and economic, social and cultural rights.[54] Adopted in 2020, the General Comment, General Comment lays out the general, specific, and core obligations of State parties and articulate duties connected with international cooperation and national implementation.[55] Another important source is subsequent state practice in the application of the ICESCR. This practice is evidence of an agreement between the parties under Article 31(3)(b) of the 1969 Vienna Convention on the Law of Treaties and therefore are a source of interpretation of treaties.[56] State practice emerges from the reports filed by State Parties as part of the monitoring process of human rights treaties, which on occasion mention the right to science.[57] The most comprehensive source of analysis of state

---

[52] It's important to note that, traditionally, cultural rights have received less attention than other kind of human rights, especially political rights. *See*, General Discussion on the Right to Take Part in Cultural Life as Recognized in Article 15 of the ICESCR, ESC, E/C.12/1992/2, at 59, para. 204.

[53] We are also mindful that the uncertainties surrounding the normative content of the right to science offer the opportunity to use indicators as tools to better define the human right standard. The matrix we drafted is itself a creative exercise that clarifies the normative content of the right. Further, if the indicators will be eventually used – by the CESCR, State Parties and civil society organizations as monitoring indicators – reporting based on these indicators will constitute state practice under the ICESCR and will be a formal source of interpretation of Article 15.

[54] See, General Comment No. 25,. Besides "assisting the States parties in fulfilling their reporting obligations," general comments are commonly considered to be the official interpretation of a right on the part of the United Nations. See, Committee on Economic. Social and Cultural Rights. Introduction, The purpose of general comments, U.N. Doc. E/1989/22, annex III at 87 (1989), reprinted in Compilation of General Comments and General Recommendations Adopted by Human Rights Treaty Bodies, U.N. Doc. HRI\GEN\1\Rev.6. 2003; Helen Keller and Leena Grover, "General Comments of the Human Rights Committee and Their Legitimacy," in *UN Human Rights Treaty Bodies: Law and Legitimacy*, ed. Geir Ulfstein and Helen Keller, Studies on Human Rights Conventions (Cambridge: Cambridge University Press, 2012), 116–198.

[55] See, General Comment No. 25, paras. 23–27, 41–52, 77–89.

[56] According to Article 31(3)(b) of the 1969 Vienna Convention on the Law of Treaties, state practice is "any subsequent practice in the application of the treaty which establishes the agreement of the parties regarding its interpretation."

[57] Rumiana Yotova and Bartha M Knoppers, "The Right to Benefit from Science and its Implications for Genomic Data Sharing," *The European Journal of International Law* 31, no. 2 (2020): 665–691. The

practice was recently completed by Yotova and Knoppers, who construct it upon reviewing all reports filed by State Parties to the ICESCR pursuant to Articles 16 and 17 of the ICESCR. A word of caution is needed in approaching state practice as a source of attributes and indicators. Since state practice emerges from periodical reports, what State Parties are asked to report is crucial. Reports are typically structured according to UN reporting guidelines, including the ones the CESCR employs.[58] If State Parties are expected to present information on the human right to science to the CESCR, but the reporting guidelines do not request information on a certain aspect of the right, State Parties are likely not to focus on, even think about, the aspect of the right that are not mentioned in said guidelines. The same may be true for civil society organizations who monitor UN monitoring efforts and State Parties' implementation efforts. What we are suggesting is that, if UN reporting guidelines do not instruct State Parties to present information about a particular aspect of the human right to science, that aspect may come to be viewed as unimportant to the right. Finally, we considered soft law instruments, such as the Venice Statement, which is the outcome of the gathering of experts in 2009 under the auspices by UNESCO,[59] the reports of Farida Shaheed in her capacity as Independent Expert and then Special Rapporteur on cultural rights,[60] and various UNESCO Declarations addressing the relationship between science and human rights.[61]

Third, we considered whether to include only indicators for which data are readily available. Data availability, of course, shapes which indicators are established, and which are not. The advantage of limiting the proposal to indicators based on existing data is that the CESCR and State Parties could promptly deploy such indicators in compliance monitoring. However, when data are not readily available about a particular aspect of a right, indicators will probably not be developed.

---

authors show that 123 of the 168 States Parties have indicated taking specific measures to implement the right to benefit from science.

[58] Guidelines on Treaty-Specific Documents to be Submitted by States Parties under Articles 16 and 17 of the ICESCR, ESC, E/C.12/2008/2, at 15, paras. 70–73.

[59] UNESCO, The Right to Enjoy the Benefits of Scientific Progress and Its Applications (Venice Statement), 2009. The Venice Statement identifies three constitutive elements of the normative content of the right to science: the creation of an enabling environment for the conservation, development and diffusion of science, enjoyment of the benefits of scientific progress, and protection from the abuse and adverse effects of scientific progress.

[60] The work of Farida Shaheed is available at www.ohchr.org/EN/Issues/CulturalRights/Pages/FaridaShaheed.aspx. See, also, Lucky Belder and Helle Porsdam, *Negotiating Cultural Rights: Issues at Stake, Challenges and Recommendations* (Cheltenham: Edward Elgar, 2017).

[61] UNESCO, Universal Declaration on the Human Genome and Human Rights (adopted at the 29th Session of the General Conference on November 11, 1997) BR/2001/PI/H/1; UNESCO, *International Bioethics Committee, Human Genetic Data: Preliminary Study by the IBC on its Collection, Processing, Storage and Use* (SHS-503/01/CIB-8/3 (Rev.2), May 15, 2002); UNESCO, Universal Declaration on Bioethics and Human Rights (adopted by the General Conference on 19 October 2005); UNESCO, Recommendation on Science and Scientific Researchers (adopted at the 39th Session of the General Conference on November 13, 2017) SHS/BIO/PI/2017/3.

Because this problem may lead to failure to measure, absence of a measure may come to be understood as indicating that aspect of the right is not important as lacking socio-legal value. Including indicators for which data are not readily available has the advantage of broadening progress monitoring to aspects of the right that are currently not captured empirically. Based on this reasoning, we decided to include indicators for which data are currently *not* available, knowing that the CESCR can request State Parties to gather and publicly share this information.[62]

15.7 A MATRIX OF RIGHT TO SCIENCE INDICATORS

Based on these key elements of human rights indicators, we have generated a matrix that applies the OHCHR framework and follows the model of the indicative indicators published in the OHCHR Guide (see Appendix A). This matrix includes attributes on the horizontal axis and structural, process, and outcome indicators on the vertical axis.

Attributes are translations of legal standards into measurable dimensions. This means that each attribute is dependent upon, albeit may not coincide with, the legal obligations that the ICESCR creates. Our reading of Article 15 of the ICESCR led us to identify three main attributes and two secondary attributes. The three main attributes are scientific freedom, access to benefits, and opportunities to participate. The secondary attributes are the duty to create an enabling environment and to facilitate international cooperation. These secondary attributes complement the three main attributes rather than creating independent obligations. For instance, an enabling environment for science "implies inter alia academic and scientific freedom"[63] and international cooperation facilitates both the exercise of scientific freedom and access to benefits. These attributes must not be construed as exhaustive of the normative content of Article 15. Although the OHCHR Guide cautions readers to identify no more than four or five attributes, more attributes can be added. In fact, access to benefits could be conceptually split into two attributes: access to scientific knowledge and access to the applications of scientific knowledge. Furthermore, access to scientific knowledge can be expanded to measure the extent to which State parties protect and foster open science practices. In our minds, the indicators we propose are meant to trigger a conversation rather than close the door to further elaboration. This point is crucial given renewed attention to the right to science, as well as evolution in science, technology and human rights.

Indicators "unpack specific aspects of implementing the standard associated with that right."[64] Structural indicators capture the acceptance, intent and commitment

---

[62] General Comment No. 25, para. 88, direct States parties to "identify appropriate indicators and benchmarks, including disaggregated statistics and time frames, which allow them to monitor effectively the implementation of the RPEBSPA."
[63] UNESCO, Venice Statement, para. 13(a).
[64] OHCHR Guide, 30.

of the State to undertake measures in keeping with its human rights obligations. In relation to the right to science, structural indicators include signing and ratifying the ICESCR and its Optional Protocol. Additionally, it captures the creation of the basic institutional mechanisms deemed necessary for the promotion and protection of the right's attributes. This includes adopting express legislative provisions to incorporate the obligations arising out of Article 15 of the ICESCR in domestic laws. Data for this indicator are partially available as they can be extracted from state reports[65] or derived from researching the laws of State Parties.[66]

Structural indicators of different kinds correspond to the three main attributes. *Scientific freedom* indicators include legislation that ensures scientists' abilities to pursue any kind of research, to engage in self-governance (through scientific societies, respecting self-regulatory instruments, and other means), to be free of censorship and other threats to their independence, to engage in collaborations, to travel domestically and internationally, and to access funding. Structural indicators should also capture whether laws and regulations meet the requirements of "legality," that is, to convey in clear terms what is lawful and what is not. *Access to benefits* indicators include legislation that ensures adequate access to scientific knowledge, translational pathways to transforming knowledge into tangible benefits (pharmaceutical drugs, innovations in the agricultural, industrial, and other sectors), and policy development mechanisms that promote the use of scientific knowledge in decision making. *Opportunities to participate* indicators include laws and regulations addressing discrimination in recruitment of participants in research, ensuring equality by gender and minority status[67] in access to scientific education and professions, promoting citizen science, and including indigenous populations and minorities in the formulation of science policy.

Process indicators capture implementation efforts to transform human rights commitments into the desired results. Evidence of these efforts include resource allocation, developing and deploying plans and programs, setting up institutional mechanisms and incentives that redress violations, stimulate compliance, and promote the realization of the right. *Scientific freedom* indicators include the number (total number and number of publicly funded) and quality of universities, research institutions, and scientific societies, percentage of GDP allocated to research and development, and number of professionals employed as researchers (in total and by government). *Access to benefits* indicators include data on

---

[65] Yotova and Knoppers, "The Right to Benefit from Science and Its Implications for Genomic Data Sharing," 677-685.

[66] See, for instance, the indicators published at www.freedomofresearch.org/right-to-science-indicators/.

[67] The OHCHR Guide notes that, generally, disaggregation in encouraged on the "sex, age, economic and social situation, race, colour, language, religion, political or other opinion, national or social origin, property, birth, disability, health status, nationality, marital and family status, sexual orientation and gender identity, place of residence, and other status." However, the Guide does not mandate a particular kind of disaggregation and leaves it open to State Parties to proceed in a way that accounts for "national circumstances." See, OHCHR Guide, 69-70.

enrollment in tertiary education, on access to and use of university library or the internet, quality of math and science education, and internet use in schools for learning purposes. *Opportunities to participate* indicators include disaggregated data (by gender and minority status) on professional and educational opportunities in the sciences, participation in research and in the formulation of science policy, citizen science, the ability to attract talent from abroad, and scientists' participation in international conferences.

Outcome indicators measure the results of the commitments and efforts in furthering the enjoyment of human rights. *Scientific freedom* indicators include reported cases of persecution of, sanctions of, or political pressure on scientists (in the absence of evidence of misconduct), number and quality of articles published in scientific journals, and availability of scientists and engineers. *Access to benefits* indicators include aggregated data on scientific literacy, educational attainment and membership in professional and scientific societies, scientific literacy, attainment or completion of a doctoral degree or equivalent, suppression of or prohibition to divulge scientific data and/or knowledge (this could also be a scientific freedom indicator), and on innovation (collaboration between business and academia, development of drugs and other translational products). Finally, *opportunities to participate* indicators include disaggregated data (by gender and minority status) on scientific literacy, educational attainment, and membership in the profession and scientific societies.

15.8 CONCLUSIONS

The human right to science may be a game changer. It has the potential to reduce discrimination when it comes to learning about and doing science. This right could strengthen scientists' freedoms to collaborate, publish, and conduct their research. It could also make possible international collaborations, which may lead to scientific advances with universal benefits.

Yet we need to know more about the impacts of the human right to science as societies move toward its realization. As this volume demonstrates, the terrain of the human right to science is vast. This chapter responds to calls for indicators of this right. Such indicators have manifold uses. Indicators will enable scholars to properly articulate the normative content of the human right to science. Indicators can be employed to assess compliance with international frameworks of human rights, which can be used to determine how nation states are performing in comparison with each other. UN bodies, nation states, and civil society actors, including watch dogs, can employ indicators to monitor implementation of the human right to science. This chapter, however, encourages experts, researchers, and leaders to maintain wariness of indicators. Although indicators are certainly useful, we must recognize their limitations, including what they do not measure. As scholarship moves forward, indicators will play key roles in understanding how science can benefit everyone.

Appendix A Proposed Compliance Indicators of Article 15 ICESCR

	Scientific freedom	Access to benefits	Opportunities to participate
Structural	• ICESCR Ratification status • ICESCR Additional Protocol ratification status • Constitutional or other forms of superior law recognizing the right to science		
	• Legislation protecting scientific freedom • Legislation ensuring the protection and safety of scientists • Significant limitations on scientific freedom (are limitations legal, necessary, and proportionate?)	• Legislation on access to scientific data, information, and knowledge, including open access initiatives • Significant limitations on access to scientific data, information, and knowledge (are limitations legal, necessary, and proportionate?)	• Legislation permitting the participation of human subjects in research • Legislation mandating nondiscrimination based on gender in hiring • Legislation establishing age differences in formal education by gender • Legal limits on conference travel
Process	• Number of universities/research institutions • Number of scientific societies • Quality of scientific research institutions • Percentage of GDP allocated to Research and Development • Rate of R&D collaboration between business and academia • Average university ranking score of countries based on their top 3 universities • Number of professionals employed as researchers (overall and by government) • Reported cases of suppression of scientific data and/or knowledge	• Enrollment in tertiary education • Proportion of population with access to university library • Proportion of population with access to internet • Percentage of the population that uses the Internet • Quality of math and science education • Internet use in schools for learning purposes	• Country's ability to attract talent from abroad • International conference participation • Enrollment in tertiary education by gender

(continued)

	Scientific freedom	Access to benefits	Opportunities to participate
Outcome	• Persecution of, sanctions of, or political pressure on scientists in the absence of evidence of misconduct • Number of scientific and technical journal articles are published each year in physics, biology, chemistry, mathematics, clinical medicine, biomedical research, engineering and technology, and earth and space sciences • Number of published articles having received at least H citations in the period 1996–2014 • Availability of scientists and engineers	• Degree of scientific literacy of 15-year-old students as measured by the Programme for International Student Assessment (PISA) • Percentage of population ages 25 and over that attained or completed a doctoral degree or equivalent	• Percentage of population ages 25 and over that attained or completed a doctoral degree or equivalent by gender • Percentage of females employed with advanced degrees out of total employed • Percentage of foreign-born professionals in tertiary education

16

Epilogue

Tensions in the Right to Science Then and Now

Christine Mitchell

Until now, a universal human right to science has not received the attention it should have. In the past, other rights may have seemed more fundamental, more urgent, easier to claim, and, perhaps, more straightforward to ensure. Yet a right to science is increasingly critical. Life, and planet earth itself, is threatened by climate change, global pandemics, exhaustion of mineral resources, mass extinction of species, human overpopulation, inequitable resource distribution, non-sustainable agriculture, and the possibilities of nuclear warfare, hostile artificial intelligence, and cosmic threats. Scientists of every sort are needed from astrophysicists to epidemiologists and sociologists to zoologists. Equally important: the understanding and participation of a wider, diverse public is essential if science is to effectively address these problems in line with shared social values.

A right to science has been included in modern visions of human rights, beginning at least from the compilation of rights in the American Declaration on the Rights and Duties of Man in 1945[1] and continuing most notably through the Universal Declaration of Human Rights (UDHR) and the International Covenant on Economic, Social, and Cultural Rights (ICESCR)[2] accepted across the globe and ratified by 171 nation states.[3]

Then, when rights were being enumerated in the 1940s, science made possible the saving of millions of lives with penicillin, as well as the mass killing of humans and all living beings with atomic bombs. These put "Science" in the United Nations Educational Scientific and Cultural Organization (UNESCO([4] and undoubtedly helped to keep a right to science among the declared human rights as many marveled at the miracles of science while also worrying about "what the scientists will do to us next."[5]

---

[1] Cesare P. R. Romano, Chapter 2 in this Volume, p. 33.
[2] www.ohchr.org/EN/professionalinterest/pages/cescr.aspx.
[3] https://treaties.un.org/Pages/ViewDetails.aspx?src=IND&mtdsg_no=IV-3&chapter=4&clang=_en.
[4] Mikel Mancisidor, Chapter 1 in this Volume, p. 17.
[5] "Miss Ellen Wilkinson included in her statement at the Conference for the Establishment of an International Agency (London, 6 November 1945) the following passage: 'Though Science was not

Now, seventy-five years later, we live in a frightful time of deaths from a global pandemic, widespread public protests about shocking social inequities, and international migration to escape political aggression in so many countries. Attention must focus on a universal right to science if we are to preserve human dignity, enable human flourishing, and address world problems. This chapter will consider what counts as science and examine two of the tensions (by no means all) built into the right to science as articulated in the UDHR and ICESCR.

What constitutes science itself has been described by Christensen[6] and authors herein, but must be noted, at least in summary, in order to see the tensions inherent in the way a right to science is understood. For, science may be, at times, (1) universally objective while also being culturally relative, and (2) practiced primarily by scientists, yet also open to the public in a variety of ways.

Science is different from the arts in that the source of its knowledge typically exists with or without human observation or intervention. Music, paintings, and novels require artists. The evolution of species, the birth and death of stars, and DNA replication happen whether or not scientists study these phenomena. As ten-year-olds are taught, "the scientific method" is applied to an already existing world. There is therefore a tendency to think of scientists as researching rather than creating. Although many scientists study existing phenomena, nevertheless, most also create. They routinely create conditions for research and new knowledge, as with e-brains,[7] or create applications of scientific knowledge, as with rocket science, or create new phenomena, such as altered genomes, or algorithms for machine learning.

In earlier times, science was understood as a quest for truths about the knowable world, often cited in western histories as starting with Aristotle[8] and including both theoretical and practical investigations aimed at discovering universal laws that apply at all times everywhere. The word "scientist" did not come into being until

included in the original title of the Organization, the British delegation will put forward a proposal that it be included, so that the title would run "Educational, Scientific and Cultural Organization." In these days, when we are all wondering, perhaps apprehensively, what the scientists will do to us next, it is important that they should be linked closely with the humanities and should feel that they have a responsibility to mankind for the result of their labours. I do not believe that any scientists will have survived the world catastrophe, who will still say that they are utterly uninterested in the social implications of their discoveries.' And as this was in fact a concern was that felt by all delegates, at the third meeting of the Conference, on 6 November, science was included in the name of what would henceforth be known as the United Nations Educational, Scientific and Cultural Organization, and the 'S' was added to the abbreviation, which became UNESCO."

Fernando Valderrana Martinez, A History of UNESCO, (1995) pp. 21–23; see also Cinzia Caporale and Ilja Richard Pavone, *International Biolaw and Shared Ethical Principles: The Universal Declaration on Bioethics and Human Rights* (New York: Routledge, 2018).

[6] Ivan Lind Christensen, Chapter 4 in this Volume.
[7] EBRAINS is a digital brain research infrastructure being developed by the Human Brain Project, publicly funded (in part) by the European Commission and based in Brussels, Belgium. https://ebrains.eu/.
[8] Aristotle, *Physics*.

the nineteenth century,[9] however, when William Whewell patronizingly chided Mary Somerville (1780–1872)[10] about her writing *On the Connexion of the Physical Sciences* which had become a bestselling popular science book[11] in 1846. Whewell argued that the sciences were inevitably disintegrating into specialties such as astronomy, geology, physics and the like, and he offered as evidence the absence of a general name for those who study the material world in all its facets. He proposed the deliberately absurd neologism "scientists," which began to catch on after his death as industrialists and educators sought to separate science from literature, humanities, and the arts. In the year of Somerville's death, *The Popular Science Monthly* was founded by Edward Youmans "to disseminate scientific knowledge to the educated layman."[12] As Henry Cowles recounts in his new book on the history of the scientific method,[13] Youmans and the authors who wrote for his magazine, championed the actual study of things using a methodology they reified – the scientific method – and this way of thinking permeated American culture in the twentieth century. Thus, scientists observe, hypothesize, predict, experiment, analyze, conclude, and report their findings about the natural world.

Science is no longer so simple, nor singular. Taking an expansive view, the Committee on Economic, Social and Cultural Rights describes "the sciences" as "a complex of knowledge, fact and hypothesis, in which the theoretical element is capable of being validated in the short or long term, and to that extent includes the sciences concerned with social facts and phenomena." As such, science encompasses both natural and social sciences, and refers both to a process following a rigorous methodology ("doing science") and to results of that process in the form of scientific knowledge and its applications.[14] Thus, scientific "knowledge should be considered as science only if it is based on critical inquiry and is open to falsifiability and testability. Knowledge which is based solely on tradition, revelation or authority, without the possible contrast with reason and experience, or which is immune to any falsifiability or intersubjective verification, cannot be considered science."[15]

What, then, is this thing that scientists do? According to UNESCO, in 2017,

> the word "science" signifies the enterprise whereby humankind, acting individually or in small or large groups, makes an organized attempt, by means of the objective

---

[9] Jessica Riskin, "Just Use Your Thinking Pump," *The New York Review of Books*, July 2, 2020, 48–50.

[10] Elisabeth Strickland, !Mary Fairfax Somerville, Queen of Science, Notices of the AMS," September 2017, 929–931 www.ams.org/publications/journals/notices/201708/rnoti-p929.pdf.

[11] Richard Holmes, "In Retrospect: On the Connexion of the Physical Sciences," *Nature*, October 22, 2014, (514), 432–433.

[12] www.gutenberg.org/wiki/Popular_Science_Monthly_(Bookshelf).

[13] Henry M. Cowles, *The Scientific Method: An Evolution of Thinking from Darwin to Dewey* (Cambridge, MA: Harvard University Press,2020).

[14] General Comment No. 25 on Article 15 of ICESCR (1), (b), (2), (3), (4), April 30, 2020 (Section II. 4.) http://docstore.ohchr.org/SelfServices/FilesHandler.ashx?enc=4slQ6QSmlBEDzFEovLCuW1ao SzabooXTdImnsJZZVQdxONLLLJiul8wRmVtR5Kxx73ioUzok13FeZiqChAWHKFuBqp%2B4RaxfUzqSAfyZYAR%2Fq7sqC7AHRa48PPRRALHB.

[15] General Comment No. 25.

study of observed phenomena and its validation through sharing of findings and data and through peer review, to discover and master the chain of causalities, relations or interactions; brings together in a coordinated form subsystems of knowledge by means of systematic reflection and conceptualization; and thereby furnishes itself with the opportunity of using, to its own advantage, understanding of the processes and phenomena occurring in nature and society.[16]

These descriptions of science hint at the tension between science as the acquisition and application of a specific sort of universal human knowledge, and science as a human enterprise that has its own practices, beliefs, and, we might add, its own customs, culture, and specialty tribes.

CULTURAL SCIENCE

Contrasting a historical understanding of science "then" with a more contemporary view of science "now," illuminates the tension created by a basic view of science that is not only universal, but true, objective, factual, perhaps seen by some as infallible, and, hence, the best way of settling arguments about the way the world is. Indeed, some scientific findings about fluid dynamics, magnetism, the structure of atoms, genes, and other phenomena may be absolute and universal across cultures, time, and place. Nevertheless, it is also the case that other things once thought to be scientifically established are not absolute. Rather, they are refined (as with Linnaeus' hierarchical taxonomy of living things), revised (as when Mendelian inheritance patterns were supplemented by genomic and proteomic science), revoked (as in the transition from Ptolemaic to Copernican cosmology), or rejected based on subsequent science, as when the theory of spontaneous generation of life from inorganic matter was replaced by an understanding of biogenesis.

Even empirically "proven" scientific findings, as well as theoretical science, are subject to incomplete, limited, culturally influenced perspectives and paradigm shifts.[17] There is more than ample evidence now, that scientific knowledge is incremental and often more relative than absolute. Mistakes even in laws of science believed to be universal can arise from incomplete knowledge, as in the transition from the Newtonian law of gravity to Einstein's theory of general relativity. What may be claimed as scientifically established can also be wrong in other ways, through error,[18] misconduct (as Roberto

---

[16] UNESCO, Recommendation on Science and Scientific Researchers, November 13, 2017, I.1.(a) (i). http://portal.unesco.org/en/ev.php-URL_ID=49455&URL_DO=DO_TOPIC&URL_SECTION=201.html.

[17] Thomas Kuhn, **The Structure of Scientific Revolutions**, Chicago: University of Chicago Press 1962, pp. 54.

[18] Andrew W. Brown, Kathryn A. Kaiser, and David B. Allison, "Issues with Data and Analyses: Errors, Underlying Themes, and Potential Solutions," PNAS, March 13, 2018, 115 (11) 2563–2570.

Andorno[19] describes in this book), and fraud,[20] but also, *relative* to its time and surrounding culture.

Culture, as used here, is a word for the way of life of a group of people, that is, the way they see the world and themselves in it – their values, beliefs, behaviors, and symbols, deeply assumed and accepted with little thought or question, and passed on by communication and imitation to members (acculturation) and new generations (enculturation).[21] Science can be "cultural" in two ways. First, science is part of culture – it is influenced by the culture in which it is situated, and it influences that culture as it did in the diffusion of "the scientific method" described earlier. In many modern societies, science plays a major role in shaping cultural beliefs, thinking patterns, and assumptions about the way the world is, as well as views of the people and other phenomena in it. Sometimes this occurs by gradual, unorchestrated diffusion of ideas from science into the culture. At other times, however, there is a conscious effort, by scientists and others, to use the authority of science to claim that scientific theories and evidence support a particular belief system or political goals. Secondly, science itself and the sciences have their own culture of beliefs about who may be a scientist, practices for doing science, and rituals marking scientific discoveries and achievements.

Although there are many examples of how science is cultural, perhaps one of the most unfavorable illustrations of its cultural boundedness is structural racism in academic sciences and the persistence of racist science. First, concerning structural racism, we note that the practice of science in many countries – especially who gets to do science – is, unfortunately, a mostly white endeavor.[22] Contemporary protests by scientists and their supporters[23] are bringing belated attention to longstanding systemic racism in science, and the ways institutional culture in the academy[24] and science itself privileges whiteness and Anglo-euro-centric worldviews and ways of knowing. Although Blacks comprise 12 percent of the US population, for example, they received just 1.8 percent of all Ph.D.s in science and engineering in the USA in 1987, and the number is declining.[25]

[19] Roberto Andorno, Chapter 5 in this Volume.
[20] Horace Freeland Judson, *The Great Betrayal: Fraud in Science.* (Orlando: Harcourt, 2004).; Daniele Fanelli, "How Many Scientists Fabricate and Falsify Research? A Systematic Review and Meta-Analysis of Survey Data," *PLOS ONE*, May 2009, 4 (5), PMID: 19478950, e5738.
[21] Interestingly, there is no formal definition of culture used by UNESCO nor described in the UDHR and ICESCR, as is acknowledged in in the Report of the independent expert in the field of cultural rights, Ms. Farida Shahed, to the Human Rights Council, fourteenth session, UN General assembly, March 22, 2010 (see II (A) (4), page 4 A/HRC/14/36).
[22] Sandra Harding (ed.), *The "Racial" Economy of Science: Toward a Democratic Future* (Bloomington: Indiana University Press, 1993).
[23] Leah Crane, "Scientists Around the World are Striking Against Racism in Academia," *New Scientist*, June 10, 2020 www.newscientist.com/article/2245743-scientists-around-the-world-are-striking-against-racism-in-academia/.
[24] Frances Henry and Carol Tator (eds.), *Racism in the Canadian University: Demanding Social Justice, Inclusion, and Equity* (Toronto: University of Toronto Press, 2009).
[25] Hugh McIntosh, "Special report: Where are Today's Black Scientists?" *The Scientist*, January 1989, www.the-scientist.com/news/special-report-where-are-todays-black-scientists-62328.

In the USA, for example, in 2018, the latest date for which data are available, Black residents were 12.3 percent of the U.S. population, but only 8.4 percent of bachelor's graduates, 8.3 percent of master's graduates and 5.5 percent of doctoral graduates.[26] As thirteen scientists, (not one of whom is Black) on the editorial board of Cell put it in 2020, "science has a racism problem."[27]

Still considering the cultural situatedness of science and widening the lens, it must be noted that three-quarters of the world's scientific publications came from Western Europe and North America. And more than 90 percent of the Nobel laureates in the natural sciences are from Western countries, despite the fact that these countries are home to only 10 percent of the world's population.[28]

The second and related example concerns racist science. Even as human rights were being discussed in many parts of the world and drafted into written documents in the twentieth century, the science of eugenics was flourishing in Nazi Germany, the USA, and elsewhere,[29] aimed at improving the quality of white "races" by denigrating and removing people deemed inferior. With the help of racial science experts, physicians, psychiatrists, anthropologists, and newly medically trained geneticists, Nazi Germany developed racial health policies that involved mass sterilization of "genetically diseased" persons resulting in approximately 400,000 forced sterilizations, over 275,000 euthanasia deaths, and the near annihilation of European Jewry.[30]

Drafters of the UDHR will have been acutely aware of medical science gone wrong through the Nuremberg Doctors Trials[31] in 1946–1947 which resulted in sixteen being found guilty and seven sentenced to death and executed on June 2, 1948. Nevertheless, Julian Huxley (1887–1975), the evolutionary biologist and Life Fellow of the (British) Eugenics Society, became the first Director-General of UNESCO and described his amended vision of "world evolutionary humanism,"[32] [33] even as the human rights

[26] Fred Guterl, "Diversity in Science: Where are the Data?," *Scientific American*, October 2014, 311 (4), 40–41.
[27] The Cell Editorial Team, "Science has a Racism Problem," *Cell*, June 25, 2020, 181, 1443–1444. www.cell.com/cell/pdf/S0092-8674(20)30740-6.pdf.
[28] Maurizio Iaccarino, "Science and Culture," *EMBO Reports*, March 2003, 4 (3): 220–223.
[29] In France, for example, the use of anthropometry and the claim of links between physiognomy and criminality, developed by Alphonse Bertillion and others, claimed to scientifically establish and predict criminality in the late 1800s, and was adopted and used by police departments in many countries before it was discredited. Similarly, theories of social Darwinism and "scientific" measurements were used during the eugenics movements in Germany, France, Brazil, and Russia. See Mark B. Adams (ed.), *The Wellborn Science: Eugenics in Germans, France, Brazil, and Russia* (New York: Oxford University Press, 1990).
[30] Francois Haas, "German Science and Black Racism – Roots of the Nazi Holocaust," *The FASEB Journal [Federation of American Societies of Experimental Biology]* 2008, 22:, 332–337; see also Unites States Holocaust Memorial Museum, www.ushmm.org/collections/bibliography/nazi-racial-science.
[31] Robert Jay Lifton, *The Nazi Doctors: Medical Killing and the Psychology of Genocide* (New York: Basic Books, Inc., 1986).
[32] Paul Weindling, "Julian Huxley and the Continuity of Eugenics in Twentieth-Century Britain," *J Mod Eur Hist*. November 1, 2012, 10 (4): 480–489. www.ncbi.nlm.nih.gov/pmc/articles/PMC4366572/.
[33] Julian Huxley, *UNESCO: Its Purpose and Philosophy*, 1946 (London: Euston Grove Press, English facsimile edition, 2010) 144 pp.

revolution brought about the UN and International Court of Justice in 1945, UNESCO in 1946, the World Health Organization in April 1948, and the Universal Declaration of Human Rights in December 1948. Still today, the search continues by some scientists for measurable biological differences between "races," despite decades of studies yielding no supporting evidence, as science absorbs and reflects back the racism in societies in which it is situated.[34]

As science is part of culture, the right to take part in cultural life includes the right *of everyone* to take part in scientific life. Readers familiar with the field of human rights and those who have read the foregoing chapters will not be surprised, since the right to science is nested within cultural rights in both the UDHR and ICESCR. As Mylene Bidault[35] explained, the right to science, contained in the right to take part in cultural life (as these together comprise article 15 of the ICESCR), is primarily a right of access to participate in science. The right to science contains correlative duties to ensure the conservation, development, and diffusion of science, to respect the freedom indispensable for scientific research, and to encourage and develop international contacts and cooperation.

It is easy to acknowledge that excellence in science requires diversity and equity, but there is far to go in achieving a diversity of perspectives in the various sciences, not only those of persons of color, but also women and LGBTQ persons, those with disabilities,[36] and other members of the public. It is necessary, therefore, to examine the tension between science as done by professional, educated, expert, science specialists, and science in which the public may effectively participate. For while science provides knowledge about the way the world "is," society is necessary for deliberating together about the way things "ought" to be.

OPEN SCIENCE

A universal right to science is not merely about respecting the freedom necessary for science and protecting the interests of scientists – though it is that. It is also the right of *everyone* to participate in that aspect of cultural life that is named science.

Passively, as first expressed in the UDHR, the right to science is a right "to share in scientific advancement and its benefits" (Article 27 (1)), and, as expressed in the ICESCR, "the right of everyone to enjoy the benefits of scientific progress and its applications" (Article 15 (1) (b)). In a time when science ranges from experiments conducted in a hadron collider to constructing artificially intelligent robots and modifying the genome of embryos, one might automatically assume on first reading that only scientists have the education and expertise to contribute to scientific knowledge. Hence, a universal right to science might be expected to relegate the rest of humanity to patiently receiving the benefits of science, as indeed some

[34] Angela Saini, *Superior: The Return of Race Science* (Boston: Beacon Press, 2019).
[35] Mylene Bidault, Chapter 8 in this Volume.
[36] Valerie Bradley, Chapter 9 in this Volume.

Epilogue

delegates argued during the drafting and discussion prior to approval of the UDHR by the General Assembly of the UN. At most, public participation would thus be primarily as consumers of science.

As Mikel Mancisidor[37] took care to explain, however, it is a misapprehension of the right to science to limit its scope to sharing in the benefits of science, such as the benefit of affordable medicine. Rather, as Mancisidor's historical hermeneutic shows, the word "share" entails action, agency, and active participation. He therefore proposes that "to share in" be considered synonymous with "to participate in" or "take part in." The right to science, he shows, "goes beyond 'benefit from' and advocates broader concepts of 'participation in'; a right which includes participation in scientific creation (citizen science, or "ordinary people doing science"[38]), the dissemination of scientific knowledge, and participation in scientific policy, among other things."[39]

A right to science that entails more robust public participation in science aligns with the original goals of the human rights drafters then, in the 1940s, and now, in the 2020s, as people in both eras aspire to enable human flourishing and peace throughout the world. Much has since been done to develop strategies for public engagement in science[40] and document the value of citizen science[41], though much remains to be done. Two examples may suffice.

When Sharon Terry's two children were diagnosed in 1994 with a rare progressive genetic disease (pseudoxanthoma elasticum PXE), she learned that neither their doctors nor scientists knew much about it. Terry[42] was a former college chaplain who had become a full-time mother, and her husband was a construction manager who had majored in drafting. Together they persuaded Harvard to let them use lab space at night and, with the informal help of generous postdoctoral students, they

---

[37] Mancisidor, Chapter 1 in this Volume, p. 17.
[38] E/c.12/GC/25 (10)
[39] Ibid. p. 9.
[40] Laura Trouille et al., "Citizen Science Frontiers: Efficiency, Engagement, and Serendipitous Discovery with Human-Machine Systems," PNAS, February 5, 2019, 116 (6): 1902–2909; see, for example, www.zooniverse.org/, a website for "people-powered research."
[41] Maria Aristeidou and Christothea Herodotou, "Online Citizen Science: A Systematic Review of Effects on Learning and Scientific Literacy," *Citizen Science: Theory and Practice*, 2030, 5(1): 1–12; Brandi Leach, et al. *Emerging Developments in Citizen Science: Reflecting on Areas of Innovation* (Rand Europe, 2020) web-only document number: RR-4401-THIS, https://doi.org/10.7249/RR4401; Committee on Designing Citizen Science to Support Science Learning, Rajul Pandya, Kenne Ann Dibner (eds.), *Learning Through Citizen Science: A Consensus Study Report of the National Academies of Sciences, Engineering, Medicine* (Washington, DC: The National Academies Press, 2018) http://nap.edu/25183.
[42] www.ted.com/speakers/sharon_terry; Terry's TED talk is entitled "Science didn't understand my kids' rare disease until I decided to study it." www.pcori.org/people/sharon-terry-ma; see a fuller description of their story in Karen Taussig, "The Molecular Revolution in Medicine," in Susan McKinnon and Sydel Silverman (eds.), *Complexities: Beyond Nature and Nurture* (Chicago: University of Chicago Press, 2005) pp. 239–241.

Also see Karen Taussig, *Ordinary Genomes: Science, Citizenship, and Genetic Identities* (Durham: Duke University Press, 2009).

learned about genes and eventually built a diagnostic test and posted data on an open online consortium, called Genetic Alliance, which Sharon Terry now runs. Genetic Alliance[43] offers tools to help other families, gives advice on how to do scientific research and how to become a political activist, and runs a participant owned and managed registry and biobank.[44]

The Terrys had to overcome numerous barriers to contribute as they did to science. The majority of science research is publicly funded through tax monies allocated through grants, by governmental agencies like the (US) National Institutes of Health and the European Commission, almost exclusively to science investigators selected by review committees of fellow scientists. Most science is done in academic and government settings or for-profit companies. Scientists who share their findings in scholarly articles, monographs, and books for the academic market are generally not paid to publish, and their data, findings, and publications are usually not freely available to the general public. Instead, scientists submit their work to journals and publishing corporations, such as Elsevier,[45] who handle scientific peer review and publication, and the information is privatized and put behind a paywall.[46] Libraries then pay an institutional fee for faculty to have access, or individuals may pay a fee per article. Sometimes authors pay publishing companies a fee as well, usually in the thousands of dollars, for their work to be freely available – typically labelled "open access"– in which case the for-profit publishing company collects fees from both the universities and authors.[47]

Given such boundaries around academic science in western countries, a second, less heartening example of opening access to science involves the young internet pioneer, Aaron Swartz,[48] whose best-known contribution is the one that also led to his death. In his teens, Schwartz was a wunderkind involved in developing RSS (which organizes web feeds), Markdown (a simple editing language for webpages),

[43] www.geneticalliance.org/about.
[44] http://geneticalliance.org/Registry_BioBank.
[45] Blair Fix, "The Legacy of Aaaron Swartz: The Fight for Open Access," December 23, 2019, https://capitalaspower.com/2019/12/the-legacy-of-aaron-swartz-the-fight-for-open-access/.
"In 2018, Elsevier's profit margin was 37%. Let's put this in perspective. Even during the peak of its profitability, Apple's profit margin never got above 27%."
[46] For information about the economics of academic publishing, see the 2018 free online documentary film *Paywall: The Business of Scholarship*, directed and produced by Jason Schmitt, which focuses on the need for open access to research and science. https://paywallthemovie.com/.
[47] Fix, note 45. "Author-funded open access has also led to the dubious practice of 'double dipping'. Companies like Elsevier give authors the option to publish their articles as open access – even in journals that are otherwise paywalled. Elsevier charges authors thousands of dollars for this privilege. But then Elsevier continues to charge universities the same subscription price for the rest of the paywalled articles. So universities effectively pay for access twice."
[48] Justin Peters, *Aaron Swartz and the Rise of Free Culture on the Internet* (New York: Scribner, 2018); See also Aaron Swartz, *Raw Thought Raw Nerve: Inside the Mind of Aaron Swartz* (New York: Discovery Publisher, 2014); see also Sean B. Palmer, *The Boy Who Could Change the World: The Writings of Aaron Swartz* (New York: The New Press, 2015); see also the documentary film "The Internet's Own Boy: The Story of Aaron Swartz" directed by Brian Knappenberger, www.youtube.com/watch?v=2MoGQww1GoY.

Reddit (now a massive news aggregation site), and Creative Commons (a nonprofit copyright-sharing system). In 2008, Swartz raised concerns about the tyranny of academic publishing in an online document entitled "Guerilla Open Access Manifesto."[49] He wrote, "The world's entire scientific and cultural heritage, published over centuries in books and journals, is increasingly being digitized and locked up by a handful of private corporations." He called for sharing information openly and freely with the whole world, not just scientists, elite universities, and citizens of the First World.

As a research fellow at Harvard, Swartz had free online library privileges. In late 2010 he hooked up his computer to the internet in an unlocked, unmarked closet at MIT, and wrote a program to download articles from behind the paywall operated by the journal storage company, JSTOR, to make them freely available around the world. He was arrested and charged with breaking and entering. Although JSTOR declined to press charges, US Federal prosecutors aggressively pursued the case, charging him with eleven violations of the computer fraud and abuse act, carrying a cumulative maximum penalty of $1 million in fines, thirty-five years in prison, asset forfeiture, restitution, and supervised release. He declined to plead guilty and plea-bargain. In 2013, Aaron Swartz hanged himself in his apartment.

The interests of scientists as authors, of science publishing companies, science communities, and the wider public, are obviously in tension even though they are contained together in the right to science articulated in Article 15 of the ICESCR. The current imbalance that prioritizes protection of the material interests of scientists could be addressed in part by applying the right to science in a manner that aligns with the order of priorities as they are listed in ICESCR. Article 15 not only recognizes the right of everyone "(c) to benefit from the protection of the moral and material interests resulting from any scientific, literary or artistic production of which he is the author," but *first* declares the right of everyone "(a) to take part in cultural life "and "(b) to enjoy the benefits of scientific progress and its applications ... " As Aaron Swartz, we, and other human rights scholars realize, redressing and restricting the "unprecedented expansion of intellectual property regimes"[50] and profits from science applications and publishing will be necessary for science to be open and public participation in science to flourish.

One encouraging follow-up to the tragedy of Aaron Swartz's death is the formation of SciHub[51] "the first pirate website in the world to provide free public access to tens of millions of research papers,"[52] Library Genesis, Open Science, and internet

---

[49] https://archive.org/stream/GuerillaOpenAccessManifesto/Goamjuly2008_djvu.txt.

[50] Effy Vayena and John Tasioulas, "We the Scientists: A *Human Right to Citizen Science*," *Philosophy & Technology*, 2015 (28), 479–485.

[51] https://scihub.to/.

[52] Sci-Hub was developed by Alexandra Elbakyan when she was a student in Kazakhstan. "Elbakyan's university couldn't afford to pay subscription fees to many of the journals that she needed to read. So to do her research, she either had to buy access to each article (typically over $30 a piece) or find friends and colleagues who had access."

sites[53] that make science and other articles and books available to those who have access to computers and the internet. Access to science publications, however, is just the foundation for open science. Robust and diverse participation in open science includes not only the most widespread forms of engagement by educating the public about science, but also forms of participation that enable communities and individuals to actively participate in science and do science themselves.

The following are examples of public participation in the development and diffusion of science internationally, across cultures:

(1) Widespread science education both in public schools for children and adolescents, and other forums for adults to examine the latest science and its implications;
(2) Participating in human research as an informed, consenting, volunteer in studies;
(3) Donating data (e.g. Open Humans)[54] or being a subject in large public research projects (institutionally reviewed and approved) for which individual consent may be waived;
(4) Serving as a member of committees, commissions and the like with scientists and funders that shape selection of problems to be studied;
(5) Being a community member of an Institutional Review Board or other research ethics review committee or data safety monitoring board;
(6) Individual (or small group) consultant, collaborator, or public partner on specific science research regarding which the public member has special interest or historical commitment;
(7) Embedding in science labs and research projects increasingly done by bioethicists, moral philosophers, humanities scholars, journalists, and others to provide an "outsider" perspective, identify ethical concerns prior to problems, and keep the general public abreast of scientific discoveries and their implications;
(8) Being a "citizen scientist" as in collecting ecological data on birds and butterflies,[55] or mapping brain slices,[56] or conducting one's own science project in a do-it-yourself lab such as DIY Science.[57]

Although these may not constitute full realization of a universal human right to enjoy, access, and participate in science, they would constitute significant progress

[53] https://openscience.com/tag/library-genesis/.
[54] Bastian Greshake Tzovaras et al. "Open Humans: A Platform for Participant-Centered Research and Personal Data Exploration," *GigaScience*, 2019, 8 (6).
[55] James Wang Wei et al., "Citizen Science and the Urban Ecology of Birds and Butterflies – A Systematic Review," *PLOS ONE*, 10 June 10, 2016 https://journals.plos.org/plosone/article?id=10.1371/journal.pone.0156425.
[56] Amy Robinson, "EyeWire, A Game to Crowdsources Brain Mapping, Citizenscience.gov," US General Services Administration www.citizenscience.gov/eyewire-brain-mapping/#.
[57] https://diybio.org/.

toward opening science to everyone. Further, the right to science explicitly includes the duty of "conservation, development and diffusion of science" (ICESCR 15 (2)) as well as "encouragement and development of international contacts and cooperation in the scientific and cultural fields" (ICESCR 15 (4)). This book, we hope, has contributed to meeting that part of the right to science.

Index

AAAS. *See* American Association for the Advancement of Science
AAC. *See* Augmentative and Alternative Communication
access, 4, 282–283. *See also* participation
  to internet, 2–3
  open, 294
  right to access to knowledge, 27–28
  in RtS, 214
  to science, 174–176
  to scientific journals, 115
accountability, 257–263
ADA. *See* Americans with Disabilities Act
advertising, 198–199
Aernie, Philipp, 5
Africa, national academies in, 226–227
African Americans, COVID-19 impacting, 178
Agenda 2030, 127–128, 136, 138–139, 156
  UNESCO on, 127–128
agriculture, 204–205
  data in, 147
algorithms, 197–198
  in media world, 198–199
All European Academies (ALLEA), 101–102
alternative facts, 195–196
American Academy of Pediatrics, 157
American Association for the Advancement of Science (AAAS), 2, 212–213, 250–251
American Declaration on the Rights and Duties of Man, 7, 66–67, 232
  aftermath of, 52–53
  Anteprojecto, 42
  Article IV, 49, 50
  Article XIII, 7, 21, 33, 49, 50, 52–53
  Article XV, 42, 43
  compliance with, 34–35
  drafting of, 35–52, 62–63
  inspirations for, 40–41

Inter-American Juridical Committee and, 36–44, 50
  language in, 34–35
  as legally binding force, 34–35
  Preamble, 49
  Preliminary Draft, 43, 46
  Resolution XI, 40–41
  RtS in, 42–44
  UDHR and, 34–35
  United States on, 35
American Disabled Persons Organization, 151–152
American Law Institute Statement of Essential Human Rights, 40–41
American Society of International Law, 38–39
Americans with Disabilities Act (ADA), 160–161
Andorno, Roberto, 8
Arab Organization of People with Disabilities, 151–152
Aral, Sinan, 196–197
Argentina, 37–38, 45–48
Aristotle, 91, 287–288
Arroyo Lameda, Eduardo, 37–38, 39
Article 15 ICESCR, 3, 4, 28, 33, 54, 57–60, 141, 195–196, 211–212, 268–269, 295
  Article 15(1), 152–153
  Article 15(2), 174, 251
  Article 15(4), 174, 258–260
Article 27 UDHR and, 147
  COVID-19 and, 169
  on cultural rights, 141
  on human rights, 279–280
  on IP rights, 54–55, 58
  proposed indicators of, 284–285
Article 27 UDHR, 1, 7, 25, 32, 52–53, 54, 57–60, 76–77, 141, 152–153, 268–269
  Article 15 ICESCR and, 147
  Berne Convention (1928) and, 60
  Bogota Convention and, 60

Index

COVID-19 and, 169
  intellectual property rights and, 54–56, 58
Article 27(1) UDHR, 33
  Humphrey involved with, 61–62
  origin of, 61–62
Article 27(2) UDHR, 54–55, 59–60, 74–75
  final draft stages of, 69–74
  origin of, 62–63
artificial intelligence, 2–3
  disabled people and, 161
  ethics of, 136–137
assistive technology (AT), 156
Association for Retarded Children, 151
AT. *See* assistive technology
Atlantic Charter, 42–43
Atom Energy Commission, 157
atomic bombs, 19
Auger, Pierre, 81, 83
  on religion, 85–86
Augmentative and Alternative Communication (AAC), 162
authenticity, 202–203
authoritarianism, Big Data and, 112
authorship, 94
autism, 157, 159
Autism Science Foundation, 157
Autistic Self-Advocacy Network, 159

Balcazar, F. E., 158–159
Baltimore, David, 98
Bauer, Henry H., 95–96
Bauman, Zygmunt, 200–201
Beall, Jeffrey, 203
bedaquiline, 262
behavior, media shaping, 199
Belgium, 22
benefits sharing, UNESCO on, 129–130
Berkeley Center for Independent Living, 151
Berne Convention (1928), 54–55, 63, 65, 74
  Article 6 of, 60
  Article 6bis of, 64
  Article 27 UDHR and, 60
  economic rights in, 64
  Inter-American Convention compared with, 66
  moral rights in, 64–65
Berne Convention on the Protection of Artistic and Literary Works (1886), 54–55
Berners-Lee, Tim, 207
Bertillion, Alphonse, 291
bias
  publication, 184
  statistical, 184
Bidault, Mylène, 9, 292
Big Data, 206

  authoritarianism and, 112
  on disabled people, 159–161
  discrimination and, 112
  ethics and, 110
  EU and, 111–112
  United States and, 111–112
Bill of Rights, US, 61
biodiversity, 29–30
bioethics, 29–30
  UNESCO on, 131–132
biogenesis, 289
biopiracy, 117–118, 119
bioprospecting, 117–118
Bluetooth, 180–181
Boggio, Andrea, 13–14
Bogota Convention, Article 27 UDHR and, 60
Bogota Declaration, 54–55
  Article XIII, 67, 68
  material interests in, 67–69
  moral rights in, 67–69
  travaux préparatoire for, 55, 74
Bok, Bart, 83
  on UDHR, 87–88
Bolivia, Constitution of 1938, 61
Boodman, Eric, 158
borderline fields, Huxley on, 84–85
Boulind, H. F., 86–87
Boutros-Ghali, B., 27–28
Brach, Marion, 99
Bradley, Valerie J., 10
Brazil, 37–38, 116
  Constitution of 1946, 61
Broad, William, 97
Bryn Mawr College, 38–39
Burundi Academy of Science and Technology, 215–216
Bush, Vannevar, 19

CABs. *See* community advisory boards
Caicedo Castilla, José Joaquín, 37–38, 39, 40
Cambridge Analytica, 206
CAME. *See* Conference of Allied Ministers of Education
Campos, Francisco, 37–38, 40
capitalism
  Coronavirus, 179–180, 181–182
  surveillance, 179
careers, in science, 95
Carton de Wiart (Count), 71–72
case-fatality rate (CFR), 167–168
Cassin, René, 6, 7, 20–21, 22, 24–25, 67, 70, 72–73
  on moral rights, 69–71
  on Nuremberg Trial, 20
del Castillo, Fernandez, 69

Centers for Disease Control and Prevention
    (CDC), 252–253
CERN, 207
CESCR. *See* Committee on Economic, Social
    and Cultural Rights
CFR. *See* case-fatality rate
Chang, P. C., 24
Chapman, Audrey, 57–58, 250, 263
Chapultepec, 35–36, 37–38, 40–41
Charter of Economic Rights and Duties of
    States, 130
children's rights, 113
Chile, 22, 24, 37–38, 39, 62–63
China, 24, 74, 258
Christakis, Nicholas M., 171
Christensen, Ivan Lind, 8, 287
citizen communcation, in science, 207–208
civil law, 51–52
Claude, Richard Pierre, 5, 24, 171
click rates, 197
climate change, 29–30
    science-based decision making and, 132–133
    UNESCO on, 132–133
Cold War, 8, 19, 78–79, 82
    Huxley on, 87–88
Colombia, 37–38, 45–48, 49–50
COMEST. *See* World Commission on the Ethics
    of Science Knowledge and Technology
Commission on Human Rights, 7, 70, 130
Committee on Economic, Social and Cultural
    Rights (CESCR), 3, 17, 25–26, 250. *See also*
    General Comment No. 25, CESCR
    General Comment No. 14, 249–250,
        263–264, 273
    General Comment No. 17, 58–59
    General Comment No. 21, 25, 142, 146, 148–149
    human rights indicators and, 272–273
    on science, 288
common law, 51–52
Common Rule, 109–110
communicable diseases, human rights and, 246
Communicator Prize, 208
community, science, 85
community advisory boards (CABs), 252–253
Community Research Advisors Group (CRAG),
    252–253, 255
complexity effects, 204–205
Comte, Auguste, on science, 82–83
Conference of Allied Ministers of Education
    (CAME), 19–20
Constitution, US, 121
Convention on the Rights of People with
    Disabilities (CRPD), 10, 150–151, 152–153, 160
    evidence-based practices and, 156–157

provisions of, 153–154
rights in, 155
RtS and, 154–156
copyright, 60. *See also* intellectual property rights
    as human right, 72–73
    in TRIPS, 56
Coronavirus Capitalism, 179–180, 181–182
Council of Europe, 142, 154
COVID-19, 3, 10, 32, 112, 125, 138–139, 185–186
    advocacy for, 265–266
    African Americans impacted by, 178
    Article 15 ICESCR and, 169
    Article 27 UDHR and, 169
    discrimination and, 177–179
    economic impact of, 177
    elimination strategies, 190, 192
    emergence of, 167
    in EU, 188–189
    fast science and, 184–188
    genomics, 190
    in Germany, 188–189
    government responses to, 182–184
    human rights and, 169
    inequality and, 175–176
    in Japan, 188–189
    mortality from, 167, 169, 183
    RtS and, 265–267
    in Russia, 189
    slow science and, 184–188
    superspreader events, 190
    testing for, 190
    Trump and, 186–187
    in United States, 173
    in Vietnam, 189
Cowles, Henry, 287–288
CRAG. *See* Community Research Advisors Group
CRISPR-Cas, 205
critical dialogue, in science, 206–207
critical thinking
    freedom and, 148
    knowledge production and, 119–120
    science and, 148
CRPD. *See* Convention on the Rights of People
    with Disabilities
Cuba, 22, 24–25, 37–38, 45–48, 70–71
cultural diversity, 145
cultural life
    defining, 123, 290
    science and, 107–108, 142–143, 144–146
    UDHR on, 108
    UNESCO on, 130
cultural rights, 48–49
    Article 15 ICESCR on, 141
    protections from, 143–144

RtS as, 29–32, 292
Shaheed on, 144
UDHR on, 1–2
as universal, 5
Curie, Marie, 71–72

Dang, Gisa, 13
Danish Committee on Research Misconduct, 99
Danish Committees on Scientific Dishonesty (DCSD), 99
Darwin, Charles, 97
data. *See also* Big Data
 in agriculture, 147
 fabrication, 97–98, 99, 100–101
 neutrality, 111–114
Data Pop Alliance, 159–160
Davis, Kevin E., 271–272, 273–274
Dawson, Charles, 97
DCSD. *See* Danish Committees on Scientific Dishonesty
Decade of Disabled People, 153
Declaration of Independence, US, 195
Declaration of International Rights of Men, 40–41
Declaration of Philadelphia of the International Labor Committee, 40–41
Declaration of the Rights of People Affected by Tuberculosis, 264
Declaration on the Right to Education
 Article 26, 22
 Soviet delegation on, 22–23
Deep Fakes, 202
definitions of science, 76, 86, 93–94, 211, 234, 287, 288–289
democracy
 education and, 4–5
 foundations of, 18–19
 general welfare in, 241–243
 RtS and, 31
Denver Principles, 254–255
Department of Health and Human Services, 98
derogation, in ICESCR, 236–237
Deutsche Forschungsgemeinschaft (DFG), 99
developing countries, TRIPS impact on, 56
DFG. *See* Deutsche Forschungsgemeinschaft
digital divide, disabled people and, 161–162
digital exclusion, 2–3
digitality, 201–202
van Dijk, Pieter, 218
Disability Rights Fund, 152
disability rights movement, history of, 151–152
disabled people
 artificial intelligence and, 161
 Big Data on, 159–161
 digital divide and, 161–162

RtS for, 150–151
 in scientific research, 158–159
 as scientific subjects, 157–158
discrimination
 Big Data and, 112
 COVID-19 and, 177–179
 racial, 177–178
dissidents, 112
do no harm, 256–257
 UNESCO on, 129–130
Donders, Yvonne, 9, 12
Down Syndrome, 157, 161
dual-use surveillance, 182
Dumbarton Oaks, 35

ECHR, Article 10, 91–92
Economic and Social Council (ECOSOC), 20–21
economic rights, in Berne Convention (1928), 64
ECOSOC. *See* Economic and Social Council
Ecuador, 22–23
EDPB. *See* European Data Protection Board
education. *See also* Right to Education
 democracy and, 4–5
 Huxley on, 85
 UNESCO on, 86–87
edX, 209–210
Eisenhower, Dwight D., 23
Elbakyan, Alexandra, 295
Electronic Frontier Foundation, 181–182
Elsevier, 294
Elzinga, Aant, 78–79
emergency powers, 181–182
Entrepreneurial Rights as Human Rights (Aerni), 5
EPO. *See* European Patent Office
ethics, 8. *See also* bioethics
 of artificial intelligence, 136–137
 Big Data and, 110
EU. *See* European Union
Euclid, 27
eugenics, 84–85
European Charter of Fundamental Rights, 91–92
European Code of Conduct for Research Integrity, 101–102
European Commission, 294
European Data Protection Board (EDPB), 180
European Patent Office (EPO), 117–118
European Union (EU)
 Big Data and, 111–112
 COVID-19 in, 188–189
Everly, Rebecca, 11–12
evidence-based practices, CRPD and, 156–157
excitation
 journalism and, 199–200

excitation (cont.)
　perceptions and, 200–201
executive distrust, of science, 182–184

Facebook, 109–110, 197, 202
　social manipulation and, 109
Facetune, 202
facial recognition, 161
Facilitated Communication (FC), 157
fair return, 43–44, 51
fake news, 196–197
fake science, 202–204
Farmer, Paul, 265
farmers, 147, 204–205. *See also* agriculture
fast science, 10–11, 171
　COVID-19 and, 184–188
FC. *See* Facilitated Communication
Fenwick, Charles, 37–39, 40
Finnemore, M., 78–79
First Founding Congress of Disabled People International, 153
Fiske, Susan, 109–110
food. *See also* agriculture; right to food
　technology, 117
Four Freedoms speech, Roosevelt, 17, 18
four-step test, 235–243
France, 25
freedom, critical thinking and, 148
freedom of expression, 50
freedom of investigation, 50
freedom of opinion, 50
French Declaration of Human Rights, 61
Fribourg Declaration on Cultural Rights, 142
Frick, Mike, 13
Fridays for Future, 200
Furin, Jennifer, 260

Gates, Bill, 209
GDP per capita, human rights and, 172–173
GDPR, 111–112
gender equality, RtS and, 30
General Comment No. 25, CESCR, 3, 26, 108–109, 112–113, 118–119, 120, 123, 142–143, 178, 188, 190–191, 238, 240, 263–264, 266–267, 268–269
　adoption of, 17
　on human rights, 190–191, 279–280
　normative implications of, 17
　paragraph 52, 184
　paragraph 54, 191
　on participation, 251
　RtS in, 170, 184
　on science, 172
　3AQ framework in, 250

General Conference in Montevideo, 84
General Day of Discussion on the New General Comment on Science, 3–4
Genetic Alliance, 293–294
Germany, 65, 199–200, 201, 206–207, 208
　COVID-19 in, 188–189
Gerst, Alexander, 206–207
GIPA. *See* greater involvement of people with AIDS
Global Innovation Index, 166
Global North, 117–118
　knowledge and language in, 113–114
Global TB Community Advisory Board (Global TB CAB), 252–253
Global Young Academy, 217
Gómez Robledo, Antonio, 37–38, 39
good participatory practice (GPP), 254
The Good Society (journal), 175
Goodstein, David, 94
　on misconduct, 95
　on scientific method, 95–96
Google, 197
　advertising and, 198–199
Google Deepmind, 205–206
Gore, Albert, Jr., 98
government relations, in national academies, 227
GPP. *See* good participatory practice
Gran, Brian, 13–14
Gray, Glenda, 246
greater involvement of people with AIDS (GIPA), 254
Guttenberg, Karl-Theodor zu, 101

H1N1 outbreak, 187–188
harms, 121–122
Harvard University, 2
Havens, W. Paul, Jr., 158
Havet, Jacques L., 7, 21, 30
Health Research Extension Act, 98
Hermann, Friedhelm, 99
Hiroshima, 19, 77
history of science, 287–288
HIV/AIDS, 56, 116, 185–186, 187–188, 246
　inclusion and research on, 254
honesty, 93, 103
HR Network. *See* International Human Rights Network of Academies and Scholarly Societies
HRBA. *See* human rights-based approach
human dignity, 91–92
human genetic modification, 2–3
human genome sequencing, TRIPS on, 57–58
human rights, 133–134
　Article 15 ICESCR on, 279–280

communicable diseases and, 246
copyright as, 72–73
COVID-19 and, 169
GDP per capita and, 172–173
General Comment No. 25 on, 190–191, 279–280
 in ICESCR, 58–60
innovation and, 121–122
IP rights and, 58–60, 115–116, 242
knowledge and, 119–120
monitoring bodies, 269–270
national academies and, 217–219, 222–224, 229
as negative rights, 74–75
Okediji on, 58–59
Roosevelt on, 18–19
RtS as, 232
science as, 31–32, 247
Stamapopoulou on, 28
in UDHR, 58–60
UNESCO on, 125–136
Western liberal conception of, 74–75
Human Rights Commission, 48, 63
Human Rights Council, 8–9, 138, 141, 269–270
human rights indicators
 CESCR and, 272–273
 defining, 271–272
 emergence of, 269–271
 outcome, 283, 284–285
 process, 282–283, 284–285
 production and, 275–277
 promulgation of, 276–277
 structural, 282, 284–285
human rights-based approach (HRBA), 126
human sciences, misconduct in, 94
Humphrey, John Peters, 6, 7, 20–21, 61–63
 on Article 27(1) UDHR, 61–62
 on RtS, 21
Hunt, Paul, 268–269, 273–274
Huxley, Julian, 77
 on borderline fields, 84–85
 on Cold War, 87–88
 on education, 85
 on scientific humanism, 80–81
hydroxychloroquine, 186–187

IAP. *See* InterAcademy Partnership
IBC. *See* International Bioethics Committee
ICCPR, 236–237, 241
ICESCR. *See* International Covenant on Economic, Social and Cultural Rights
ICT. *See* information and communication technologies
IGBC. *See* Intergovernmental Bioethics Committee

IHME. *See* Institute for Health Metrics and Evaluation
Imanishi-Kari, Thereza, 98
impact factors, 203
inclusion
 HIV/AIDS research and, 253–256
 TB research and, 253–256
India, 56
indigenous peoples, 117
 IP rights and, 117–118
industrial property, 56–57
industrialization, 55–56
inequality
 COVID-19 and, 175–176
 in science, 174–176
information and communication technologies (ICT), 110, 113–114, 122–123
Information Society Project, 27–28
informed consent, 150
innovation, human rights and, 121–122
Instagram, 202
Institute for Health Metrics and Evaluation (IHME), 167
Instituto Hispano-Luso-Americano de Derecho Internacional, 40
intellectual property (IP) rights, 51
 Article 15 ICESCR on, 54–55, 58
 Article 27 UDHR and, 54–56, 58
 human rights and, 58–60, 115–116, 242
 indigenous peoples and, 117–118
 in Latin America, 66–67
 moral rights and, 56, 65
 origins and growth of, 55–58
 right to food and, 116–117
 Shaheed on, 59–60
InterAcademy Partnership (IAP), 217
Inter-American Bar Association, 36
Inter-American Commission of Jurists, 50
Inter-American Commission on Human Rights, 34–35
Inter-American Convention on the Rights of the Author in Literary, Scientific and Artistic Works, 66
 Article XI, 66–67
 Berne Convention (1928) compared with, 66
Inter-American Court of Human Rights, 34–35
Inter-American Juridical Committee, 24, 46, 61, 66–67
 American Declaration and, 36–44, 50
 Article XV of, 62–63
 drafts of, 50
 members of, 37–38
 role of, 36–37

Inter-American Juridical Committee (cont.)
  second draft of, 45–48
interdisciplinary relationships, 120–123
Intergovernmental Bioethics Committee (IGBC), 124–125
International Bioethics Committee (IBC), 124–125, 131–132
international cooperation, UNESCO on, 129–130
International Covenant on Economic, Social and Cultural Rights (ICESCR), 213
  Article 2, 11, 233, 235
  Article 2(1), 233
  Article 2(2), 178
  Article 4, 11, 148, 238–239, 241
  Article 15, 3, 4, 28, 33, 54
  Article 15.3, 42
  Article 15(1), 1
  Article 15(1)(b), 11, 54, 144–146
  Article 15(2), 11
  Article 15(4), 233
  countries signing, 232, 233
  derogation in, 236–237
  General Comment No. 25, 3
  human rights in, 58–60
  IP rights in, 58–60
  retrogressive measures and, 237–238
  UDHR enshrined by, 1–2
International Declaration on Human Genetic Data, 131
International Disability Alliance, 151–152
International Disability Caucus (IDC), 152
International Federation of Hard of Hearing People, 151–152
International Human Rights Network of Academies and Scholarly Societies (HR Network), 218–219, 230
international law, on text interpretation, 25
International League of Societies for the Mentally Handicapped, 151–152
International Organization of the Francophonie, 142
international trade fairs, 55–56
International Year of Disabled Persons, 153
internet, access to, 2–3
Internet Governance Lab, 160
inventions, classification of, 54
IP rights. *See* intellectual property rights

Jacob, Francois, 218
Japan, COVID-19 in, 188–189
Joint Appeal for Open Science, 136–137
Joint Civil Society Statement, 181–182
journalism, as excitation business, 199–200
JSTOR, 295

Kahneman, Daniel, 170
Kakkar, Raman, 261–262
Kaplan, D. L., 158–159
Kaye, David, 111
Keys, C. B., 158–159
Khan, Nadia, 208–209
Khan, Salman, 208–209
Khan Academy, 209
Kingsbury, Benedict, 271–272, 273–274
knowledge, 143–144
  beliefs separated from, 144
  critical thinking and production of, 119–120
  defining, 113–114
  in Global North, 113–114
  human rights and, 119–120
  science as global, 107–108
  traditional, 119
Krieger, 78–79

The Lancet, 187
language, in Global North, 113–114
Latin America, 35, 38, 52
  IP rights in, 66–67
League of Nations, 77–78, 83
LGBTQ+ community, 177–178, 292
Library Genesis, 295–296
Life Prize, 258–260
liquid modernity, 200–201
Lomborg, Bjørn, 99–100
L'Oréal, 128–136
Luca Coscioni Association, 215

Macchiarini, Paolo, 101
MacDonald, K. E., 158–159
Mancisidor de la Fuente, Mikel, 3–4, 6, 293
  on sharing, 50–51
Manheim, Karl, 81–82
March for Science, 196
Marshall, George C., 48
Massachusetts Institute of Technology (MIT), 196–197
material interests, in Bogota Declaration, 67–69
Mayor Zaragoza, Federico, 31
Mazibrada, Andrew, 8–9
MDGs. *See* Millennium Development Goals
meaningful consent, 109, 110–111
measles, mumps, and rubella (MMR) vaccine, 100
media
  algorithms in, 198–199
  behavior shaped by, 199
  perceptions shaped by, 196–198
medicine, misconduct in, 94
MedRxiv, 185–186
Mendel, Gregor, 97

Mental Patients Liberation Front, 151
Merkel, Angela, 189
Merry, Sally Engle, 270–272, 273–274
Merton, Robert K., 8, 88
Metaphysics (Aristotle), 91
Mexico, 37–38, 45–48, 70–71
migrant workers, 113
military industrial complex, 23
Millennium Development Goals (MDGs), 127–128
Miller, 270–271
Millikan, Robert, 97
misconduct
  defining, 93–96
  Goodstein on, 95
  historical perspective on, 96–102
  in human sciences, 94
  in medicine, 94
  participation as protection from, 252
  in social sciences, 94
missing link, 97
MIT. *See* Massachusetts Institute of Technology
MMR. *See* measles, mumps, and rubella vaccine
Montréal Declaration on the Responsible Use of Artificial Intelligence, 111
moral rights, 63
  of authors, 60
  in Berne Convention (1928), 64–65
  in Bogota Declaration, 67–69
  Cassin on, 69–71
  IP rights and, 56, 65
  origins of, 64–65
Mortchev, Mina, 211

Nagasaki, 19, 77
national academies, 215–217
  in Africa, 226–227
  barriers in study on, 225–227, 230
  characteristics of, 221
  civil and political rights focus of, 219
  collaborative efforts in, 228–229, 230
  cross-regional interests, 228
  functions of, 216–217
  government relations in, 227
  human rights and, 217–219, 222–224, 229
  methodology of study on, 220–221
  non-Western, 219
  organizational structure of, 226–227
  RtS and, 224–229
National Institutes of Health (NIH), 98, 159, 255–256, 294
National Young Academies (NYAs), 217, 220–221, 230
Nature Science Index, 166

Nawrot, Anna Maria Andersen, 5
NDR. *See* Norddeutscher Rundfunk
Needham, Joseph, 19–20, 77, 83
  on science, 80, 81
negative rights, 55–56
  human rights as, 74–75
New Urban Agenda, 125, 127–128
New Zealand, 73–74
Newton, Isaac, 97
NGOs. *See* non-governmental organizations
Nieto del Río, Felix, 37–38, 39
NIH. *See* National Institutes of Health
Ninth Conference of American States, 45–52
non-governmental organizations (NGOs), 152
Norddeutscher Rundfunk (NDR), 203
nuclear science, 87–88
Nuremberg Trial, 7
  Cassin on, 20
NYAs. *See* National Young Academies

OAS Charter, 34–35
objectivity, science and, 82–84
Obregón Tarazona, Liliana, 38
Office of the High Commissioner for Human Rights (OHCHR), 123, 136–137, 271, 273, 275–277, 278–279
Okediji, Ruth L., 59–60
  on human rights, 58–59
On the Connexion of the Physical Sciences (Somerville), 287–288
open access, 294
open science, 136–137, 292–297
Optional Protocol to the Convention, 153–154
Orešković, Stjepan, 10–11
O'Toole, Margaret, 98
outcome indicators, 283, 284–285

Pai, Madhukar, 260
Palais Chaillot, 20–21
Pan-American Union, 35–36
Pan-European Privacy-Preserving Proximity Tracing Project, 180–181
parapsychology, 84–85
Paris Convention on the Protection of Industrial Property, 56–57
participation, 108–111, 120, 148, 296
  defining, 108–109
  General Comment No. 25 on, 251
  for misconduct protection, 252
  opportunities for, 282–283
  in RtS, 25, 26, 146–149
  scientific progress and, 251–253
Pasteur, Louis, 97

patents, 115
  holders, 54, 56
  for seeds, 116–117
Patents, Human Rights and Access to Science (Plomer), 5
patterning, 157
Pavlov, Alexei, 22, 73
Pavlov, Ivan, 22
Peru, 37–38, 45–48, 74
Perutz, Max, 218
Petijean, Patrick, 78
Philadelphia Declaration of the International Labour Organization, 68
  travaux préparatoire for, 68, 69
Piltodwn Man forgery, 97
plagiarism, 94
Plato, 215–216
Plomer, Aurora, 5
PNAS. *See* Proceedings of the National Academy of Sciences
Poland, 73
The Popular Science Monthly, 287–288
Porsdam, Helle, 12
Porsdam Mann, Sebastian, 10–11, 12, 153
Preliminary Report of the Commission to the Study the Organization of Peace, 40–41
pretomanid, 260–261
principle of national treatment, 56
privacy rights, 180
private funding, public funding and, 114–119
Proceedings of the National Academy of Sciences (PNAS), 109–110
process indicators, 282–283, 284–285
property rights, 62–63
pseudoscience, 3, 84–85
  UNESCO on, 85
public consultation, 120
public funding, private funding and, 114–119
public good, 260
  science as, 107–108, 172–174
Public Health Service, 98–99
publication bias, 184
Putin, Vladimir, 2

QR codes, 180

racial discrimination, 177–178
  in science field, 290–291
realism, political, 78
REBSP, 28. *See* right to enjoy the benefits of scientific progress and is applications
reciprocity, TB research and, 256–257
religion, Auger on, 85–86

Report of the Working Group of Human Rights, 48
retrogressive measures, ICESCR and, 237–238
Rigamonti, Cyrill P., 64–65
right to access to knowledge, 27–28
Right to Education, 22
  RtS and, 30
right to enjoy the benefits of scientific progress and is applications (REBSP), 26–27, 28
right to food, 116
  IP rights and, 116–117
Right to Food, RtS and, 30
Right to Health, 27
  RtS and, 30
right to participate in and to enjoy the benefits of Scientific Progress and its Applications (RPEBSPA), 26–27
Right to Science (RtS), 2, 76–77
  abbreviation of, 27
  access in, 214, 249–251
  in American Declaration, 42–44
  benefits in, 24, 25, 26, 214
  COVID-19 and, 265–267
  CRPD and, 154–156
  as cultural right, 29–32, 292
  defining, 211–212, 213–214, 215, 244
  democracy and, 31
  for disabled people, 150–151
  formal reasons for, 141
  full implementation of, 4–5
  future potential of, 263–265
  gender equality and, 30
  in General Comment No. 25, 170, 184
  historical neglect of, 3, 231–233
  history of, 152–153, 268–269, 286–287
  as human right, 232
  Humphrey on, 21
  indicators, 273–283
  limitation of, 236–241
  literature review, 213–215
  naming, 26–29
  national academies and, 224–229
  normative content of, 3, 234–235
  participation in, 25, 26, 146–149
  Right to Education and, 30
  Right to Food and, 30
  Right to Health and, 30
  Right to Water and Sanitation and, 30
  sharing in, 50–51
  significant impacts of, 143–146
  strategic litigation for, 261–263
  substantive reasons for, 141–143
  in UDHR, 17–18
  UNESCO and, 20
  in UNESCO Constitution, 20–21

right to share in scientific advancement and its benefits (RSSAB), 26–27
Right to Water and Sanitation, RtS and, 30
rights of priority, 56
rights of science, 7
Rio de Janeiro, 33, 36–38
Roberts, Ed, 151
Roman law, 64–65
Romano, Cesare P. R., 7
Roosevelt, Franklin D.
　Four Freedoms speech, 17, 18
　on human rights, 18–19
Rose, 270–271
RPEBSPA. *See* right to participate in and to enjoy the benefits of Scientific Progress and its Applications
RSSAB. *See* right to share in scientific advancement and its benefits
RT-PCR, 190
RtS. *See* Right to Science
Russell, Bertrand, on science, 29
Russia, COVID-19 in, 189
Rwanda Academy of Science, 215–216

Salk, Jonas, 158, 265–266
Samarasan, Diana, 152
Sanderson, Grant, 209
SARS-CoV-2. *See* COVID-19
Satabello, Maya, 159
Saudi Arabia, 24
Schabas, William A., 213
science, technology and innovation (STI), 127–128
Science Barometer, 207–208
Science in the Service of Human Rights (Claude), 5
science-based decision making, climate change and, 132–133
scientific advancement, 234
Scientific Advisory Board, 125
scientific freedom, 132, 282–283
scientific humanism, Huxley on, 80–81
scientific integrity, defining, 93–96
scientific journals, access to, 115
scientific literacy, lack of, 3
scientific method, 287, 290
　Goodstein on, 95–96
　as ideal, 96
　as myth, 95–96
scientific progress, 234
　applications of, 234–235
　benefits of, 235–236, 251–253
　participation and, 251–253
SciHub, 295–296
search engine optimization (SEO), 197

self-image of science, 210
Shaheed, Farida, 5, 8–9, 28, 58–59, 141, 146, 249, 251, 279–280
　on cultural rights, 144
　on IP rights, 59–60
sharing, Mancisidor on, 50–51
Shaver, Lea, 27, 28–29, 51–52, 108
Silva, Cerda, 66
Silva, Diego, 256
Singapore Statement on Research Integrity, 102
Singer, H. S., 157
Skype, 220
slow science, 10–11, 171
　COVID-19 and, 184–188
Slow Science Academy, 185
Sluga, Glenda, 78–79
smartphones, surveillance from, 113
social manipulation, Facebook and, 109
social networks, 11
Social Relations of Science Movement (SRSM), 81
social sciences, misconduct in, 94
society, science and, 171–172
Somerville, Mary, 287–288
South Africa, 56
Soviet Union, 24, 73
　on Declaration of the Right to Education, 22–23
　United States rivalry with, 19
space research, 206–207
SRSM. *See* Social Relations of Science Movement
Stack, E., 158–159
Stalin, Joseph, 23
Stamatopoulou, Elsa, 28
Stapel, Diederik, 100–101
State Department, US, 172–173
statistical -bias, 184
STEM, 166
Stengers, Isabelle, 185–186
Stephenson, J. P., 86
STI. *See* science, technology and innovation
Stobbe, Mike, 158
Stoepler, Teresa M., 11–12
structural indicators, 282, 284–285
Suarez Balcazar, Y., 158–159
Süddeutsche Zeitung (SZ), 203
Sulston, John, 57
Surgisphere Corporation, 187
surveillance
　Big Data and, 112
　dual-use, 182
　from smartphones, 113
surveillance capitalism, 179
Sustainable Development Goals, 31, 125, 127–128
Swartz, Aaron, 294–295
SZ. *See Süddeutsche Zeitung*

TAG. *See* Treatment Action Group
Tararas, Konstantinos, 9
Tate, Jack, 48–49
TB. *See* tuberculosis
10/90 gap, 242
Terry, Sharon, 293–294
text interpretation, international law on, 25
Thierse, Wolfgang, 199–200
Timmermann, Cristian, 256–257
TKDL. *See* Traditional Knowledge Digital Library
TMS. *See* transcranial magnetic stimulation
Toussaint, Henri, 97
Trade Related Agreement on Intellectual Property Rights (TRIPS), 55–56, 64
 Article 27(1), 57–58
 copyright in, 56
 developing countries impacted by, 56
 on human genome sequencing, 57–58
traditional knowledge, 119
Traditional Knowledge Digital Library (TKDL), 117–118
transcranial magnetic stimulation (TMS), 156
transparency, 121–122, 197–198
travaux préparatoire, 17–18, 50–51
 for Bogota Declaration, 55, 74
 for Philadelphia Declaration, 68, 69
Treatment Action Group (TAG), 13, 248, 251, 258–260
Trewin, S., 161
Tripathi, Kaushal, 262–263
TRIPS. *See* Trade Related Agreement on Intellectual Property Rights
TRIPS Agreement, 54
Trump, Donald, COVID-19 and, 186–187
trust, in science, 170, 188–191, 205–206
tuberculosis (TB), 13, 247, 252–253
 activists, 250–251
 advocacy for, 257–263
 conservation and, 258–261
 drug-resistant, 258, 262
 inclusion and research on, 253–256
 reciprocity and, 256–257
 research on, 247–249
 strategic litigation for, 261–263
 UN on, 257–258
TWAS. *See* The World Academy of Sciences
Twitter, 197

UAE. *See* United Arab Emirates
UDHR. *See* Universal Declaration of Human Rights
Ukraine, 73
UN. *See* United Nations
UN Committee on the Rights of the Child, 113

UN Human Rights Commission, 39
UN Human Rights Office, 3–4
UN Preparatory Committee, 34
UNESCO. *See* United Nations Educational, Scientific and Cultural Organization
UNESCO Constitution
 Article 1, 9, 124
 Preamble, 82–83
 RtS in, 20–21
Unified Growth Theory, 176
United Arab Emirates (UAE), 258
United Nations (UN), 211
 global frameworks, 127–128
 Guiding Principles on Business and Human Rights, 111
 Scientific Advisory Board, 134–136
 on TB, 257–258
United Nations Division of Human Rights, 20–21
United Nations Educational, Scientific and Cultural Organization (UNESCO), 8, 204
 on Agenda 2030, 127–128
 on benefits sharing, 129–130
 on bioethics, 131–132
 on climate change, 132–133
 Conference on the Dissemination of Science, 85
 creation of, 19–20
 on cultural life, 130
 Declaration of Ethical Principles in Relation to Climate Change, 132–133
 on do no harm, 129–130
 enemies of progress and, 84–86
 Field Science Cooperation Offices, 87
 General Conference, 76–77, 131
 history of, 79–80
 on human rights, 125–136
 Human Rights Strategy, 126
 on international cooperation, 129–130
 mandate of, 125–127
 Medium-Term Strategy, 126
 Natural Science Sector, 77, 79–80, 86–87
 Program For Women in Science, 128–136
 on pseudoscience, 85
 Recommendation on Science and Scientific Researchers, 76–77, 102, 119, 129, 133–134, 214
 RtS and, 20
 on science, 76–77, 78–80, 82–84, 86–88, 128–137, 234
 on science education, 86–87
 Statement on Science and Scientific Researchers, 188
 Venice Statement, 212–213
 Wilkinson on, 20
 on world unity, 80–82

Index

United States, 37–38, 45–48
  on American Declaration, 35
  Big Data and, 111–112
  COVID-19 in, 173
  Soviet rivalry with, 19
  in UDHR drafting, 48–49
Universal Declaration of Human Rights (UDHR), 1, 6, 17, 33, 42–43, 83, 124, 204. *See also specific articles*
  American Declaration and, 34–35
  Article 18, 91
  Article 19, 91
  Article 29(1), 62
  benefits in, 24
  binding nature of, 1, 232
  Bok on, 87–88
  compliance with, 34–35
  on cultural life, 108
  on cultural rights, 1–2
  drafting of, 34, 45–48, 291–292
  historical context of, 17–21
  human rights in, 58–60
  ICESCR enshrining, 1–2
  IP rights in, 58–60
  objects of rights in, 24–26
  role of science in, 22–23
  RtS in, 17–18
  on science, 108
  United States in drafting of, 48–49
  working drafts of, 20–21
Universal Declaration on Bioethics and Human Rights, 131–132
Universal Declaration on the Human Genome and Human Rights, 131
Universal Periodic Review (UPR), 34–35, 257, 269–270
Uruguay, 45–48
  Constitution of 1942, 61
The Utopian Human Right to Science and Culture (Nawrot), 5

Venezuela, 37–38, 45–48
Venice Statement on the Right to Enjoy the Benefits of Scientific Progress and its Applications, 126–127
Venkat, Bharat, 264–265
Venter, J. Craig, 57
Verma, Iner M., 109
Vienna Convention on the Law of Treaties
  Article 31(1), 231–232
  Article 31(3), 231–232
  Article 32, 6, 18

Vietnam, COVID-19 in, 189
Vitullo, M. W., 213
vocation, science as, 95

Wade, Nicolas, 97
Wakefield, Andrew, 100
Wallace, Alfred Russell, 97
WDR. *See* Westdeutscher Rundfunk
Weigers Vitullo, Margaret, 11–12
Weisenberg, Nathaniel, 11–12
Westdeutscher Rundfunk (WDR), 203
WHA. *See* World Health Assembly
WhatsApp, 202
Whewell, William, 287–288
WHO. *See* World Health Organization
Wiesel, Torsten, 218
Wilkinson, Ellen, 19–20, 77, 286–287
  on UNESCO, 20
WIPO. *See* World Intellectual Property Organization
The World Academy of Sciences (TWAS), 228
World Bank, Doing Business Index, 270
World Blind Union, 151–152
World Commission on the Ethics of Science Knowledge and Technology (COMEST), 124–125
World Federation of the Deaf, 151–152
World Health Assembly (WHA), 156
World Health Organization (WHO), 136–137, 156, 168, 172–173, 247–248
World Intellectual Property Organization (WIPO), 58–59, 115–116, 122
World Justice Report, 270
World Network of Users and Survivors of Psychiatry, 151–152
World Programme of Action concerning Disabled Persons, 153
World Trade Organization (WTO), 54, 57–58, 115–116
World War II, 18, 33
World Wide Web, invention of, 207
WTO. *See* World Trade Organization
Wyndham, J. M., 11–12, 213

Yogeshwar, Ranga, 11
Youmans, Edward, 287–288
YouTube, 197, 209
Yugoslavia, Constitution of, 61

Ziaee, Julia, 211
Zuckerberg, Marc, 205–206

Printed in the United States
by Baker & Taylor Publisher Services